CHINESE PRIVATE INTERNATIONAL LAW

Written with the assistance of a team of lecturers at the Shanghai University of Political Science and Law, this book is the leading reference on Chinese private international law in English. The chapters systematically cover the whole of Chinese private international law, not just questions likely to arise in commercial matters, but also in family, succession, crossborder insolvency, intellectual property, and competition (antitrust). The chapters do not merely cover the traditional conflict of law areas of jurisdiction, applicable law (choice of law), and enforcement. They also look into conflict of law questions arising in arbitration and assess China's involvement in the harmonisation of private international law globally and regionally within the Belt and Road Initiative. Similarly to the Japanese and Indonesian volumes in the series, this book presents Chinese conflict of laws through a combination of common and civil law analytical techniques and perspectives, providing readers worldwide with a more profound and comprehensive understanding of Chinese private international law.

Volume 3 in the series Studies in Private International Law – Asia

Studies in Private International Law – Asia

Editor: Anselmo Reyes
Advisory Editor: Paul Beaumont

Much has been written about private international law in the EU and the US. Less is known about the conflict of laws in Asia. Thus, little attention has been paid so far to the modernisation of private international law codes and rules that has been taking place over the last decade all over Asia. That trend continues. Now is the time to take stock of those reforms that have already taken place and suggest further improvements for the future.

Published under the celebrated series *Studies in Private International Law*, this monograph sub-series provides a forum for discussion and analysis of private international law in Asia. The series is not solely a survey of jurisdictions for practitioners. Comprising in-depth thematic and country-specific studies, each volume considers the private international law of Asian countries from a variety of perspectives. An underlying assumption is that private international law in different jurisdictions follow broad discernible patterns. Each volume in this sub-series highlights those patterns and discusses how rules in different Asian jurisdictions are either converging with, or diverging from, the patterns identified. Such an analytical framework will assist academics, judges, lawyers and legislators to envisage ways in which laws affecting cross-border relationships can be harmonised across jurisdictions and be made more responsive to the needs of citizens in Asia and elsewhere.

Volume 1: Recognition and Enforcement of Judgments in Civil and Commercial Matters
Edited by Anselmo Reyes

Volume 2: Indonesian Private International Law
Afifah Kusumadara

Volume 3: Chinese Private International Law
Edited by Xiaohong Liu and Zhengyi Zhang

Chinese Private International Law

Edited by

Xiaohong Liu

and

Zhengyi Zhang

•HART•

OXFORD • LONDON • NEW YORK • NEW DELHI • SYDNEY

HART PUBLISHING

Bloomsbury Publishing Plc

Kemp House, Chawley Park, Cumnor Hill, Oxford, OX2 9PH, UK

1385 Broadway, New York, NY 10018, USA

29 Earlsfort Terrace, Dublin 2, Ireland

First published in Great Britain 2021

Reprinted 2021, 2022

A catalogue record for this book is available from the British Library.

Library of Congress Cataloging-in-Publication data

Names: Liu, Xiaohong (Law teacher), editor. | Zhang, Zhengyi (Law teacher), editor.

Title: Chinese private international law / edited by Xiaohong Liu and Zhengyi Zhang.

Description: Oxford, UK : New York, NY Hart Publishing, an imprint of Bloomsbury Publishing, 2021. | Series: Studies in private international law – Asia; volume 3 | Includes bibliographical references and index.

Identifiers: LCCN 2021002341 (print) | LCCN 2021002342 (ebook) | ISBN 9781509924370 (hardback) | ISBN 9781509924387 (pdf) | ISBN 9781509924394 (Epub)

Subjects: LCSH: Conflict of laws—China. | International law—China.

Classification: LCC KNQ480 .C49 2021 (print) | LCC KNQ480 (ebook) | DDC 340.90951—dc23

LC record available at https://lccn.loc.gov/2021002341

LC ebook record available at https://lccn.loc.gov/2021002342

ISBN: HB: 978-1-50992-437-0
ePDF: 978-1-50992-438-7
ePub: 978-1-50992-439-4

Typeset by Compuscript Ltd, Shannon
Printed and bound in Great Britain by TJ Books Limited, Padstow, Cornwall

To find out more about our authors and books visit www.hartpublishing.co.uk. Here you will find extracts, author information, details of forthcoming events and the option to sign up for our newsletters.

FOREWORD

Chinese Private International Law is the second volume in the *Studies in Private International Law: Asia* series to focus on the conflict of laws as practised in a specific Asian country. This volume is the product of academics and lawyers associated with Shanghai University of Political Science and Law ('SHUPL'), working under the editorship of Professor Xiaohong Liu (the President of SHUPL and herself one of China's foremost authorities on private international law) and Zhengyi Zhang (SHUPL's Deputy Director of International Affairs). In recent years SHUPL has been establishing itself as a leading university in China for study and research into public and private international law. This book is tangible evidence of SHUPL's efforts in that direction.

Like the first volume, much of this book was written during the COVID-19 pandemic. That period corresponded with heightened tensions between China and the US and to a like or lesser extent between China and other developed countries. The tensions have not gone away and will probably be with us for some time. The tensions have resulted in China's motives in the international sphere being regarded with deep suspicion. Ironically, this scepticism about China has come at a time when it has been seeking to boost its commercial, financial and economic relations with the rest of the world through its Belt-and-Road Initiative ('BRI'). Against this background of mistrust, the chapters in this book prompt three reflections. First, despite China being a socialist state, the cross-border issues in commercial, family and other areas of the law that face its citizens and businesses are strikingly similar to those faced by citizens and businesses everywhere in the capitalist world. It will be apparent from the text that the ways in which Chinese law and the Chinese courts have sought to resolve those issues have been analogous to the approaches taken in leading common and civil law jurisdictions. Thus, at the level of the mundane situations that all of us have to contend with in our daily lives, there is actually more that unites China with (rather than separates it from) the world beyond its borders. Second, despite China being very old in terms of history and civilisation, private international law in the codified form applied there today is a recent phenomenon, only dating to the 1980s. While China has made strides in the articulation of conflict of law principles domestically over the past 40 years, its private international law remains a work in progress. Its judges, legal practitioners and academics look to conflicts of law practice and theory in other jurisdictions (in particular, the US, the UK, Germany and France) to inform and guide themselves on how gaps in the law may be filled. This familiar process of developing law by comparing what has been done abroad and 'picking and choosing' from among best practices adopted elsewhere, again unites China with the world at large. Third, the scale and ambition of the BRI means that, if it is to succeed, China will have to cooperate closely with other nations to coordinate approaches to cross-border legal bottlenecks (especially, commercial ones) so as to foster an environment which will motivate entrepreneurs to invest in the countries comprising the BRI. This is all the more so given the worldwide economic recession that has come in the wake of COVID-19. The development of a harmonised system of private international law is therefore as much a priority for China as it is for everyone else.

If there is so much that unites China with the rest of the world, especially at the level of ordinary lives, one might ask why is there at the same time so much at the level of international politics threatening to divide? That is a complex question which it is plainly not within the scope or function of this book to answer. What this book instead does is to highlight the evolving state of Chinese private international law: where it has been, what it is now, and where it should be going. Such a snapshot will not by itself lead to a relaxation of international tensions. But it can at least help counter stereotypical views of each other and lead to a better mutual understanding. In that sense, this volume on the conflict of laws can serve as a step, however modest or tentative, towards mitigating the political and ideological conflicts that currently beset China's relations with the world.

Anselmo Reyes
Kyoto
1 December 2020

ACKNOWLEDGEMENTS

Numerous persons have been involved in the publication of this book. We sincerely thank all of them. But we hope that they will not mind if we do not mention them all by name. We instead confine ourselves here to acknowledging the assistance of Dr Roberta Bassi, Rosemarie Mearns, Wilson Lui, Dilrabo Abdullayeva, Hanyan Li, Ziwen Xu, Cuishan Su, Haomiao Chen, Yilin Cao, Jiabao Chen, Qiwei Wu, Yiwei Dong, Shengyang Zou. Special thanks go to our assistant editors Adrian Mak, Sherson Ng, Nicholas U Jin, Ameer Ismail, Dolly Xu and Liam McKenna, as without their efforts this book would not have been possible.

Xiaohong Liu
Zhengyi Zhang
Shanghai
31 August 2020

CONTENTS

LIST OF CONTRIBUTORS

Xin Cai is a Lecturer in the School of International Law at Shanghai University of Political Science & Law (SHUPL) and a Council Member of the Chinese Society of Private International Law.

Yang Cao is a Professor and the Director of the Intellectual Property and the Technology & Law Centers at SHUPL, an Executive Director of the China Technology & Law Association, and a Research Fellow at the Berkman Klein Center at Harvard University.

Jun Chen is a Lecturer of the School of International Law at SHUPL.

Maozhong Ding is a Professor at SHUPL.

Min Han is an LLM candidate at SHUPL.

Lin Jia is an Associate Professor at SHUPL and a Council Member of the Chinese Society of Private International Law.

Xiaolin Li is a Lecturer of the School of International Law at SHUPL.

Xiaohong Liu is the President of and a Professor at SHUPL. She is also Vice-Chairperson of the China Society of Private International Law, Vice- President of the Shanghai Law Society, Chief Expert of the Collaborative Innovation Center of the China (Shanghai) Pilot Free Trade Zone, and Member for the International Commercial Expert Committee of the Supreme People's Court.

Yannan Liu is an LLM candidate at SHUPL.

Jianping Shi is an Associate Professor of the School of International Law at SHUPL.

Shuo Feng is a PhD candidate and a Research Fellow at the East China University of Political Science and Law.

Junrong Song is an Associate Professor at SHUPL.

Dan Wang is a Chinese attorney. She holds an LLM from SHUPL.

Guojian Xu is Distinguished Dean and a Professor of the School of International Law at SHUPL. He is a Founding Partner of Boss & Young, Attorneys-at-Law, Shanghai and the Vice-Chairperson of the China Society of Private International Law.

Qingkun Xu is a Professor at SHUPL, a Council Member of the Chinese Society of Private International Law, and an arbitrator at the Qingdao Arbitration Commission.

Qingxuan Wu is an LLM candidate at SHUPL.

Zijun Zhai is an LLM candidate at SHUPL.

Jingning Zhang is an LLM candidate at SHUPL.

Zhen Zhang is an LLM candidate at SHUPL.

Zhengyi Zhang is an Associate Professor at SHUPL, a Council Member of the Chinese Society of Private International Law, and an arbitrator at the Shanghai International Arbitration Center (SHIAC).

LIST OF ABBREVIATIONS

SMGS	1951 Agreement on the International Goods Transport by Rail
New York Convention	1958 Convention on the Recognition and Enforcement of Foreign Arbitral Awards
Hague Service Convention	1965 Hague Convention on the Service Abroad of Judicial and Extrajudicial Documents in Civil or Commercial Matters
Hague Evidence Convention	1970 Convention on the Taking of Evidence Abroad in Civil or Commercial Matters
CLC Convention	1992 International Convention on Liability for Oil Pollution Damage
Montreal Convention	1999 Convention on the Unification of Certain Rules for International Aviation
2005 Hague Convention	2005 Hague Convention on Choice of Court Agreements
2010 Choice of Law Act	Act of Application of Law to Foreign Civil Relations
TRIPs	Agreement on Trade-Related Aspects of Intellectual Property Rights
ALI Global Rules	ALI Global Rules on Conflict-of-Laws Matters in International Insolvency Cases
Branch of CCB	Anhui Branch of China Construction Bank Co. Ltd.
Anhui	Anhui Foreign Economic Construction (Group) Co. Ltd.
Anhui subsidiary	Anhui Foreign Economic Construction Central America Co. Ltd.
1987 Answers	Answers of the Supreme People's Court Concerning the Application of Foreign Economic Contract Law
Gibbs	Antony Gibbs & Sons v Société Industrielle et Commerciale des Métaux
Macao Arrangement	Arrangement between the Mainland and the Macau SAR on Reciprocal Recognition and Enforcement of Arbitration Awards
Mutual Recognition Arrangement of Civil and Commercial Judgments	Arrangement on Mutual Recognition and Enforcement of Judgments in Civil and Commercial Cases between the Mainland and Hong Kong Special Administrative Region Courts

Marriage and Family Arrangements	Arrangement on Mutual Recognition and Enforcement of Marriage and Family Civil Cases between the Mainland and Hong Kong Special Administrative Region Courts
Arrangement on Jurisdiction of Agreements	Arrangement on the Judgment of Civil and Commercial Jurisdictions under the Mutual Recognition and Enforcement of the Agreement of the Parties between the Mainland and the Hong Kong Special Administrative Region Courts
Hong Kong Arrangements	Arrangements of the Supreme People's Court on the Mutual Enforcement of Arbitral Awards between the Mainland and the Hong Kong Special Administrative Region
AIIB	Asian Infrastructure Investment Bank
ASEAN	Association of Southeast Asian Nations
Aoda	Beijing Sunshine Aoda Auto Sales Co. Ltd.
BRI	Belt and Road Initiative
BCI	Benchmark Chambers International
BIT	Bilateral Investment Treaty
District Court	Changping District Court
CIETAC Arbitration Rules	China International Economic and Trade Arbitration Commission Arbitration Rules
CIETAC	China International Economic and Trade Arbitration Commission
CUPL	China University of Political Science and Law
CSPIL	Chinese Society of Private International Law
1995 CAA	Civil Aviation Act of 1995
Civil Aviation Law	Civil Aviation Law of the People's Republic of China
Civil Procedure Law	Civil Procedure Law of the PRC
1999 CA	Contract Act
Immunity Convention	Convention on Jurisdictional Immunities of States and Their Property
ICSID Convention	Convention on the Settlement of Investment Disputes between States and Nationals of Other States
DBS	DBS Bank Ltd
ECUPL	East China University of Political Science and Law
ESCAP	Economic and Social Commission for Asia and the Pacific
IPRS	Enforcing intellectual property rights

Enterprise Bankruptcy Law	Enterprise Bankruptcy Law of China
ECJ	European Court of Justice
EIR	European Insolvency Regulation
Rome II Regulation	European Regulation on the Law Applicable to Non-contractual Obligations
1985 FECA	Foreign Economic Contract Act
Foreign Investment Law	Foreign Investment Law of the People's Republic of China
FTAIA	Foreign Trade Antitrust Improvements Act
FBB	Fortis Bank SA/NV
Gates	Gates Fluid Power Technologies (Changzhou) Co., Ltd.
1986 GPCL	General Principles of Civil Law of 1986
General Principles of Civil Law	General Principles of the Civil Law of the People's Republic of China
HCCH	Hague Conference on Private International Law
CFA	Hong Kong Court of Final Appeal
HKSAR	Hong Kong Special Administrative Region
UCP600	ICC's Uniform Customs and Practices for Documentary Credits
Oriental	Inmobiliaria Palacio Oriental S.A.
IP	Intellectual property
ICSID	International Centre for the Settlement of Investment Disputes
ICC Arbitration Rules	International Chamber of Commerce Arbitration Rules (2017 Amendment)
ICC	International Chamber of Commerce
ICJ	International Court of Justice
2012 Judicial Interpretation I	Interpretation I by the Supreme People's Court on Issues Concerning the Application of the Choice of Law Act
Interpretation of Civil Procedure Law	Interpretation of the Supreme People's Court on the Application of Civil Procedure Law
Application Law Interpretation (I)	Interpretations of the Supreme People's Court on Several Issues Concerning Application of the Law of the People's Republic of China on Choice of Law for Foreign-Related Civil Relationships I
ISDS	investor-state dispute settlement

Succession Law	Law of Succession of the People's Republic of China
Application Law	Law of the People's Republic of China on Choice of Law for Foreign-related Civil Relationships
Foreign Investment Enterprise Law	Law of the People's Republic of China on Wholly Foreign-Owned Enterprises 1986
Foreign Economic Contract Law	Law of the People's Republic of China on Economic Contracts Involving Foreign Interest
Law on Chinese-Foreign Joint Ventures	Law on Chinese-Foreign Equity Joint Ventures
Legislation Law	Legislation Law of the People's Republic of China
L/C	letter of credit
L/G	letter of guarantee
LCIA Arbitration Rules	London Court of International Arbitration Rules
LY	Luo Yanqing
1992 MA	Maritime Act of 1992
Maritime Law	Maritime Law of the People's Republic of China
Bankruptcy Minutes	Minutes of the National Courts' Meeting on Bankruptcy Adjudication
Model Law	Model Law of Private International Law of the People's Republic of China
Bean	Murray Edward Bean
NPC	National People's Congress
Instruments Law	Negotiable Instruments Law of the People's Republic of China
Opinions on the Implementation	Opinions on Several Issues Concerning the Implementation of the General Principles of the Civil Law of the People's Republic of China for Trial Implementation
Organic Law of the Court	Organic Law of the People's Courts of the People's Republic of China
PRC	People's Republic of China
China Ping An	Ping An Life Insurance Company of China, Limited; Ping An Insurance (Group) Company of China, Limited
PICC	Principles of International Commercial Contracts
CLIP Principles	Principles on Conflict of Laws in Intellectual Property
PLs	provisional liquidators

Taiwan Provisions	Provisions of the Supreme People's Court on Recognition and Enforcement of the Arbitral Awards of the Taiwan Region
REIO	Regional Economic Integration Organisation
2007 Rules	Rules of the Supreme People's Court on the Relevant Issues Concerning the Application of Law in Hearing Foreign-Related Contractual Dispute Cases in Civil and Commercial Matters
HB	Shanghai Hengyi Battery Co., Ltd.
SCIA	Shenzhen International Arbitration Court
GE	Sihui City Gaofeng Electronic Co. Ltd.
SIAC	Singapore International Arbitration Centre
Sino-Environment	Sino-Environment Technology Group
SAR	Special Administrative Region
Part IV	Special Provisions on Foreign Civil Procedures
SAFE	State Administration of Foreign Exchange
SPC	Supreme People's Court of the People's Republic of China
1988 Opinions	Supreme People's Court on Issuing Opinions on Several Issues concerning the Implementation of the General Principles of the Civil Law of the People's Republic of China
China-Germany BIT	The Agreement between the Federal Republic of Germany and the People's Republic of China on the Encouragement and Reciprocal Protection of Investments
Canada-China BIT	The Agreement Between the Government of Canada and the Government of the People's Republic of China for the Promotion and Reciprocal Protection of Investments
Canada-China BIT	The Agreement Between the Government of Canada and the Government of the People's Republic of China for the Promotion and Reciprocal Protection of Investments
China-South Korea BIT	The Agreement Between the Government of the People's Republic of China and the Government of the Republic of Korea on the Promotion and Protection of Investments
China-Belgium-Luxembourg Economic Union BIT	The Agreement Between the Government of The People'S Republic of China and the Belgium-Luxemburg Economic Union on the Reciprocal Promotion and Protection of Investments
China-Singapore BIT	The Agreement Between the Government of the People's Republic of China and the Government of the Republic of Singapore on the Promotion and Protection of Investments

Peru-China BIT	The Agreement Between the Government of the People's Republic of China and the Government of the Republic of Peru Concerning the Encouragement and Reciprocal Protection of Investments
ASEAN-China Investment Agreement	The Agreement on Investment of the Framework Agreement on Comprehensive Economic Cooperation Between the People's Republic of China and The Association of Southeast Asian Nations
Spain-Mexico BIT	The Agreement on the Reciprocal Promotion and Protection of Investments signed by the Kingdom of Spain and the United Mexican States
Civil Code	The Civil Code of the People's Republic of China
Monopoly civil disputes	The civil disputes caused by monopoly
AML	The PRC Anti-Monopoly Law
AUCL	The PRC Anti-Unfair Competition Law
TFEU	Treaty on the Functioning of the European Union
Convention on Mauritius Transparency	UN Treaty Arbitration Based on Transparency Between Investors and the National Convention
UNCITRAL Model Law	UNCITRAL Model Law on Cross-Border Insolvency
UNCITRAL Model Law	UNCITRAL Model Law on International Commercial Arbitration 1985 With amendments as adopted in 2006
UNCITRAL Arbitration Rules	United Nations Commission on International Trade Law Arbitration Rules (as revised in 2010)
UNCITRAL	United Nations Commission on International Trade Law
CISG	United Nations Convention on Contracts for the International Sale of Goods
UNDP	United Nations Development Programme
WHO	World Health Organization
WMMP	Wuhan Marine Machinery Plant Co. Ltd.
Humei	Wuxi Humei Thermal Power Engineering Co., Ltd.
YDM	YDM Shipping Co. Ltd.

TABLE OF CASES

China

United States

United Kingdom

Hong Kong

ICSID

PCIJ

Europe

New Zealand

TABLE OF LEGISLATION

International Instruments

Bilateral treaties and agreements

Primary legislation, secondary legislation and other materials

United States

Albania

Hong Kong

European Union

Germany

Switzerland

1

Subject Matter of Private International Law

XIAOHONG LIU, XIN CAI

Private international law deals with legal issues that cross national lines. The subject matter of private international law is civil and commercial legal relationships containing foreign-related factors. These are also known as the 'international civil and commercial legal relationship[s]', 'transnational civil and commercial legal relationship[s]', 'civil and commercial legal relationship[s] with international factors', or 'private international law relationship[s]'.[1] Traditional Chinese private international law theories and judicial practice determine whether a case is subject to private international law mainly based on two factors: first, whether the legal relationship is civil and commercial; second, whether there is a 'foreign-related' or 'international' factor in the case.

I. Definition of the Civil and Commercial Legal Relationships

Civil and commercial legal relationships recognised by private international law refer to the personal property and non-property relations that occur between equal parties.[2] Chinese scholars and practitioners generally adopt an enlarged understanding of civil and commercial relationships. This understanding includes foreign-related property relationships, debt relationships, intellectual property relationships, marriage and family relationships, and inheritance relationships, as well as company legal relationships, instrument legal relationships, maritime legal relationships, insurance legal relationships, and bankruptcy legal relationships.[3]

II. Definition of the Foreign-Related or International Factors

Chinese private international law scholars typically define 'foreign-related' or 'international' factors as being composed of three elements, which together constitute the 'three elements test'. These are: (i) the parties; (ii) the subject matter; and (iii) the juristic fact. As long as there is a foreign-related factor in any one of the three elements, the legal relationship is determined to be foreign-related.[4] The 'three-element-test' is generally endorsed by legislation. Article 178 of

[1] DP Han, *Guoji Sifa* [*Private International Law*] (Higher Education Press & Peking University Press, 2014).

[2] EX Wan, *Understanding and Application of 'Law of the People's Republic of China on Choice of Law for Foreign-related Civil Relationships* (China Legal Publishing House, 2011) 12.

[3] WZ Chen, *Bijiao Guoji Sifa* [*Comparative Private International Law*] Law Press China, 2012) 6.

[4] Han (n 1) 1.

the Opinions on Several Issues Concerning the Implementation of the General Principles of the Civil Law of the People's Republic of China for Trial Implementation (hereinafter referred to as the 'Opinions on the Implementation') provides that:

> Where either party or both parties in a civil legal relationship is an alien, a stateless person, or a foreign legal person, and the object of the civil legal relationship is within the territory of a foreign country, and the legal facts that produce, alter, or annihilate the civil relations of rights and obligations occur in a foreign country, such relationship shall be called foreign-related civil relations.[5]

In 1992, the Supreme People's Court issued Some Issues Concerning the Application of the Civil Procedure Law of the People's Republic of China. In Article 304, it clarifies the identification of 'foreign-related civil cases' from the perspective of procedural law. It provides that:

> Civil cases in which one party or both parties are foreigners, stateless persons, foreign enterprises or organizations, or the legal facts for establishment, alteration, or termination of a civil legal relationship between the parties concerned takes place abroad, or the subject matter of an action is located abroad, are civil cases involving foreign elements.[6]

The two judicial interpretations are consistent with the criteria for foreign-related factors, and all adopt the 'three-element-test'. In judicial practice, most judges also use the three-element-test to determine whether a case should be included in the scope of private international law, especially when the parties have foreign-related factors. According to an empirical study on Chinese foreign-related commercial cases, in 1,000 foreign-related civil and commercial cases concluded by Chinese courts, there were 483 cases involving foreign parties, accounting for 48.3 per cent of all foreign-related cases. There were 463 cases involving Hong Kong, Macao, and Taiwan, accounting for 46.3 per cent of all foreign-related cases. However, the traditional 'three-element-test' and related judicial interpretations have gradually exposed some problems in practice. According to this test, the determination of whether a case has foreign-related factors can only be made on the basis of the parties, the subject matter, or the juristic facts. At the same time, there were irrationalities in early judicial interpretations. Those opinions only considered the element of nationality when determining whether the parties were foreign-related. Whereas for determining the foreign-related nature of the subject matter and juristic facts, they adopted expressions that were not very accurate, such as the 'foreign field' or 'in the foreign country'. These have been criticised by scholars and it is generally believed that the understanding of the 'foreign-related factors' standard should be broader. It cannot be limited to the three traditional situations: parties, subject matter, and juristic facts.[7] Some scholars have pointed out the complexity of foreign-related factors step-by-step and believe that it is necessary to consider 'hidden foreign-related cases', 'false foreign-related cases', and 'special types of foreign-related cases' under special circumstances.[8]

Subsequently, in 2011, The Law of the People's Republic of China on Choice of Law for Foreign-related Civil Relationships (the 'Application Law') was promulgated. It serves as the

[5] Opinions of the Supreme People's Court on Several Issues concerning the Implementation of the General Principles of the Civil Law of the People's Republic of China (Trial Implementation) (Supreme People's Court, Fa Ban Fa (1988) 6, adopted on 26 January 1988 and promulgated on 2 April 1988).

[6] Opinions of the Supreme People's Court on Some Issues Concerning the Application of the Civil Procedure Law of the People's Republic of China (Supreme People's Court, Fa Fa (1992) 22, adopted on 14 July 1992).

This was replaced by Interpretations of the Supreme People's Court on Applicability of the Civil Procedure Law of the People's Republic of China (Supreme People's Court, Zhu Shi (2015) 5, adopted on 18 December 2014, promulgated on 4 February 2015).

[7] YP Xiao, *Principle of Private International Law* (Law Press China, 2003) 3.

[8] T Du, *Principles of Private International Law* (Fudan University Press, 2018) 3–4.

current legislation. Article 1 states that the object of adjustment of the law is 'foreign-related civil relations', but it does not directly stipulate how to determine the 'foreign-related' factor.[9] In 2012, the Supreme People's Court of the People's Republic of China (SPC) issued the Interpretations of the Supreme People's Court on Several Issues Concerning Application of the Law of the People's Republic of China on Choice of Law for Foreign-Related Civil Relationships I (the 'Application Law Interpretation (I)'). It clearly defines how to determine a 'foreign-related' factor. Article 1 of the Application Law Interpretation (I) stipulates that:

> Where a civil relationship falls under any of the following circumstances, the people's court may determine it as foreign-related civil relationship: 1. where either party or both parties are foreign citizens, foreign legal persons, or other organizations or stateless persons; 2. where the habitual residence of either party or both parties is located outside the territory of the People's Republic of China; 3. where the subject matter is outside the territory of the People's Republic of China; 4. where the legal fact that leads to the establishment, change, or termination of civil relationship happens outside the territory of the People's Republic of China; and 5. other circumstances under which the civil relationship may be determined to be a foreign-related civil relationship.[10]

The provisions of the Application Law Interpretation (I) are more comprehensive and complete than previous judicial interpretations. On the one hand, the traditional three-element system has been followed, but it has been expanded and partially improved. For example, in addition to the previous nationality standard, the place of habitual residence is now also used as a criterion for judgment. At the same time, the expression 'foreign' has been changed to 'outside the realm of the People's Republic of China', which is more rigorous and thorough. On the other hand, the miscellaneous provisions have been added. Application Law Interpretation (I) provides a more flexible space for judging foreign-related issues in judicial practice.

III. Case Studies

A. Foreign-Related Factor According to the Nationality of the Parties[11]

In the Xiao 1 and Xiao 2 inheritance dispute appeal case, one of the parties, Xiao 3, was a Canadian citizen. The court held that Article 1(1) of the Application Law Interpretation (I) required that Xiao 3 be considered a foreign citizen, so the civil legal relationship in this case was a foreign-related civil legal relationship.

B. Foreign-Related Factor According to the Residence of the Parties[12]

In the Wu Yubin and Xiong Wanyi contract dispute case, Xiong Wanyi and Li were husband and wife. The two registered their marriage on 30 April 2002. Wu Yubin's investment dispute with

[9] The Law of the People's Republic of China on Choice of Law for Foreign-related Civil Relationships, adopted at the Seventeenth Session of the Eleventh Standing Committee of the National People's Congress of the People's Republic of China on 28 October 2010, and took effect on 1 April 2011.

[10] Interpretation of the Supreme People's Court on Several Issues Concerning the Application of the 'Law of the People's Republic of China on the Law Applicable to Foreign-Related Civil Relationships' (I) (Supreme People's Court, Fa Shi (2012) 24, adopted on 10 December 2012 and took effect on 7 January 2013).

[11] Beijing Municipality Intermediate People's Court No 1 Decision *Xiao v Xiao and Xiao* (2017) Jing-01 Min Zhong No 9314.

[12] Guangzhou Intermediate People's Court Decision *Wu Yubin v Xiong Wanyi* (2017) Yue-01 Min Zhong No 15952.

Li, Wei, and Huang occurred during the marriage between Xiong Wanyi and Li. The court held that Xiong Wanyi should pay the debt arising from Li's obligation to return of Wu Yubin's investment of 1 million yuan and interest of 24,464 yuan. The court found that, because Xiong Wanyi had worked and lived in the US for a long time, the provisions of Article 1(2) of the Application Law Interpretation (I) required that the case be considered as a foreign-related civil case.

C. Foreign-Related Factor According to the Nationality of a Legal Person[13]

In the Paul Frank Industries LLC and Beijing Yichengshun Trading Co Ltd copyright infringement dispute case, Paul Frank was the copyright owner of two works of art, 'Julius' and 'Paul Frank Official Logo', and enjoyed the copyright of the two works of art. In 2017, Paul Frank found that unauthorised sales by Beijing Yichengshun Trading Co Ltd consistently utilised the overall image and visual effects of the 'Julius' and 'Paul Frank Official Logo' art works. Paul Frank sued Beijing Yichengshun to stop the infringement and seek compensation for its losses. The court held that Paul Frank LLC was registered at 10100 Santa Monica Boulevard, Los Angeles, California, so there were foreign-related factors and the case was subject to the Application Law Interpretation (I).

D. Foreign-Related Factor According to the Nationality of a Legal Person[14]

In the Château Lafite Rothschild and Shanghai Mellowines Development Co Ltd trademark infringement case, the plaintiff alleged that the two defendants had imported and sold a large number of wines with the 'Lafitte Manor' and 'Chateau Moron Lafitte' logos through their official website and promoted, displayed, and sold the alleged infringing goods on the Tmall website. The plaintiff asked the court to order the defendant to stop the infringement and compensate the plaintiff for its loss. The court held that, as the plaintiff was an enterprise established in France, the case involved a foreign-related civil relationship under the first paragraph of Article 1 of the Application Law Interpretation (I).

E. Foreign-Related Factor According to Juristic Facts[15]

In the Hu Chao and Li Gen private pending dispute case, the two parties were friends. From 7–13 May 2016, they went to Macau to gamble with Peng and Luo. After shopping, they went to the casino to gamble. Capital chips were borrowed. On 11 May, Li Gen wanted to go to the casino to gamble again and asked Hu Chao to lend him 100,000 yuan. Hu Chao did not agree at first, but Li Gen persisted, so Hu withdrew RMB 100,000 from his bank at Macao. Li Gen promised to repay in instalments but failed to do so. He instead asked Hu to delay the repayment period.

[13] Beijing Fengtai District People's Court Decision *Paul Frank Industries v Beijing Yichengshun Trading* (2017) Jing-0106 Min Chu No 22134.

[14] Shanghai Intellectual Property Court Decision *Château Lafite Rothschild v Shanghai Mellowines Development* (2015) Hu Zhi Min Chu Zi No 518.

[15] Pingxiang Intermediate People's Court Decision *Hu Chao v Li Gen* (2018) Gan-03 Min Zhong No 6.

Hu did not agree and took the case to court. The court held that, even though both parties were Chinese, the loan between them had been made in the Macau Special Administrative Region of the People's Republic of China. Accordingly, under Article 1, Paragraph 4 of the Application Law Interpretation (I), which states that 'where the legal fact that leads to the establishment, change, or termination of a civil relationship happens outside the territory of the People's Republic of China', the case must be treated as involving foreign-related civil relations.

F. Foreign-Related Factors Based on the Location of the Subject Matter[16]

In the Jiangsu Hongyu Solar Energy Industry Co Ltd, Shen Zhui and Fan Jinmei property disputes case, Jiangsu Hongyu alleged that the company had sent a solar water heater worth US$25,683.68 to Shen Zhui in September 2009. The water heater had been transported to and stored in Romania and then sold with Shen Zui's assistance. After Shen Zhui received the goods in Romania, he stored the goods in a warehouse leased under his name. On 29 December 2009, after Shen Zhui returned to China, Hongyu Company asked Shen Zhui to disclose the whereabout of the goods and to provide storage information about them. But Shen Zhui refused. Fan Jinmei was the wife of Shen Zhui, which meant that Fan was jointly responsible for Shen's debts during the marriage. Shen Zhui and Fan Jinmei jointly argued that Shen Zhui had no relationship with Hongyu Company, nor did he conduct any transactions, nor did he receive, store or transfer any goods in Romania. They submitted that Hongyu Company's legation lacked a factual basis so the court should reject its claims. The court held that the solar water heater had been exported to Romania as shown by an import bill of lading provided by Hongyu Company and the import declaration materials provided by Shen Zhui, so the case had foreign-related factors.

G. Foreign-Related Factors According to Miscellaneous Provisions[17]

In the Siemens International Trade (Shanghai) Co, Ltd and Shanghai Golden Landmark Co case, Siemens applied for recognition and enforcement of a foreign arbitration award. Siemens and Golden Landmark were both wholly foreign-owned enterprises registered in the Shanghai Pilot Free Trade Zone. On 23 September 2005, Siemens and Golden Landmark signed a contract for the supply of goods by tender, stipulating that Siemens should ship the equipment to Golden Landmark's site by 15 February 2006. The contract provided that disputes were to be submitted to the Singapore International Arbitration Centre (SIAC). A dispute arose between the parties regarding performance of the contract. Golden Landmark Company submitted to SIAC arbitration, requesting the termination of the contract and payment. Siemens filed a counterclaim requesting payment of all purchases, interest and compensation for other losses. In November 2011, the SIAC issued an award rejecting the Golden Landmark's request and supporting Siemens' counterclaim. Golden Landmark Company paid a portion of the amount. The unpaid payment and interest under the arbitral award was RMB5,133,872. Pursuant to the 1958 New York Convention on the Recognition and Enforcement of Foreign Arbitral Awards, Siemens asked the Shanghai

[16] Jiangsu High People's Court Decision *Jiangsu Hong Yu Solar Energy Industry Ltd v Shen Zhui and Fan Jinmei* (2011) Su Shang Wai Zhong Zi No 57.

[17] Shanghai Intermediate People's Court No 1 Decision *Siemens International Trade (Shanghai) Co v Shanghai Golden Landmark Co.* (2013) Hu Yi Zhong Min Ren Wai Zhong Zi No 2.

No 1 Intermediate People's Court to recognise and enforce the SIAC award. Golden Landmark argued that the award should not be recognised on the grounds that both parties were Chinese legal persons and the contract had been performed in the People's Republic of China. It submitted that the relevant civil relations did not have foreign-related factors, rendering the agreement for international arbitration invalid and the recognition and enforcement of the award contrary to China's public policy. However, the court held that the contract was not a typical foreign-related situation. The performance characteristics of the contract differed from the ordinary domestic contract, leading to its identification as a foreign-related civil legal relationship.

The differences were as follows. First, the parties had certain foreign-related characteristics. Although Siemens and Golden Landmark were Chinese legal entities, their registered places were within the Shanghai Pilot Free Trade Zone and they were wholly foreign-owned enterprises. The capital sources, ultimate interests of the companies, and their respective business decisions were closely related to their foreign investors. Therefore, they were obvious foreign-related factors when compared with ordinary domestically funded companies. Given the background of reform to promote international investment and trade in the Pilot Free Trade Zone, the abovementioned foreign-related factors should be given more weight. Second, the performance characteristics of the contract involved foreign-related factors. Although the subject matter equipment under the contract required delivery at a domestic site, the equipment had first to be shipped from overseas to the Pilot Free Trade Zone (formerly the Shanghai Waigaoqiao Free Trade Zone). Contract performance required timely customs clearance procedures to complete the import process, so the transfer process also had certain international cargo trading characteristics.

Therefore, the performance of the contract was distinguishable from that of general domestic sales contracts. Based on the above, the court held that the contractual relationship was in line with the 'other circumstances that can be recognised as foreign-related civil relations' stipulated in Paragraph 5 of Article 1 of the Application Law Interpretation (I), and the contractual relationship had foreign-related elements. The arbitration clause was accordingly valid. This case is typical of the situations in which the court flexibly uses Article 1 of the Application Law Interpretation (I) to identify 'other circumstances under which the civil relationship may be determined as a foreign-related civil relationship'. If the traditional 'three-element test' had been used, there would be no foreign-related factor in respect of the parties, subject matter, and juristic facts. However, in the specific circumstances of the case, it was plainly inappropriate to treat it as a purely domestic civil law case. The court comprehensively considered the facts of the case and applied the 'other circumstances' clause to classify the case as falling within the scope of private international law.

H. Cases Involving Hong Kong, Macau and Taiwan

As a multi-jurisdictional country, China generally interprets 'foreign-related' as 'involving foreign jurisdiction'. Cases involving Hong Kong, Macau, and Taiwan are treated in the same way as other cases involving foreign factors. Article 19 of the Application Law Interpretation (I) stipulates that: 'Issues concerning the application of law in connection with civil relationships involving the Hong Kong Special Administration Region and the Macau Special Administration Region are subject to these Interpretations by analogy.' In practice, a large number of foreign-related cases determined by Chinese courts fall into this category. For example, in a dispute between Xu Wen and Hu Guisheng about the validity of contract,[18] Xu Wen and Hu Guisheng made

[18] Guizhou High People's Court Decision *Xu Wen v Hu Guisheng* (2015) Qian Gao Min San Zhong Zi No 7.

an appointment in Macau to invest in the transcode business services of the gaming industry and the two sides signed a 'cooperation agreement'. According to the agreement, Xu Wen paid RMB8,181,000 to Hu Guisheng, and Hu Guisheng began to operate after receiving the payment. The parties fell into arguments about management operations and dividends, so Xu sued Hu in the Guizhou court to resolve their disputes. The court held that the contract between the two parties having been signed in Macau and the main business activities having occurred in Macau, there was a foreign-related contractual relationship under Article 1(4) of the Application Law Interpretation (I). This was a case 'where the legal fact that leads to the establishment, change or termination of the civil relationship happened outside the territory of the People's Republic of China' so that Article 19 of the Application Law Interpretation (I) was engaged.

2

Sources of Law

XIN CAI

The sources of law refer to something that provides the authority for judicial decisions and for legislation. As each country's private laws differs, so do the sources of their laws. Private international law is generally believed to have two sources based on the foreign-related nature of its subject matter: domestic law and international law.[1] Specifically, the domestic sources of private international law include domestic legislation and precedent, while international sources include international treaties and customs. Authoritative academic doctrines and international practice have also been put forward as sources of law of private international law by some scholars.

I. Domestic Sources

Domestic legislation is the main form of law in civil law countries and is also the most important source of Chinese private international law. At present, the legislative system of private international law in the international community can be roughly divided into code-based legislation and decentralised legislation. There are a few special private international law statutes, while the bulk of relevant regulations are scattered among various domestic civil law statutes. In recent decades, with the rise of the codification of private international law, more and more countries have begun to formulate special international private law codes.[2] China's private international law is also in the form of decentralised legislation. Most statutes are embodied in Chapter VIII of the 'General Principles of the Civil Law of the People's Republic of China' (the 'General Principles of Civil Law'), comprising nine articles, mainly concerning choice of law rules.[3] In addition, there are also some conflicts of law rules in the Law of Succession of the People's Republic of China (the 'Succession Law'),[4] the Civil Aviation Law of the People's Republic of China (the 'Civil Aviation Law'),[5] the Maritime Law of the People's Republic of China

[1] DP Han, *Guoji Sifa* [*Private International Law*] (Higher Education Press & Peking University Press, 2014) 20.

[2] SC Symeonides, *Codifying Choice of Law around the World: An International Comparative Analysis* (Oxford University Press, 2014).

[3] Passed at the Fourth Session of the Sixth National People's Congress of the People's Republic of China on 12 April 1986 and was implemented on 1 January 1987. It is invalidated by the Civil Code of the People's Republic of China (issued on 28 May 2020, effective on 1 January 2021).

[4] Passed on 10 April 1985, at the Third Session of the Sixth National People's Congress of the People's Republic of China and was implemented on 1 October 1985. Article 36 of the Succession Law has been replaced by the Application Law because of conflicts with the relevant provisions.

[5] Adopted on the Sixteenth Session of the Eighth Standing Committee of the National People's Congress of the People's Republic of China on 30 October 1995, and five amendments were made in 2009, 2015, 2016, 2017 and 2018.

(the 'Maritime Law'),[6] and the Negotiable Instruments Law of the People's Republic of China (the 'Instruments Law').[7] On 28 October 2010, the Seventeenth Session of the 11th Standing Committee of the National People's Congress passed the Application Law, which became effective on 1 April 2011. This law is the first independent private international law statute in the history of the PRC. The law consists of eight chapters and 52 articles, including general provisions, civil subjects, marriage and family, inheritance, real property rights, creditor's rights, intellectual property rights, and supplementary provisions. The law mainly focuses on choice of law rules, and it provides a more centralised and comprehensive stipulation of the application of relevant laws. However, the law is not a complete private international law code. It needs to be supplemented with the conflict rules in other separate laws.

II. Judicial Interpretations

The Supreme People's Court has issued a large number of interpretations of the text and spirit of relevant domestic legislation. Judicial interpretations clarify the ambiguities of, and bridge the gaps in, the statutory provisions. According to Article 104 of the Legislation Law of the People's Republic of China (the 'Legislation Law'):

> Interpretations on the specific application of law in adjudication or procuratorate work issued by the Supreme People's Court or Supreme People's Procuratorate shall primarily target specific articles of laws, and be consistent with the goals, principles, and significance of legislation. Where encountering the situation provided for in the second paragraph of Article 45 of this Law, a request for a legal interpretation, or a proposal to draft or amend relevant law, shall be submitted to the National People's Congress Standing Committee. Specific interpretations on the application of law in adjudication or procuratorate work made by the Supreme People's Court or Supreme People's Procuratorate, shall be reported to the Standing Committee of the National People's Congress for recording within 30 days of their being released.[8]

This provision requires the Supreme People's Court to seek the advice of the Standing Committee of the National People's Congress before issuing judicial interpretations. A judicial interpretation must thereafter be reviewed by the Standing Committee of the National People's Congress to ensure its legitimacy.

The legal basis for judicial interpretation is derived from the Organic Law of the People's Courts of the People's Republic of China (the 'Organic Law of the Court').[9] Article 18 of the Law stipulates that the Supreme People's Court may explain the specific application of law at the trial. At the same time, the Resolution of the Standing Committee of the National People's Congress Providing an Improved Interpretation of the Law stipulates that: 'Interpretation of questions involving the specific application of laws and decrees in court trials shall be provided by the Supreme People's Court.'[10] Based on the above principles, Article 5 of Provisions of the

[6] Adopted on the Twenty-eighth Session of the Seventh Standing Committee of the National People's Congress of the People's Republic of China on 7 November 1992 and took effect on 1 July 1993.

[7] Adopted at the Thirteenth Session of the Eighth Standing Committee of the National People's Congress of the People's Republic of China on 10 May 1995 and amended in 2004.

[8] Passed at the Third Session of the Ninth National People's Congress of the People's Republic of China on 15 March 2000 and was amended in 2015.

[9] Passed on 1 July 1979, at the Second Session of the Fifth National People's Congress of the People's Republic of China, and revised three times in 1983, 1986, 2006, and 2018.

[10] Resolution of the Standing Committee of the National People's Congress Providing an Improved Interpretation of the Law, adopted at the Nineteenth Session of the Fifth Standing Committee of the National People's Congress of the People's Republic of China on 10 June 1981.

Supreme People's Court on Judicial Interpretation Work provides that judicial interpretations issued by the Supreme People's Court shall have full legal force. Article 27 stipulates that: 'Where any judicial interpretation is taken by the people's court as a ruling basis after it is promulgated, it shall be quoted in the judicial documentation.' Judicial interpretations issued by the Supreme People's Court are therefore an important source of Chinese private international law.[11] Judicial interpretations issued by the Supreme People's Court relating to private international law can be divided into two broad categories. The first is judicial interpretation in the field of choice of law, the most important of which is the Application Law Interpretation (I). The other is the judicial interpretation of international civil procedure law, such as the Interpretation of the Supreme People's Court on the Application of Civil Procedure Law (the 'Interpretation of Civil Procedure Law').[12] However, judicial interpretations of foreign-related civil relations will be invalid insofar as they violate the Application Law, according to the Notice of the Supreme People's Court on Earnestly Studying and Implementing the Law on Choice of Law for Foreign-related Civil Relationships.[13]

III. International Treaty

International treaties are written international agreements concluded by subjects (primarily states and international organisations) that establish their respective rights and obligations. International treaties are one of the important sources of private international law. Article 142(2) of General Principles of Civil Law provides that:

> If any international treaty concluded or acceded to by the People's Republic of China contains provisions differing from those in the civil laws of the People's Republic of China, the provisions of the international treaty shall apply, unless the provisions are ones on which the People's Republic of China has announced reservations.

There are similar provisions in the Civil Procedure Law, the Instruments Law, the Maritime Law, and the Civil Aviation Law. According to these provisions, international treaties take precedence over domestic law in the absence of reservations to the former. Article 4 of the Application Law Interpretation (I) stipulates:

> Where the application of law of any foreign-related civil relationship involves the application of any international treaty, the people's courts shall allow the application thereof in accordance with Article 142(2) of the General Principles of Civil Law of the People's Republic of China, Article 95(1) of the Negotiable Instruments Law of the People's Republic of China, Article 268(1) of the Maritime Law of the People's Republic of China, and Article 184(1) of the Civil Aviation Law of the People's Republic of China, except those international treaties on intellectual property that have been or are required to be transformed into domestic laws.

Article 9 has a further stipulation:

> Where parties to a contract invoke any international treaty not yet binding upon the People's Republic of China, the people's court may determine the rights and obligations between the parties in accordance

[11] Provisions of the Supreme People's Court on the Judicial Interpretation Work (Supreme People's Court, Fa Fa [2018] 12).

[12] Interpretation of the Supreme People's Court on the Application of the Civil Procedure Law of the People's Republic of China (Supreme People's Court, Fa Shi [2015] 5). The judicial interpretation was adopted by the 1636th meeting of the Supreme People's Court Judicial Committee on 18 December 2014, and took effect on 4 February 2015.

[13] Notice of the Supreme People's Court on Earnestly Studying and Implementing the Law of the People's Republic of China on Choice of Law for Foreign-related Civil Relationship (Supreme People's Court, Fa Fa [2010] 52).

> with the content of such international treaty, provided that such international treaty is not in violation of the social public interests of or mandatory provisions in the laws and regulations of the People's Republic of China.

However, some scholars have argued that Article 9 does not recognise international treaties that are not yet binding upon the PRC, as sources of private international law. International treaties on private international law in China can be classified as bilateral and multilateral treaties. Chinese bilateral treaties mainly focus on international civil procedure law, especially judicial process. Although there are many bilateral treaties, multilateral treaties are to some extent more important, because they cover a broader range of matters, including the legal status of foreign nationals, choice of law, international civil litigation and international commercial arbitration. Among them, the conventions formulated by the Hague Conference on Private International Law (HCCH) have had the greatest influence.

The contents of a treaty may be invoked in an agreement between two or more parties by incorporation as contractual terms.[14]

IV. International Custom and Practice

Article 142(3) of General Principles of Civil Law stipulates:

> International practice may be applied on matters for which neither the Law of the People's Republic of China nor any international treaty concluded or acceded to by the People's Republic of China has any provisions.

Similar provisions to Article 142(3) are Article 268(2) of the Maritime Law, Article 184(2) of the Civil Aviation Law, and Article 96(2) of the Instruments Law. Many scholars cite Article 142(3) of the General Principles of Civil Law in support of the position that international practice is the source of Chinese private international law.[15] It is necessary, however, to distinguish between international custom and international practice. In China, there are certain similarities between the two concepts, but their definitions are different. Custom is a tendency or social custom that has been formed over a long period of time and is not easily changed. Practice means a generally accepted way of doing something. These differences have the consequence that international custom is a narrower concept than international practice. Article 38 of the Statute of the International Court of Justice (ICJ) is generally recognised as the authoritative statement of the sources of public international law. Article 38(1) recognises 'international custom as evidence of a general practice accepted as law'. Based on Article 38(1), international custom involves two elements: the actual practice of states and the acceptance by states of that practice as a matter of *opinio juris*. Obviously, Article 38(1) entails a narrow definition for international custom. In contrast, there is no consensus as to the meaning of international custom in private international law. More importantly, international custom (for instance, the principle that the *lex situs* should apply to property and the principle of party autonomy in international arbitration) have already been incorporated into statutes. Thus, even if international custom is regarded as a source of law, it would not seem to be relevant in most contexts.

Consequently, international custom is not generally a source of private international law in China, but can at best supplement the application of law in specific situations. On the other

[14] T Du, *Principles of Private International Law* (Fudan University Press, 2018) 21.
[15] ibid, 27–29.

hand, a number of scholars have argued that international practice cannot be a source of private international law. According to them, the provisions in the General Principles of Civil Law and other laws instead imply that international practice may be considered by the people's court where there is no operative provision in domestic law or in international treaties. Provisions in the General Principles of Civil Law and other laws also imply that international practice is not legally binding.[16] The scholars further contend that references to international practice in provisions such as Article 142(3) of the General Principles of Civil Law do not refer to private international law at all. but instead concern substantive law and are simply meant to plug gaps in the civil law.

Where the parties to a contract invoke an international custom in their contract, the people's court should enforce the same as the parties' choice. The parties have the burden of proving their choice.

V. Judicial Precedent and Authoritative Academic Theory

A. Judicial Precedent

In China, neither legislative nor judicial practice is deemed to be the source of international law. *Stare decisis* does not exist in China. This means that the judgments of other courts at any level do not bind judges in cases involving similar facts and issues. Although the Supreme People's Court regularly publishes model cases in the *Gazette* of the Supreme People's Court, these model cases are not binding on other people's courts. Disadvantages of this principle appear when different courts deal with cases involving similar facts and issues in different ways and with sometimes contradictory results. Inconsistencies even exist in the judgments of different divisions of the same court. Litigants therefore cannot predict the legal effects of the earlier cases. Although the civil law system in general takes statute law as the main source of law, it has gradually adopted a more open attitude towards precedent. Influenced by this trend, Chinese courts have in recent years begun to explore the guiding role of precedent. The Supreme People's Court has issued a Notice on Issuing Provisions on Case Guidance. The Notice provides that:

> In order to sum up trial experience, unify the application of law, enhance the quality of trials, and maintain judicial justice, these Provisions regarding case guidance are formulated in accordance with the Law of the People's Republic of China on the Organization of the People's Courts and other legal provisions.[17]

To this end, the Supreme People's Court has issued a series of provisions giving case guidance. But, at present, judicial precedent is not a source of Chinese private international law.

B. Authoritative Academic Theory

Before the Interpretation of Application Law (I) was unveiled in 2011, provisions on private international law in China's domestic law were mainly found in the General Principles of Civil Law and other departmental laws. At that time, many scholars would cite the Model Law of Private

[16] WZ Chen, *Bijiao Guoji Sifa [Comparative Private International Law]* (Law Press China, 2012) 69.

[17] Notice of the Supreme People's Court on Issuing the Provisions on Case Guidance (Supreme People's Court, Fa Fa [2010] 51).

International Law of the People's Republic of China (the 'Model Law').[18] The Chinese Society of Private International Law began drafting the Model Law in 1993. After many discussions and revisions, the sixth version was adopted as the final version. Although the Model Law has the word 'Law' in its title, it is not actually law but is academic in nature and only used as a reference by the legislative and judicial branches, by government departments engaged in foreign-related affairs, by law schools, and by law research institutes. Like academic theory, the Model Law cannot be regarded as a source of private international law but can be used as a reference to help understand and explain Chinese private international law.

[18] China Society of Private International Law, *Model Law of Private International Law of the People's Republic of China* (Law Press, 2000).

3

History of Private International Law

XIN CAI

I. Private International Law in Ancient China

Chinese private international law originally dates back to the *Yonghui* Law of the Tang dynasty.[1] The *Yonghui* Law was promulgated in 651 CE and is the earliest and most complete law code known to have existed in China. There are 12 chapters and 502 articles. Article 6 of Chapter *Mingli* stipulates: 'If both parties to an infringement belong to the same foreign ethnic group, the customary law of their own shall apply; if the parties belong to different ethnic groups, the law of the Tang Empire shall apply.'[2] Historical materials record that the Tang Government set up *Fan Fang* in Guangzhou as a residence for Arab and Persian merchants. The Arab merchants wrote travel notes and one record is as follows:

> Soliman the Merchant relates that, at Canfu, which is the principal Scale for Merchants, there is a Mohammedan appointed Judge over those of his Religion, by the Authority of the Emperor of China, and that he is Judge of all the Mohammedans who retort to these Parts. Upon Festival Days he performs the public Service with the Mohammedans, and pronounces the Sermon or Kotbat, which he concludes, in the usual form, with Prayers for the Sultan of the Moslems, [or Muselmen.] The Merchants of Irak who trade hither, are no way dissatisfied with his Conduct, or his Administration in the Post he is invested with, because his Actions, and the Judgments he gives, are just and equitable, and conformable to the Koran [or Alcoran,] and according to the Mohammedan Jurisprudence.[3]

Many Chinese scholars believe that the lack of a distinction between the civil and criminal law in ancient China facilitated the application of foreign law in foreign-related cases or at least in foreign-related tort cases.[4] Hence, the *Mingli* may be regarded as the world's oldest choice of law rules. But this view has been challenged in recent years by some scholars who argue that the statute is just a Tang dynasty criminal code and does not relate to private international law.[5] They argue that the rule in the first section of the *Mingli* was similar to the general principles of criminal law at the time. Other scholars argue that the *Mingli* mainly reflected foreign policy and

[1] DP Han, *Guoji Sifa* [*Private International Law*] (Higher Education Press & Peking University Press, 2014) 53; YG Guo, 'Summary of the Evolution of Private International Law in China' (2015) 2 *Tsinghua Law Review* 3–4; T Du, *Principles of Private International Law* (Fudan University Press, 2018) 12.

[2] SY Li, *China's General Theory of Private International Law* (Law Press, 2006) 82–83.

[3] Abu Zayd Hasan ibn Yazid Sirafi and S al-Tajir, *Ancient Accounts of India and China* (Printed for S. Harding, 1733) 7–8.

[4] Han, (n 1).

[5] LM Wang, 'The Article of the Law of the Tang Dynasty on the Incrimination of Foreigners Belongs to the Question of Private International Law and Discusses the Nature of the Criminal Code of the Tang Dynasty' (2017) 8 *Legal Science* 98.

a specific method of dealing with foreign-related problems. Given the legal techniques available at the time, the *Mingli* could not be put into practice. Even in terms of the international communication and technological methods now available, proof of foreign law remains cumbersome.[6]

The Song dynasty inherited this early choice of law rule from the Tang dynasty. The principles of Song dynasty criminal law were similar to those in the *Tang Lu Shu Yi*. The *Xing Tong Shi Wen* stated that if the parties were from the same country, the proper law should be their country's law. But if they were from different countries, the proper law should be Song dynasty law. The rule changed after the Yuan dynasty. The Ming dynasty's law did not distinguish among parties from different nations and all cases applied the law of the Mong dynasty. The Qing Code of 1646 CE adopted the law of the Ming dynasty. Some opinions hold that the laws of the Ming and Qing dynasties law were regressive by comparison with Tang dynasty law, which itself had reverted back from a combination of the territorial principle and the principle of nationality to an absolute principle of nationality.

II. Transition to Modern Private International Law

The Beiyang Government (that is, the Chinese Government between 1912 and 1928) promulgated the Application of Law Ordinance on 5 August 1918. The Application of Law Ordinance was greatly influenced by Japanese law and is recognised as a step in the modernisation of Chinese law.[7] The Application of Law Ordinance is detailed and complete. However, it did not work well in practical terms because of consular jurisdiction.[8] Western countries had consular jurisdiction in some parts of China, notably in Shanghai and the northwest, so their natural and legal persons were under the jurisdiction of their own consulates. Some scholars point out that the influence of consular jurisdiction should not be overstated.[9] It is necessary to consider the Chinese legal system in the context of that time, including the background, mindset and objectives of the then Chinese judiciary; the negotiations between China and foreign countries; and the content of the Application of Law Ordinance itself. All of these factors limited the role played by the Application of Law Ordinance in judicial practice.[10] On 12 August 1927, the Application of Law Ordinance was suspended by the Nanjing National Government. In 1949, the Application of Law Ordinance was abolished in mainland China with the establishment of the People's Republic of China, but it remained binding in the Taiwan region of China until 1953.

III. Private International Law in the PRC

With the founding of the People's Republic of China in 1949, the relevant laws of the Guomindang Government, including the Application of Law Ordinance and the unequal treaties signed with foreign countries, were abolished. China began a comprehensive study of the socialist legal system.

[6] JF Bai, 'Zhongguo Xiewai Falü Fazhan Kaolun'[On the Development of Foreign-Related Laws in China] [2006] *Master Thesis of China University of Political Science and Law* 8–10.

[7] HP Li, *Selected Works of Li Haopei* (Law Press, 2000), 45–46; L Haopei, *Collected Law Works of Li Haopei* (Law Press, 2006) 463.

[8] J Huang, *Private International Law* (Law Press, 1999) 163; Tao (n 1) 13.

[9] D Bao, 'The Misunderstanding of Extraterritoriality' in J Wang, *Western Law and Eastern Law and the Modern Reform of Chinese Law* (China University of Political Science and Law Press, 2001) 281–284.

[10] Bai (n 6) 40–42.

However, for a long time there were no significant laws on foreign-related civil and commercial relations. In 1951 the provisions related to private international law were found sporadically in legal texts, such as the Interim Opinions on the Marriage of Aliens and between Aliens and Chinese, and the Sino-Soviet Consular Treaty. Generally speaking, there was no Chinese private international law.

After 1978, China's reform and foreign policy required corresponding legal protection, so private international law gained attention at the legislative level. The Law on Chinese-Foreign Equity Joint Ventures promulgated in 1979 was the first to confirm the legal status of foreign nationals engaged in civil activities in China.[11] In 1982, the Constitution of the People's Republic of China explicitly permitted foreign legal persons to invest in China and protected the legitimate rights and interests of foreign nationals. The Trademark Law, the Patent Law, and other statutes similarly contain provisions on the legal status of foreign nationals. On the choice of law, the State Council promulgated the Regulation on the Implementation of the Law of the People's Republic of China on Chinese-Foreign Equity Joint Ventures in 1983. The latter provided that: 'The conclusion, effectiveness, interpretation, and execution of the contract regarding an equity joint venture and the settlement of disputes in relation thereto shall be governed by the Chinese laws.'[12] It is a unilateral conflicts rule and shows that China had not lost sight of the need for choice of law rules in foreign-related civil and commercial legal activities.

The Law of the People's Republic of China on Economic Contracts Involving Foreign Interest (the 'Foreign Economic Contract Law')[13] and the Law of Succession were promulgated in 1985. In 1986, based on the experience of civil activities since the reform and opening up policy had begun, the General Principles of Civil Law was promulgated. Chapter VIII contained provisions on foreign-related matters, including general principles, the preservation of public order, capacity for civil conduct, real rights, creditor's rights, marriage, and family relations. Although there are only nine provisions in Chapter VIII, to a certain extent, these nine provisions demonstrate the legislators' attention to private international law by effectively stipulating rules for foreign-related civil cases. It also laid the foundation for the formulation of choice of law rules in the Maritime Law, the Instruments Law, the Civil Aviation Law, and other statutes. Detailed provisions on the application of law to foreign-related civil and commercial cases were set out in the Response of the Supreme People's Court to Certain Questions Concerning the Application of the Foreign Economic Contract Law of 1987 and the Opinions on the Implementation of 1988.[14] The Application Law of 2010 was a landmark in Chinese private international law as special legislation on choice of law. It articulated the principle of party autonomy, the principle of closest relationship, and the principle of the protection of the party with weaker bargaining power.

Relevant laws and regulations have also been formulated in civil procedure and international commercial arbitration. The Opinions on the Implementation promulgated in 1982 included a section that clarified civil procedure in foreign-related matters. The Civil Procedure

[11] Adopted at the second session of the Fifth National People's Congress of the people's Republic of China on 1 July 1979, amended in 1990, 2001 and 2016.

[12] Promulgated by the State Council of the people's Republic of China on 20 September 1983, amended in 1986, 1987, 2001, 2011 and 2014. Invalidated by the Foreign Investment Law of the People's Republic of China (issued on 15-03-2019 Effective on 01-01-2020); Regulation for Implementing the Foreign Investment Law of the People's Republic of China (Issued on 26-12-2019 Effective on 01-01-2020).

[13] Adopted at the 10th Session of the Standing Committee of the Sixth National People's Congress of the People's Republic of China on 21 March 1985. On 15 March 1999, Law of the People's Republic of China on Economic Contracts Involving Foreign Interest was replaced by the Contract Law of the People's Republic of China.

[14] Response of the Supreme People's Court to Certain Questions Concerning the Application of the Foreign Economic Contract Law. The response was repealed by the Supreme People's Court (the Third Batch) by virtue of the Catalogue of Certain Judicial Interpretations issued before the end of 1999.

Law, promulgated in 1991, was intended to safeguard developments in the civil procedure relating to foreign-related matters and to protect the litigation rights of foreign nationals. The Civil Procedure Law contains 33 articles in Chapter VI that cover the litigation status of foreign nationals, jurisdiction, service of judicial documents, property preservation, foreign-related arbitration, judicial assistance, and other provisions. Revisions have since been made to the Civil Procedure Law to make it conform to contemporary developments. At the same time, China became a party to the 1965 Hague Convention on the Service Abroad of Judicial and Extrajudicial Documents in Civil or Commercial Matters (the 'Hague Service Convention'), the 1970 Hague Convention on the Taking of Evidence Abroad in Civil or Commercial Matters (the 'Hague Evidence Convention'), along with other private international law instruments. It also signed bilateral treaties on judicial assistance with other countries. In addition to legislation, the Supreme People's Court has issued judicial interpretations on the Civil Procedure Law and interregional judicial assistance involving Hong Kong, Macao, and Taiwan, and has played an important role in developing the principles of China's private international law. As for international commercial arbitration, the National People's Congress ratified and acceded to the 1958 Convention on the Recognition and Enforcement of Foreign Arbitral Awards in 1986 (the 'New York Convention'), which places Chinese international commercial arbitration in line with practice around the world. In 1991, the Arbitration Law was promulgated with provisions on foreign-related arbitration and was included in Chapter VII.[15] In recent years, the Chinese Government has committed to promoting diversified dispute resolution mechanisms, including arbitration. The Supreme People's Court has issued a number of judicial interpretations to clarify the relationship between litigation and arbitration, to support the development of arbitration and to provide explanations, approvals, responses and notices on issues of international commercial arbitration.

[15] It was adopted at the ninth session of the eighth Standing Committee of the National People's Congress of the People's Republic of China on 31 August 1994 and amended in 2009 and 2017.

4

Classification

XIN CAI

I. Definition

In private international law, the terms 'qualification' and 'classification' refer to the process of characterising the facts of a case for the purpose of identifying applicable choice of law rules. The terms will be used interchangeably here. Classification is thus the first step in analysing the facts of a case involving foreign elements. The facts are classified into specific legal categories before the application of law. From this perspective, classification is not unique to private international law but extends to all fields of law. But in the context of domestic law, a court can analyse the facts without considering foreign law. In private international law, foreign-related issues enable the laws of different states to be applied to different aspects of a case. There may be different outcomes to a case depending on how its facts are classified and the choice of law rule applied in consequence of such classification. As a result, there may be problems arising from conflicting classifications.

II. Characterisation Conflict

Classification conflicts may result from the following circumstances: (1) Different states may attach different legal consequences to the same set of facts. (2) The laws of different states may classify the same legal issues differently. (3) A state may have legal concepts that are unique to it. Most scholars and courts favour the *lex fori* approach to resolve conflicts, but some scholars advocate the *lex causae* approach. Under the former approach, the court (that is, the forum hearing a case) determines how the facts are classified. Under the latter approach, the facts are classified in accordance with the law applicable to the cause of action, typically, the law of the place of closest connection to the facts of a case. Prior to the Application Law of 2010, neither statute nor judicial interpretation covered the question of characterisation except for purposes of limitations. Article 8 of the Application Law now provides: 'The classification of foreign-related relationships shall be governed by the law of forum.' But the Application Law does not provide a solution when a foreign-related claim is not recognised by the law of the forum. Although, as a matter of theory, scholars dispute the rationality of the simple application of the *lex fori* in determining classification, the Application Law has clearly stipulated that only the law of the court is applicable for classification. Consequently, the application of the *lex fori* for the purposes of classification has become the common practice in Chinese courts.

III. Case Studies

In *Toshiba Corporation v Grande Holdings Limited*, Grande was a company registered in Bermuda.[1] Tomei Shoji was a British Virgin Islands company. Toshiba was a Japanese company. Toshiba International Procurement Hong Kong Ltd was a Hong Kong company. The case involved a dispute over processing contracts with Hong Kong and foreign elements. The court held that, that the *lex fori* should apply to the classification of the foreign-related civil relations and thus the People's Republic of China law should determine the classification of the dispute in accordance with Article 8 of the Application Law.

In *Jiangsu Hongyu Solar Industry Co Ltd v Shen Zhui and Fan Jinmei*), Jiangsu Hongyu claimed that it had sent a solar water heater worth US$25,683.68 to Shen Zhui in September 2009 and the heater had been stored, transported and made available for sale by Shen Zhui in Romania.[2] Jiangsu Hongyu further alleged that, after Shen received the goods in Romania, he stored the goods in a warehouse leased under his name. On 29 December 2009, after Shen returned to China, he was asked by Jiangsu Hongyu to provide information about the goods' location and storage. Shen refused. Fan Jinmei, as Shen's spouse, was jointly responsible under the law for Shen's debts during their marriage. The husband and wife were thus potentially liable to pay the amount due on the heater. However, Shen and Fan argued that Shen had no relationship with Jiangsu Hongyu. They said that Shen had not conducted any relevant transactions in relation to the heater. Shen denied that he had received, stored, or transferred the goods in Romania on behalf of Jiangsu Hongyu. A focal dispute in the case was thus whether there was a civil legal relationship between Jiangsu Hongyu and Shen. In accordance with the provisions of Article 3 of the Application Law, the court held that: 'The law of the forum shall apply to the determination of the nature of foreign-related civil relations.' Thus, PRC law should determining how the facts should be classified as a step towards the applicable law and determining whether here was a civil relationship between the parties.

[1] Supreme People's Court Decision *Toshiba Corporation v The Grande Holdings Limited* (2016) Zui Gao Fa Min Xia Zhong No 245.

[2] Jiangsu High People's Court Decision *Jiangsu Hongyu Solar Energy Industry Ltd v Shen Zhui and Fan Jinmei* (2011) Su Shang Wai Zhong Zi No 57.

5

Preliminary Question

XIN CAI

I. Definition

Preliminary question, also known as incidental question, refers to questions that must be resolved before a primary legal question can be satisfactorily determined. Traditional Chinese private international law textbooks draw on the views of British scholars and state that there are three basic elements constituting a preliminary question: (1) The main issue must be governed by the law of some foreign country. (2) A preliminary question must arise involving foreign elements, but which is capable of arising in its own right and for which there is a separate choice of law rule. (3) The law governing the preliminary question must result in a different outcome from the law governing the main issue.[1] Some scholars further believe that, if these three elements are not met, there will be no conflict in the application of law and no need to engage in a conflicts of law analysis.[2] According to this view, many cases that are considered to have an incidental question at first blush cannot be regarded as actually involving a preliminary question as a matter of private international law. Therefore, in recent years, many domestic scholars have questioned such strict requirements.[3] It is argued that strict constitutive requirements will limit the utility of a preliminary question analysis, thereby leading to a failure to identify disputes as involving preliminary and main questions. This could have the result of parties having to bring separate actions, wasting their own and judicial resources. Some academics have also discussed the distinction between broad and narrow senses of the preliminary question. They distinguish between preliminary questions in private international law and preliminary questions in substantive law.[4] There has been no conclusion to the current debates over the concept of the preliminary question.

II. Solution of Preliminary Question Problems

There are two main techniques for solving preliminary question problems. One approach is to use the legal system specified by the choice of law rules of the state to which the main problem

[1] DP Han, *Guoji Sifa* [*Private International Law*] (Higher Education Press & Peking University Press, 2014) 120.

[2] L Collins, *Dicey, Morris and Collins on Conflict of Law* vol 1, 14th edn (Sweet & Maxwell 2006) 52–53.

[3] YM Wu, 'Guoji Sifa Zhong di Xianjue Wenti: Luojixue Shang de Chongxin Shenshi' [A Preliminary Question in Private International Law: A Re-examination of Logic] (2013) 1 *Western Law Review*; YN Liu, S Chen and JG Yuan, 'The Preliminary Question in Private International Law' (2007) 3 *Journal of Yanshan University* (Philosophy and Social Sciences Edition).

[4] BS Wang, *Guoji Sifa zhong di xianjuewenti yanjiu* [*Research on Preliminary Questions in Private International Law*] (Law Press, 2007).

is subject in order to determine the appropriate law. The purpose of this method is to unify the application of the law and thus achieve consistent results. The other approach is to apply the legal system specified by the choice of law rules of the state in which the court is located as the prerequisite law. This view essentially considers the problem of a preliminary question as separate from the main issue, and resolves it independently without considering its relationship with the law governing the main issue.

III. Current Practice in China on Preliminary Question Problems

The Application Law does not directly address the preliminary question problem. According to Article 12 of the Application Law Interpretation (I), where the resolution of a foreign-related civil dispute hinges on the confirmation of another foreign-related civil relationship, the people's court shall determine the applicable law in accordance with the nature of the latter issue. As can be seen, the Application Law Interpretation (I) did not adopt the strict three elements test posted by academic theory. It only stipulates that the preliminary question is to be regarded as a separate legal issue. A court must first separately apply the law applicable to that issue, before the court solves the main problem of the case by reference to the outcome of the preliminary question problem.

IV. Case Studies

In *Mountain Breeze (Barbados) SRL v Beijing Zhongtian Hongye Real Estate Consulting Co, Ltd*,[5] Mountain Breeze was established in Barbados in January 2006, iXinbaiyi (Hong Kong) Investment Co Ltd was a shareholder. Xinbaiyi's shares were in turn held by SBI Holdings Inc (Korea). Beijing Zhongtian was a wholly foreign-owned enterprise established on 24 April 2006. Its shareholder (founder-member) was Mountain Breeze. According to Zhongtian Hongye's registered industrial and commercial information, its legal representative had been changed from Huang Huajie to Min Fengzhen on 21 April 2008. Its directors in 2010 were Min Fengzhen, Jin Hongying, and Min Caixing. Its supervisor was Song Changqing. Mountain Breeze claimed to be Zhongtian Hongye's sole shareholder since the latter's establishment. In order to ascertain Zhongtian Hongye's operating status and balance sheet and exercise its shareholder rights, Mountain Breeze submitted a request to inspect and copy Zhongtian Hongye's articles of association, minutes of shareholders' meetings, board resolutions, minutes and resolutions of supervisors' meetings, financial accounting reports, accounting books, and related documents. Mountain Breeze Ltd delivered a written request to Zhongtian Hongye for access to the foregoing documents on 27 June 2012. Zhongtian Hongye refused to provide the requested documents. Mountain Breeze therefore applied to the court for an order that Zhongtian Hongye produce the documents.

Underlying the dispute was a conspiracy between Woori Bank Korean and the developer of Zhonghui Plaza, Beijing Zhongdi Real Estate Development Co Ltd. They attempted to embezzle monies from Zhonghui Plaza (with a market value of more than RMB 7 billion), infringing the rights and interests of Zhongtian Hongye and its ultimate shareholder, Min Fengzhen. Zhongtian Hongye argued that the main qualification documents submitted by Mountain Breeze could not

[5] Beijing Municipality Intermediate People's Court No 2 Decision (2016) Jing-02 Min Chu No 93.

prove that Jin Xiurong, Cui Rongshou and their successors (namely, Zhang Xuefeng, Liu Huilu, and Li Hong) were legal directors of Mountain Breeze. The appointments of Mountain Breeze's directors should therefore be regarded as invalid and the alleged directors had no right to file a lawsuit on behalf of Mountain Breeze. Zhongtian Hongye further submitted that shareholders can only inquire about accounting books, but cannot copy them according to the law. The result was that the documents sought could not be investigated or copied and Mountain Breeze had no basis for its demands. The court treated the case as a dispute over the shareholder's right to know. Since Zhongtian Hongye was a People's Republic of China (PRC) company established as a wholly foreign-owned enterprise, the dispute should be governed by PRC law in accordance with Article 4 of the Application Law, Article 4 of Law on Wholly Foreign-Owned Enterprises, and Article 2 of the Detailed Rules for the Implementation of the Law on Wholly Foreign-owned Enterprises. However, to determine whether Mountain Breeze had a right to know as a shareholder, it was necessary to confirm the identity of Mountain Breeze's directors and to determine the law that should be applied to that issue. Article 14 of the Application Law stipulates: 'The laws at the locality of registration shall apply to such items as the civil rights capacities, civil acts capacities, organizational institutions, rights and obligations of shareholders, etc. of a legal person and its branch.' Article 16 of the Application Law Interpretation (I) further provides: 'The people's courts shall determine the place of incorporation registration of the legal person as the place of registration of the legal person as prescribed in the Law on Choice of Law for Foreign-Related Civil Relationships.' The court consequently held that because Mountain Breeze was a legal entity established in Barbados, Barbados law should be applied to matters such as Mountain Breeze's civil rights, civil capacity, organisation, and rights and obligations as shareholder.

In *Allianz Global Corporate & Specialty SE v NHE Shipping Inc*,[6] the preliminary question involved a determination of the legal relationship between NHE and Allianz, in particular their status in respect of an insurance policy. One of NHE's claims was that Allianz had not proven that it was the insurer under the policy and enjoyed subrogation rights thereunder. Pursuant to Article 12 of Application Law Interpretation (I), the court treated this issue as a preliminary question and the applicable law was applied separately from the law governing the main issue (namely, the legal effect of a contract for the carriage of goods by sea). The court could not determine from the evidence whether NHE and Allianz had specifically agreed on the law governing their relationship under the insurance policy. However, NHE and Allianz were both German legal entities. Further, according to a clause in the insurance policy, the German General Rules for Marine Insurance should apply. Therefore, in keeping with Article 41 of the Application Law, the court held that the preliminary question called for the application of German law. As far as the law governing the contract of carriage of goods by sea was concerned, the court applied PRC law since both parties had agreed to that.

In *Guo Zongxi, Li Shuzhen v Qingdao Changlong Stationery Co Ltd*,[7] the main issue was the inheritance relationship between Li Shuzhen and Guo Yinwei. In accordance with Article 31 of the Application Law, the law of the habitual residence of the deceased at the time of death applied to the question of inheritance. Guo Yinwei, the deceased, had passed away in Taiwan, but he lived and worked in Qingdao for a long time prior to his death. Therefore, Guo's residence at the time of death was mainland China. It followed that inheritance to Guo's estate should be governed by the law of mainland China. However, the court took the view that, in order to

[6] Tianjin High People's Court Decision *Allianz Global Corporate v NHE Shipping Incorporated* (2016) Jin Min Zhong No 138.

[7] Shandong Province High People's Court Decision *Guo Zongxi, Li Shuzhen v Qingdao Changlong Stationery Co Ltd* (2016) Lü Min Zhong No 2270.

determine the inheritance relationship, it must first determine whether there was a valid marriage relationship between Guo and Li Shuzhen. This preliminary question was not subject to the law governing succession to Guo's estate. According to Article 22 of the Application Law, that part of the legal relationship was to be confirmed in accordance with the law of Taiwan. On 25 November 1990, the marriage between Li and Guo was certified before a notary in the Taipei District Court. The marriage conformed with Article 982 of the Taiwan Civil Law which provided that a valid marriage requires a public ceremony and more than two persons as witnesses. Thus, the marriage between Li and Guo had been validly contracted.

In *Zeng Haiquan and Zhuhai Jiantai Real Estate Development Co Ltd*,[8] Zeng Haiquan signed a Cooperation Agreement with Oriental International Enterprise Ltd. He also furnished a letter confirming that he held a 15 per cent stake in Jiantai Company and that requested Oriental International Enterprise Ltd to fulfil its equity transfer obligations as stipulated in the 'Cooperation Agreement'. The Cooperation Agreement and the letter were apparently both issued on behalf of Zhong Xiaojian. Therefore, the issue was whether the two documents gave rise to any contractual obligations between Zeng and Oriental. The Cooperation Agreement, having been signed before the implementation of the Application Law, that statute was not pertinent. The court referred instead to Article 2 of the Application Law Interpretation (I). This provides that, in cases for which there are no applicable laws at a relevant time, the applicable law may be determined by reference to the Application Law. The court thus determined the applicable law by reference to the Application Law and the relevant provisions of its judicial interpretation. According to Article 12 of the Application Law Interpretation (I), where the settlement of a foreign-related civil dispute is conditional on the validity of another foreign-related civil relationship, the people's court shall determine the applicable law in accordance with the nature of that initial issue. Thus, Article 8 of the Application Law stipulates that the *lex fori* shall apply to the determination of the nature of foreign-related civil relations and PRC law should apply to the determination of the nature of a dispute. According to the Company Law of the PRC, matters relating to a company's organisational structure and legal responsibilities are issues concerning the scope of a company's civil capacity. On that basis, the court held that the Macao Law, as the law of Oriental's place of registration, should be applied to resolve the preliminary problem. That would be in accordance with Article 14 of the Application Law which states: 'The laws at the locality of registration shall apply to such items as the civil rights capacities, civil acts capacities, organizational institutions, rights and obligations of shareholders, etc. of a legal person and its branch.'

[8] Guangdong High People's Court Decision *Zeng Haiquan v Zhuhai Jiantai Real Estate Development Co Ltd* (2016) Yue Min Zhong No 588.

6

Dépeçage

XIN CAI

I. Definition

Dépeçage, colloquially referred to as 'picking-and-choosing', is also known as choice of law by legal division. The term comes from French and means 'cutting up, dismembering, carving up'.[1] Broadly, it refers to the application of different laws to the substantive and procedural issues of a case. More specifically, in the field of private international law, *dépeçage* refers to the division of a complicated conflict of law problem into several issues, so as to apply different laws to each separate issue.[2] Recent years have seen a trend of expanding the role of *dépeçage*. There are a variety of reasons for this. First, traditional private international law focuses on the unity, integrity, and internal consistency of the application of law. It emphasises the single connection between cross-border civil or commercial cases and specific countries and advocates the identification of a connection between a given situation and a specific state for the purpose of determining the law applicable to the situation.[3] Therefore, it is common practice to choose one specific applicable law for a given case. *Dépeçage* only occasionally appears as an exception. Modern *dépeçage* was born in the twentieth century out of the American conflicts of law revolution. At that time, it was generally believed that for each specific issue in a case, the court should apply the law that has the closest connection with the issue. In many cases, there may be multiple issues involving conflicts of law.

The relevant choice of law rule may also be different for each issue. Therefore, implementation of the principle requires separate legal choices for each issue. Second, the use of *dépeçage* can prevent evasion of law. According to the traditional approach, the final result applies only one specific law (except for procedural issues which apply the *lex fori*). This often yields unsatisfactory results for the handling of complex cases. In order to avoid such results, many judges often resort to classification, public policy, and other methods to achieve a just result. This in turn increases the uncertainty and unpredictability of conflicts of law outcomes. The use of *dépeçage*, which facilitates the fair resolution of the case, should therefore reduce the need to 'get around' the law. Third, for some complicated cases, multiple states have interests that lead them to apply their laws. The traditional conflicts method only applies the law of one state to resolve all the issues of

[1] Guangdong High People's Court Decision *Zeng Haiquan v Zhuhai Jiantai Real Estate Development Co Ltd* (2016) Yue Min Zhong No 588.

[2] Cheshire and North, *Private International Law* 11th edn (Butterworth, 1987) 56; WLM Reese, 'Dépeçage: A Common Phenomenon in Choice of Law' (1973) 73 *Columbia Law Review* 58.

[3] YP Xiao, *Principle of Private International Law* (Law Press China, 2003) 280.

a case. This may damage the interests of other states. By employing *dépeçage*, an issue-by-issue method, a state's interest can be safeguarded by applying its law to the issues of a case that are closely linked to that state. Finally, *dépeçage* is the inevitable result of the development of satisfactory choice of law rules.

Traditional choice of law principles are mostly general rules. For example, a rigid rule such as the application of the *lex loci delicti* in the field of tort does not guarantee a fair result in every case. New types of cases have emerged with the growth in international civil and commercial exchanges. This has led to criticism of traditional jurisdiction-selection rules which ignore the outcome of a case. The changing circumstances of today's world require new approaches. Compared with traditional conflicts rules, the new types of conflicts rules are more numerous but are also narrower in scope.[4] The purpose of developing such rules is to address specific issues in a case. Applying satisfactory choice of law rules in this way requires the application of different laws to the different issues of the case. If *dépeçage* is rejected, it will inevitably lead to the exclusion of such new rules. Correspondingly, the certainty, predictability, and convenience of application will not be realised. Therefore, it is submitted that *dépeçage* is a prerequisite for the development of satisfactory choice of law rules.

Not surprisingly, *dépeçage* has been criticised for its flexibility and lack of limitation. Criticism has concentrated on several points. First, critics suggest that *dépeçage* is essentially the use of an amalgam of different choice of law rules to come up with a 'mixed rule' for the determination of a case. In this way, it is argued that it would be more appropriate to speak of *dépeçage* as the 'legislation' of a new rule rather than the application of a variety of 'choice of laws'. Second, there is no limit to the extent to which a court can break a case down into its component parts for the purpose of applying different choice of law rules to each part. This can lead to overly complicated legal analyses. The lack of a clear standard as to the extent to which a case may be broken down appears to be the principal objection to *dépeçage*. On the one hand, when the court applies *dépeçage*, it can manipulate its analysis to reach a desired result. *Dépeçage* would thus be susceptible to being employed as a means to escape certain legal consequences. On the other hand, due to the lack of limitations to the method, the court may distort the underlying rationale of an applicable law when resorting to *dépeçage*. Therefore, it is important to impose restrictions on *dépeçage*. At the same time, given the diversity and complexity of cross-border cases, it is unrealistic specifically to regulate *dépeçage*. Finally, if the court adopts *dépeçage*, there could be a lack of predictability to the outcome of a case. This is because the court may apply the laws of many states in its analysis and thereby reach a result that would not be in accordance with the parties' expectations. Ultimately, the flexibility inherent in *dépeçage* is both its strength and its weakness. Flexibility may give rise to uncertainty. But flexibility enables judges to select the appropriate law for each issue of a case, maximising the potential to achieve a just and reasonable result in the specific circumstances of the case.

II. Legislation and Practice on *Dépeçage* in China

Although Chinese conflicts of law legislation does not mention *dépeçage*, certain statutes reveal a tendency to favour its use. For example, on marriage, Articles 21 and 22 of the Application Law respectively break down the requirements for a valid marriage to essential and formal elements.[5]

[4] WLM Reese, 'Choice of Law: Rules or Approach' (1972) 57 *Cornell Law Review* 319.

[5] The Law of the People's Republic of China on Choice of Law for Foreign-related Civil Relationships, adopted at the Seventeenth Session of the Eleventh Standing Committee of the National People's Congress of the People's Republic of China on 28 October 2010, and took effect on 1 April 2011.

Articles 23 and 24 respectively refer to the personal and property relationships of husband and wife. In Article 28, the conditions for adoption, the procedures for adoption, and the effectiveness of adoption are all separately specified. In addition, there are similar regulations in the fields of inheritance, contracts, and infringement of intellectual property. The Application Law thus tacitly affirms the approach of dividing a specific legal institution (such as marriage or adoption) into its component parts and applying a different law to each part. The Application Law Interpretation (I) promulgated in 2012 offers further insight into the tacit use of *dépeçage* in Chinese private international law.[6] Article 13 stipulates that, where a case involves two or more foreign-related civil relationships, the people's court shall respectively determine the applicable laws thereof. Unlike the preliminary question, the provisions of Article 13 do not require that the multiple legal relationships be related to each other. As long as the judge decides that there are multiple foreign-related relations, she can apply the law separately. In essence, the law paves the way for courts to use *dépeçage*. According to Article 13, if the judge determines that there are multiple legal relationships, it is not necessary to apply only one choice of law rule. Instead, different laws can be applied separately for each relevant relationship identified.

III. Case Studies

In *Lin Jiansheng v Wang Jianming and others*,[7] Lin Jiansheng, was a resident of Macao. On 5 March 2013, Wang Jianming as borrower entered into a loan contract for RMB 7 million with Lin as lender in Zhuhai. The loan was for nine months at a monthly interest rate of 50 per cent. The contract was governed by Macao law. On 8 March 2013, in accordance with the contract and pursuant Wang Jianming's instruction, Lin remitted RMB 7 million to Wang Haiquan's account through a bank in Zhuhai. On the same day, Wang Jianming issued a 'receipt' to Lin for the above loan. On 5 March 2013, Yuhua Company Guangdong Branch issued a Commitment Letter to Lin in the name of the company. The Commitment letter stated that, if Wang Jianming could not repay the loan on time, Yuhua would pay the relevant compensation and late payments fee to Lin and assume full repayment responsibility for the loan. The court held that the case actually involved two related disputes, namely: (1) a dispute between Lin Jiansheng and Wang Jianming on the loan contract; and (2) a dispute over whether Wang Haiquan and Yuhua Company should bear any responsibility upon non-payment of the loan. On the first matter, the court held that, since Lin was a Macao resident, the case was a dispute over a loan contract with a Macao connection. Further, the loan contract clearly provide for the application of Macao law. According to Article 145 of the General Principles of the National Law and Articles 3 and 41 of the Law of Application Law, the principle of party autonomy meant that Macao law governed the rights and obligations of Lin and Wang Jianming under the contract. As to whether Wang Haiquan and Yuhua were jointly and severally liable for unpaid loan monies, the court decided that the law of Mainland China had the closest connection to the pertinent civil relationships in accordance with Article 13 of the Applicable Law Interpretation (I) ('Where a case involves two or more foreign-related civil relationships, the people's court shall respectively determine the applicable laws thereof') and Article 2 of the Application Law. It will be seen that the court did not apply

[6] Interpretation of the Supreme People's Court on Several Issues Concerning the Application of the 'Law of the People's Republic of China on the Law Applicable to Foreign-Related Civil Relationships' (I) (Supreme People's Court, Fa Shi (2012) 24, adopted on 10 December 2012 and took effect on 7 January 2013).

[7] Zhuhai Municipality Intermediate People's Court Decision *Lin Jiansheng v Wang Jianming* (2016) Yue-04 Min Chu No 28.

the Macao law to the whole case. It instead broke down the case into its specific legal issues and applied different laws to the issues identified in accordance with *dépeçage*.

In *Asia Steel (Investments) Limited v Wuhan Yagang Metal Co Ltd*[8] iSteel Asia and Asia Steel (Investments) Limited were Hong Kong companies. They became embroiled in a commercial dispute with Wuhan Yagang. According to Article 19 of the Application Law Interpretation (I), the Application Law and its judicial interpretation shall apply. At the same time, the case involved several legal issues, namely the legal effect of a guarantee letter and the civil capacity of iSteel Asia Trading Co Ltd. On the validity of the guarantee, the court referred to the first paragraph of Article 14 of the Application Law: 'The laws at the locality of registration shall apply to such items as the civil rights capacities, civil acts capacities, organizational institutions, rights and obligations of shareholders, etc. of a legal person and its branch.' Therefore, the civil capacity of Asia Steel to enter into a guarantee were governed by Hong Kong law. However, Asia Steel's civil capacity to enter into the guarantee and the validity of guarantee were distinct issues, so the applicable laws had to be determined separately. According to Article 41 of the Application Law states: 'The parties concerned may choose the laws applicable to contracts by agreement.' The court found that the guarantee expressly provided for the application of Chinese law. Therefore, the validity of the guarantee was governed the law of Mainland China.

In *Guo Zongxi, Li Shuzhen and Qingdao Changlong Stationery Co Ltd*,[9] the court pointed out that the case involved multiple legal relationships. First, Guo Yinwei and Qingdao Changlong Stationery Co Ltd had shareholder rights and obligations. Second, there was the legal inheritance relationship between Guo Zongxi, Li Shuzhen, and Guo Yinwei. Third, there was the relationship between Guo Yinwei and Li Shuzhen. Fourth, there was Guo Yinwei and Li Shuzhen's property relationship. The court applied different choice of law rules for each relationship and applied different laws in accordance with the choice of law rules employed.

[8] Hubei Province High People's Court Decision *Asia Steel (Investments) Ltd v Wuhan Yagang Metal Co Ltd* (2017) E Min Shen No 2157.

[9] Shandong Province High People's Court Decision *Guo Zongxi, Li Shuzhen v Qingdao Changlong Stationery Co Ltd* (2016) Lv Min Zhong No 2270.

7

Renvoi

XIN CAI

Choice of law rules will sometimes direct the judge to apply the laws of a foreign state. The judge must then determine whether the choice of law rule requires the application of the substantive law of the foreign state or whether one must have regard to the choice of law rules of that state. This has led to the problem of *renvoi* (from the French, meaning 'send back' or 'to return unopened') in private international law. *Renvoi* can generally be divided into three categories:

(1) Remission: In accordance with its choice of law rule on a given matter, a court in state X refers to the law of state Y including the latter's choice of law rules. Where state Y's choice of law rule provides for the application of the law of state X in the matter, then the court in state X accepts the *renvoi* and applies the substantive law of state X to the matter.
(2) Transmission: As in (1), the court in state X refers to the law of state Y, including the latter's choice of law rules, on a matter. Where state Y's choice of law rule provides for the application of the substantive law of state Z in the matter, then the court in state X follows the transmission and applies the substantive law of state Y to the matter.
(3) Indirect remission: As in (1), the court in state X refers to the law of state Y, including the latter's choice of law rules on a matter. Where state Y's choice of law rule provides for the application of the law of state Z and the law of state Z provides for the application of the law of state X in the matter, then the court in state X accepts the *renvoi* from state X via state Z and applies the substantive law of state X to the matter.

Renvoi arises because different countries have different choice of law rules. There is a long-standing controversy over whether *renvoi* should play any part in private international law. Thus, it would always be possible to decline a *renvoi* by treating a choice of law rule as solely referring to the substantive law of a foreign state. In such cases, the court would pay no heed to the choice of law rules of the foreign state, but simply apply its substantive law in a given matter. However, proponents of *renvoi* believe that the application of *renvoi* is conducive to achieving international consistency among judgments, expanding the scope of judges' abilities to achieve fair results in cases and creating greater opportunity to apply the law of the forum. Opponents emphasise the unpredictability and the inextricable circular logic underlying the doctrine of *renvoi*.

Before the implementation of the Application Law in 2011, neither Chapter 8 of the General Principles of Civil Law nor other laws contained choice of laws rules, much less explicit provisions on *renvoi* and transmission.[1] Article 178, paragraph 2 of the 1988 Opinions on the

[1] The Law of the People's Republic of China on Choice of Law for Foreign-related Civil Relationships, adopted at the Seventeenth Session of the Eleventh Standing Committee of the National People's Congress of the People's Republic of China on 28 October 2010, and took effect on 1 April 2011.

Implementation states that, when a people's court hears a case concerning a foreign-related civil relationship, it shall determine the substantive law to be applied in accordance with Chapter VIII of the General Principles of Civil Law.[2] Since Chapter 8 of the General Principles of Civil Law stipulates the choice of law rules relating to specific foreign-related civil relations,[3] it implies that a judge only needs to consider the substantive provisions of the foreign legal system designated by an operative choice of law rule without having to consider the choice of law rules of that foreign legal system. This means rejecting the possibility of *renvoi*. Some scholars thus interpret the text and purpose of the General Principles of Civil Law as excluding remission and transmission.[4] However, since judicial interpretation is not explicit on this point, some courts continue to use *renvoi*.

The implementation of the Application Law in 2011 clearly shows the attitude of the legislators towards *renvoi*.[5] Article 9 of the law stipulates that foreign laws used in foreign-related civil relations do not include the choice of law rules of such foreign law and only its substantive law is to be used. This fundamentally rejects the possibility of *renvoi* and transmission. *Renvoi* previously was primarily used to reconcile conflicts between the laws of a person's domicile and nationality. But the Application Law of 2011 adopts the doctrine of habitual residence as its basic connection factor, so this reduces the need to resort to *renvoi*. By excluding *renvoi* and transmission, the court can enhance certainty and predictability in the determination of the applicable law.[6]

[2] Opinions of the Supreme People's Court on Several Issues concerning the Implementation of the General Principles of the Civil Law of the People's Republic of China (Trial Implementation) (Supreme People's Court, Fa Ban Fa (1988) 6, adopted on 26 January 1988 and promulgated on 2 April 1988).

[3] Passed at the Fourth Session of the Sixth National People's Congress of the People's Republic of China on 12 April 1986 and was implemented on 1 January 1987. It is invalidated by the Civil Code of the People's Republic of China (issued on 28 May 2020, effective on 1 January 2021).

[4] DG Xu, *Guoji Sifa Qushi Lun* [*Trend of International Private Law*] (Peking University Press, 2005) 80.

[5] The Law of the People's Republic of China on Choice of Law for Foreign-related Civil Relationships, adopted at the Seventeenth Session of the Eleventh Standing Committee of the National People's Congress of the People's Republic of China on 28 October 2010, and took effect on 1 April 2011.

[6] WZ Chen, 'Shewai Minshi Guanxi Falü Shiyong Fazhan Shi Da Liang Dian' [Ten Highlights of the Application law for Foreign-related Civil Relations] (2010) *Legal Daily*; WZ Chen, 'Shewai Minshi Guanxi Falü Shiyong di Zhongguo Te Se' [Chinese Characteristics of the Law Applicable to Foreign-related Civil Relations] (2011) *Applicable Law* 48–52.

8

Point of Contact

XIN CAI

Point of contact is also known as connecting factor. It refers to the basis for determining the law applicable to a civil relation involving foreign elements. The most common points of contact include nationality, residence, habitual residence, and the place of the forum.

I. Nationality

Nationality is the identity of an individual with respect to his or her political status and allegiance to a state. In the context of private international law, nationality may be used to determine legal personality and plays a major role in matters of capacity, marriage, family, and inheritance of natural persons. For example, the Application Law refers to nationality as a connecting factor in marriage, relationships between husband and wife, and relationships between parents and children. Article 19 of the Application Law provides that:

> If the *lex patriae* applies in accordance with this law, where a natural person has two or more nationalities, the *lex patriae* of the country of his or her habitual residence shall apply. Where he or she is not habitually resident in a country of which he or she is a national, the *lex patriae* of the country having the most significant relationship with him or her shall apply. In the case of a stateless natural person or a natural person without clear nationality, the law of his or her habitual residence shall apply.[1]

Thus, where there is a conflict among the laws of a person's nationalities, the law of the country of nationality coinciding with the person's habitual residence needs to be identified. If there is no habitual residence in one or other of the person's countries of nationality, the judge needs to determine the applicable law by reference to the principle of the closest connection. Where a person has no nationality or the person's nationality is unclear, the country of habitual residence is to be regarded as the country of nationality.

II. Habitual Residence

Early Chinese private international law legislation, such as the General Principles of Civil Law, chose residence as the connecting factor. With the enactment of the Application Law, there

[1] The Law of the People's Republic of China on Choice of Law for Foreign-related Civil Relationships, adopted at the Seventeenth Session of the Eleventh Standing Committee of the National People's Congress of the People's Republic of China on 28 October 2010, and took effect on 1 April 2011.

has been a movement away from nationality and residence as connecting factors and towards using habitual residence as the main factor to determine personal law. Habitual residence appears in the 25 articles of the Application Law for a total of 44 times, but its definition is not clear.[2] 'Habitual residence' is similar to the connecting factor used by the Hague Conference of Private International Law in its various conventions. The fundamental purpose of using habitual residence as a connecting factor is to reconcile differences between nationality and domicile principles of personal law in different countries. The resort to habitual residence is thus a product of the unified private international law movement. The determination of habitual residence is often considered to be a question of fact. Therefore, international treaties do not specify the criteria for habitual residence. There are few definitions of 'habitual residence' in the laws of different countries. For example, there is an abstract provision in German and Swiss laws, which emphasises that 'habitual residence' should be a 'life centre'. The 2012 Application Law draws on the Opinions on the Implementation and Interpretation of the Supreme People's Court on the Application of the Civil Procedure Law[3] to define 'habitual residence'. Article 15 of the Application Law states:

> Where a natural person has lived continuously for more than one year [in a state] as at the time of the creation or alteration or termination of a foreign-related civil relationship and [such state] is the centre of his life, the people's court may determine [such state to be] the permanent residence of the natural person as stipulated in the applicable law of foreign-related civil relations, except [where the natural person's residence in the relevant state has been the purposes of] for medical treatment, labour dispatch, official duties, etc.

A number of matters need to be clarified. First, the time limit is defined as at the point of 'starting or changing or terminating foreign-related civil relations'. A year of continuous residence in a locality prior to that point is plainly necessary. However, whether that one-year period must be an absolutely uninterrupted period is not explained in the article. In judicial practice, courts treat the one-year period loosely and do not require a continuous uninterrupted residence for one year. Second, there is the question of what is meant by 'life centre'. The article does not directly define the concept, but merely identifies what would not count towards establishing a 'life centre' (namely, residence for the purposes of medical treatment, labour dispatch, and official duties). Otherwise, judges must use their discretion in determining whether a locality may be characterised as a person's 'life centre'.

[2] HF Du, 'Chinese-style Choice, Judgment, and Application of Natural Persons' Law and Current Residence – Comment on the Article 15 of Law of the People's Republic of China on Choice of Law for Foreign-related Civil Relationships' (2015) 3 *The Jurist* 152–163.

[3] Opinions on Several Issues concerning the Implementation of the General Principles of the Civil Law of the People's Republic of China (For Trial Implementation), art 9: The place where citizens leave their homes for more than one year in a row, is a place of permanent residence. That is, except for hospital treatment; Interpretation of the Supreme People's Court on the Application of the Civil Procedure Law of the People's Republic of China, art 4: The permanent residence of citizens refers to the place where citizens have left their homes until they have been in residence for more than one year at the time of prosecution, except where citizens are hospitalised for medical treatment.

9

Ascertainment of Foreign Law

XIN CAI

The ascertainment of foreign law is an essential part of private international law. When the choice of law rules direct the court to a foreign law, the judge must determine whether such law exists and what the contents of that law are.

I. Nature of Foreign Law

In the ascertainment of foreign law, the first question is the practical one of whether the determination of foreign law is to be regarded as a question of 'fact' or a question of 'law'. If the foreign law is deemed to be a matter of fact, the burden of proof would be upon the plaintiff to prove the existence and contents of that foreign law as a matter of fact in accordance with basic principles of civil litigation. If the foreign law is a matter of law, the judge is responsible for ascertaining what the relevant foreign law is in accordance with the principle of *iura novit curia*. Chinese law does not give a clear answer to the question. Article 7 of the Civil Procedure Law stipulates that: 'The people's courts must take the facts as the basis and take the law as the criterion when adjudicating civil cases.' In light of this statement, some scholars have suggested that the distinction between foreign law as a matter of fact and as a matter of law is meaningless in the Chinese context.[1]

II. Method of Ascertaining Foreign Law

A. Judges Ascertain Foreign Law by Authority

Article 10 of the Application Law stipulates that the foreign laws applicable to foreign-related civil relations shall be ascertained by the people's courts, arbitration institutions, or administrative organs dealing with a case. Where the parties choose to apply foreign law, they are to provide the court with the content of the same.[2] In contrast, Article 178, paragraph 2 of the Opinions on the

[1] J Huang, *Private International Law* (Law Press, 1999).
[2] The Law of the People's Republic of China on Choice of Law for Foreign-related Civil Relationships, adopted at the Seventeenth Session of the Eleventh Standing Committee of the National People's Congress of the People's Republic of China on 28 October 2010, and took effect on 1 April 2011.

Implementation stipulates that, when a people's court hears a case concerning a foreign-related civil relationship, it shall determine the substantive law to be applied in accordance with the provisions of Chapter VIII of the General Principles of Civil Law.[3] According to the latter provisions, in the absence of the exercise of party autonomy, the burden of ascertaining foreign law shall be on the court. At the same time, in cases where a choice of law rule identifies the applicable foreign law, the judge must ascertain it *ex officio* even if the parties do not ask the court to apply the foreign law.[4] The Application Law does not directly specify the means by which judges are to ascertain foreign law. Article 17 of the Application Law Interpretation (I) merely says that:

> If the people's court still fails to obtain foreign laws through the channels provided by the parties, the means of international treaties that have entered into force for the People's Republic of China, and Chinese and foreign legal experts, it may conclude that foreign law cannot be ascertained.[5]

Although the thrust of the article is to identify when a judge may conclude that foreign law cannot be ascertained, several methods of ascertainment are implicit in the article. These include the following: (1) The parties inform the court about ('provide' the court with) the content of the relevant foreign law. (2) The foreign law is determined by using the means set out in an operative treaty. (3) The foreign law is identified with the assistance of Chinese and foreign legal experts. At the same time, Article 193 of the Opinions on the Implementation states that applicable foreign laws can be ascertained though various sources, namely: (1) the parties; (2) an authority specified in a mutual legal assistance agreement between China and a relevant foreign state; (3) the Chinese embassy or consulate in the relevant country; (4) the relevant country's embassy in China; and (5) Chinese and foreign legal experts. Compared with the ways listed in the Application Law Interpretation (I), the Opinions on the Implementation add mutual legal assistance and diplomatic means. In practice, courts use multiple methods to ascertain foreign law. Some well-known foreign laws can be ascertained by a court taking judicial notice of their existence and content. The scope of extraterritorial law is not limited to statutory law. Authoritative legal commentary, academic textbooks, and cases with guiding significance can be used as important references for the existence and content of foreign law. In recent years, many Chinese courts, universities, research institutions and think-tanks have signed agreements on the ascertainment of foreign law. In 2014, the Shanghai High People's Court and the East China University of Political Science and Law (ECUPL) signed a special cooperation agreement for the ascertainment of foreign laws and established the Foreign Law Ascertainment Research Center of East China University of Political Science and Law. The Ningbo Intermediate People's Court signed a cooperation agreement with ECUPL, whereby legal experts in the latter can help to identify the content of foreign law in foreign-related civil and commercial trials. In early 2015 the Supreme Court and the China University of Political Science and Law (CUPL) jointly established a foreign law ascertainment research database. In August of the same year, the Supreme People's Court engaged Benchmark Chambers International (BCI) to assist in discerning Hong Kong, Macau, Taiwan, and foreign law. In 2017, the Shanghai and Guangzhou Maritime Courts signed an ascertainment of foreign law cooperation agreement with relevant universities.

[3] Opinions of the Supreme People's Court on Several Issues concerning the Implementation of the General Principles of the Civil Law of the People's Republic of China (Trial Implementation) (Supreme People's Court, Fa Ban Fa (1988) 6, adopted on 26 January 1988 and promulgated on 2 April 1988).

[4] P Xu, *Chongtu Guifan Renyixing Shiyong Yanjiu* [*A Study on Facultative Application of Conflict Rules*] (Xiamen University Press, 2010).

[5] Interpretation of the Supreme People's Court on Several Issues Concerning the Application of the 'Law of the People's Republic of China on the Law Applicable to Foreign-Related Civil Relationships' (I) (Supreme People's Court, Fa Shi (2012) 24, adopted on 10 December 2012 and took effect on 7 January 2013).

In *Magyar Exporthitel Biztosító Zrt v Xia Jingjun and others*,[6] the court applied the closest law of connection, Hungarian law, to an international sales agreement and a contract of insurance. The court entrusted the determination of Hungarian law to ECUPL in accordance with Article 10, paragraph 1 of the Application Law and Article 193 of the Opinions on the Implementation. ECUPL identified relevant provisions of Hungarian law and the court adopted its report.

In *Allianz Global Corporate & Specialty SE v NHE Shipping Incorporated Maritime*,[7] the parties had chosen Chinese law as the law governing their contractual relationship. Nonetheless, the court found *ex officio* that the case also raised issues of German law. The court therefore consulted the German Civil Code, commentaries on relevant codes, academic works on German contract and insurance law, and German case precedents to determine the content of the applicable German law.

B. Parties Provide Foreign Law

Article 10, paragraph 1 of the Application Law stipulates that parties shall provide information on the laws of the relevant foreign country, if they choose to have their relationship governed by foreign laws. Article 17 of the Application Law Interpretation (I) allows the court to hold that foreign law cannot be ascertained if the parties are unable to provide the same within a reasonable period of time designated by the court. Since the ascertainment of foreign law will normally require expertise in the foreign law, the parties usually engage Chinese and foreign legal experts to provide opinions on the foreign law relating to specific issues. The parties or their experts may also refer to foreign law materials. However, such legal opinions and other types of foreign law materials must be certified by the notarial office of the relevant country, and the notarised documents and related annexes must be submitted to the Chinese consulate for certification. The Chinese authorities will then translate those materials into Chinese. After the foregoing procedures, the parties can submit the corresponding Chinese and English translations to the court. It might be found that the foreign laws provided by different parties are inconsistent with each other, due to the conflicting views of the parties and their experts. In such circumstances, the court should hear both parties and their experts and make a final decision in accordance with Article 18 of the Application Law Interpretation (I).

In *Eventint International Ltd v Haojie Investment Co Ltd and others*,[8] Eventint (a BVI company) and Haojie (a Hong Kong company) agreed that Hong Kong law would apply to their loan contract. The court found that there was nothing in the contract that violated the public policy of Mainland China and therefore applied Hong Kong law. The court also held that, although not explicitly stated, Hong Kong law governed the parties' subsidiary agreements. There was an issue as to whether the loan contract was legally valid. The plaintiff engaged the Shenzhen Lanhai Modern Legal Service Development Center to provide an opinion on Hong Kong law. Shenzhen Lanhai then instructed a Hong Kong barrister to prepare the opinion on the effect of the Hong Kong Money Lenders Ordinance (Cap.163) on the loan contract. Applying Hong Kong law as so advised to the facts established by the evidence, the court found the loan contract and its supplementary agreements to be valid.

[6] Zhejiang Province Intermediary People's Court Decision *Magyar Exporthitel Biztosító Zrt v Xia Jingjun and other insurers* (2015) Zhe Tong Shang Wai Chu Zi No 181.

[7] Tianjin Municipality High People's Court Decision *Allianz Global Corporate & Speciality SE v NHE Shipping Incorporated* (2016) Jin Min Zhong No 138.

[8] *Xinjiang Uyghur Autonomous Region Urumqi Intermediate People's Court Decision Evenint International Ltd v Haojie Investment Co Ltd and others* (2015) Wu Zhong Min San Chu Zi No 64.

In *Bank D v Company L*,[9] there was a leasing contract between D and L which had been signed in Hong Kong. The parties had agreed that disputes in connection with their contract were to be resolved in accordance with Hong Kong law. After suit had been commenced before the Chinese court, an attempt was made to resolve the matter through mediation in Hong Kong. The parties reached a settlement agreement to pay rent and various expenses in RMB instalments in accordance with Hong Kong law. The people's court in the Shenzhen Qianhai Cooperation Zone reviewed the settlement agreement and found it to be in accordance with Hong Kong law. To assist the court in its review, D submitted a legal opinion from a lawyer of 30 years' experience in Hong Kong. The opinion had been certified in Hong Kong by a Chinese notary and transmitted to the court by China Legal Services (Hong Kong) Co Ltd. L did not object to D's Hong Kong law expert or to the contents of his legal opinion. In the course of its review, the court noted that both Chinese and foreign legal experts could be used for the ascertainment of foreign law under Article 193 of the Opinions on the Implementation.

In *Zeng Haiquan v Zhuhai Jiantai Real Estate Development Co Ltd*,[10] there was a preliminary question on whether a Cooperation Agreement was binding on Dongfang Entrepreneur Co (a Macau company). According to the Application Law, the law of the place of Dongfang's registration governed the preliminary question. Referring to Article 193 of the Opinions on the Implementation, the court requested the parties to submit evidence of the relevant provisions of Macau law. Among the materials received from the parties as a result were the Macau Civil and Commercial Codes and opinions from Macau lawyers. The court noted that the parties agreed that Article 236 of the Macau Commercial Code was applicable and that there was no dispute as to the text of the relevant articles. But the parties' Macau law experts held different opinions on the application of Article 236. After reviewing the competing views, the court preferred one view over the other.

C. Failure to Prove Foreign Law

Article 10 of the Application Law provides: 'In the event that foreign laws are unable to be ascertained or contain no relevant provisions, the laws of the People's Republic of China shall apply.' Article 17 of the Application Law Interpretation (I) states that, pursuant to Article 10, a party is to provide evidence of the applicable foreign law and, if it fails to do so without reasonable cause within a reasonable period as designated by the people's court, the court may conclude that it is unable to ascertain the foreign law.

In *Guan Shijun v Li Zhengjian*,[11] Li assigned some of the equity in Myanmar Mengla Jinguan International Trade Co Ltd (a Myanmar company) to Guan. The latter argued that Myanmar law governed the assignment and succeeded on that basis at first instance. On appeal, the court held that Myanmar Mengla had been established and registered in the Fourth Special Zone of Myanmar's Eastern Shan State (the 'Fourth Zone'). The latter zone was found by the court to be under the control of armed groups and Myanmar Mengla's business licence stated that it was issued 'in accordance with the industrial and commercial tax law of the Fourth Special Zone of Eastern Shan State'. The court requested Guan to provide evidence of the industrial and commercial tax law of the Fourth Zone. Guan could not do so and was in any event uncertain as to

[9] Shenzhen Qianhai Cooperation Zone People's Court Decision *Bank D v Company L and the Guarantors* (2016) Yue-0391 Min Chu No 713.

[10] Guandong Province High People's Court Decision (2016) Yue Min Zhong No 588. See also ch 5, section IV above.

[11] Yunnan Province High People's Court Decision (2016) Yun Min Zhong No 795.

whether there were any such laws. As a result, the court held that it was inappropriate to apply the company law of Myanmar and PC law should be applied instead.

In *Guangdong Tianhe v HSBC*,[12] a loan contract provided for the application of Hong Kong law. HSBC argued that PRC law should apply instead. Tianhe was of the view that Hong Kong law should apply, but did not provide evidence of the relevant Hong Kong laws. The court at first instance was unable to ascertain the relevant Hong Kong law. Consequently, the court applied PRC law.

In *Delixy Energy Pte Ltd v Dongming Petro China fuel Petrochemical Co Ltd*,[13] the contract provided for 'British law' to apply, but Dongming did not submit evidence of such law. Although Delixy adduced an expert report on UK law, the court held that the opinion only expressed the author's subjective view and, in any event, the case as presented in the report differed from the actual circumstances of the case. Further, the report had not been notarised, thereby diminishing its probative value. PRC law was accordingly applied to the case.

In *Shenyang Shenyang Amusement Park Co Ltd v Export-Import Bank of Malaysia Berhad*,[14] the loan agreement signed by the parties stipulated:

> [T]he laws of Malaysia as the governing law of this agreement shall be interpreted in accordance with the laws of Malaysia; if Malaysian law does not apply or is not enforceable, the parties shall apply applicable laws of China Law or other applicable laws recognized by the Export-Import Bank to govern disputes, and the laws applicable to all security documents are subject to this same rule.

The bank claimed that PRC law should apply. Shenyang argued to the contrary that the parties had agreed to apply Malaysian law. But Shenyang failed to provide evidence of the relevant provisions of Malaysian law. Therefore, the court refused to apply Malaysian law.

[12] Guangdong Province Guangzhou Intermediary People's Court Decision (2016) Yue-01 Min Zhong No 14763.
[13] Shandong Province High People's Court Decision (2016) Lü Min Zhong No 1891.
[14] Supreme People's Court Decision (2017) Zui Gao Ren Min Zhong No 636.

10

Public Order, Mandatory Rules and Evasion of Law

XIN CAI

I. Public Order

A. Definition

Public order, also known as public policy, means that the court can exclude the application of foreign law when such law would otherwise apply under conflicts rules, if the court finds that the application of the foreign law would lead to an outcome which is contrary to the forum's fundamental principles of law, fundamental principles of morality, or fundamental interests. The reservation of public order can be traced back to Savigny, who distinguished between the *statuta favorabilia* and the *statuta odiosa* of other states. In Savigny's theory, the general principle is that the law of the seat or forum should be applied, including its conflicts rules which might require the application of foreign law. However, Savigny also proposed the reservation of public order as an exception to this universal principle.

B. Content of Public Order

Although the reservation of public order has largely been adopted by legal systems around the world,[1] a unified international standard for the identification of public order is impossible because of the different political, economic, religious, and cultural conditions of various countries. It is may be difficult to define precisely what constitutes public order even within a given country. For this reason, although most countries' conflict laws include a public order exception, they generally only set out procedures for what should be done after a decision is taken to exclude the application of foreign law on public order grounds. The definition of what constitutes the public order is left to judges to decide.

C. Standard of Violation of Public Order

There are two theories for determining whether a foreign law to be applied under conflict rules violates domestic public order. According to the subjective theory, the foreign law specified by

[1] Cheshire and North, *Private International Law* 11th edn (Butterworth, 1987), 700–705.

the conflict rules can be excluded as long as its content is in conflict with the public order of the forum, regardless of the outcome of its application. This criterion does not consider the result of the final application of foreign law to the case and focuses on the foreign law itself. This approach has been heavily criticised. On the other hand, the objective theory provides that the application of foreign law specified in the conflicts rules may only be excluded when it results in conflict with the public order of the forum country. The content of the law itself does not provide a valid reason for excluding the application of foreign law. Most countries have adopted the objective theory, which emphasises the conflict between the outcome of applying foreign law and domestic public order.

D. Practice of Applying the Reservation of Public Order to Exclude Foreign Law

The direct result of applying the reservation of public order is to exclude foreign law which should otherwise have been applied under conflicts rules. But this leaves open how a specific case is actually to be resolved. Resort to the *lex fori* is the most common solution. This approach is relatively simple, although some scholars worry that this approach will lead judges to use the reservation of public order as a means to exclude foreign law.[2]

E. Regulations and Practice of Reservation of Public Order in China

China takes a positive attitude towards the preservation of public order. For instance, as early as 1950, the Opinions on the Marriage between Chinese and Aliens, Aliens and Aliens provided that the application of the Marriage Law shall not violate the public order, public interest, and fundamental policies of China.[3] In 1986, the General Principles of Civil Law for the first time dealt with the reservation of public order in private international law. Article 150 of that statute provides that the application of foreign law or international practice should not violate the PRC's social and public interest.[4] Article 276 of the Maritime Law and Article 190 of the Civil Aviation law have similar provisions. Article 282 of the Civil Procedure Law provides that, in determining the enforceability of foreign judgments, the people's court shall review relevant international treaties and, in accordance with the principle of reciprocity, consider whether a foreign judgment violates the fundamental principles of the PRC's sovereignty, laws, security and social and public interest before ordering enforcement. Article 5 of the Application Law, which came into force in 2011, provides that if the application of foreign law will undermine the PRC's social and public interest, then PRC law shall apply.[5]

The foregoing legislation adopts an objective test for determining whether foreign law is contrary to public order. However, as in other countries, the legislation does not define public

[2] ZX Huo, *Private International Law* 2nd edn (China University of Political Science and Law Press, 2020), 142.

[3] *Guanyu Zhongguoren yu Waiqiao Waiqiao yu Waiqiao Tonghun Wenti de Yijian* [*Opinions on the Marriage between Chinese and Aliens, Aliens and Aliens*] (Legal Committee of the Central People's Government (1950)).

[4] Passed at the Fourth Session of the Sixth National People's Congress of the People's Republic of China on 12 April 1986 and was implemented on 1 January 1987. It is invalidated by the Civil Code of the People's Republic of China (issued on 28 May 2020, effective on 1 January 2021).

[5] The Law of the People's Republic of China on Choice of Law for Foreign-related Civil Relationships, adopted at the Seventeenth Session of the Eleventh Standing Committee of the National People's Congress of the People's Republic of China on 28 October 2010, and took effect on 1 April 2011.

order and the 2012 Application Law Interpretation does not address this issue. It is up to the judge to decide. The Interpretation and Application of the Provisions of the Law of the PRC on the Application of Laws to Foreign-related Civil Relations, compiled by the Supreme People's Court, explains the meaning of public order as comprising the following matters: (1) the fundamental policy of the PRC Constitution; (2) China's national sovereignty and security; (3) international treaties concluded or acceded to by China, including obligations under multilateral and bilateral treaties; (4) universally recognised principles of fairness and justice in international law; (5) fundamental legal principles of Chinese law, such as good faith, counter-terrorism, prohibition of cults, prohibition of human trafficking, prohibition of money-laundering, prohibition of gambling, etc; (6) China's fundamental moral norms; and (7) China's fundamental and overall interests.[6] Although the seven criteria remain vague, they give judges more guidance than the simple 'public interest' in provisions.

II. Mandatory Rules

A. Definition

Mandatory rules refer to obligatory provisions of a country's domestic law. These are to be directly applied to the private international law cases when the relevant conditions are met, regardless of choice of law rules. Mandatory rules have long been classified as a category of public order. They may be regarded as part of 'positive' public order (that is, relating to the application of specific legislation regardless of a choice of law rule) in contrast to the public order principles discussed in the previous section which illustrate 'negative' public order (that is, concerning the exclusion of foreign law for lack of compatibility with the domestic public order).

B. Chinese Legislation on Mandatory Rules

Article 4 provides that mandatory provisions on foreign-related civil relations prescribed by the law shall directly apply. This is elaborated in Article 10 of the 2012 Application Law Interpretation:

> The people's courts shall determine that the following situations constitute mandatory provisions involving the public interest of the PRC, as stipulated in Article 4 of the Law of the PRC on the Application of Laws to Foreign-related Civil Relations, and cannot be excluded by agreement of the parties nor by conflicts rules; (1) involving the protection of labourers' rights; (2) involving food or public health safety; (3) involving environmental safety; (4) involving financial security, such as foreign exchange control; (5) involving anti-monopoly or anti-dumping; (6) involving other circumstances that shall be recognised as mandatory provisions.

In *Daxin Bank Co, Ltd v Hong Kong Sanxing Industrial Development Co, Ltd and others*,[7] a financial guarantee expressly provided for the application of Hong Kong law. Foreign guarantees in Mainland China must be approved by the State Administration of Foreign Exchange (SAFE).

[6] Interpretation of the Supreme People's Court on Several Issues Concerning the Application of the 'Law of the People's Republic of China on the Law Applicable to Foreign-Related Civil Relationships' (I) (Supreme People's Court, Fa Shi (2012) 24, adopted on 10 December 2012 and took effect on 7 January 2013).

[7] Jiangxi Province Intermediary People's Court Decision *Daxin Bank Co Ltd v Hong Kong Sanxing Industrial Development Co Ltd and others* (2016) Gan-04 Min Chu No 123.

Since the signatories of the financial documents had not observed the necessary approval from SAFE, the guarantee was invalid. This was pursuant to Article 6 of the *Judicial Interpretation of the Supreme People's Court on Some Issues Regarding the Application of Security Law of the People's Republic of China* which states: 'A foreign guarantee contract shall be invalid if it has not been approved or registered by the competent State Department concerned.' The law of Mainland China was applied to the guarantee as a mandatory rule, regardless of the parties' express choice of law.

In *Guan Enjun v Yan Chenglong and others*,[8] Guan Enjun had been engaged in the timber business in Russia. Yan Chenglong joined the business in February 2012 as a piecework labourer. Yan did not sign a contract with Guan. In May 2012, Yan was injured while working at a timber processing station. He was hospitalised for 25 days. Yan Guo sued Guan for the cost of medical treatment and lost wages. The court found that, because Yan had been injured in Russia, the case was foreign-related. Russian law would normally have been applicable as the *lex loci delicti*. However, because laws involving the protection of workers' rights form part of the PRC's mandatory norms according to the Application Law Interpretation (I), the court decided that PRC law should apply to the dispute.

In *Gao Delong v Nanjing Jinsha Industrial Co Ltd*[9] Gao signed a 'Project Investment Agreement' whereby he would provide Nanjing Jinsha with HK$3 million for one year at an interest rate of 18 per cent per annum. Nanjing Jinsha failed to repay the money upon the expiry of the agreement. The issue was whether the agreement was an investment agreement or a foreign loan agreement. The court held that, although the parties' contract described itself as an 'Investment Agreement,' it stated that Gao only had a fixed income and did not bear operational risks. Therefore, the agreement was not one of sharing profits, losses and risks as would have been characteristic of an investment agreement. The parties' contract was therefore a loan agreement. Article 10 of the Application Law Interpretation (I) provides that matters relating to financial security, such as foreign exchange control, are to be treated as subject to the mandatory rules of the PRC. Further, by Article 18 of the Regulation on Foreign Exchange Administration, foreign debts must be registered with SAFE. The relevant loan being a foreign debt, the agreement was subject to the mandatory provisions of PRC law.

In *Bank D v Company L*[10] the question was on the effect of mandatory provisions in respect of financial security on a cross-border guarantee of a Hong Kong-related financial lease. The settlement currency of the financial lease was originally to be Hong Kong dollars. The plaintiff creditor was registered in Hong Kong, while the defendant was registered in Mainland China. There was a subsequent mediation in which the parties agreed to change the settlement currency from Hong Kong dollars to Chinese RMB. The court held that the relevant SAFE regulations on the foreign exchange administration of cross-border guarantees were legally binding on the guarantor to the creditors. According to those regulations, the guarantor had to go through registration and filing procedures with SAFE. However, the court found that the regulations did not on their terms affect the validity of the cross-border guarantee administrative penalties if violated. The financial leasing agreement in question was signed on 1 September 2014. The provision therefore applied to this case. Whether the parties had fulfilled the relevant registration or filing procedures did not affect the validity of the contract. Failure to comply with the regulations would simply

[8] Hulun Buir City Intermediary People's Court Decision *Guan Enjun v Yan Chenglong and others* (2016) Nei-07 Min Zhong No 1202.

[9] Nanjing Municipality Intermediary People's Court Decision *Gao Delong v Nanjing Jinsha Industrial Co Ltd* (2014) Ning Shuang Wai Chu Zi No 26.

[10] Shenzhen Qianhai Cooperation Zone People's Court Decision *Bank D v Company L and the Guarantors* (2016) Yue-0391 Min Chu No 713.

give rise to the payment of penalties. To assist in deciding the matter, the People's Court of the Qianhai Cooperation Zone in Shenzhen wrote to SAFE's Shenzhen branch, requesting information on SAFE's view as to whether the relevant regulations were mandatory and whether the change of settlement currency into RMB violated the regulations. SAFE replied that, in its view, non-compliance with the operative legislation 'will not affect the validity of guarantee contracts, [but] it may affect the enforceability of guarantee contracts'. On the change in currency denomination, SAFE's opinion was that 'the mediation agreement … did not violate the relevant regulations of the People's Bank'.

III. Evasion of Law

A. Definition

Evasion of law refers to the situation where a party artificially creates or alters a connecting factor in order to avoid the application of a law to which a transaction would normally be subject. This is usually done so that a law which is more favourable to the party will be applied to the transaction. There will typically be evasion of law where the following elements are present in a transaction: (1) The evasion is attributable to the conduct of at least one of the parties to a transaction. (2) Such party has the subjective objective to evade a certain law. (3) The law to be avoided is a mandatory or prohibitive provision that would normally apply to the transaction under a choice of law rule. (4) The party or parties involved have attempted to evade the law by artificially structuring the relevant transaction so as to manipulate an operative connecting factor. (5) The relevant conduct has been completed and, if left unchecked by the court, will result in a more favourable law being applied to the transaction in question. Because the party or parties involved will have a fraudulent intent, in accordance with the maxim *fraus omnia corrumpit*, their acts of evasion are generally treated as invalid. However, there remain disputes as to how to treat evasion of law. Consequently, there are three legislative approaches: (1) Only the evasion of domestic law is regarded as evasion of law. (2) Conduct seeking to evade mandatory rules of domestic law will not be recognised, while the evasion of foreign law is not addressed at all by the legislation. (3) All evasions of law are treated as void acts.

B. Relevant Legislation

The Application Law does not contain rules governing evasion of law. However, Article 194 of the 1988 Opinions in the Implementation of the General Principles of Civil Law states that the acts of parties to evade the compulsory or prohibitive legal norms of the PRC will result in foreign laws not being applied.[11] Article 11 of the 2012 Application Law Interpretation (I) offers a little more detail. According to this provision, if a party intentionally creates a connecting point in foreign-related civil relations to evade the mandatory provisions of PRC law, the people's court will not apply foreign law. The article then sets out the means by which attempts may be made to evade the law and stipulates that evasion of law also relates to mandatory provisions in administrative regulations.

[11] Opinions of the Supreme People's Court on Several Issues concerning the Implementation of the General Principles of the Civil Law of the People's Republic of China (Trial Implementation) (Supreme People's Court, Fa Ban Fa (1988) 6, adopted on 26 January 1988 and promulgated on 2 April 1988).

11

Jurisdiction in Personam

JIANPING SHI AND ZIJUN ZHAI

As the first issue the courts will encounter when adjudicating international civil cases, establishing jurisdiction is the starting point of international civil procedure. Jurisdiction is the pre-condition for courts to accept and try a case. It is also a pre-condition which influences the recognition and enforcement of judgments by other states. It is thus directly related to the vindication of the parties' rights and the exercise of a nation's sovereignty. Jurisdiction in international civil procedure refers to the authority of the courts or other organs of a state having judicial power to accept and try cases with international factors. It is the legal basis for a state's court to accept and try cases with foreign-related factors. The determination of jurisdiction of international civil litigation in regard to China involves two issues: (1) whether Chinese courts have jurisdiction; and (2) if so, which Chinese court will specifically exercise jurisdiction.[1]

I. General Principles

The enforcement of jurisdiction by a state over an international civil case is usually based on two principles: the principle of personal jurisdiction and the principle of territorial jurisdiction. The principle of personal jurisdiction is based on the connecting points of personal law to the subject of a legal relationship, such as the plaintiff's or defendant's nationality, habitual residence, or presence in his or her state. Civil procedure relating to matters of personal relationship or status, such as divorce, adoption, and inheritance, usually also adopt this principle. At present, countries adopting the principle of personal jurisdiction include the European countries following the Roman law-based systems as exemplified by France, Spain and Portugal. The principle of territorial jurisdiction is based on the fact that international civil cases have a certain relationship with a specific country's legal system. More precisely, the exercise of jurisdiction comes about due to: (1) the presence of juristic facts based on the relationship in question;[2] or (2) the location or occurrence of the subject matter regarding which the parties have engaged in civil procedures within the territory of a particular state. This principle of jurisdiction is a manifestation of the national territorial principle in international civil procedure and is commonly and broadly adopted by

[1] W Li, 'The Analysis on Jurisdiction of Transnational Civil Litigation: Evaluating the Provisions on Jurisdiction of Transnational Civil Litigation in Civil Procedure Law of P. R. China (Amended in 2012)' (2014) 1 *Chinese Review of International Law*.

[2] Civil Procedure Law of the People's Republic of China, promulgated on 9 April 1991 ('Civil Procedure Law'), s 2.

countries around the world. China is no exception. Matters of personal status or relationship apart, China typically adheres to the principle of territorial jurisdiction. Thus, for instance, the territorial principle arises in connection with tort, contract, and disputes over property rights. In this respect, China has always followed the principle that the plaintiff should be accommodating to the defendant's circumstances in determining jurisdiction. This means that jurisdiction is determined by the defendant's domicile. For example, if the defendant resides in Mainland China, the PRC court would have jurisdiction under the territorial principle.

A. Jurisdiction of the Chinese People's Court

China has no specific legislation on the jurisdiction as a matter of international civil procedure. However, a special chapter in the Civil Procedure Law of the PRC (the 'Civil Procedure Law') contains provisions on the issue. Meanwhile, the Special Maritime Procedure Law stipulates the jurisdiction in maritime cases. The latter will be dealt with in the next section.

Since its enactment, the Civil Procedure Law has adopted the model of separate legislation on international and domestic jurisdiction. Articles 259 and 260 of Part IV of the Special Provisions on Foreign Civil Procedures ('Part IV') have created a brief framework on jurisdiction. Article 259 stipulates: 'The provisions of this Part shall apply to foreign-related civil actions within the territory of the People's Republic of China. Where this Part is silent, other relevant provisions of this Law shall apply.' Article 260 stipulates that 'Where there is any discrepancy between an international treaty concluded or acceded to by the People's Republic of China and this Law, the provisions of the international treaty shall prevail, except clauses to which the People's Republic of China has declared reservations.' In fact, to date, China has become party to only a few treaties on jurisdiction. These include the 1951 Agreement on the International Goods Transport by Rail (SMGS) and the 1999 Convention on the Unification of Certain Rules for International Aviation (the Montreal Convention) and the 1992 International Convention on Liability for Oil Pollution Damage (the CLC Convention).

In addition, China signed (but has yet to ratify) the 2005 Hague Convention on Choice of Court Agreement in September 2017. This means that jurisdiction in international civil cases other than those covered by those few treaties are to be determined in accordance with the Civil Procedure Law. Articles 265 and 266 of Chapter 24 contain the provisions on jurisdiction in Part IV. Article 265 has special provisions on contract disputes or disputes over property rights. Article 266 has special provisions on exclusive jurisdiction. Otherwise, the general provisions on jurisdiction in Chapter 2 of the Civil Procedure Law (Articles 17–38) will apply to foreign-related procedure matters. The Supreme People's Court issued an Interpretation on the Application of the Civil Procedure Law of the PRC (the Interpretation of the Civil Procedure Law) in 2015 with observations on jurisdiction which are also applicable to foreign-related matters.[3]

From the perspective of legislation and judicial practice, China's jurisdiction over foreign-related civil cases can be divided into four types: general territorial jurisdiction, special territorial jurisdiction, exclusive jurisdiction, and agreed jurisdiction.

[3] Opinions of the Supreme People's Court on Some Issues Concerning the Application of the Civil Procedure Law of the People's Republic of China (Supreme People's Court, Fa Fa (1992) 22, adopted on 14 July 1992).

This was replaced by Interpretations of the Supreme People's Court on Applicability of the Civil Procedure Law of the People's Republic of China (Supreme People's Court, Zhu Shi (2015) 5, adopted on 18 December 2014, promulgated on 4 February 2015).

B. Territorial Jurisdiction: General Territorial Jurisdiction

As noted, China's approach to jurisdiction in international cases (as with many countries) follows the principle that the plaintiff should accommodate the defendant's circumstances. Article 21 of the Civil Procedure Law accordingly provides:

> A civil action instituted against a citizen shall be under the jurisdiction of the people's court at the place of domicile of the defendant; or if the defendant's place of domicile is different from his or her place of habitual residence, the civil action shall be under the jurisdiction of the people's court at the place of habitual residence of the defendant. A civil action instituted against a legal person or any other organization shall be under the jurisdiction of the people's court at the place of domicile of the defendant. Where the places of domicile or places of habitual residence of several defendants in the same action are located within the jurisdictions of two or more people's courts, both or all of such people's courts shall have jurisdiction over the action.

While the Civil Procedure Law in general priorities the principle of the plaintiff accommodating the defendant, the law may also take into consideration the plaintiff's domicile and habitual residence. Article 22 of the Civil Procedure Law stipulates that a personal action against a person whose whereabouts are unknown or who has been declared missing shall be under the jurisdiction of the people's court at the place of the plaintiff's domicile or habitual residence. Another example is found in Article 15 of the Interpretation of the Civil Procedure Law which states:

> Where both spouses are Chinese citizens but one lives abroad and the other lives in China, the people's court at the place of domicile of the spouse who lives in China shall have jurisdiction over a divorce action between them, regardless of which spouse institutes a divorce action in a people's court. Where the spouse who lives abroad institutes an action in a court of the country of residence of the spouse, and the spouse who lives in China institutes an action in a people's court, the people's court in which the action is instituted shall have jurisdiction over the divorce case.

C. Territorial Jurisdiction: Special Territorial Jurisdiction

Special territorial jurisdiction rules are based on the fact that certain types of international civil litigation are connected with particular countries. Article 265 of the Civil Procedure Law reads:

> Where an action is instituted against a defendant which has no domicile within the territory of the People's Republic of China for a contract dispute or any other property right or interest dispute, if the contract is signed or performed within the territory of the People's Republic of China, the subject matter of action is located within the territory of the People's Republic of China, if the defendant has any impoundable property within the territory of the People's Republic of China, or the defendant has any representative office within the territory of the People's Republic of China, the people's court at the place where the contract is signed or performed, where the subject matter of action is located, where the impoundable property is located, where the tort occurs, or where the domicile of the representative office is located may have jurisdiction over the action.

In addition, Articles 23 to 32 of the Civil Procedure Law contain provisions of special jurisdiction, which enable Chinese courts to assert jurisdiction over international civil and commercial cases. The specific provisions will be discussed below.

D. Territorial Jurisdiction: Exclusive Jurisdiction

Exclusive jurisdiction means that a country's courts will have jurisdiction over specified types of foreign-related civil cases, to the exclusion of the courts in all other countries, in accordance with domestic legislation or international treaties. Exclusive jurisdiction prevents parties from going to some other court or asserting the jurisdiction of other courts in relation to their case.[4] Exclusive jurisdiction is a reflection of a country's national judicial sovereignty. It emphasises that a designated domestic court is to have unconditional jurisdiction over civil cases that are closely concerned with the fundamental interests of the country and people. Typically, national public policy or important political and economic issues will be involved. If one party does not abide by a country's rules on exclusive jurisdiction and submits the case to another country's court, the judgment of the latter court will not normally be recognised and enforced in the country exerting exclusive jurisdiction. However, this doctrine may cause conflicts in the adjudication of international civil cases since the scope of exclusive jurisdiction is not consistent in different countries. Article 266 of Part IV is a clause providing for foreign-related exclusive jurisdiction:

> Actions instituted for disputes arising from the performance of contracts for Chinese-foreign equity joint ventures, Chinese-foreign contractual joint ventures, or Chinese-foreign cooperative exploration and exploitation of natural resources in the People's Republic of China shall be under the jurisdiction of the people's courts of the People's Republic of China.

Some scholars take the view that not all of the three categories of foreign-related contracts mentioned in Article 266 are intended to be subject to exclusive jurisdiction, particularly the first two classes of contract, which are not substantially different from general foreign-related contracts and have no obvious connection with the public interest of the PRC.[5] In addition, by Article 33 of the Civil Procedure Law, the following cases fall under the exclusive jurisdiction of the people's courts: (1) an action instituted in a real estate dispute involving land in China; (2) an action instituted in a dispute relating to harbour operations in China; (3) an action instituted in an inheritance dispute, where the deceased passed away while domiciled in China or the bulk of the deceased's estate is located in China. Disputes relating to harbour operations are divided into two categories: the first comprises cargo handling and storage disputes associated with the harbour, while the second covers damage compensation disputes due to torts committed in the course of harbour operations. Inheritance disputes involve conflicts over private rights. Notably, there is no inevitable connection between these disputes and China's political and economic interests. Focusing narrowly on jurisdiction does not ensure the recognition or enforcement of judgments abroad, In this light, it is arguably unnecessary cases relating to harbour operations and inheritance to be treated as matters falling with the exclusive jurisdiction of the Chinese court.

E. Territorial Jurisdiction: Agreed Jurisdiction

Agreed jurisdiction (also known as consensual jurisdiction) occurs where parties are allowed to select the court which will exercise jurisdiction over an international civil dispute. An increasing number of countries no longer insist on exercising jurisdiction over cases that have little connection with that country or society. Thus, countries have gradually recognised and established a

[4] SY Li, *Private International Law* 3rd edn Beijing University Publishing House, 2011) 315.

[5] LF Tao and YF Gao, 'Reconstruction of the Exclusive Jurisdiction Clause over the Three Types of Contract Disputes Involving Foreign Element in China' (2013) 4 *International Business Research*.

system of agreed jurisdiction in their legislative and judicial practice.[6] Article 34 of the Civil Procedure permits agreed jurisdiction:

> Parties to a dispute over a contract or any other right or interest in property may, by a written agreement, choose the people's court at the place of domicile of the defendant, at the place where the contract is performed or signed, at the place of domicile of the plaintiff, at the place where the subject matter is located, or at any other place actually connected to the dispute to have jurisdiction over the dispute, but the provisions of this Law regarding hierarchical jurisdiction and exclusive jurisdiction shall not be violated.

The provision, in addition to acknowledging the existence of agreed jurisdiction in Chinese law, imposes limits on what can be agreed: (1) Where matters such as civil status, personal relations, legal capacity, and domestic relations are concerned, the parties may not choose the court to hear their dispute. (2) An agreement on jurisdiction must be written and the court selected by the agreement must have an actual connection with the dispute. (3) The jurisdictional agreement can only change general and special jurisdiction and cannot be contrary to exclusive jurisdiction provisions. (4) The parties can only choose the court of first instance by agreement and should not contravene provisions of hierarchical jurisdiction. (5) The jurisdictional agreement must be the result of equal consultation between the parties so that, if one party obtains agreement by deception, coercion, etc, the court will treat the ostensible choice as invalid.

In *Cathay United Bank Co Ltd v Gao*,[7] Gao objected to the court's jurisdiction, maintaining that the parties had agreed in their contract that the law of Taiwan should be applied as the governing law and that the Taiwan District Court should be the court of jurisdiction. The case was not within the exclusive jurisdiction of the people's court. The courts of first and second instance in Shanghai dismissed Cathay's action. Cathay applied for retrial to the Supreme People's Court. The latter rejected the application for retrial, holding that the contractual jurisdiction clause was clear and the application of the clause was not improper. In coming to its decision, the court noted that it was unnecessary for a jurisdiction agreement to specify a particular court within a given jurisdiction. It was enough for the parties' agreement to designate the state which was to have jurisdiction over disputes arising out of a particular civil relationship. In this case, with Cathay being domiciled in Taiwan, there was a factual link between a party and the designated jurisdiction. Further, the dispute between the parties was not one reserved to the exclusive jurisdiction of the PRC court. The jurisdiction agreement was exclusive. Under Article 3(b) of the 2005 Hague Choice of Court Agreements Convention (see further section J below), 'a choice of court agreement which designates the courts of one Contracting State or one or more specific courts of one Contracting State shall be deemed to be exclusive unless the parties have expressly provided otherwise'. In light of that guidance, the key to whether a choice of court is exclusive is whether the terms of the parties' agreement provide so clearly. The agreement here unambiguously stipulated that in 'any litigation arising out of or in connection with this contract, the Taiwan District Court shall be the court of first instance'. Nowhere did the parties state otherwise. It followed that the people's court had no jurisdiction.

F. Hierarchical Jurisdiction

Hierarchical jurisdiction identifies which court will have jurisdiction to hear a case from first instance onwards and is determined according to the nature, complexity, and effect of a case.

[6] XH Liu and Q Zhou, 'The Principle of Actual Connection in the System of Agreement Jurisdiction and the Principle of Inconvenient Court' (2012) 12 *Law Science*.

[7] See *Cathay United Bank v Gao*, Shanghai High Court, (2016) Hu Min Xia Zhong No 99.

Articles 17 to 20 of the Civil Procedure Law[8] deal with hierarchical jurisdiction. The court of first instance for a foreign-related civil case will typically be a base level court and only a 'major' foreign-related civil case may fall within the jurisdiction of an intermediate or higher people's court. Article 1 of the Interpretation of the Civil Procedure Law defines a 'major' foreign-related case as one in which a large number of issues are in dispute, complex cases, or cases involving many parties who live abroad.

Following China's accession to the WTO, the Supreme People's Court passed *Regulations on Several Issues Concerning the Jurisdiction of Foreign-related Civil and Commercial Cases* on 25 December 2001 to implement a system for centralised jurisdiction over specific civil and commercial cases.[9] Under these new regulations, foreign civil and commercial cases of the first instance will come within the jurisdiction of the following people's courts:

(1) people's courts within economic and technological development zones approved by the State Council;
(2) intermediate people's courts in the provincial capital, an autonomous region's capital, or a municipality under the Central Government;
(3) intermediate people's courts in special economic zone and municipalities with independent planning status;
(4) other intermediate people's courts designated by the Supreme People's Court; and
(5) higher people's courts.

The Regulations apply to the following cases:

(1) foreign-related contracts and cases of tort;
(2) letters of credit disputes;
(3) applications for the revocation, recognition or enforcement of international arbitral awards;
(4) applications for the review of foreign-related arbitration agreements; and
(5) applications for the recognition and enforcement of civil and commercial judgments of foreign courts.

For foreign-related cases not mentioned above, hierarchical jurisdiction pursuant to previous rules.

G. Forum Non Conveniens

The principle of *forum non conveniens* refers to instances where a court has jurisdiction to hear an international civil case but declines to exercise such jurisdiction, because it would be inconvenient or unfair to do so and it be more convenient and appropriate for the parties to litigate

[8] Article 17. The basic people's courts shall have jurisdiction over civil cases as a court of first instance, except as otherwise provided for in this Law.

Article 18. The intermediate people's courts shall have jurisdiction over the following civil cases as a court of first instance: (1) Major foreign-related cases. (2) Cases which have a major impact within their respective jurisdictions. (3) Cases which are under the jurisdiction of the intermediate people's courts as determined by the Supreme People's Court.

Article 19. The higher people's courts shall have jurisdiction over civil cases which have a major impact within their respective jurisdictions as a court of first instance.

Article 20. The Supreme People's Court shall have jurisdiction over the following civil cases as a court of first instance: (1) Cases which have a major impact nationwide. (2) Cases which the Supreme People's Court deems shall be tried by itself.

[9] (Supreme People's Court, Fashi (2002) 5 Hao). Adopted at the 1,203rd Session of the Judicial Committee of the Supreme People's Court on 25 December 2001; effective as of 1 March 2002.

their dispute before a court in another country.[10] Article 532 of the Interpretation of the Civil Procedure Law states:

> Where a foreign-related civil case falls under all the following circumstances, the people's court may render a ruling to dismiss the plaintiff's action, and direct the plaintiff to institute an action in a more convenient foreign court:
>
> (1) The defendant raises a claim that the case shall be subject to the jurisdiction of a more convenient foreign court, or raises an objection to jurisdiction.
> (2) The parties do not have an agreement specifying the jurisdiction of a court of the People's Republic of China.
> (3) The case does not fall under the exclusive jurisdiction of a court of the People's Republic of China.
> (4) The case does not involve the national interest or the interest of any citizen, legal person or any other organization of the People's Republic of China.
> (5) The people's court has great difficulty in the determination of facts and the application of laws since major facts of the dispute in a case did not occur within the territory of the People's Republic of China and the laws of the People's Republic of China do not apply to the case.
> (6) A foreign court has jurisdiction over the case and it is more convenient for the court to try the case.

The rationale for applying a doctrine of *forum non conveniens* is as follows: (1) It is helpful in resolving conflicts of international civil jurisdiction, especially for disputes that are not strongly connected with China or are inconvenient to resolve in China. (2) It is beneficial to optimise the allocation of judicial resources, so as to reduce unnecessary burdens on the Chinese courts and better balance the interests of the parties. (3) Insofar as Hong Kong, Macao, and Taiwan are concerned, their legal systems differ from that of Mainland China so that the application of *forum non conveniens* may resolve inter-regional jurisdictional conflicts, avoid conflicting judgments rendered by different regions within China, and aid in the maintenance of consistency within the PRC legal system.

H. Lis Alibi Pendens

Lis alibi pendens is a Latin term meaning that an action on the same cause of action is pending elsewhere. When two courts hear the same dispute, they can reach inconsistent decisions. The doctrine of *res judicata* provides that, once a case has been determined, it is final subject only to appeal. No party to the case can commence another case on the same dispute in another court. When a case is pending, no other case on the same issue should be commenced in another court. *Lis alibi pendens* is based on international comity. It permits a court to refuse to exercise jurisdiction when there is parallel litigation pending in another jurisdiction. However, when the other litigation is about materially different issues, documents and parties, the doctrine of *lis alibi pendens* will not apply. In most common law jurisdictions (for example, England, Singapore, Hong Kong, Malaysia), *lis alibi pendens* is not a distinct doctrine on its own, but merely one of several factors for a court to take into account when applying the doctrine of *forum non conveniens.*[11] In the US, however, *lis alibi pendens* and *forum non conveniens* are distinct doctrines. In China, there are only two provisions in the Interpretation of the Supreme People's Court on the Application of the Civil Procedure Law of the PRC dealing with *lis alibi pendens.*[12] In Chinese

[10] XL Zhao, *Private International Law* (China University of Political Science and Law Press, 2000) 366.

[11] JJ Fawcett, *Declining Jurisdiction in Private International Law* (Oxford, Clarendon Press 1995) 10.

[12] Article 15. Where both spouses are Chinese citizens but one lives abroad and the other lives in China, the people's court at the place of domicile of the spouse who lives in China shall have jurisdiction over a divorce action between them,

practice, if the courts of two countries have jurisdiction over a certain case, they may exercise their respective jurisdictions concurrently. The people's court may accept a party's claim, without checking whether the defendant has filed a lawsuit in the court of another state or whether the court of another state is trying the same matter. Some scholars believe that, even if a foreign court has rendered final judgment in a case, it will not preclude the Chinese court from hearing the case according at the suit of one of the parties. After China's court has rendered judgment, the foreign court's judgment will not be recognised or enforced in China.[13]

I. Interim Measures

Interim measures in civil procedure are temporary protective measures against the person or property of a party issued before or during the process of accepting and hearing civil cases. Interim measures typically ensure that when final judgment is rendered in favour of a party, it will not be an empty judgment because the successful party is unable to enforce the judgment against the assets of the losing party. Often interim measures are sought at an early stage of litigation, in order to prevent a defendant from hiding away its assets. They are temporary in the sense that they are only valid from the time when they are made until the time of final judgment. They may also be subject to review from time to time depending upon the circumstances. Such temporary protection enforcement measures are accordingly designed to guarantee the smooth conduct of a trial and the effective enforcement of future judgments.[14] As a matter of international civil procedure, the jurisdiction to grant interim measures is exercised pursuant to international treaties and domestic laws.

In China's Civil Procedure Law, there are two types of foreign-related property preservation measures: pre-litigation preservation of property and preservation of property in litigation. Article 31 of Interpretation of the Civil Procedure Law stipulates:

> For the preservation of property before the institution of an action, the party concerned shall file an application with the people's court at the place where the property is located. If an applicant files a lawsuit after a people's court took measures for preservation of property before the institution of an action, the lawsuit may be filed with the people's court that took the measures for preservation of property before the institution of an action or any other competent people's court.

However, Article 32 states:

> If the party concerned fails to file a lawsuit within the statutory term after applying for preservation of property before the institution of an action, and a lawsuit has resulted from the loss of property to the party against whom the application is filed, the lawsuit shall be under the jurisdiction of the people's court that took the measure for preservation of property before the institution of an action.

regardless of which spouse institutes a divorce action in a people's court. Where the spouse who lives abroad institutes an action in a court of the country of residence of the spouse, and the spouse who lives in China institutes an action in a people's court, the people's court in which the action is instituted shall have jurisdiction over the divorce case.

Article 533. For a case over which both a people's court of the PRC and a foreign court have jurisdiction, if one party institutes an action in the foreign court whereas the other party institutes an action in the people's court of the PRC, the people's court may accept the case. If, after a judgment is rendered, the foreign court or a party requests the people's court's recognition and enforcement of the judgment or ruling rendered by the foreign court concerning this case, the people's court shall not consent to the request, unless it is otherwise prescribed by an international treaty concluded or acceded to by both countries.

[13] See Y Ma, *Explanation of the Opinions on the Application of the Civil Procedure Law*, (China Procuratorate Publishing House, 1994) 217 ff.

[14] P Liu, 'Study on Jurisdiction of Temporary Protection Measures in International Civil Litigation' (2009) 9 *Journal of Litigation Law* 489.

It appears from the two articles that the court that has jurisdiction over the substance of the case and the court where the property is located both have jurisdiction to issue property preservation measures.

J. Jurisdiction under the 2005 Hague Choice of Court Agreements Convention

i. Basic Provisions of the Convention

The twentieth Diplomatic Conference of the Hague Conference on Private International Law adopted the 2005 Hague Convention on Choice of Court Agreements (the 2005 Hague Convention) on 30 June 2005. The instrument came into force on 1 October 2015. On 12 September 2017, China signed the 2005 Hague Convention. China actively participated in the negotiation and drafting of the 2005 Hague Convention. It is anticipated that China will soon ratify the Convention,[15] to which there are currently 32 contracting states (including the EU as a Regional Economic Integration Organisation (REIO).

The 2005 Hague Convention gives detailed provisions on the recognition and enforcement of: (1) choice of court agreements designating a specific court to decide disputes arising under an international commercial contract; and (2) the judgments of the court so designated. By Article 1, the instrument applies to international civil and commercial cases in which exclusive choice of court agreements have been concluded. Article 2 lists the situations in which the instrument does not apply. Article 3(a) sets out the requirements that an exclusive choice of court agreement must meet to fall within the ambit of the 2005 Hague Convention. Essentially, the agreement must be in writing (including in electronic or analogous format). It must designate, as the forum to decide a dispute arising under the parties' cross-border commercial relationship, to the exclusion of the courts of any other state: (1) the courts of a contracting state; or (2) one or more courts of a contracting state. In the absence of an express indication to the contrary, a choice of court agreement will be presumed to be exclusive in nature (Article 3(b)). The validity of the exclusive choice of the court agreement cannot be contested solely on the ground that the contract in which it is found is not valid (Article 3(d)). Article 5(1) provides that the court or courts of a contracting state designated in an exclusive choice of court agreement shall have the right to determine a relevant dispute, unless the choice of court agreement is null and void. There is no requirement that the designated court should have a substantial connection with a relevant dispute.

ii. Positive Impact of the 2005 Hague Convention

Acceding to the 2005 Hague Convention should improve China's consensual jurisdiction system. There are differences between the scope of the instrument and that of current statutes. First, choice of court agreements in China are primarily in writing. The 2005 Hague Convention, however, clarifies that a broad range of communications (including in electronic form) can qualify as 'written' choice of court agreements. Moreover, '[i]f the agreement is in conformity with the conditions of the Convention, no further requirements under domestic law shall be

[15] Official Website of the Ministry of Foreign Affairs of the People's Republic of China www.fmprc.gov.cn accessed 25 March 2019.

imposed'.[16] Thus, a written agreement within the terms of the 2005 Hague Convention shall be effective, regardless of any additional requirements imposed by China's Civil Procedure Law or the Interpretation of the Supreme People's Court on the Application of the Civil Procedure Law of the PRC. However, the above documents do not specify the form the written provision must take. Second, the 'actual connection principle' in PRC law serves as a restriction on foreign-related contractual jurisdiction clauses. Chinese courts will refuse to exercise jurisdiction, pursuant to a choice of court agreement, if they lack an actual connection to the dispute at hand. This would contract the obligation of a designated court under the 2005 Hague Convention to accept jurisdiction. On the other hand, a Chinese court that has not been designated but which in fact has a connection with the case will exercise jurisdiction in accordance with domestic law. Third, Chinese legislation has no presumption as to whether consensual jurisdiction is or is not exclusive in nature, making it difficult for courts to judge whether or not the parties intended a chosen court to exercise exclusive jurisdiction.

While in most cases, Chinese courts have held contractual jurisdiction to be exclusive, the relevant provisions of the 2005 Hague Convention on contractual jurisdiction will cater for potential uncertainty. The 2015 Interpretation of the Supreme People's Court on the Application of the Civil Procedure Law permits the choice of two or more people's courts in places with substantial connection to a dispute.[17] This raises an issue regarding exclusive jurisdiction. If two competent courts can be chosen at the same time, can it be said that there is 'exclusivity'? The 2005 Hague Convention sheds light on this question. By Article 3(a), parties may designate 'the courts of one Contracting State or one or more specific courts of one Contracting State to the exclusion of the jurisdiction of any other courts'.

iii. Negative Impact of the 2005 Hague Convention

Before a country implements the 2005 Hague Convention, it must ensure that its application will conform to the interests of that country. If the 2005 Hague Convention is to be implemented in full in China, then certain existing laws will need to be adjusted. Accordingly, China will need to consider whether the implementation of the 2005 Hague Convention will conform to its interests and so justify making any necessary changes to existing laws. At least three areas will need to be examined. First, China's legislation concerning consensual jurisdiction is rigid in comparison to the flexible provisions of the 2005 Hague Convention as well as the practices of other countries. The requirement for the parties to choose a court that has a substantial connection with the dispute excludes the possibility of choosing a court in a neutral jurisdiction which has no link at all with the parties to a cross-border relationship apart from the choice of court agreement. As a result, parties negotiating an international commercial contract may not reach agreement on a court to resolve their disputes. Under PRC law, the jurisdictions that parties may choose is relatively limited. It is unclear whether the emphasis on a connection between a designated court and the circumstances of a case necessarily will result in superior dispute resolution or have the opposite result. PRC law does not in fact clearly define 'places that have a practical connection with the dispute', resulting in difficulties in applying the principle. In judicial practice, identifying

[16] M Dogauchi and TC Hartley, 'Explanatory Report on the 2005 Hague Choice of Court Agreements Convention' (Hartley Report), 61.

[17] Interpretation by the Supreme People's Court on the Application of the Civil Procedure Law, (Supreme People's Court, 30 January 2015) (2015 Interpretation), Article 30(2). It stipulates that:

> Where a jurisdiction agreement provides that two or more people's courts at places with substantial connection to a dispute shall have jurisdiction over the dispute, the plaintiff may institute an action in one of the people's courts.

'places that have a practical connection with the dispute' is often determined by the views of the judge hearing a case. This can lead to inconsistencies in the ruling.[18]

Second, there may be conflicts in circumstances where, under existing law, a PRC court has exclusive jurisdiction in a given matter, especially where the national interest is involved. To what extent, if at all, should a choice of court agreement designating some other court in such a situation be enforceable in China pursuant to the terms of the 2005 Hague Convention?

Third, there may be a mismatch between what is regarded as an 'international' commercial case under the 2005 Hague Convention on the one hand and current PRC law on the other. In general, under the former, as long as a case is not purely domestic-related, then it will fall within the international sphere. This would be broader than the present position in China. Thus, implementing the 2005 Hague Convention, may lead to Chinese courts having to deal with more 'international' cases (as defined in the 2005 Hague Convention) that they are currently accustomed to handling.

In short, there are differences between existing law and provisions of the 2005 Hague Convention which will surely pose a major challenge to Chinese ratification.

K. Service Abroad

Service abroad refers to the situation where the judicial authorities of one country deliver judicial and extrajudicial documents to parties or litigants living in another country in accordance with the domestic legislation of the latter country or the provisions of an international treaty.[19] China's position regarding service abroad is shaped by international treaties, bilateral treaties, and domestic laws. As a party to the 1965 Hague Service Convention, China has signed mutual legal assistance agreements with more than 30 countries. The procedures for serving judicial documents to parties outside China follow those set out in the 1965 Hague Service Convention and notices issued by the Supreme People's Court, the Ministry of Foreign Affairs and the Ministry of Justice.[20] The procedure can be cumbersome and inefficient. The success rate of service abroad has been relatively low. By way of improvement, in September 2003 the Supreme People's Court issued a notice on the designation of the High Courts of Beijing, Shanghai, Guangdong, Zhejiang, and Jiangsu Provinces, pursuant to the 1965 Hague Service and 1970 Hague Evidence Conventions, as the PRC's Central Authorities for transmitting mutual legal assistance requests and related materials to foreign Central Authorities. The notice further provides that the courts at all levels in the foregoing five provinces and municipalities may transmit judicial documents to the Central Authorities of the 1965 Hague Service Convention's Member States through the High Court of their respective provinces, without the need to report to the Supreme People's Court and the Ministry of Justice. This has had the effect of simplifying procedures and shortening the time needed for service. If a state that has signed a legal assistance agreement with China wishes to request the people's court to facilitate service from abroad, the Central Authority of the requesting state shall submit a form to that effect. The relevant materials should thereafter be forwarded by the Ministry of Justice, reviewed by the Supreme People's Court, and submitted to the relevant High Court. The intermediate people's court designated by the High Court will then be responsible for the service.

[18] YH Wu, 'On the stipulation of Article 34 of the New Civil Procedure Law to the Law Application of Foreign-related Contractual Jurisdiction' (2016) 5 *Journal of Northwest University of Political Science and Law*.

[19] J Huang, *Private International Law* (Legal Publishing House, 1999) 918.

[20] QS He, *Research on the Service Abroad* (Peking University Press, 2006) 199.

II. Special Rules

A. Jurisdiction in Foreign-Related Contractual Claims

According to provisions of the 1991 Civil Procedure Law[21] and its judicial interpretations, there are two types of judicial jurisdiction over foreign-related contract litigation: agreed jurisdiction and legal jurisdiction. The parties have the right to choose the court to deal with their dispute by agreement. Chinese courts will apply the provisions of Article 34 of the Civil Procedure Law to determine the validity of the parties' jurisdictional agreement. Additionally, there must be compliance with Article 266 of the Civil Procedure Law. See sections I.D and I.E above. Where the parties have not designated a court in their agreement, jurisdiction will depend on whether the defendant is domiciled in the PRC. If so, the plaintiff may file a suit in the people's court where the defendant is domiciled or where the contract is to be performed. The place of contractual performance can be determined by reference to Articles 18 to 21 of the Supreme People's Court's 2015 Interpretation of the Civil Procedure Law.[22] If the defendant is not domiciled in the PRC and either: (1) the contract was signed or is to be performed in China; (2) the subject matter of the action is situated in the PRC; (3) the defendant has property available for seizure in the PRC; or (4) the defendant has a representative office in the PRC, then the people's court having jurisdiction is the one located: (a) where the contract was signed; (b) where the contract is to be performed; (c) where the subject matter of the action is situated; or (d) where the defendant's property is available for seizure.

It may be difficult in some cases to determine where a contract is to be performed. In Chinese civil procedure law, the concept of the place of performance is narrowly defined. To a large extent, it is only a procedural concept designed to facilitate the easy determination of the court of jurisdiction, while substantive law regarding the place of performance simply guides parties in paying their debts at the correct place, encourages performance in accordance with the terms of a contract, and helps to reduce disputes over the performance of a contract. For the litigation process, the

[21] Civil Procedure Law of People's Republic of China, as amended in 2007 and 2012.

[22] The 2015 Interpretation provides as follows:

> Article 18. If the contract stipulates the place of performance, the agreed place of performance shall be the place of performance. If the place of performance is not specified in the contract or the agreement is not clear and the subject of the dispute is the payment currency, the place of performance of the contract shall be the place where the party receiving the currency is located. If the real estate is delivered, the place where the real estate is located is the place where the contract is performed; For other subjects, the place where the party performing the obligation is located is the place where the contract is performed. For contracts that are settled immediately, the place of transaction is the place where the contract is performed. If the contract is not actually performed and both parties' domiciles are not in the place agreed upon in the contract, the jurisdiction of the people's court in the place where the defendant is domiciled shall be exercised.
>
> Article 19. Property lease contracts and finance lease contracts shall be performed in the place where the leased property is used. If the contract has an agreement on the place of performance, the agreement shall prevail.
>
> Article 20. If the subject matter of a sales contract concluded through an information network is delivered through the information network, the place of performance shall be the place of domicile of the buyer; If the subject matter is delivered by other means, the place of receipt is the place of performance of the contract. If the contract has an agreement on the place of performance, the agreement shall prevail.
>
> Article 21. A lawsuit brought over a dispute over a property insurance contract may be under the jurisdiction of the people's court of the place where the transportation vehicle is registered, the transportation destination and the place where the insurance accident occurred if the subject matter of the insurance is the transportation vehicle or the goods in transit. A lawsuit brought over a dispute over a personal insurance contract may be under the jurisdiction of the people's court in the place where the insured is domiciled.

'place of performance' will be regarded as ambiguous if the contract merely provides for the jurisdiction of the court in the place of performance in the event of a dispute. According to Article 1 of the Regulations of Beijing Higher People's Court on Several Issues concerning Jurisdiction over Civil Proceedings and the first paragraph of Article 18 of the 2015 Interpretation of the Civil Procedure Law, 'if the place of performance has been agreed upon in the contract, the agreed place of performance shall be the place of performance of the contract'. But there will only be an 'agreed place of performance' where the 'place of performance of the contract' is expressly identified in the parties' contract. Contractual terms on the place of delivery, place of payment, and alternative places of performance of a contractual obligation cannot be the basis for determining the place of performance for the purpose of establishing jurisdiction. Therefore, an agreement that 'the court in the place of performance' is to have jurisdiction would be an unclear agreement and would not be sufficient to establish jurisdiction. By Article 30 of the 2015 Interpretations of the Supreme People's Court on Application of the Civil Procedure Law, in the absence of a valid jurisdictional agreement, the provisions of the 1991 Civil Procedure Law would be applicable and suit should be commenced in the people's court where the defendant is domiciled.

Suppose now that the parties' agreement provides that 'either party may directly bring an action to the people's court in the place where the plaintiff is located'. It might be suggested that the clause is unclear, because it would not be possible at the time of contracting to know which party (if either) will be the plaintiff. If both parties sue at the same time, there would then be two courts having jurisdiction under the agreement. However, the agreement would be valid. Although the parties have potentially agreed on two or more courts having jurisdiction in the event of a dispute, according to the second paragraph of Article 30 of the 2015 Interpretations of the Supreme People's Court on the Application of the Civil Procedure Law, 'where two or more people's courts substantively related to a dispute are stipulated in a jurisdiction agreement, the plaintiff may file a lawsuit at any of such people's courts'.

B. Jurisdiction in Foreign-Related Tort Claims

With the development of science and technology and the deepening of international interactions, new types of rights infringement are constantly emerging. In addition to the traditional types of infringement, there are now maritime infringements, aviation infringements, product liability infringements, transnational network infringements, etc. In cases of foreign-related tortious disputes, the first step is to determine whether the infringement is a wrong relating to property rights. If so, Article 265 of the Civil Procedure Law on 'Special Territorial Jurisdiction' will apply. See section I.C above. As for the other types of tortious infringement, the general rule is that suit should be brought before the court in the place where the infringement occurred or where the defendant is domiciled. This rule applies to actions for damages from railway, highway, water, and aviation accidents as well as ship collisions and other maritime accidents. The Civil Procedure Law and its judicial interpretations provide:[23]

(1) Determination of the place of infringement

The place of infringement includes the place where the act of infringement is committed and the place where the result of the infringement occurred.

[23] See Civil Procedure Law of the People's Republic of China Section 2 Territorial Jurisdiction and Interpretations of the Supreme People's Court on Application of the 'Civil Procedural Law of the People's Republic of China.

(2) Jurisdiction over disputes of product quality

The people's court in the place where the product is manufactured, sold, used, or where the defendant is domiciled has jurisdiction over a lawsuit brought due to the defective product that causes property or personal injury.

(3) Determination of jurisdiction over reputation cases

Reputation cases shall be under the jurisdiction of the court in the place where the infringement occurred or where the defendant is domiciled.

(4) Determination of jurisdiction over copyright infringement cases

(a) A lawsuit brought for copyright infringement shall be under the jurisdiction of the people's court of the place where the infringement was committed, the place where the infringing copies were stored, or the place where the seizure or detention took place, or the place where the defendant is domiciled.
(b) The plaintiff may choose the court in the place where the infringement by one of the defendants is committed to have jurisdiction over the joint lawsuit brought against multiple defendants engaged in different places where the infringement is committed. The people's court in the place where the defendant's infringement was committed has jurisdiction only over the lawsuit against any one of the defendants.
(c) The place where infringing copies are stored refers to the place where a large number of infringing copies are stored or hidden for business purposes. The place of seizure or detention refers to the place where the customs, copyright, industry and commerce, and other administrative organs seize or detain infringing copies according to law.

(5) Jurisdiction over patent infringement cases

(a) A lawsuit brought for infringement of a patent right shall be under the jurisdiction of the people's court in the place where the infringement occurred or where the defendant is domiciled.
(b) If the plaintiff only brings a lawsuit against the manufacturer of the infringing product instead of the seller, and the manufacturing site of the infringing product is inconsistent with the place of sale, the people's court for the manufacturing site shall have jurisdiction. If the manufacturer and the seller are co-defendants, the people's court at the place of sale shall have jurisdiction. If the seller is a manufacturing branch, the people's court of the place of sale has jurisdiction if the plaintiff sues the manufacturer of infringing products for manufacturing or selling.

(6) Trademark infringement cases

Civil actions brought for infringement of registered trademark rights shall be under the jurisdiction of the people's court of the place where the infringement was committed, the place where the infringing goods are stored, the place where the seizure was made, or the place where the defendant is domiciled.

In *Suntech Power Holding Co Ltd v Suntech Power Investment Co Ltd*,[24] both parties were registered outside China. The defendant objected to jurisdiction on the ground that the parties had neither agreed to the jurisdiction of the Chinese court nor chosen Chinese law. In addition, the main circumstances of the dispute happened outside China. The relevant evidence was also located outside China. Further, a related case had been filed and accepted by the Singapore court. The Shanghai Court dismissed the lawsuit by Suntech Holding. It held that, although it

[24] Shanghai Higher People's Court Decision *Shang De Dian Li Kong Gu You Xian Gong Si v Shang De Dian Li Tou Zi You Xian Gong Si* (2015) Hu Gao Min Er (Shang) Zhong Zi No 7.

had jurisdiction over the case, the main facts of the case had occurred outside China and so the dispute was governed by foreign law. It was more appropriate, applying the doctrine of *forum non conveniens*, for the foreign court to hear the case. On appeal, the second-instance court reversed the ruling, finding that the focus of the dispute was whether the conditions for the operation of *forum non conveniens* in paragraphs 1(4), (5) and (6) of Article 532 of the Interpretations of the Supreme People's Court on the Application of the Civil Procedure Law had been met. The appellate court declined to apply *forum non conveniens* on the following grounds:

(1) The case involved the interests of Chinese citizens, legal persons, and organisations. Although the parties overseas companies, their business was conducted in China.
(2) There were no major difficulties for the people's court to ascertain the facts and apply the law. The main issues related to China.
(3) China was a convenient forum for hearing the case. Interim measures had been taken to protect the defendant's enforceable property in China. The hearing of the case by the people's court was conducive to the execution of the judgment. If the Singapore court heard the case, the rights and interests of the parties would be sufficiently protected because the bilateral judicial assistance treaty between China and Singapore did not include the reciprocal enforcement of judgments.

In *New Times International Transport Service Co Ltd Shanghai Branch (NTS SH) v National Air Cargo Middle East FZE & National Air Cargo Group Inc*,[25] FZE was a UAE company, a subsidiary of the US Grupe Group. The defendants objected to jurisdiction, claiming that the case was a foreign-related dispute governed by international treaties and that the parties had agreed that 'any lawsuit arising out of or in connection with this contract, shall be submitted to the court in Dubai, UAE which has jurisdiction'. The Shanghai court held that the dispute concerned whether an international treaty should be applied to determine jurisdiction and concluded that the PRC court had no jurisdiction. The reasons were as follows:

(1) The case concerned a foreign-related civil relationship. By the first paragraph of Article 1 of the Interpretation (I) of the Supreme People's Court on Several Issues Concerning the Application of the Law of the PRC on the Application of Laws to Foreign-Related Civil Relations, the relationship involved one or more parties who were foreign legal persons.
(2) Pursuant to the second paragraph of Article 142 of the General Principles of the Civil Law, if any international treaty to which China is a party differs from domestic civil law, the provisions of the treaty are to apply. China, the UAE and the US are all parties to the Montreal Convention. In the case, goods were transported from China to the US and so the facts fell within the scope of the Montreal Convention. Therefore, the treaty applied to determine jurisdiction.
(3) The court had no jurisdiction over the case. Under Article 33 of the Montreal Convention, an action for damages must be brought, at the plaintiffs' option, in a court of the contracting state: (a) where the carrier has its domicile or principal place of business; (b) where the carrier has its place of business through which the contract was made is located; or (c) where the cargo was destined. Since none of the foregoing places were in the PRC, the people's court had no jurisdiction.

[25] Shanghai Pudong Xin Qu District People's Court Decision *Xin Shi Dai Guo Ji Yun Shu Fu Wu You Xian Gong Si Shanghai Fen Gong Si* (2015) Pu Min Er (Shang) Chu Zi Di S No 5130.

C. Jurisdiction in Foreign-Related Family Litigation

China's regulations on jurisdiction over foreign-related divorces are messy. There are two principal sources. The first is the Civil Procedure Law and its Judicial Interpretation. The second is the Response of the Supreme People's Court. The Civil Procedure Law has no special provisions on jurisdiction over foreign-related divorces, but stipulates in Article 22:

> The people's court in the place where the plaintiff is domiciled shall have jurisdiction over lawsuits concerning identity relations brought against persons who do not reside within the territory of the People's Republic of China. If the domicile of the plaintiff is inconsistent with his habitual residence, the people's court of the plaintiff's habitual residence shall exercise jurisdiction.

Articles 13 to 17 of the Judicial Interpretation of the Civil Procedure Law regulates arrangements for jurisdiction over foreign-related divorces. However, those five articles mainly cover parties with or without Chinese nationality. Their scope of application is narrow, and it cannot completely resolve the question of jurisdiction in foreign-related divorce cases where the parties have different nationalities. There is no uniform standard of jurisdiction. This situation therefore allows for the occurrence of parallel litigation. Further, China's divorce jurisdiction does not distinguish between divorce and the annulment of a nuptial relationship. The rules of jurisdiction apply to all issues of property distribution and child support in foreign-related divorce proceedings.

In *Cai v Wang*,[26] Cai, a Hong Kong resident, married Wang. They registered their marriage in Jinjiang City, Fujian Province and settled in Hong Kong with their children. In January 1997, Cai filed for a divorce lawsuit in the people's court in Jinjiang. Wang objected, claiming that the reason for divorce was Cai's bigamy. This lawsuit was not an ordinary divorce case. It involved bigamy in Hong Kong and thus a Hong Kong marriage as well as a Fujian marriage, both of which could be tried together by a Hong Kong court. The parties and their children's household registration was in Hong Kong and all of them lived in Hong Kong. It was more practical to submit the dispute to the court in Hong Kong for settlement in accordance with Hong Kong law. Most of the joint real estate owned by the parties during the marriage was either in Hong Kong or Macao, adding to the argument that it was more convenient to litigate in Hong Kong. Wang applied to the Hong Kong court in connection with the parties' divorce. The Jinjiang court rejected Wang's objection, holding that, as the marriage had been contracted in Jinjiang, it had jurisdiction. On appeal, the Quanzhou Intermediate People's Court overturned the first instance ruling, holding that the parties should litigate in Hong Kong. The court noted that, following Article 22 of the Civil Procedure Law, Cai should accommodate Wang's circumstances and initiate proceedings in Hong Kong the place of Wang's domicile. Further, given that the parties and their children lived in Hong Kong and their property was also situated there, Hong Kong was the more appropriate forum for the determination of their dispute.

D. Jurisdiction in Cross-Border Corporate Bankruptcy Claims

Jurisdiction over cross-border corporate bankruptcy is a prerequisite for the commencement of cross-border corporate insolvency proceedings and an important guarantee for their smooth development.[27] The Enterprise Bankruptcy Law of the PRC, which came into effect on 1 June 2007,

[26] See Hong Kong Resident *Cai Mouzou v Wang Mouzou* Divorce Litigation Jurisdictional Objections, a virtual case for teaching.

[27] MM Liu, 'Reconstruction of China's Cross-border Bankruptcy Jurisdiction Distribution System' [2016] *Daqing Social Science* 1.

regulates the bankruptcy of enterprise legal persons in China. The provisions in this area of law and the corresponding judicial interpretations have been nullified by the Civil Procedure Law. Thus, the Enterprise Bankruptcy Law now provides a complete code on matters of corporate insolvency. Article 3 of that statute covers jurisdiction in domestic and cross-border insolvency cases. According to the article, domestic and cross-border bankruptcy cases are under the jurisdiction of the people's court of the debtor's domicile. The debtor's domicile is the place where its main office is located according to the judicial interpretation of the Civil Procedure Law. If that cannot be determined, the court in the place where the legal person is registered will have jurisdiction. It can be seen that cross-border bankruptcy jurisdiction in China applies the single standard of 'debtor's domicile'. Once established, a court's jurisdiction in bankruptcy will cover all of a debtor's asset, wherever in the world they may be situated.

In the future, China will likely join cross-border insolvency treaties and cooperate with other countries on cross-border bankruptcy jurisdiction.

E. Jurisdiction in Competition Law Claims

For anti-monopoly civil litigation cases, China currently applies the ordinary rules of jurisdiction. The specific jurisdiction provisions are mainly reflected in the Judicial Interpretation on the Supreme People's Court on the Application of Law in the Trial of Civil Disputes Caused by Monopolistic Acts, which was formally implemented on 1 June 2012. According to Article 1 of the Judicial Interpretation:

> The civil disputes caused by monopoly (hereinafter referred to as monopoly civil disputes) mentioned in these provisions refer to civil litigation cases brought to the people's court by natural persons, legal persons, or other organisations who have suffered losses from monopoly and who are engaged in disputes arising from the violation of anti-monopoly laws.

Article 3 of the Judicial Interpretation sets out jurisdictional rules at different levels. In first instance civil disputes, jurisdiction is to be exercised by the intermediate people's court in: (1) the city where the government of a province, autonomous region, or municipality is located; or (2) a city specifically designated in an operative State Plan. Cases may also be brought before an intermediate people's court designated by the Supreme People's Court. With the approval of the Supreme People's Court, the grass-roots people's court may have first instance jurisdiction in civil disputes relating to monopolies. Article 4 of the Judicial Interpretation contains provisions on regional jurisdiction. That is typically determined according to the specific circumstances of a case, civil procedure law, and judicial interpretations of jurisdiction in tort, contract and analogous disputes. As to the jurisdiction of the Chinese courts over conduct overseas that has the effect of restricting competition, there is currently no legal provision.

12

Jurisdiction in Shipping Claims

JIANPING SHI AND ZIJUN ZHAI

I. Jurisdiction of the Chinese Maritime Courts

The Special Maritime Procedure Law of the PRC states that:

> Whoever engages in maritime litigation within the territory of the People's Republic of China shall apply the Civil Procedure Law of the People's Republic of China and this Law. Where otherwise provided for by this Law, such provisions shall prevail.

Therefore, the Special Maritime Procedure Law, as special legislation on litigation procedures, is applied in preference to the Civil Procedure Law of the PRC in maritime matters. According to the Special Maritime Procedure Law, maritime disputes include maritime tortious disputes, maritime contract disputes, and other maritime disputes.

A. Exclusive Jurisdiction

Article 7 of the Special Maritime Procedure Law stipulates that:

> The following maritime litigation shall be under the exclusive jurisdiction of the Maritime Courts specified in this Article,
>
> (1) A lawsuit brought over a dispute regarding harbour operations shall be under the jurisdiction of the Maritime Court of the place where the harbour is located;
>
> (2) A lawsuit brought over a dispute regarding pollution damage from a ship's discharge, omission or dumping of oil or other harmful substances, or maritime production, operations, ship scrapping, or repairing operations shall be under the jurisdiction of the Maritime Court of the place where the oil pollution occurred, where the result of the injury occurred, or where preventive measures were taken;
>
> (3) A lawsuit brought over a dispute regarding the performance of a maritime exploration and development contract within the territory of the People's Republic of China and the waters under its jurisdiction shall be under the jurisdiction of the Maritime Court of the place where the contract is performed.

In fact, among the three categories of 'exclusive jurisdiction' listed in Article 7, only the third truly falls within the internationally exclusive jurisdiction of the Chinese Maritime Court to the exclusion of other courts. See further section D below.

B. Prescribed Jurisdiction

Article 8 of the Special Maritime Procedure Law of the People's Republic of China provides:

> Where the parties to a maritime dispute are foreign nationals, stateless persons, or foreign enterprises or organisations, and the parties, through written agreement, choose the Maritime Court of the People's Republic of China to exercise jurisdiction, the Maritime Court of the People's Republic of China shall also have jurisdiction over the dispute even if the place which has practical connections with the dispute is not within the territory of the People's Republic of China.

Compared with the Civil Procedure Law of the PRC, the conditions for establishing jurisdiction by agreement in foreign-related maritime cases may vary from case to case. When the parties are foreign nationals, their jurisdiction agreement may designate the Chinese Maritime Court, even if the latter has no actual connection with their case. However, when one or more of the parties is a Chinese national, their jurisdiction agreement is subject to the provisions of the Civil Procedure Law. This means that 'actual connection' is an important condition for the validity of the jurisdiction agreement.

C. Jurisdiction Over Maritime Tort Cases

Maritime tort disputes refer to claims due to ship collisions or other accidents due to ships and their navigation. Claims will typically include compensation for damage from ship collisions, collisions with offshore facilities, oil pollution from spillages, and so on.[1] The maritime court's jurisdiction over maritime torts is different from that of the ordinary courts in relation to general tort disputes. With maritime torts, it is often difficult to determine the precise time and place when the wrong occurred, so other places that have actual connection with the case must be taken as the basis for determining the maritime court having jurisdiction. An example of such a connecting factor would the first port where a vessel arrives following a collision. In addition to complying with the jurisdictional conditions in Articles 29 to 31 of the Civil Procedure Law, the basis of determining jurisdiction has to comply with Article 6 of Special Maritime Procedure Law. The latter would include consideration of one or more of the places where a defendant is domiciled, the place where the vessel first arrived, the place where a collision occurred, the place where a vessel first arrived following a collision, the place where the vessel at fault is detained, the place where a salvaged vessel first arrives, the place of salvage, and the place of port registry. In short, the jurisdictional provisions of maritime tort cases are flexible and similar to the 'minimum links' in US maritime jurisdiction.

D. Jurisdiction Over Maritime Contract Disputes

Maritime contract disputes include litigation in relation to contracts for the carriage of goods by sea, ship mortgages, charterparties, marine insurance policies, crewing contracts, maritime guarantees, and so on.[2] These disputes may be under the jurisdiction of the people's court of the place where a voyage originated, the destination of a voyage, or the defendant's domicile

[1] Provisions of the Supreme People's Court on the Scope of Cases to be Accepted by Maritime Courts (Supreme People's Court, 1 March 2016).

[2] ibid.

in accordance with the provisions of Article 27 of the Civil Procedure Law. At the same time, according to the Special Maritime Procedure Law, several types of maritime contracts may also fall under the jurisdiction of the Maritime Courts:

(1) A lawsuit brought over a maritime transportation contract may also be under the jurisdiction of the Maritime Court of the place for its port of re-transportation.
(2) A lawsuit brought over maritime charter parties may be under the jurisdiction of the Maritime Court for its port of ship delivery, port of ship return, port of ship registry, or port where the defendant is domiciled.
(3) A lawsuit brought on a maritime protection and indemnity contract may be under the jurisdiction of the Maritime Court of the place where the object of the action is located, the place where the accident occurred, or the place where the defendant is domiciled.

II. Preservation Measures in Support of Maritime Claims

In maritime claims, maritime courts may issue compulsory preservation measures against defendants' properties in order to ensure the successful exercise of certain rights when applied for by maritime claimants. This includes interlocutory applications for the arrest of ships (except those engaged in military or government duties) and the sequestration of a ship's cargo fuel and supplies. Parties may also apply for the freezing of funds or the sealing of property pending litigation. A claimant may apply to a maritime court for preservation measures regardless of any jurisdictional agreements or arbitration agreements between the relevant parties relating to the said maritime claims. Before bringing a lawsuit, a claimant must file an application with the maritime court of the place where the property to be arrested, sequestered or preserved is located. This typically refers to the place where the ship or cargo is located. Where a party applies for the preservation of cargo that has already been unloaded but remains under the control of the carrier, if the location of the cargo is not within the jurisdictional area of a maritime court, the party may file its claim with the maritime court of the place of discharge or with the local people's court of the place where the cargo is located.[3]

[3] See Civil Procedure Law of the People's Republic of China, Art 30.

13

Immunities from Jurisdiction

JIANPING SHI AND ZIJUN ZHAI

Jurisdictional immunity reflects the principle of state sovereignty in international civil procedure. It refers to the principle that the state cannot be a defendant in a foreign court or that state-owned property cannot be the object of actions in a foreign court.[1] China lacks explicit legislation to determine the civil status of foreign states before China's courts, that is, whether and to what extent foreign states enjoy immunity from jurisdiction. Article 261 of the Civil Procedure Law only provides that:

> Civil actions instituted against foreign nationals, foreign organisations, or international organisations which enjoy diplomatic privileges or immunities shall be governed by the relevant laws of the People's Republic of China and the international treaties concluded or acceded to by the People's Republic of China.

I. Sovereign Immunity

China is one of the countries that insists on absolute sovereign immunity. This position has been repeatedly affirmed by its central government on various occasions.[2] On 16 December 2004, the UN General Assembly adopted the Convention on Jurisdictional Immunities of States and Their Property (the Immunity Convention). Its preamble states that the principle of jurisdictional immunity of states and their property is 'a generally accepted principle of customary international law'. Article 6 of the Immunity Convention additionally makes it clear that 'a state shall refrain from exercising jurisdiction in its courts over proceedings brought by another state.' However, Article 5 of the Immunity Convention provides that a state and its property enjoy immunity from jurisdiction in the courts of another state in accordance with the provisions of the Immunity Convention. Part III of the Immunity Convention qualifies that a state and its property shall not enjoy immunity in eight situations, including commercial transactions.[3] On 14 September 2005, the then Chinese Foreign Minister Li Zhaoxing signed the Immunity Convention on behalf of the Chinese Government. This has been taken by some observers as signalling that China is

[1] DP Han and YP Xiao, *Private International Law* 1st edn (People's Court Press & China Social Science Press, 2004) 34.

[2] *Russell Jackson et al v People's Republic of China* 794 F2d 1490 (11th Cir 1986) 1494. See also the Memorandum sent by the Chinese Embassy in Washington DC in *Morris v People's Republic of China* 478 F Supp 2d 561 (SDNY 2007).

[3] The eight situations are: Commercial transactions, Contracts of employment, Personal injuries and damages to property; Ownership possession and use of property; Intellectual and industrial property; Participation in companies or other collective bodies; Ships owned or operated by a State; Effect of an arbitration agreement.

switching to a restrictive approach in relation to the application of the principle of state immunity. However, in *FG Hemisphere Associates v Democratic Republic of Congo*,[4] the Hong Kong Court of Final Appeal (CFA), before deciding on the issue of state immunity, ruled that a reference had to be made to the Standing Committee of the National People's Congress (NPC) pursuant to Article 158 of the Basic Law of Hong Kong. As the Standing Committee of the NPC is China's national legislature, its legislative decisions have the legal status of national law. The Standing Committee of the NPC gave its answer by issuing a legislative interpretation on 26 August 2011, clarifying that 'state immunity concerns whether the courts of a state have jurisdiction over foreign states and their properties', and 'directly relates to the state's foreign relations and international rights and obligations'. Thus, as the issue of sovereign immunity falls within the realm of foreign affairs, the Chinese central Government has the power to decide on this issue and Hong Kong courts are bound to follow the PRC's practice in adopting the absolute approach. Consequently, the CFA formally disposed of the case by allowing the appeal by the Congo on 8 September 2011.[4] Some scholars believe that this position of the Chinese Government is not only inconsistent with international trends, but also inconsistent with its own practice.[5] Some scholars believe that the *FG Hemisphere* case has firmly situated the application of state immunity rules within the 'one country, two systems' context and thereby ensured that China as a whole speaks with one voice on the matter. However, considering that it is not necessarily disadvantageous for China to adopt restrictive immunity, China may consider changing its position in the future.[6] Therefore, it is still too early to conclude that China has abandoned the doctrine of absolute immunity and instead chosen to embrace a restrictive approach along the lines of the Immunity Convention. It should be noted in this connection that the Standing Committee of the NPC has yet to ratify the Immunity Convention and there is nothing to suggest that it will be doing so in the foreseeable future.

II. Jurisdictional Immunity of State-Owned Enterprises

China has always adhered to the international law principle that a state and its property enjoy immunity. Therefore, Chinese law distinguishes between actions of a state from those of state-owned enterprises. It holds that state-owned enterprises are economic entities with independent legal status and do not enjoy immunity. However, there are still many cases in which Chinese state-owned enterprises claim that they are 'part of state institutions' and so enjoy jurisdictional immunity. For instance, in *Animal Science Products Inc v China Minmetals Corp*,[7] sovereign immunity was a defence raised by Chinese state-owned Minmetals. The US court recognised Minmetals as China's 'agency or media'. But the court ruled out the application of sovereign immunity on the basis that Minmetals was engaged in commercial transactions. The Immunity Convention adopts the principle of restrictive immunity. With regard to sovereign immunity, a 'state' in Article 2 of the Convention includes:

(1) various organs of the state and its government;
(2) constituent units or political branches of the state that have the right to exercise sovereign power and act in that capacity;

[4] FACV No 5 of 2010 (8 June 2011).

[5] YL Ding, 'Absolute, Restrictive, or Something More: Did Beijing Choose the Right Type of Sovereign Immunity for Hong Kong' (2012) 29 *Emory International Law Review* 997.

[6] YJ Guo and YY Liu, 'On the case of *FG Hemisphere Associates LLC v the Democratic Republic of the Congo and others*' (2012) 2 *Law of the Times*.

[7] *Animal Science Products Inc v China Minmetals Corp* 654 F3d 462 (3rd Cir, 2011).

(3) agencies or media or other entities of the state, which have the right to exercise and are actually exercising the sovereign rights of the state; and,
(4) representatives acting in the capacity of state representatives.

According to the principle of *par in parem imperium non habet*, the most important feature of persons who enjoy sovereign immunity is the exercise of state power. Therefore, it is only when state-owned enterprises exercise sovereign power that they can be protected by sovereign immunity. Only at that point are the sovereign immunity exceptions taken into consideration. In the future, China should further define the jurisdictional immunity of state-owned enterprises and highlight they are normally independent from the state. However, when state-owned enterprises are authorised to engage in governmental or managerial activities on behalf of the state, their sovereign immunity should be recognised.

14

Law of Obligations

QINGKUN XU

I. Contracts

Contractual disputes account for the largest portion of cases dealing with foreign elements in China.[1] Accordingly, more choice-of-law rules have been enacted in the area of contracts than in any other area: Article 5 of the Foreign Economic Contract Act (1985 FECA),[2] Article 145 of the General Principles of Civil Law of 1986 (1986 GPCL),[3] Article 269 of the Maritime Act of 1992 (1992 MA),[4] Article 188 of the Civil Aviation Law of 1995 (1995 CAL),[5] Article 126 of the Contract Law (1999 CL),[6] Articles 41–43 of the Act of Application of Law to Foreign Civil Relations (2010 Choice of Law Act).[7] In addition, the Supreme People's Court has issued two Judicial Interpretations addressing choice-of-law rules for contractual obligations: the Answers of the Supreme People's Court Concerning the Application of Foreign Economic Contract Law (1987 Answers)[8] and the Rules of the Supreme People's Court on the Relevant Issues Concerning the Application of Law in Hearing Foreign-Related Contractual Dispute Cases in Civil and

[1] YJ Guo and JT Xu, 'A Statistical Analysis of Judicial Practice on Foreign-Related Cases in Civil and Commercial Matters in China' (2008) 11 *Chinese Yearbook of Private International Law & Comparative Law* 122, 125.

[2] Foreign Economic Contract Act of the People's Republic of China, promulgated on 21 March 1985(1985 FECL). Art 5 of the 1985 FECL provides in three clauses:

> The parties to a contract may choose the proper law applicable to the settlement of contract disputes. In the absence of such a choice by the parties, the law of the country which has the closest connection with the contract shall apply.
>
> The law of the People's Republic of China shall apply to contracts that are to be performed within the territory of the People's Republic of China, namely contracts for Chinese-foreign equity joint ventures, Chinese-foreign contractual joint ventures and Chinese-foreign cooperative exploration and development of natural resources.
>
> For matters that are not covered in the law of the People's Republic of China, international usages shall be followed.

[3] General Principle of the Civil Law of the People's Republic of China, promulgated on 16 April 1986 (1986 GPCL); trans in P Hay, RJ Weintraub and PJ Borchers, *Comparative Conflict of Laws: Conventions, Regulations and Codes* (Foundation Press, 2009) 316–7.

[4] Maritime Act of the People's Republic of China, promulgated on 7 November 1992 (1992 MA).

[5] Civil Aviation Law of the People's Republic of China, promulgated on 30 October 1995 (1995 CAL).

[6] Contract Law of the People's Republic of China, promulgated on 15 May 1999 (1999 CL). See also M Zhang, 'Freedom of Contract with Chinese Legal Characteristics: A Closer Look at China's New Contract Law' (2000) 14 *Temple International and Comparative Law Journal* 237.

[7] Act of the People's Republic of China of Application of Law, adopted on 28 October 2010 (2010 Choice of Law Act); trans in 'Law of the People's Republic of China on the Laws Applicable to Foreign-related Civil Relations' (2013) 1 *Chinese Journal of Comparative Law* 185.

[8] Answers of the Supreme People's Court Concerning the Application of Foreign Economic Contract Law (Supreme People's Court, 19 October 1987) (1987 Answers).

Commercial Matters(2007 Rules).[9] This chapter begins by clarifying the relationships between these various rules. It then discusses general choice-of-law rules, before finally analysing the special choice-of-law rules that apply to consumer contracts, employment contracts, contracts for the carriage of goods by sea or air, negotiable instruments, and agency.

A. Relationships among Legal Sources

The hierarchy between the various statutes on conflicts of laws is relatively straightforward. The rules provided by the Acts listed above are not always consistent. Where they conflict, it is necessary to determine which rule takes precedence. In some instances the hierarchy is clear, such as where later legislation expressly replaces an earlier regime. For example, Article 5 of the 1985 FECA was replaced by Article 126 of the 1999 CA (governing general contracts),[10] Article 269 of the 1992 MA (governing contracts for the carriage of goods by sea), and Article 188 of the 1995 CAA (governing contract for the carriage by air). Alternatively, later legislation might specify that it takes effect subject to the provisions of earlier Acts. For example, the provisions which replace Article 5 of the 1985 FECA take priority over Article 41 of the 2010 Choice of Law Act.[11] This is confirmed in Interpretation I by the Supreme People's Court (SPC) on Issues Concerning the Application of the Choice of Law Act, which was issued on 28 December 2012 (2012 Judicial Interpretation I).[12] Elsewhere, the hierarchy is more obscure. For example, it is difficult to determine the relationship between Article 145 of the 1987 GPCL, Article 126 of the 1999CA, and Article 41 of the 2010 Choice of Law Act. All three were enacted by the NPC and regulate similar subject matters. They are essentially different at least in one respect: only the 2010 Choice of Law Act adopts the doctrine of characteristic performance.[13] Hence, with respect to the relationship between these statutes, the 2012 Judicial Interpretation I provides that the 2010 Choice of Law Act prevails over the 1987 and 1999 statutes where the provisions in the former are different from those in the latter.[14] This interpretation conforms to the principle *lex posterior derogat priori*.[15] However, Section 2 of Article 126 of the 1999 CA, which stipulates the applicable law for three types of foreign investment contracts, remains effective because it is a special provision addressing the matters not covered by the 2010 Choice of Law Act.[16] Fortunately, the problem of the relationship between the Article 145 of the 1987 GPCL, Article 126 of the 1999 CA, and Article 41 of the 2010 Choice of Law Act ceased to exist from 1 January 2021 as the 1987 GPCL and the 1999 CA were repealed by the 2020 Civil Code.[17] It is worth noting that Section 2

[9] Rules of the Supreme People's Court on the Relevant Issues Concerning the Application of Law in Hearing Foreign-Related Contractual Disputes Cases in Civil and Commercial Matters (Supreme People's Court, 23 July 2007) (2007 Rules); Hay, Weintraub and Borchers, *Comparative Conflict of Laws*, (n 3) 312–5.

[10] 1999 CA, Art 428.

[11] 2010 Choice of Law Act, Art 2.

[12] Interpretation I by the Supreme People's Court on Issues Concerning the Application of the Act on Choice of Law for Civil Relation with Foreign Elements, (Supreme People's Court, 28 December 2012) (2012 Judicial Interpretation I), Art 3.

[13] 2010 Choice of Law Act, Art 41.

[14] 2012 Judicial Interpretation I, Art 3.

[15] GH Sun and JW Zhu, *Jurisprudence* 4th edn (China Renmin University Press, 2015) 112; WX Zhang, *Jurisprudence* 4th edn (Higher Education Press 2011) 63.

[16] 2012 Judicial Interpretation 1, Art 3(2). It provides that where any other statute provides applicable law for a civil relation with foreign elements and the 2010 Choice of Law Act is silent on the matter, the provision of the other statute shall apply.

[17] Civil Code of the People's Republic of China, promulgated on 28 May 2020 (2020 Civil Code). Art 1260 provides that the 2020 Civil Code shall come into force as of 1 January 2021, and the 1987 GPCL and the 1999 CA shall be repealed simultaneously.

of Article 126 of the 1999 CA is retained as Section 2 of Article 467 of the 2020 Civil Code, so that three types of foreign investment contracts performed in China will continue to be governed by Chinese law.[18]

The extent to which the two judicial interpretations have binding force is complex. Formally, both have been annulled. The 1987 Answers were expressly abolished by the SPC on 13 July 2000 because the 1985 FECA – the subject of the 1987 Answers – had been replaced by the 1999 CA.[19] Prior to the issuance of the 2007 Rules, some leading commentators argued that the 1987 Answers should continue to guide judicial practice.[20] They argued that, though the 1987 Answers lacked formal force, their provisions were reasonable and had been widely accepted by courts for many years, so were of persuasive authority. In practice, some courts adopted this argument and continued to invoke the 1987 Answers to justify decisions even after the Answers had been abolished.[21] The 2007 Rules, which retained most choice-of-law rules of the 1987 Answers, were declared invalid on 8 April 2013 because some of the Rules' provisions were incompatible with the 2010 Choice of Law Act.[22] To date, no new judicial interpretation has been issued, or announced as forthcoming. This is unfortunate, as the provisions of the 2010 Choice of Law Act remain vague, making it difficult for the courts to apply them to the numerous cases involving conflicts of contract laws that emerge every day. Therefore, it is understandable that courts continue to consult the 2007 Rules, sometimes citing them expressly.[23]

B. Contracts in General

Article 41 of the 2010 Choice of Law Act provides:

> The parties may choose the law applicable to their contract. In the absence of a choice by the parties, the contract shall be governed by the law of the country where the party whose obligation of performance is characteristic of the contract has his habitual residence, or such law that is most closely connected with the contract.[24] (Author's translation)

This simple provision contains three principles: party autonomy; the closest connection; and characteristic performance. These concepts are elaborated on in other statutes and related judicial interpretations (I.B.ii-I.B.iii), which Article 41 of the 2010 Act must be read alongside. In addition, the provision is implicitly underlain by the requirement of the internationality of the contract.

[18] ibid, Art 467(2). It provides that the law of the People's Republic of China shall apply to contracts that are to be performed within the territory of the People's Republic of China, namely contracts for Chinese-foreign equity joint ventures, Chinese-foreign contractual joint ventures and Chinese-foreign cooperative exploration and development of natural resources.

[19] The List of Abolished Judicial Interpretations Issued before the End of 1999 by the Supreme People's Court (III) (Supreme People's Court, 13 July 2020).

[20] DP Han and YP Xiao, *Private International Law* 2nd edn (Higher Education Press, 2007).

[21] Hubei High People's Court Decision *CMACGM France v Hunan Province Technology Imp & Exp Co Ltd* (2004) E Min Si Zhong Zi No 17 (8 May 2004).

[22] Decision of the Supreme People's Court on Abolishment of Some Judicial Interpretations Issued From 1 July 1997 and 31 December 2011 (Supreme People's Court, 26 February 2013).

[23] The author found 7 case decisions after searching the database of CHINALAWINFO www.lawinfochina.com/ accessed 28 January 2019, where the 2007 Rules were expressly applied even when the facts occurred after 8 April 2013. See also Futian District of Shenzhen People's Court Decision *Xunbang Technology & Intl Co Ltd v Shenzhen Guoxun Technology Co Ltd* (2014) No 11527 (1 March 2014).

[24] 2010 Choice of Law Act, Art 41.

i. Internationality of Contract

The internationality of the contract is an implicit requirement for the application of conflicts law to that contract.[25] There is no special rule for identifying internationality in the case of contracts; the general rule for defining civil relations with foreign elements applies. Article 1 of the 2012 Judicial Interpretation I provides criteria for defining 'foreign':

> The people's court may determine a civil relation as a civil relation with foreign elements under any of the following elements:
>
> (1) Where either party or both parties is/are foreign citizen(s), foreign juridical person(s), or any other entity or stateless person;
> (2) Where the habitual residence of either party or both parties is/are situated outside the territory of the People's Republic of China;
> (3) Where the subject matter is outside the territory of the People's Republic of China;
> (4) Where the juristic fact that leads to the creation, change, or termination of a civil relation happens outside the territory of the People's Republic of China; and
> (5) Other circumstances that may be determined as a civil relation with foreign elements.[26] (Author's translation)

Hence, three elements feed into internationality: the parties, the subject matter, and juridical fact. This provision is therefore based on the three-element doctrine of legal relations,[27] and refines the similar provision found in the 1988 Opinions.[28] The 2012 Judicial Interpretation contains two additional considerations not found in the 1988 Opinions. Habitual residence is added because it is the primary personal connecting factor in the 2010 Choice of Law Act.[29] 'Other circumstances' are considered in order to leave room for the future development of conflicts law.[30]

ii. Party Autonomy

The principle of party autonomy has been employed in China to deal with conflicts of contract law for just over a century. Article 23(1) of the Act on Application of Law (the 1918 Act) provides: 'The formation and effects of an obligation created by a juridical act shall be governed by the law determined according to the parties' intention.'[31] Since 1918, the principle has been consistently employed and regarded as the primary principle governing conflicts of contract law.[32] Although the 2007 Rules were abolished, some of the rules concerning party autonomy were incorporated into the 2012 Judicial Interpretation I.[33] It is worth noting that Article 41 of the 2010 Choice of Law Act provides that the parties may choose the *law* rather than the *law of a state*,[34] with the

[25] ibid, Art 1 (stating that choice-of-law rules only apply to civil relation with foreign elements). See also DP Han and YP Xiao, *Private International Law* 3rd edn (Higher Education Press 2014) 34.

[26] 2012 Judicial Interpretation I, Art 1.

[27] Han and Xiao, *Private International Law* (n 25) 3.

[28] Several Opinions Concerning Implementation and Application of the General Principles of the Civil Law of China (For Trial Implementation) (Supreme People's Court, 18 Aug 1988) (1988 Opinions), Art 178(1); trans in Hay, Weintraub and Borchers, *Comparative Conflict of Laws* (n 3).

[29] 2010 Choice of Law Act. Out of 52 articles in the 2010 Choice of Law Act, habitual residence is employed in 25.

[30] Chief Judge GX Liu, 'Keynote Address' (2015 Annual Meeting of Chinese Society of Private International Law, 14 November 2015). He argued that where two companies incorporated in mainland China conclude a contract and shareholders of one of the companies are from Hong Kong, the investment from Hong Kong might be covered by 'other circumstances' though all other factors relating to the contract are situated in mainland China.

[31] HB Ma, *Private International Law: General Part and Special Parts* 3rd edn (Ma Hanbao, 2014) 377.

[32] Han and Xiao, *Private International Law* (n 25) 207.

[33] 2007 Rules, Art 4.

[34] 2010 Choice of Law Act, Art 41.

implication that non-state norms can be chosen by the parties, whether they are found in international treaties or international usages.[35]

Four types of limitation are imposed on party autonomy:

(1) The application of foreign law chosen by the parties should not prejudice the social and public interests of China.[36]
(2) For matters or issues governed by mandatory rules of China, the parties may not make a choice of foreign law.[37]
(3) The parties should not abuse choice-of-law rights to evade Chinese law.[38]
(4) Contracts for foreign investment performed within the territory of China shall be exclusively governed by Chinese law.[39]

The last limitation merits further analysis. This limitation was first adopted in the 1985 FECA,[40] and a similar provision was accepted by the 1999 CA, which provides:

> The law of the People's Republic of China shall govern a contract for a Chinese-foreign equity joint venture, a contract for a Chinese-foreign cooperative joint venture, or a contract for the Chinese-foreign joint exploration and development of natural resources which is to be performed within the territory of the People's Republic of China.[41]

The 2007 Rules extended this provision to include six other types of foreign investment contracts.[42] Meanwhile, the Civil Procedure Act stipulates that Chinese courts have exclusive jurisdiction over disputes arising from the three types of contracts set out in the 1985 FECA.[43] This combination of exclusive jurisdiction and application of Chinese law aims to ensure complete legal control over the activities of foreign investors in China. There are two main reasons for this: first, activities of foreign investors occurring in China can affect China's sovereignty and national economic security; second, contracts of foreign investment into China have their closest geographic connection with China.[44] At the early stage of opening up to the outside world these provisions were considered reasonable and necessary because China was inexperienced in the regulation of foreign investments. However, it is now questionable whether such provisions should remain. As China has adopted a comprehensive opening-up policy, doctrines such as mandatory rules are sufficient to protect public interests.[45]

iii. The Closest Connection and Characteristic Performance

The relationship between the principles of the closest connection and characteristic performance was once clear. The closest connection, though it has the merit of flexibility, is too vague by itself

[35] 2012 Judicial Interpretation I, Art 9. See also T Du, *Comments on the Act of the People's Republic of China of Application of Law to Foreign Relations* (China Legal Publishing House, 2011) 273–4.

[36] 2010 Choice of Law Act, Art 5.

[37] ibid, Art 4.

[38] 2012 Judicial Interpretation I, Art 11.

[39] 1999 CA, Art 126.

[40] 1985 FECA, Art 5(2).

[41] 1999 CA, Art 126.

[42] 2007 Rules, Art 8.

[43] Civil Procedure Act of the People's Republic of China, promulgated on 9 April 1991 and most recently amended on 31 Aug 2012, Art 266.

[44] MZ Yao, *Textbook of Foreign Investment Enterprise Law* 2nd edn (Law Press, 1994) 32, 232–3.

[45] QS He, *International Civil Litigation in Comparative Perspective* (Higher Education Press, 2015) 128–30 (arguing against exclusive jurisdiction over foreign investment enterprise contract performed in China).

to provide guidance for the courts. It has been sharply criticised as a 'give-it-up formula'[46] that means 'nothing except, perhaps, that the answer is not ready at hand'.[47] Therefore, in order to objectively determine which law has the closest connection with a contract, the principle of characteristic performance, a term 'coined in the Swiss literature and developed in the practice of the Swiss Federal Tribunal',[48] was introduced into Chinese law in the 1987 Answers.[49] This principle was applied, sometimes in conjunction with other factors, to determine the applicable laws for 13 types of contracts.[50] The 2007 Rules extended the principle to apply to more types of contracts.[51] In the two judicial interpretations, the principle of characteristic performance was employed to determine the place that has the closest connection with the contract, ie the place where the characteristic performer has their domicile or place of business. But such a determination is a presumption and can be rebutted if another place can be shown to be more closely connected to

[46] AA Ehrenzweig, 'The Second Conflicts Restatement: A Last Appeal for Its Withdrawal' (1964–1965) 113 *University of Pennsylvania Law Review*1230, 1241.

[47] FK Juenger, *Choice of Law and Multistate Justice* (Special edn, Transnational Publishers, 2005) 58.

[48] K Lipstein, 'Characteristic Performance – A New Concept in the Conflict of Laws in Matters of Contract for the EEC' (1982) 3 *Northwestern Journal of International Law & Business* 402, 405.

[49] 1987 Answers, Art 2 (6).

[50] ibid.

[51] Art 5 of 2007 Rules provides:

> In the absence of choice of law by the parties for a contractual dispute, the law of the country or region which has the closest connection with the contract shall apply.
>
> In determining the applicable law for a contractual dispute in accordance with the principle of the closest connection, the people's court shall make the determination based on the special nature of contract and such factors as the obligation performed by a party which essentially reflects the characteristics of the contract.
>
> (1) A sale contract is governed by the law of the place where the seller has their domicile at the time of the conclusion of the contract; or the law of the place where the buyer has their domicile if the contract was negotiated and concluded at that place or the contract expressly provides that the goods shall be delivered by the seller at that place.
> (2) A contract on processing with supplied materials, assembling with supplied parts or other processing works is governed by the law of the place where the processor has their domicile.
> (3) A contract for supply of plant equipment is governed by the law of the place where the equipment was installed.
> (4) A contract for sale, lease or mortgage of immovable property is governed by the law of the place where the immovable property is situated.
> (5) A contract for the lease of movable property is governed by the law of the place where of the lessor has their domicile.
> (6) A contract for the pledge of movable property is governed by the law of the place where the pledgee has their domicile.
> (7) A loan contract is governed by the law of the place where the lender has their domicile.
> (8) An insurance contract is governed by the law of the place where the insurer has their domicile.
> (9) A financial lease contract is governed by the law of the place where the lessee has their domicile.
> (10) A contract for construction project is governed by the law of the place of the place where the construction project is situated.
> (11) A warehousing or safekeeping contract is governed by the law of the place where the warehouse keeper has their domicile.
> (12) A guaranty contract is governed by the law of the place where the guarantor has their domicile.
> (13) An agency contract is governed by the law of the place where the agent has their domicile.
> (14) A contract for the issuance, sale or assignment of bonds is governed by the law of the place where the bonds were issued, sold or assigned.
> (15) An auction contract is governed by the law of the place where the auction took place.
> (16) A commission contract is governed by the law of the place where the commissioned party has their domicile.
> (17) A brokerage contract is governed by the law of the place where the broker has their domicile.
>
> Where it is clear that any contract above is more closely connected with a place other than that indicated above, the law of that other country shall apply.
>
> (Author's trans).

the contract. The 2010 Choice of Law Act also incorporates the principle of characteristic performance. However, the Act juxtaposes characteristic performance with the principle of the closest connection,[52] blurring the two principles and making their relationship confusing. The word 'or' in Article 41 of the 2010 Act ('… the contract shall be governed by the law of the country where the party whose obligation of performance is characteristic of the contract has his habitual residence, or such law that is most closely connected with the contract') demonstrates that courts have some discretion in selecting either principle to determine the applicable law.[53] In practice, judges often employ whichever principle leads to the application of Chinese law.[54] The 2010 Act's treatment of these principles has been criticised by some Chinese commentators as a step backwards in the codification of contract conflicts law.[55]

In *Wuxi Humei Thermal Power Engineering Co Ltd V DBS Bank Ltd*,[56] the DBS Bank Ltd (DBS), a Singaporean company, issued a letter of credit (L/C) in favour of Wuxi Humei Thermal Power Engineering Co Ltd (Humei), a company in Jiangsu Province, PR China in June 2013. On 29 November 2013, Humei presented the required documents to DBS but the latter rejected the documents on 5 December because the FOB price in the Certificate of Origin was the same as the CIF price in the invoice. The parties had agreed that the L/C was to be governed by the latest version of the ICC's Uniform Customs and Practices for Documentary Credits (UCP 600). The Jiangsu Higher People's Court, the court of the first instance, determined the applicable law according to Article 41 of the 2010 Choice of Law Act. On the one hand, the parties' choice of law was effective and the L/C was governed by the UCP 600. On the other hand, the issues not covered by the UCP 600 were found to be governed by the law of the country where the party whose obligation of performance was characteristic of the contract had their habitual residence, or such other law that was most closely connected with the contract. Under a L/C, the obligation of a beneficiary is to present the documents specified by the account party, while the obligation of an issuing bank is to make payment after confirming the documents' conformity on their face to the terms of the credit. The court considered that the beneficiary's obligation best reflected the characteristics of a L/C relationship. Therefore, the law of the country of the beneficiary's habitual residence, in this case the Chinese law, governed the issues not covered by the UCP 600. This conclusion was confirmed by the SPC.

iv. Formal Validity

An obvious defect of the 2010 Choice of Law Act is that it provides no rules for determining the formal validity of contracts with international elements. This defect could easily have been avoided, as Article 26 of the proposed draft by the Chinese Society of Private International Law (CSPIL) contained a provision addressing the formal validity of juristic acts, including the formal

[52] 2010 Choice of Law Act, Art 41.

[53] ibid.

[54] The author collected 486 contract cases decided in 2014, in which the parties did not make a choice of law. The principle of the closest connection was employed in 250 case decisions, the principle of characteristic performance was employed in 24 decisions, both principles were employed in 3 decisions, Article 41 of the 2010 Choice of Law Act was generally referred to in 202 decisions, and 7 decisions mentioned the 2010 Choice of Law Act but did not apply any particular article. The case decisions are available at www.court.gov.cn/zgcpwsw/ accessed 21 August 2020.

[55] LZ Zhang, 'A Revisit to the Relationship between the Doctrine of Characteristic Performance and the Principle of the Closest Connection – with a Comment on Article 41 of the Act of the People's Republic of China of Application of Law to Foreign Civil Relations' (2013) 15 *Chinese Yearbook of Private International Law & Comparative Law* 98, 120–3.

[56] Supreme People's Court Decision *Wuxi Humei Thermal Power Engineering Co Ltd v DBS Bank Ltd* (2017) Minzhong No 327 (26 July 2017). See also (2018) 11 *Supreme People's Court Gazette* 24, 24–31.

validity of contracts.[57] Furthermore, it may surprise some readers that similar choice of law rules existed in Article 26 of the 1918 Act, nearly 100 years before the promulgation of the 2010 Choice of Law Act.[58] Unfortunately, the legislature of the 2010 Choice of Law Act overlooked the proposed draft and the former provision. In codifications of private international law around the world, it has become a trend to favour the formal validity of juridical acts.[59] Because of this global trend and the fact that the substantive Chinese law of contracts does not require contracts to be in writing, some commentators propose that China should adopt the rule of *favournegotii*, ie when there is conflict between the law of country A, which upholds the formal validity of contract, and the law of country B, which denies the formal validity of contract, the law of country A shall apply.[60]

v. Capacity

As in the case of formal validity, the 2010 Choice of Law Act contains no special choice-of-law rules governing the capacity to make a contract. Capacity to enter into contracts will therefore be determined by the general choice-of-law rules determining a person's capacity to enter into juridical acts, found in Article 12 (capacity of natural persons) and Article 14 (capacity of legal persons).[61] According to Article 12, contractual acts of a natural person are governed by the law of the person's habitual residence or, if the person lacks capacity under this law, the law of the place of action. Hence, Article 12 is in line with the world trend of favouring the validation of juridical acts.[62] Article 14 provides that contractual acts of a legal person are governed by the law

[57] Chinese Society of Private International Law (CSPIL), Art 26. It provides:

> The formal validity of juridical acts is governed by the lex loci actus or the law of the state that governs the substance of juridical acts.
>
> But the preceding provision does not govern the formal validity of juridical acts relating to creation and disposal of right in rem or other rights which need to be registered.
>
> (Author's trans).

See also J Huang, *The Proposed Draft of and Comments on Act of the People's Republic of China of Application of Law to Foreign Relations* (China Renming University Press, 2011) 15.

[58] Ma, *Private International Law* (n 31) 377. It provides:

> The formality of juridical acts, except otherwise provided, is governed by *lex loci actus*. However, the formality, which satisfies the requirements of the law applicable to the substance of the act, is also effective.
>
> The formality of juridical acts to exercise or preserve rights on a negotiable instrument is merely governed by *lex loci actus*.
>
> (Author's trans)

[59] SC Symeonides, *Codifying Choice of Law around the World: An International Comparative Analysis* (Oxford University Press, 2014) 256–9.

[60] Du, *Comments on the Act* (n 35) 293.

[61] 2010 Choice of Law Act. Art 12 provides:

> A natural person's capacity to enter into juridical acts is governed by the law of their habitual residence.
>
> Where a natural person entering into a juridical act lacks such capacity under the law of their habitual residence, but has capacity under the law of the place of act, the law of the place of act applies, unless the act is related to the issues of marriage, family or succession.

Art 14 provides:

> Such matters of a legal person and its branches as its capacity to have civil rights, its capacity to enter into juridical acts, its organization, rights and duties of its shareholders, are governed by the law of the place of registration.
>
> Where the principle place of business is different from the place of registration, the law of the principle place of business may apply. The principle place of business of a legal person is deemed to be its habitual residence.

[62] Symeonides, *Codifying Choice of Law* (n 59) 259.

of the place of its registration or the law of its principal place of business when its principal place of business is different from the place of registration.

C. Specific Contracts

i. Consumer Contracts

After years of extensive debate and exhortation by academics,[63] a special statutory choice-of-law provision for consumer contracts was finally enacted. Article 42 of the 2010 Choice of Law Act provides:

> A consumer contract is governed by the law of the place where the consumer has his habitual residence. If the consumer makes a choice of the law of the place where goods or services are provided, or the business operator does not pursue any related commercial activity in the place where the consumer has his habitual residence, the law of the place where goods or services are provided shall apply.[64] (Author's translation)

In contrast to Article 56 of the proposed draft by CSPIL,[65] the parties are deprived of the right to collectively make a choice-of-law. Such a right can be unilaterally exercised by the consumer, whose choice is limited to the law of the consumer's habitual residence or the law of the place where the goods or services are provided. This limitation of choice serves two purposes. First, to protect the weaker party, ie the consumer.[66] The consumer may choose the law that is more beneficial to themselves and, in the absence of such a choice, the law of their habitual residence will apply. Second, to protect the reasonable expectations of the business operator.[67] If the business operator does not pursue any related commercial activity in the place of the consumer's habitual residence, then they would not expect to be governed by the law of that place, so the law of the place where goods or services are provided will apply instead. In other words, this provision endeavours to balance the interests of the consumer and of the business operator.

However, several issues remain unresolved. First, the Act provides no definition of a 'consumer contract'.[68] A 'consumer contract' is not an autonomous concept and it is necessary to determine clearly who can be treated as an eligible consumer or as a professional.[69] Although domestic law

[63] QK Xu, 'The Conflicts Method to Protect Consumers' (2006) 6 *Political Science & Law* 74–8. See also YP Xiao, *The Basics of Private International Law* (Law Press, 2003) 184–5.

[64] 2010 Choice of Law Act, Art 42.

[65] Huang, *The Proposed Draft* (n 57) 21. Art 56 provides:

> A consumer contract is governed by the law of the place where the consumer has their habitual residence, or the law where goods or services are provided.
>
> The parties to a consumer contract may make a choice of the law which has a reasonable connection with consumption. Where the business operator pursues marketing activities by any medium in the place where the consumer has their habitual residence, or makes an invitation specifically to the consumer at the place thereof, or receives the order from the place thereof, the choice of law by the parties shall not be incompatible with mandatory rules of the place where the consumer has their habitual residence, except that the consumer receives goods or services by actively visiting the place where the business operator is situated and with no relation with the marketing activities by the business operator.
>
> (Author's translation)

[66] J Huang and RJ Jiang, *Act of the People's Republic of China of Application of Law to Foreign Civil Relations: Interpretations and Analysis* (Law Press, 2011) 230.

[67] ibid, 235.

[68] 2010 Choice of Law Act, Art 41.

[69] cf Council Regulation (EC) 593/2008 on the Law Applicable to Contractual Obligations (Rome I Regulation) [2008] OJ L177/6, Art 6(1).

contains a definition of 'consumer',[70] it is doubtful whether this definition can be used in conflicts law. Because foreign-related consumer contracts are more complicated than domestic ones, it is necessary for the SPC to clarify the definition. Second, it is unclear whether Article 42 applies to all kinds of consumer contracts. The Article does not expressly exclude any type of contract. But similar provisions in other jurisdictions do not treat consumer contracts universally. For example, the Rome I Regulation excludes contracts such as contracts of carriage, insurance contracts, and contracts relating to a right *in rem* in immovable property.[71] Third, it is difficult to determine whether a business operator is pursuing a 'related commercial activity'. For instance, should the mere fact that the business operator's website can be accessed in the place of the consumer's habitual residence be treated as a decisive factor?[72] No answer for such questions can be found. Finally, Article 42 does not satisfactorily deal with the problem of whether a consumer can, as a weaker party, make a meaningful choice of law. Because of language barriers and a lack of knowledge pertaining to foreign law, it may be entirely impractical for most consumers to choose a law that is more beneficial to them.

In *Beijing Sunshine Aoda Auto Sales Co Ltd v Zhang Dong*,[73] the Appellant Beijing Sunshine Aoda Auto Sales Co Ltd (Aoda), a company situated in Beijing, sold a car to the Respondent Zhang Dong (Zhang), a Canadian citizen, and made the vehicle registration for Zhang on 17 July 2015. However, Zhang found that his car could not go through its annual inspection at the Vehicle Administration Office of the Beijing Government in July 2017, because the vehicle's appearance did not conform to mandatory requirements and was different from that recorded in the Vehicle Administration Office. Subsequently, Zhang filed an action at the Changping District Court (District Court), alleging that Aoda's sale of an illegal vehicle constituted fraud and that punitive damages, three times that of the purchase price, should be paid by Aoda pursuant to the Contract Law of the People's Republic of China and the Law of the People's Republic of China on the Protection of Consumer Rights and Interests. The District Court issued a judgment in favour of Zhang, which Aoda appealed to the Beijing No 1 Intermediate People's Court. The appellant court held that the applicable law should be decided on the basis of Article 42 of the 2010 Choice of Law Act. Zhang, as a consumer, had the right to choose the law of the place where goods or services are provided. Because he sought damages according to the Contract Law of the People's Republic of China and the Law of the People's Republic of China on the Protection of Consumer Rights and Interests, the applicable law should be the law of the place where the vehicle was provided, ie Chinese law. Finally, the judgment by the District Court was confirmed and Zhang obtained punitive damages amounting to RMB1,980,000.

ii. Employment Contracts

As in the conflicts law for consumer contracts, no special choice-of-law rule for employment contracts was provided in any statute prior to the 2010 Choice of Law Act. Even the Draft Civil Code failed to address employment contracts.[74] Fortunately, academics realised the significance

[70] Act of the People's Republic of China on Protection of Rights and Interests of Consumer, promulgated on 31 October 1993 and most recently amended on 25 October 2013, Art 2 (defining the consumer as a person who purchases and uses goods or receives services for daily consumption).

[71] cf Rome I Regulation, Art 6(4), recital (32).

[72] cf Rome I Regulation, recital (23).

[73] Beijing Intermediate People's Court No 1 Decision *Beijing Sunshine Aoda Auto Sales Co Ltd v Zhang Dong* (2019) Jing 01 Min Zhong No 5533 (17 June 2019).

[74] WD Zhu, 'China's Codification of the Conflict of Laws: Publication of a Draft Text' (2007) 3 *Journal of Private International Law* 283, 294–6. See also Huang and Jiang, (n 59) 123–32.

of such a rule, and employment contracts were dealt with in the proposed draft by the CSPIL.[75] In Article 57 of the proposed draft, the policy of protecting the weaker party was fully reflected.[76] However, the proposed article was not completely accepted by the legislature. Article 43 of the 2010 Choice of Law Act provides:

> An employment contract is governed by the law of the place where the employee carries out his work or, if that place cannot be determined, by the law of the principal place of business of the employer. The labour dispatch may also be governed by the law of the place where the labour is dispatched.[77] (Author's translation)

In contrast with the article proposed by the CSPIL, Article 43 of the 2010 Act fails to grant the parties the right to make a choice of law, and the phrase 'favourable to the employee' has been omitted.[78] Considering that the law of the place where the employee carries out their work or the place of the employer's principal place of business may not be beneficial to the employee in all situations, it is difficult to conclude that such a provision truly reflects the policy of protecting the weaker party.[79] Comparison with Article 8 of the Rome I Regulation highlights three further flaws in Article 43 of the 2010 Act. First, the Chinese provision does not distinguish between an individual employment contract and a collective employment contract.[80] Domestically a trade union is not treated as the weaker party in negotiations with the employer,[81] so it is unnecessary to employ a special conflicts rule for a collective employment contract.[82] It is submitted that the Chinese provision should therefore expressly limit its scope to individual employment contracts. Second, the meaning of 'the place where the employee carries out their work' is ambiguous. An employee may work in several countries for shorter or longer periods. Thus, qualifiers such as 'habitually' or 'from which' would be helpful in determining the workplace.[83] Finally, the Chinese provision leaves no room for the principle of the closest connection and this inflexibility may lead to injustice in particular cases.[84]

The final sentence of Article 43, addressing labour dispatch, is full of Chinese characteristics and worthy of further analysis. A labour dispatch arrangement involves three parties: the dispatching company, the dispatched employees, and the host employer. It also involves two contracts: an employment contract between the dispatching company and the dispatched employees, and

[75] Huang and Jiang, *Act of the People's Republic* (n 66) 21.

[76] ibid. Art 57 provides:

> An employment contract is governed by the law of the place where the work is carried out or the law of the place of business of the employer, whichever is more favourable to the employee.
>
> The parties of the employment contract may make a choice of the law which has a reasonable connection with the work. However, the choice of law by the parties shall not be incompatible with mandatory provisions under the law of the place where the work is carried out or, if the place thereof cannot be determined, under the law of the place of business of the employer.
>
> (Author's translation).

[77] 2010 Choice of Law Act, Art 43.

[78] cf Huang and Jiang, *Act of the People's Republic* (n 66) 21.

[79] SC Symeonides, *Private International law at the End of the 20th Century: Progress or Regress?* (Kluwer Law International, 2000) 60.

[80] cf Rome I Regulation, Art 8.

[81] QX Wang, *Employment Law* 3rd edn (Law Press, 2008) 208.

[82] AV Dicey, JHC Morris, LA Collins, and A Briggs, *Dicey, Morris and Collins on the Conflict of Laws* 15th edn (Sweet & Maxwell, 2012) 2025.

[83] cf Rome I Regulation, Art 8(2) (qualifying the workplace as 'the country in which or, failing that, from which the employee habitually carries out his work in performance of the contract').

[84] cf Rome I Regulation, Art 8(4).

a dispatch contract between the dispatching company and the host employer.[85] A question then arises as to the meaning of 'labour dispatch'. Does it cover both contracts or refer only to the employment contract? In the author's opinion, the parties to the dispatch contract usually have equivalent bargaining power so the conflicts rule for contracts in general should apply. Under Article 43, the employment contract between a dispatching company and dispatched employees is governed by the law of the place where the employee carries out their work or, if this place cannot be identified, the law of the principal place of business of the employer, or the law of the place where the labour is dispatched.[86]

In *Murray Edward Bean v Gates Fluid Power Technologies (Changzhou) Co Ltd*,[87] Murray Edward Bean (Bean), a Canadian citizen, entered into an individual employment contract on 19 November 2011 with the Gates Fluid Power Technologies (Changzhou) Co, Ltd (Gates), a Sino-US joint venture situated in Changzhou City, Jiangsu Province, PR China. Bean served Gates as a manager from 1 January 2012 to 31 December 2012. On 8 October 2012, Bean sent an email to Gates to declare that he would not renew the contract. After the termination of the contract, Bean did not obtain his bonus and other compensation he claimed was owed for his resignation, because he did not take part in a performance appraisal. Bean filed an action for his bonus and the other compensation. The Changzhou Intermediate People's Court held that the case was a foreign-related dispute because Bean was a Canadian citizen, and the applicable law should be determined according to Article 43 of the 2010 Choice of Law Act. Since the place where Bean carried out his work was within the territory of the PRC, Chinese law should apply to the dispute. Per the Labour Contract Law of the People's Republic of China, the court ordered that Gates pay Bean the bonus of RMB224,000, but found that Bean could not obtain compensation since he actively resigned from, as opposed to being dismissed by, Gates.

iii. Contracts for the Carriage of Goods by Sea or Air

Although the 1992 MA and the 1995 CCA contain separate choice-of-law rules for contracts of carriage by sea and contracts of carriage by air,[88] the wording of both provisions is almost the same as that of Article 145 of the GPCL.[89] Therefore, even if the articles for contracts of carriage by sea or by air had been deleted, application of the general rule for contracts in the GPCL would have reached the same result. However, since 1 April 2011, Article 145 of the GPCL has been replaced

[85] J Li, 'China's New Labor Contract Law and Protection of Workers' (2008-2009) 32 *Fordham International Law Journal* 1083, 1121–2.

[86] 2010 Choice of Law Act, Art 43. See also Huang and Jiang, *Act of the People's Republic* (n 66) 237.

[87] Changzhou Intermediate People's Court Decision *Murray Edward Bean v Gates Fluid Power Technologies (Changzhou) Co Ltd* (2014) Chang Min Zhong Zi No 351 (1 December 2014).

[88] 1992 MA, Art 269. It provides:

> The parties to a contract may choose the law applicable to their contract, unless otherwise provided by law. In the absence of such a choice by the parties, the law of the country which has the closest connection with the contract shall apply. (Author's trans).

See also 1995 CAA, Art 188. It provides:

> The parties to a contract of carriage by air may choose the law applicable to their contract, unless otherwise provided by law. In the absence of such a choice by the parties, the law of the country which has the closest connection with the contract shall apply. (Author's trans).

[89] 1986 GPCL, Art 145. It provides:

> The parties to a contract involving foreign elements may choose the law applicable to their contract, unless otherwise provided by law.
>
> In the absence of such a choice by the parties, the law of the country which has the closest connection with the contract shall apply.
>
> (Author's trans).

by Article 41 of the 2010 Choice of Law Act. The old rule and the new rule significantly diverge in the latter's adoption of the doctrine of characteristic performance. Since the choice-of-law rules for contracts in the 1992 MA and the 1995 CCA are based on Article 145, it is reasonable to question why those rules do not follow the development of the choice-of-law rule for contracts in general. The answer to this question now appears in the draft of the revised Maritime Act. The latest version of the draft Act not only absorbs the new elements of Article 41 of the 2010 Choice of Law Act, but also extends the scope of application of Chinese law.[90]

iv. Agency

Article 16 of the 2010 Choice of Law Act provides that agency is governed by the law of the place where the act of agency occurred, but the relationship between the principal and agent is governed by the law of the place where the relationship of agency was created, while the parties may agree to choose the law applicable to the commissioned agency.[91] The relevant provisions contain three notable features. First, the principle of party autonomy may apply to the commissioned agency. Second, if there is no choice of law by the parties for the commissioned agency, the relationship between the principal and the agent is governed by the law of the place where the relationship of agency was created. Third, other issues relating to agency are governed by *lex actus*, ie law of the place where the act of agency took place. Unlike the Hague Convention of 14 March 1978 on the Law Applicable to Agency, the above Chinese provisions do not distinguish between the outer relationship and the inner relationship of agency. Different issues are mixed together and governed by vague rules. The relationship between these provisions is ambiguous and may puzzle the courts.[92]

II. Torts

Choice-of-law rules for torts are scattered across three statutes: the 2010 Choice of Law Act, the 1992 MA, and the 1995 CAA. Prior to the 2010 Choice of Law Act, Article 146 of the 1986 GPCL provided three basic rules for torts in general: the *lex loci delicti* rule; the common domicile or nationality exception; and the rule of double actionability.[93] This Article played an important

[90] The Revised Maritime Act (Draft for Public Comments), Art 16(2). It provides:

> The parties to a contract may choose a law applicable to their contract, unless otherwise provided by law. In the absence of a choice by the parties, the contract is governed by the law of the country where the party whose obligation of performance is characteristic of the contract has their habitual residence, or other laws which are most closely connected with the contract.
>
> Notwithstanding the provisions of the preceding section, Chapter Four of this Act applies to contracts of international carriage of goods by sea if the port of loading or the port of discharge, agreed or actual, is a Chinese port.
>
> (Author's trans).

[91] 2010 Choice of Law Act.

[92] WZ Chen, *Comparative Private International Law* (Law Press, 2012) 293–4.

[93] 1986 GPCL, Art 146. It provides:

> The compensation for the losses arising from tort is governed by the law of the place of the tort. If the parties have the same nationality or their domiciles are in the same country, the law of the country of the nationality or the domicile may also apply.
>
> If an act occurring outside of the territory of the People's Republic of China is not treated as tort under the law of the People's Republic of China, the act shall not be actionable.
>
> (Author's translation).

role in the development of conflicts law for torts. Looking backwards, it retained the main elements (the *lex loci delicti* rule and the double actionability rule) of Article 25 of the 1918 Act.[94] Looking forwards, it significantly influenced the enactments of Article 273 of the 1992 MA[95] and Article 189 of the 1995 CAA.[96] However, the defects of Article 146 of the 1986 GPCL were obvious. Its wording limited the scope of its application to compensation, leaving other issues relating to torts unaddressed. The double actionability rule became obsolete after it was largely abolished in the UK, where the rule originated, in 1995.[97] Therefore, Article 146 of the 1986 GPCL was expressly repealed and replaced by Article 44 of the 2010 Choice of Law Act.[98] The choice-of-law rules for particular torts in the 1992 MA and the 1995 CAA remain effective as special provisions. In addition to choice-of-law rules for torts in general, the 2010 Choice of Law Act provides special choice-of-law rules for product liability and infringement of personality rights. These rules will be discussed below in detail.

A. Torts in General

Article 44 of the 2010 Choice of Law Act provides:

> Tort liability is governed in the first place by the law of the place of the tort. If the parties have a common habitual residence, the law of the common habitual residence shall apply. If the parties make a choice of law by agreement after the tortious act has occurred, the law chosen shall apply.[99] (Author's translation)

This new provision differs from Article 146 of the 1986 GPCL in at least four aspects. First, the scope of application is extended from compensation to tort liability. Second, habitual residence replaces nationality and domicile as the personal connecting factor. Third, the double actionability rule was abandoned. Finally, the principle of party autonomy is introduced into the rules on conflicts of tort laws. In contrast to Article 4 of the European Regulation on the Law Applicable

[94] Ma, *Private International Law* (n 31) 377. Art 25 of the 1918 Act provides:

> The obligation arising from a wrongful act is governed by the law of the place of the tort. However, the law thereof does not apply if the act is not wrongful under Chinese law.
>
> Claims for damages and other remedies resulting from the wrongful act mentioned above are limited to those provided under Chinese law.
>
> (Author's translation).

[95] 1992 MA, Art 273. The *lex loci delicti* rule and common nationality exception are introduced into art 273:

> Compensation for losses arising from the collision of ships is governed by the law of the place of the tort.
>
> Compensation for losses arising from the collision of ships on the high sea is governed by the law of the forum.
>
> If the colliding ships have the same nationality, regardless of where the collision occurred, claims for compensation are governed by the law of the flag state.
>
> (Author's translation).

[96] 1995 CAA, Art 189. It provides:

> If an aircraft caused losses to a third party on the ground, compensation for the losses is governed by the law of the place of the tort.
>
> If an aircraft flying over the high sea caused losses to a third party on the surface of water, the law of the forum shall apply.
>
> (Author's translation).

[97] Dicey, Morris, Collins and Briggs, *Dicey, Morris and Collins* (n 82) 2206.
[98] 2010 Choice of Law Act, Arts 44, 51.
[99] 2010 Choice of Law Act, Art 44.

to Non-contractual Obligations (Rome II Regulation),[100] Article 44 of the 2010 Choice of Law Act does not adopt the principle of the closest connection as an escape clause, and therefore lacks the flexibility that adoption of this principle would provide. Furthermore, some elements of Article 44 are ambiguous, as will be analysed below.

i. The Lex Loci Deliciti Rule

As mentioned above, the *lex loci delicti* rule has been consistently adopted as a basic conflicts rule for torts.[101] Although the rule seems simple, the meaning of 'the place of the tort' is difficult to define and codifications around the world provide differing solutions.[102] Article 187 of the 1988 Opinions provided that the place of tort included the place of the tortious act and the place of damage, and the court could choose either of these when they were in different countries.[103] This judicial interpretation was issued specifically to clarify the meaning of *locus delicti* in Article 146 of the 1986 GPCL. Therefore it should cease to have binding force following the annulment of Article 146. Some Chinese commentators suggest that the SPC should embrace the *favor laesi* principle in future judicial interpretations on conflicts of tort laws.[104]

In *Anhui Foreign Economic Construction (Group) Co Ltd v Inmobiliaria Palacio Oriental S.A., the Bank of Costa Rica and Anhui Branch of China Construction Bank Co Ltd(Third Parties),*[105] Anhui Foreign Economic Construction (Group) Co Ltd, as the contractor (Anhui), and Anhui Foreign Economic Construction Central America Co Ltd (Anhui subsidiary), as the performing party, concluded a construction contract, on 16 January 2010, with the Inmobiliaria Palacio Oriental S.A. (Oriental), as the employer, for a project in San José, Costa Rica. The Bank of Costa Rica issued a performance bond to Oriental for Anhui's guarantee of good performance, and the Anhui Branch of China Construction Bank Co Ltd (Branch of CCB) made a counter-guarantee to the Bank of Costa Rica. On 7 February 2012, the Anhui subsidiary initiated arbitration in Costa Rica in respect of Oriental's default of payment for the project. On 10 February, Oriental demanded payment by the Bank of Costa Rica under the performance bond. Anhui filed an action in China, claiming that Oriental's demand of payment constituted a fraud of the letter of guarantee (L/G). The SPC held that as the dispute concerned the L/G fraud, the place of damage should be the place where the Branch of CCB was situated, because the Branch of CCB issued the counter-guarantee. Even though the guarantee and the counter-guarantee were governed by the ICC Uniform Rules for Demand Guarantees, the issue of fraud was beyond the Uniform Rules' scope. The applicable law was instead determined according to Article 44 of the 2010 Choice of Law Act, ie the law of the People's Republic of China. Under Chinese law, breach of contract by the beneficiary under the underlying contract does not necessarily constitute a fraudulent claim

[100] Council Regulation (EC) 264/2007 on the Law Applicable to Non-contractual Obligations (Rome II Regulation) [2007] OJ L199/40.

[101] Rome II Regulation Accompanying Notes, 82–4.

[102] Symeonides, *Codifying Choice of Law* (n 59) 59.

[103] Several Opinions on the Implementation and Application of the General Principles of the Civil Law of China (For Trial Implementation) (Supreme People's Court, 18 August 1988) (1988 Opinions); trans in Hay, Weintraub and Borchers, *Comparative Conflict of Laws* (n 3) 317–9.

[104] QK Xu, 'On the Trend of Justice in Conflicts Law for Torts in General and the Formulation of China's Judicial Interpretation' (2013) 3 *The Jurist* 128, 137. See also GY Zou, 'The Evolution and the Latest Developments of Chinese Conflicts Law for Torts' (2014) 9 *Frontiers of Law in China* 582, 588.

[105] Supreme People's Court Decision *Anhui Foreign Economic Construction (Group) Co Ltd v Inmobiliaria Palacio Oriental SA, the Bank of Costa Rica and Anhui Branch of China Construction Bank Co Ltd (Third Parties)* (2017) Supreme Fa Min Zai No 134 (14 December 2017). See also (2018) 3 *Supreme People's Court Gazette* 18, 18–33.

under the independent L/G. Hence, it is not sufficient in and of itself to constitute a L/G fraud. Therefore, Anhui's claim was rebutted.

ii. Common Habitual Residence Exception

At least two aspects distinguish the common habitual residence exception in the 2010 Choice of Law Act from the similar exception in the Rome II Regulation. First, in the Rome II regulation this exception is subject to the principle of the closest connection,[106] while under the 2010 Act the law of the parties' common habitual residence applies whenever the parties have a common habitual residence.[107] Second, the 2010 Act provides that the law of the parties' common habitual residence applies to all issues relating to tort liability, including conduct-regulation and loss-allocation.[108] In contrast, Article 17 of the Rome II Regulation requires that 'account shall be taken' of the 'rules of safety and conduct'.[109] There is no such a provision in the 2010 Act. Comparison with American rules suggests scope for refinement of the Chinese common habitual residence exception. In the US, there is wide acceptance of the distinction between conduct-regulation rules and loss-distribution rules.[110] Conduct-regulation is usually governed by the law of the place of the tort, for this law has 'a predominant, if not exclusive, concern' about standards of conduct, whereas loss-distribution is usually governed by the law of common domicile, as this law caters for 'the benefits and the burdens' of the parties.[111] This distinction is considered as 'one of the major breakthroughs in American conflicts thought' and 'one of its major contributions to international conflicts thought'.[112] Hence it is unfortunate that the Chinese legislature did not learn from the American experience, and Chinese commentators have suggested that the SPC should accept this American distinction in future judicial interpretations.[113]

iii. Party Autonomy

The adoption of the principle of party autonomy in the development of Chinese conflicts law in tort has been a breakthrough. The feasibility of allowing parties to make a choice of law for torts was discussed as early as the 1980s.[114] The principle was first introduced into Article 116 of the Model Law of Private International Law drafted by CSPIL in 2000, but the law that could be chosen by the parties was limited to *lex fori*.[115] This provision was followed by Article 81 of Book Nine of the Draft Civil Code.[116] The limitation to *lex fori* was deleted in the bill for the second reading at the Standing Committee of the 11th NPC in 2010.[117] Under Article 44 of the 2010 Choice of Law Act, the parties to a tort suit may freely choose any law, including *lexfori*, even if the law has no factual connection with the tort.[118] However, the choice can be made only after the

[106] Rome II Regulation, Art 4.
[107] 2010 Choice of Law Act, Art 44.
[108] ibid.
[109] Rome II Regulation, Art 17.
[110] P Hay, PJ Borchersand SC Symeonides, *Conflict of Laws* 6th edn (West Academic Publishing, 2018) 786.
[111] ibid, 785, 787–8.
[112] SC Symeonides, 'Problems and Dilemmas in Codifying Choice of Law for Torts: The Louisiana Experience in Comparative Perspective' (1990) 38 *American Journal of Comparative Law* 431, 441.
[113] Xu, 'On the Trend of Justice' (n 104) 137–8.
[114] J Ning, 'The Choice-of Law Principles for Torts' (1989) 3 *Anhui University Journal* 70, 74.
[115] Hay, Weintraub and Borchers, *Comparative Conflict of Laws* (n 3) 355.
[116] Huang, *The Proposed Draft* (n 57) 131.
[117] ibid, 136.
[118] 2010 Choice of Law Act, Art 44.

tort occurs.[119] This time requirement follows the prevailing trend of legislation internationally.[120] Unfortunately, Article 44 does not require that the choice should not prejudice the rights of third parties, in contrast to the Rome II Regulation.[121]

B. Specific Torts

i. Product Liability

In recent years, Chinese courts have decided numerous cases relating to product liability, in which some defendants were renowned transnational companies.[122] The lack of special choice-of-law rules made it difficult to determine the appropriate law in product liability cases, producing wasteful litigation and embarrassing the courts.[123] In response to the urgent practical need, a conflicts rule for product liability was introduced in Article 45 of the 2010 Choice of Law Act, which provides:

> Product liability is governed by the law of the place where the victim has their habitual residence. The law of the tortfeasor's principal place of business or the law of the place of injury shall apply if the victim makes a choice of the law of the tortfeasor's principal place of business or the law of the place of injury, or if the tortfeasor did not pursue any related commercial activity in the place where the victim has their habitual residence.[124] (Author's translation)

This special rule aims to strike a reasonable balance between protecting victims of torts and acknowledging the reasonable expectations of the tortfeasor. The rule protects victims by allowing them to apply the familiar law of their habitual residence. It also gives victims the unilateral right to choose the law of the tortfeasor's principal place of business or the law of the place of injury if they are not satisfied with the result of applying the law of their habitual residence. At the same time, the rule takes into consideration the interests of the tortfeasor by providing that if they did not pursue any related commercial activity in the place of the victim's habitual residence, and so could not reasonably foresee the application of that law, the law of that place will not apply, even if this law would be beneficial to the victim. However, it is questionable whether the aim of balancing the interests of victims and tortfeasors has been achieved. The victim's interests seem to be weighted much more heavily than the tortfeasor's interests.[125] The victim has significant freedom to make a choice among three different laws. Conversely, the sole method left for the tortfeasor to defeat the application of the law of the victim's habitual residence is to prove that they did not engage in any business activity in that place. In addition, it is worth noting that the phrase 'pursue any related commercial activity' is different to the phrase 'reasonably foresee the marketing of the product' used in the Rome II Regulation.[126] It is possible for a tortfeasor to pursue related commercial activity in the place of the victim's habitual residence without reasonably foreseeing the marketing of their product by another importer.[127] Finally, in contrast to

[119] ibid.
[120] Symeonides, *Codifying Choice of Law* (n 59) 101.
[121] Rome II Regulation, Art 14.
[122] Du, *Comments on the Act* (n 35) 372–3.
[123] ibid, 373.
[124] 2010 Choice of Law Act, Art 45.
[125] Du, *Comments on the Act* (n 35) 375.
[126] cf Rome II Regulation, Art 5.
[127] Du, *Comments on the Act* (n 35) 375–6.

Article 5 of the Rome II Regulation, the Chinese rule leaves little discretion for a court to strive for justice in an individual case, as it is not subject to the common habitual residence exception and the closer connection exception.[128]

In *Wuhan Marine Machinery Plant Co Ltd v YDM Shipping Co Ltd*,[129] the YDM Shipping Co Ltd (YDM), a company registered in Kingstown, Saint Vincent, concluded a contract in September 2009 with the Zhejiang Zhenghe Shipbuilding Co Ltd, a Chinese company, to purchase a vessel. The shipboard cranes were manufactured by the Wuhan Marine Machinery Plant Co Ltd (WMMP), situated in Hubei Province, PRC. The vessel had to return from an Indonesian port to a Chinese shipyard to be repaired, because of a malfunction of the shipboard cranes in February 2010. About nine months later, a second repair occurred in another Chinese shipyard, also as a result of defects with the cranes. In January 2012, the YDM filed an action against WMMP in the Wuhan maritime court, claiming for economic losses caused by the defects of the cranes. The court ruled in favour of the YDM; subsequently, the WMMP appealed to the Hubei Higher People's Court. The appellate court held that the case was about product liability. Though the facts of the case occurred before the date on which the 2010 Choice of Law Act became effective, the applicable law could be determined with reference to Article 45 of the 2010 Choice of Law Act according to Article 2 of the 2012 Judicial Interpretation I, as there was no special choice of law rule for product liability at that time. The tortfeasor's principal place of business in this case was Wuhan, Hubei Province, People's Republic of China. During litigation, the YDM made a choice of Chinese law. In accordance with Article 45 of the 2010 Choice of Law Act, the YDM's choice of law was effective. The final judgment was made in favour of the YDM, awarding damages amounting to over RMB4,253,569.92 with interest.

ii. Infringement of Personality Rights

The Rome II Regulation refrains from providing any conflicts rule for violations of personality rights. Instead, it only directs the European Commission to issue a study, most likely because of the complexity of the issue.[130] In contrast, the Chinese legislature enacted a simple choice-of-law rule for infringement of personality rights. Article 46 of the Choice of Law Act provides:

> Infringement of such personality rights as the rights to name and image, the right of reputation, and the right of privacy, whether via the Internet or by other approaches, is governed by the law of place where the victim has their habitual residence.[131] (Author's translation)

This provision is consistent with the choice-of-law rule for the content of personality rights and both of them adopt habitual residence as the main connecting factor.[132] In comparison with Article 139 of the Swiss PIL Act, the Chinese provision does not provide several laws from which the victim may make a choice, even though the law of the victim's habitual residence is not always favourable to the victim.[133] In addition, the Chinese provision does not make the tortfeasor's reasonable expectations as to applicable law a condition for the determination of the applicable law.[134]

[128] cf Rome II Regulation, Art 5.

[129] Hubei Higher People's Court Decision *Wuhan Marine Machinery Plant Co Ltd v YDM Shipping Co Ltd* (2015) E'min Fourth Final Zi No 00066 (12 April 2016).

[130] Rome II Regulation, Art 30(2).

[131] 2010 Choice of Law Act, Art 46.

[132] cf ibid, Art 15.

[133] cf Bundesgesetz Uber Das InternationalePrivatrecht [Federal Law on Private International Law], promulgated on 18 December 1987, Art 139.

[134] ibid.

III. Unjust Enrichment and Negotiorum Gestio

The first conflicts rule on unjust enrichment and *negotiorum gestio* appeared in the 1918 Act, which provided that obligations arising from *negotiorum gestio* and unjust enrichment should be governed by the law of the place where the actions giving rise to the claim occurred.[135] After the founding of the PRC and the abolishment of the 1918 Act, there were no conflicts of law in this area until the 2010 Choice of Law Act. In practice, the courts usually treated unjust enrichment as a quasi-tort and applied the law of the state where the event occurred.[136] The 2010 Choice of Law Act filled the gap and adopted a much more complex rule than the 1918 Act. Article 47 of the 2010 Act provides:

> Obligations arising from unjust enrichment or *negotiorum gestio* are governed by the law chosen by the parties. In the absence of such a choice, the law of the parties' common habitual residence applies. Failing which, the law of the place where the unjust enrichment or *negotiorum gestio* occurred applies.[137] (Author's translation)

This provision follows the approach adopted by the 1918 Act in that the same law applies to both unjust enrichment and *negotiorum gestio*. Meanwhile, it is very similar to Article 44 of the 2010 Choice of Law Act, concerning choice-of-law for torts. Both Articles contain three elements, ie, the principle of party autonomy, the law of common habitual residence, and the *lex loci actus*. One minor difference is the provision on party autonomy. Article 47 allows the parties to make a choice of law at any time. In contrast, Article 44 allows the parties to make a choice of law only after the tort has occurred.[138] Though Article 47 has been clearly influenced by the Rome II Regulation, several differences exist between them. First, the Rome II Regulation contains two separate rules for unjust enrichment and *negotiorum gestio*,[139] while the 2010 Choice of Law Act treats both under the same rule. Second, the Rome II Regulation distinguishes between obligations related to an existing relationship between the parties, such as one arising out of a contract or a tort/delict that is closely connected with the unjust enrichment or *negotiorum gestio*, and obligations which are not related to an existing relationship.[140] There is no such distinction in the 2010 Choice of Law Act. Third, several limitations are imposed on the principle of party autonomy in the Rome II Regulation,[141] while the 2010 Choice of Law Act has very few limitations on the principle of party autonomy, except the formal requirement on choosing the applicable law imposed by Article 3.[142]

In *Shanghai Hengyi Battery Co Ltd v Sihui City Gaofeng Electronic Co Ltd& Luo Yanqing*,[143] Sihui City Gaofeng Electronic Co Ltd (GE) was a one-person company situated in Guangdong Province, Mainland China. Its single shareholder was Luo Yanqing (LY), a Hong Kong resident. On 12 April, 2018, GE wrongly received RMB150,000 online from the Shanghai Hengyi Battery Co Ltd (HB) because of mistakes made by the financial staff of HB. The record of the money

[135] Ma, *Private International Law* (n 31) 377.

[136] EX Wan, *Interpretation and Application of the Provisions in the Act of Application of Law to Foreign Civil Relations* (China Legal Publishing House, 2011) 339.

[137] 2010 Choice of Law Act, Art 47.

[138] cf ibid, Art 44.

[139] Rome II Regulation, Arts 10–11.

[140] P Stone, *Stone on Private International Law in the European Union*, 4th edn (Edward Elgar, 2018) 590–3.

[141] Rome II Regulation, Art 14.

[142] 2010 Choice of Law Act, Art 3. It provides: 'The party or parties may expressly choose the law applicable to a civil relation with foreign elements in accordance with the provisions of law' (Author's trans).

[143] Zhaoqing Intermediate People's Court Decision *Shanghai Hengyi Battery Co Ltd v Sihui City Gaofeng Electronic Co Ltd & Luo Yanqing* (2019) Guangdong 12 Minchu No 46 (29 May 2019).

transfers stipulated that payment was made for the sale of goods. However, no business transactions had been concluded between the two parties. On 26 April, HB requested that GE provide restitution.GE refused this request. The Zhaoqing Intermediate People's court held that the case was about an unjust enrichment dispute, and that the applicable law should therefore be determined according to Article 47 of the 2010 Choice of Law Act. Accordingly, the parties enjoyed the right to make a choice of law. The two defendants were served with legal documents but refused to appear in court at the trial. During litigation, HB chose the law of Mainland China as the applicable law. Therefore, the dispute was governed by the law of Mainland China, under which the court ordered the two defendants to provide restitution of RMB150,000 with interest.

15

Law of Property

LIN JIA, QINGXUAN WU, ZHENGYI ZHANG

I. Immovable Property

The general international practice is for foreign-related immovable property to be governed by the law of the property's locality (*lex situs*).[1] This application of *lex situs* is relatively uncontroversial, and has been adopted by China.[2] However, the increasing frequency of international trade exchanges has had the effect of both obfuscating the nature of foreign-related civil and commercial relations and increased the complexity of their content, resulting in more numerous and complex legal conflicts. Hence, while *lex situs* remains the primary law applicable to property rights over foreign-related realty, it is sometimes necessary to depart from the *lex situs*, choosing and applying the law flexibly in response to new situations and new problems, which has not shown in judicial practice.

A. Foreign-Related Immovable Property

Whether a legal relationship requires the application of law governing foreign-related realty depends on three elements: the subject, the object and the content of the legal relationship. So long as one or more of these three elements is foreign, the law governing foreign-related realty is engaged. 'Immovable property' is generally considered to refer to property that cannot be moved physically, or which if moved would have its economic value damaged and its attributes harmed.[3] China's existing laws and regulations recognise the concept of 'immovable property', but do not clearly define the concept. The Civil Code of the People's Republic of China (the 'Civil Code') divides 'property' into movable property and immovable property,[4] and stipulates that the establishment, alteration, transfer and termination of the real right of immovable property must be registered according to regulations.[5] The Notice of the Supreme People's Court on Issuing Opinions on Several Issues concerning the Implementation of the General Principles of the Civil Law of the People's Republic of China ('1988 Opinions') also clearly stipulates that

[1] J Huang, 'Lun Guoji Sifa Shang De Wuquan Wenti' [On the real right in private international Law] (1995) 3 *Studies in Law and Business* 51.

[2] ibid.

[3] LM Wang, *Wuquanfa Yanjiu* [*A Study of Property Law*] 3rd edn (Renmin University of China Press, 2013) 67.

[4] The Civil Code of the People's Republic of China, Art 115.

[5] ibid, Art 208.

land, appurtenant easements, and the appertaining equipment of other appurtenant construction are classified as real estates.[6]

i. Varieties of Realty Rights in China

China's Civil Code defines a real right as the right holder's exclusive right to directly dominate a specific thing in accordance with the law. For example, the rights of ownership, usufruct, and security interests[7] which all enjoy an absolute right over a thing good against the world.

B. Legislation on the Application of Laws on the Right of Foreign-Related Realties

The law governing the application of laws to foreign-related realties is dispersed throughout a number of legislative enactments. The General Principles of Civil Law 1986 stipulates: 'The ownership of immovable property shall be bound by the law of the place where it is situated.'[8] The 1988 Opinions expanded the scope of application of the law of the location of real estate: 'The law of the place where a real property is located shall apply to such civil relationships as the property right, sales, tenancy, mortgage and use of the property.'[9] The Law on the Law Applicable to Foreign-Related Civil Relationships (the '2010 Choice of Law Act') also clearly stipulates: 'The laws at the locality of immovables shall apply to the right of immovables.'[10] In addition, The Model Law of Private International Law of China (the 'Model Law') provides that the law of the location of the immovable property should be applied to the ownership, co-ownership, and registration of the property, the validity of the property right certificate, and to the distinction between movable and immovable property.[11] The Model Law was drafted by the China Society of Private International Law, a body of academics, and has not been adopted by the Chinese legislature. It therefore has no binding force. However, it is nonetheless referred to by legislative, judicial or other government departments engaged in foreign-related affairs, as well as law schools and scientific research institutes.[12] It can be said that the Model Law of Private International Law of China reflects the general opinions of Chinese academic circles on the application of laws on foreign-related real estate in earlier times.[13]

China's legislation on the application of the law to disputes over foreign-related immovable property is unrefined. It is necessary to sort through provisions across acts to determine the applicable law. Taking the acts together shows a trend of gradual expansion: from ownership to civil relations such as sale, lease, mortgage and use, and then to the real right in immovable property in the 2010 Choice of Law Act.

[6] Notice of the Supreme People's Court on Issuing the Opinions on Several Issues concerning the Implementation of the General Principles of the Civil Law of the People's Republic of China (Supreme People's Court, 2 April 1988) (Opinions on General Principles of the Civil Law), Art 186.

[7] The Civil Code of the People's Republic of China, Art 114.

[8] The General Principles of the Civil Law of the People's Republic of China, Art 144.

[9] Notice of the Supreme People's Court on Issuing the Opinions on Several Issues concerning the Implementation of the General Principles of the Civil Law of the People's Republic of China (Supreme People's Court, 2 April 1988) (Opinions on General Principles of the Civil Law), Art 186.

[10] 2010 Choice of Law Act, Art 36.

[11] 'The Model Law of Private International Law of China' (China Society of Private International Law, 29 April 2014) Arts 76–8, 90 www.cspil.org/Plus/m_default/Cms/docDetail.php?ID=208 accessed 17 August 2020.

[12] J Huang, 'Zhongguo Shewai Minshi Guanxi Falv Shiyongfa De Zhiding Yu Wanshan' [Enactment and improvement of the Law on the Law Applicable to Foreign-Related Civil Relationships] (2011)5 *Tribune of Political Science and Law* 7.

[13] ibid.

C. Disputes Over Foreign-Related Realty: Rights *in rem* and Contractual Obligations

'Real estate disputes' may be used in two senses. Used narrowly, the term refers only to disputes over proprietary rights. Used broadly, the term encompasses all disputes involving real estate, including contractual disputes. That is, disputes not over ownership but over personal obligations relating to the real estate. China's Choice of Law Act 2010 stipulates that its use of 'real estate disputes' is in the narrower, proprietary, sense.[14] The provisions of the Choice of Law Act 2010 on foreign-related immovable property treat all proprietary rights without distinction, from the real right of the creditor's security interest.[15] Article 36 of the Choice of Law Act 2010 states that '[r]ights *in rem* in immovable property are governed by the law of the place where the immovable property is located'. In practice, most recent foreign-related real estate disputes in China involve real estate transactions, eg the sale of housing or disputes over leasing and mortgage contracts.[16] They therefore involve proprietary rights, contractual obligations, and proprietary rights generated by contract, such as leases. Hence, in deciding these disputes, judges often waver between Article 36 of the Choice of Law Act 2010, which concerns rights *in rem*, and Article 41, which concerns contractual obligations. This leaves wide scope for judicial discretion and judgments are often difficult to reconcile with one another, both in their reasoning and their results.

Where Article 36 requires the application of the law of the place where the property is located, Article 41 permits the parties to make a choice of law in their contract. If the parties do not make a choice of law, the law of the habitual residence of the party whose performance is most characteristic of the contract will apply, or the law that is most closely connected with the contract.[17] This can be illustrated by considering three cases, each of which involved dispute over the lease of a house, and in each of which the court reached a different conclusion on the applicable law. First, in *YUYAOTAI v Li Peng* (2020),[18] the Guangdong Guangzhou Intermediate People's Court, after recognising the case as a foreign-related housing lease dispute, decided that Article 36 of the Choice of Law Act 2010 required the application of Chinese law. Second, in the case between *Liu Xiaozhang v Fang Hanzhao*,[19] the court noted that the two parties had agreed that disputes concerning the lease would be governed by the laws of China. The court accepted this choice of law, and the case was governed by the laws of China. Third, in *Guangzhou Xingzhong Vegetable United Corporation v KWONCHUNGKYEOM*,[20] the parties' rental contract did not stipulate the applicable law. However, the court nonetheless applied the provisions of Article 41 rather than Article 36, deciding that the principle of the closest connection therefore decided the applicable law. Accordingly, since the leased item involved was in China, Chinese law was applied.

[14] 2010 Choice of Law Act, Art 36.

[15] ibid.

[16] HY Tian, 'Dashuju Shiye Xia Shewai Minshi Falv Guanxi Shiyong Fa Shishi Zhong Cunzai De Wenti Ji Jiejue Cuoshi' [Problems and Solutions in the Implementation of the Law Applicable to Foreign-related Civil Relations Law – From the Perspective of Big Data] (2018) 3 *Social Science Journal* 96–7.

[17] 2010 Choice of Law Act, Art 41. It provides:

> The parties concerned may choose the laws applicable to contracts by agreement. If the parties do not choose, the laws at the habitual residence of the party whose fulfillment of obligations can best reflect the characteristics of this contract or other laws which have the closest relation with this contract shall apply.

[18] Guangdong Guangzhou Intermediate People's Court Decision *YUYAOTAI v Li Peng* (2020) Yue-01 Min Zhong No 21 (20 March 2020).

[19] Guangdong Zhongshan Intermediate People's Court Decision *Liu Xiaozhang v Fang Hanzhao* (2018) Yue-20 Min Zhong No 5663 (30 October 2019).

[20] Guangdong Guangzhou Intermediate People's Court Decision *Xingzhong Vegetable United Corporation v KWONCHUNGKYEOM* (2019) Yue-01 Min Zhong No 894 (16 April 2019).

According to Chinese judicial interpretation and practice, there are no strict distinctions between disputes over real rights and disputes over creditor's non-proprietary rights.[21] However, disputes over real rights and disputes over creditors' rights are two different categories of disputes, raising different considerations. It is therefore important to distinguish between them.[22] The basic principle for the application of law in relation to creditor's right disputes is party autonomy. Therefore, party autonomy should be given primacy, with the law of the location of real estate should be applied secondarily.[23]

II. Transfer of Movable Property

Article 37 of the Choice of Law Act 2010 stipulates that '[t]he parties may by agreement choose the law applicable to rights *in rem* in movable property. Absent any choice by the parties, the law of the place where the property is located when the legal fact occurs shall be applied.'[24] This provision replaced the common practice of simply taking the place of the relevant chattel as the determining factor, introducing the principle of party autonomy into the field of property rights in China's private international law.[25] Recognition of party autonomy is not without difficulties, insofar as it contradicts the *numerus clausus* principle.[26] Private international law is a part of domestic law, and cannot be discussed in isolation from the overall framework of civil and commercial legal norms. If the values underlying closely related legal norms are inconsistent with each other, so that the norms conflict when applied to the same legal fact, the law cannot ignore this inconsistency. It must be determined which norm is fundamental; and the other, inconsistent norm should be amended or repealed. The principle of *numerus clausus* is foundational in Chinese property law.[27] It is a mandatory norm and protects important interests of the legal order. The principle of party autonomy, which enables the rights *in rem* in individual items of property located in China to be treated under different legal regimes, appears to contradict this foundational principle. This conflict has become the focus of significant academic comment.[28]

A. Law Applicable to the Real Right in General Foreign-Related Movable Property

i. *Principle of* numerus clausus

The principle of *numerus clausus* means that the law only recognises a 'closed list' of property rights. Individual parties are not able to create new types of property right, nor alter the type,

[21] Tian, 'Problems and Solutions' (n 17).

[22] ibid, 92–101.

[23] XL Han, 'Lun Shewai Budongchan Hetong De Falv Shiyong' [On the law application of foreign real estate contract] (2012) 3 *Cross-strait Legal Science* 103.

[24] 2010 Choice of Law Act, Art 37.

[25] SY Li, HB Zhou, JH Huang, 'Qutong Zhizhong Jian Chayi – Lun Jinyibu Fengfu Woguo Guoji Sifa Wuquan Falv Shiyong Wenti De Yanjiu Neirong' [Differences are seen in convergence – On Further Enriching the Research Content of the Application of the Real Right of Chinese Private International law] (2002)1 *China Legal Science* 137–149.

[26] JA Zhu, SJ Fan, 'Lun Wuquan Fading Yu Yisi Zizhi Zhi Huanhe – Ping Woguo Shewai Wuquan Falv Shiyong Zhong Yinru Yisi Zizhi De Helixing' [On the Moderation of Numerus Clausus and Party Autonomy: On the Rationality of the Introduction of Party Autonomy into the Application of Law over China's Foreign-related Property Right] (2020) 3 *Journal of Northwest University (Philosophy and Social Sciences Edition)* 62.

[27] ibid.

[28] ibid.

content, effect and publication method of existing property rights.[29] China's Civil Code adopts the *numerus clausus* principle, stipulating that 'the types and contents of property rights shall be prescribed by law'.[30] If parties attempt to create a property right not recognised by law, or to vary the content of a recognised right outside the legal limits of that right, their provision will be invalid. A court will determine what, if any, property rights the parties succeeded in creating, and the scope and content of those rights, according to the list of rights recognised in law. Hence, it seems that there is little room for party autonomy in the field of property rights, as foreign laws may differ from Chinese law in the types and contents of real rights they recognise, and in the regulation of those rights.[31] That there is a conflict between *numerus clausus* and party autonomy is uncontroversial. But the picture is complicated by increasing criticism in recent years of the *numerus clausus* principle. There is a view that the autonomy of individuals, rather than *numerus clausus*, is and should be the core principle in civil law.[32] The principle of *numerus clausus*, by restricting autonomy, prevents the civil subject from creating new property rights on their assets according to their free decision.[33]

ii. The Principle of Party Autonomy

Party autonomy is an extension of the principle of autonomy in private law to the field of private international law. In general, whether private international law recognises party autonomy depends on the character of the field of civil law it is regulating. In a field where permissive norms are dominant, and mandatory rules supplementary, private international law is minded to recognise the principle of party autonomy. In a field where mandatory rules are dominant and permissive norms supplementary, private international law is less likely to recognise the principle of party autonomy.[34] The principle of autonomy of will is now recognised in the fields of contract, matrimonial property, wills and tort. In particular, contract law most broadly recognises party autonomy; private international law on contract conflicts usually takes the autonomy of will as the primary consideration in determining the applicable law. In contrast, the transfer and protection of real rights in the Chinese Civil Code are generally governed by mandatory rules, with permissive norms playing a supplementary role. From this perspective, the law on the conflict of property rights in principle cannot recognise the principle of party autonomy. Put at its most broad, rights *in rem* are normally governed principally by mandatory law, while autonomy is dominant in relation to rights *in personam*. Property rights, as rights *in rem*, are therefore an inappropriate field for the application of principles of party autonomy.

As mentioned above (at I.C), immovable property is governed by the law of the place where the property is located. The principle of party autonomy is not recognised. However, party autonomy is of greater significance in the context of movable property. France and Japan adopt the 'principle of will' as the mode of real right alienation. Under this mode, both creditor's rights and property rights are created as soon as the contract is established. In recent years, with the mutual

[29] Q Fu, 'Wuquan Fading Santing' [Three Questions on real right law] (1999) 1 *Law and Social Development* 30–4; HX Liang and HB Chen, '*Wuquan Fa*' [*Property Law*] (Law Press China, 2005) 20, 38.

[30] The Civil Code of the People's Republic of China, Art 116.

[31] Zhu and Fan, 'On the Moderation of Numerus Clausus' (n 27) 63.

[32] DX Yang, 'Wuquan Fading Yuanze Pipan – Jianping Zhonghua Renming Gongheguo Wuquan Fa Di Wu Tiao' [Critique of the Numerus Clausus Principle: In Addition Commenting Article 5 of Real Right Law of PRC] (2007) 4 *Law and Social Development* 20–31.

[33] ibid.

[34] X Song, 'Yisi Zizhi Yu Wuquan Chongtu Fa' [Autonomy of Will and conflict of Property rights law] (2012) 1 *Global Law Review* 82.

influence and interaction between the real right and the credit,[35] the traditional characteristics of a real right such as 'one thing, one right' and *numerus clausus* have gradually dissipated.[36] One example of the increasing recognition of party autonomy is the case of *Wenzhou Guocai Packaging Co Ltd v Sumitomo Mitsui Financial Leasing Co Ltd*.[37] Sumitomo Mitsui Co Ltd was a foreign company that stipulated the application of the laws of the PRC, with no objections from the Guocai Packaging Company. Therefore, the court applied Chinese law in accordance with Article 37 of the Choice of Law Act 2010. Hence, China's private international law now places the principle of party autonomy in a prominent position, allowing the parties to choose the applicable law of foreign-related civil legal relations by agreement in a wide range of fields. Many Chinese scholars have expressed the view that this kind of flexibility is excessive and should be restricted through judicial interpretation.[38]

iii. Lex situs *Rule*

Lex situs is the law of the location of the property. Application of the *lex situs* is one way of determining the applicable law where a conflict of property laws arises.[39] Before the Choice of Law Act 2010 was promulgated, Chinese legislation did not stipulate general conflict rules regarding the ownership of movable properties and other real rights, but only addressed certain special movable properties such as property rights over sea vessels in the Maritime Law and civil aircraft property rights in the Civil Aviation Law.[40] Today, *lex situs* is applicable to immovable property unless the parties have by agreement chosen a different applicable law,[41] or the property is in transit (in which case the law of the place of destination applies[42]). Some scholars believe that real rights, by their nature, can only be governed by the law of the place where the property is located, and cannot be agreed by the parties.[43]

B. The Moderating Space between Party Autonomy and *numerus clausus*

It can be seen from the above that, the types of real rights, their content and their publication method are all enumerated by the Chinese legislation on property law, which reflects the principle

[35] QH Li, 'Lun Zhaiquan Wuquanhua Qushi' [The Analysis on The Trend of Creditor's Rights Turning into Property Right] (2005) 7 *Contemporary Law Review* 69, 69–71. See also MM Gong, 'Wuquan He Zhaiquan Xianghu Ronghe Zhi Qushi Fenxi' [The Analysis on the trend of the integration of real right and creditor's right] (2008) 6 *Knowledge Economy* 16–7.

[36] QH Li, 'Lun Wuquan De Zhaiquanhua Qushi' [Discussion on the Trend of Obligatory Rights Ization of Real Right] (2006) 6 *Higher Education Forum* 55–7.

[37] Zhejiang Higher People's Court Decision *Guocai Packaging Co Ltd v Sumitomo Mitsui Financial Leasing Co Ltd* (2018) Zhe Min Zhong No 878 (13 March 2019).

[38] GJ Chen, 'Lun Yisi Zizhi Zai Dongchan Shiyong Zhong De Xianzhi' [On the limitation of the principle of Autonomy of Will in the application of the law of real right of chattel] (2017) 5 *Political Science and Law* 122, 122–131; WZ Chen, 'shewai Minshi Guanxi Falv Shiyong Fa De Zhongguo Tese' [The Chinese Characteristics of Law on the Application of Law in Foreign-related Civil Relations] (2011) 11 *Legal Forum* 48, 48–52; T Du, 'Lun Wuquan Guoji Sifa Zhong Dangshiren Yisi Zizhi De XianDu – Jianping Shewai Minshi Guanxi Falv Shiyong Fa Di 37 Tiao' [On the Limits of Party Autonomy in International Real Right Law: Analysis of Article 37of the Law of the Application of Law for Foreign-related Civil Relations of the People's Republic of China] (2012) 5 *Journal of Shanghai University of Finance and Economics* 31–8.

[39] XY Zeng, LM Wang, *Guoji Sifa* [*International Law*] (China Renmin University Press, 2007).

[40] Maritime Law of the People's Republic of China, Arts 270–2; Civil Aviation Law of the People's Republic of China, Arts 185–7.

[41] Article 37 of the Law of the Application of Law for Foreign-related Civil Relations of the People's Republic of China.

[42] Article 38 of the Law of the Application of Law for Foreign-related Civil Relations of the People's Republic of China.

[43] HF Du, 'Lun Woguo Shewai Wuquan Falv Shiyong De Wanshan' [On the Improvement of The Application of The Law on Real Right in Foreign Affairs in China] (2013) 2 *Contemporary Law* 141.

of *numerus clausus*. However, in respect of the transfer of real rights in movables, both legislative norms and judicial interpretations have telegraphed a trend of moderation between party autonomy and *numerus clausus*, leaving a large gap for party autonomy.

i. Delivery of Chattels

China's Civil Code stipulates that the creation or transfer of a property right in a chattel becomes valid upon delivery.[44] This principle is called 'realistic delivery' (*xian shi jiao fu*) and is mandatory law.[45] The Civil Code provides for three forms of delivery: simple delivery, designated delivery and possession reformulation.[46] Parties may choose between these modes of delivery. This choice creates space for party autonomy in the transfer of rights in chattels. It is stipulated that if delivery is completed by designated delivery (*zhi shi jiao fu*), the relevant property right will transfer when the parties' mutual intentions on the transference of the right by designated delivery become effective. In other words, where a third party has possessed a movable before the real right in the movable is created or transferred, the person who is obliged to deliver the movable may transfer the right to request a third party to return the original property to replace the delivery.[47]

ii. Real Rights for Security

A security interest in a chattel is established by the will of the parties. For example, a mortgage in a chattel is created at the time when the mortgage contract becomes valid, and if it is not registered, it shall not be set up against a bona fide third party.[48]

iii. Ownership Reservation

The Interpretation of the Supreme People's Court on Issues Concerning the Application of Law for the Trial of Cases of Disputes over Sales Contracts stipulates that the rules for the sale of ownership reservation are only applicable to movable property, and both parties to a contract of sale can agree to retain the ownership of movable property.[49]

Although Chinese property laws are fundamentally compulsory, as demonstrated in the above examples (II.B.i–iii), recent developments have seen a degree of weakening of the mandatory rules in terms of effectiveness over the transfer of movable property rights. There exists a moderation between *numerus clausus* and party autonomy, and the rules governing transfer of the real right of a chattel is the embodiment of this moderation. However, the balance between these two competing principles is arguably unsettled. The recognition of party autonomy in the Choice of Law Act 2010 goes much further than the corresponding weakening of the principle of *numerus clausus* in substantive domestic law.[50] Therefore, the Choice of Law Act 2010's openness to party autonomy is arguably excessive and should be restricted.

[44] The Civil Code of the People's Republic of China, Art 224.

[45] Zhu and Fan, 'On the Moderation of Numerus Clausus' (n 27) 64.

[46] The Civil Code of the People's Republic of China, Arts 226–8.

[47] ibid, Art 227.

[48] The Civil Code of the People's Republic of China, Art 403.

[49] Interpretation of the Supreme People's Court on Issues Concerning the Application of Law for the Trial of Cases of Disputes over Sales Contracts (Supreme People's Court, Fa Shi (2012) 7, 7 January 2012), Art 34.

[50] GJ Chen, 'Lun Yisi Zizhi Yuanze Zai Dongchan Wuquan Falv Shiyong Zhong De Xianzhi' [On the Limitation of the Party Autonomy in the Application of the Law of Real Right of Chattel] (2017) 5 *Political Science and Law* 122–131.

C. The Dispute between the Party Autonomy and the *lex situs*

Commentators have expressed concern that, in comparison with *lex situs*, the biggest drawback of an autonomy-centred approach is that it will lead to a split in the applicable law of property rights.[51] Consider a contract for the international sale of goods. On an autonomy-centred approach, both parties to the contract can agree on the law applicable to their personal obligations, but also to the real right of the goods. As regards the personal obligations this is unobjectionable, as these obligations are good only between the parties. However, property rights are good against the whole world. It would thus be objectionable if the parties, by their bilateral agreement, could vary the law governing the real right of the goods, in so doing varying the legal positions of third parties to the contract. Hence, the parties' agreement on the applicable law can only be valid between themselves. It cannot govern the applicable law as between the buyer or seller and any third party. The result of this is that the same legal relationship – the real right of property – may be subject simultaneously to the laws of two countries. This complicates the real right relationship and is both practically and in principle undesirable. If the parties to the contract of sale were not entitled to make a choice of law with regard to the real right of the property, the property right will consequently be more stable and clear. Both internal and external relations will be uniformly governed by *lex situs*, the law of the location of the thing.[52]

This view is not universally held. Other scholars have expressed the belief that the 'split' of the applicable law of property rights is caused not by the application of party autonomy, but by the inevitable uncertainty created by the transfer of movable property in two or more countries in the international trade of goods.[53] Rather than causing uncertainty, recognising party autonomy ameliorates uncertainty, as the law chosen by the parties is at least predictable to both parties in the transaction. These scholars accept that this poses a difficulty for third parties, but argue that the same difficulties arise if party autonomy is rejected and *lex situs* applied rigorously.[54] An example illustrates the point. Consider an international sale where the domestic seller has effectively sold the goods twice, once to a domestic buyer and once to an international buyer. The goods are transported to the international buyer, in foreign territory. The domestic buyer, on learning what has happened, may seek to enforce against the seller their property rights according to domestic law. However, since the goods have been shipped to a foreign port, they will be frustrated in their attempt to enforce their domestic rights. *Lex situs*, the law of the location of the international buyer, will apply. Hence the domestic buyer's expectations of their rights would be bound to fall through, since they would have been unable to foresee this international transfer of the movable property. This case illustrates that, though scholars accept that application of the party autonomy principle may 'split' the rights to movable property, producing uncertainty, application of lex situs also produces uncertainty and may frustrate the expectations of third parties.

The law of the locality of the applicable property cannot effectively protect the expectations of the third party. The purpose of party autonomy is to protect the interests of the parties to a transaction and to overcome rigidity and unreasonableness resulting from the application of *lex situs*. Simultaneously, party autonomy is conducive to the convenience and security of a transaction, ensuring that the parties have a clear understanding of the content and passage of the real right.

[51] T Du, 'On the Limits of Party Autonomy' (n 39).

[52] ibid.

[53] HC Zhou, 'Wuquan Chongtufa Zhong De Yisi Zizhi Yu Disanren Liyi Baohu'[Autonomy in Real Right Conflict Law and Protection of the Third Party's Interest] (2014) 6 *Journal of Henan University of Economics and Law* 108–115. Zhu and Fan, 'On the Moderation of Numerus Clausus' (n 27) 63–68.

[54] Zhu and Fan, 'On the Moderation of Numerus Clausus' (n 27) 65.

This is desirable practically, as it helps to avoid transactional failures and increases convenience in transacting, and in principle, as it better promotes parties' freedom. As for protecting third party rights, restrictive provisions are needed to protect the expectations of third parties. Party autonomy should be respected in disputes between the parties over the real right of chattel, but not in disputes between the parties and persons not party to their transaction.

D. Application of Law to Real Rights in Movables in Foreign-Related Transportation

The Choice of Law Act 2010 contains provisions on the law applicable to determining the real right in movables in transportation.[55] The parties concerned may choose the laws applicable to any change of the right over the movables taking place in transportation via mutual agreement. This reflects the prioritisation of the principle of party autonomy. If the parties do not agree on what laws to apply, the laws of the destination of transportation will apply by default.[56] Therefore a dispute over the real right in movables in foreign-related transportation, in the absence of a party-agreed choice of law, will not be resolved until the destination of the goods in transit is determined. This application of the law of the destination of transportation for settlement is in line with the private international law principle of the place of closest connection.

E. The Law Applicable to Pledges of Rights and Negotiable Securities

The Choice of Law Act 2010's provisions on negotiable securities reflect the private international law principle of the place of closest connection.[57] The law of the place where the right of the security is realised – or other laws that are most closely related to the security – will apply to negotiable securities. Whether the rights of holders of securities can be recognised, acquisitions and transfers of securities, and the legality of the realisation of these rights are all ultimately determined by the place where the rights are realised. Legal authorities have confirmed, with caveats, that this conforms to the *lex situs* principle. One example can be found in the case of *Nanyang Commercial Bank (China) Co Ltd Guangzhou Branch, etc v Guangzhou Dacheng Trade Development Co Ltd*, regarding an objection to the implementation of a distribution plan.[58] The object of the dispute was the distribution of Guangzhou Bank shares held by the Yangcheng Group after an auction. As the stock was made up of negotiable securities, and the law of its place of realisation was within the jurisdiction of the court of first instance (that is Guangzhou), the law of the PRC was applied. Finally, note that the provisions of the Choice of Law Act 2010 only involve the legal application of the rights embodied in the securities, not the legal application of the real rights to the securities themselves. Further, although the application of the law under the system of direct holding of securities is addressed, the application of the law under the system of indirect holding of securities is not.

[55] 2010 Choice of Law Act, Art 38.
[56] ibid.
[57] ibid, Arts 39–40.
[58] Guangdong Guangzhou Intermediate People's Court Decision *Nanyang Commercial Bank (China) Co Ltd Guangzhou Branch, etc v Guangzhou Dacheng Trade Development Co Ltd* (2015) Sui Zhong Fa Min Fourth Final Zi No 124 (25 September 2016).

Certain academic writers have argued that it is necessary to distinguish between the two kinds of rights to negotiable securities: real rights and the right of pledge.[59] For ownership, possession and other real rights to negotiable securities, the applicable law of the real right (generally the law of the place where the negotiable securities are located) or the law of the country where the negotiable securities may usually be found should be applied.[60] This applies to the ownership and hypothec of a security, the effectiveness and conditions of the transfer of securities, the relationship between the security owner and third parties, the security mortgage guarantee, etc. Conversely, the right of pledge – that is, the right to pledge negotiable instruments, bonds, bills of lading, stock rights and any other rights that can be pledged – is governed by the law of the place where the pledge is established.[61] The variety of types of rights which may be pledged, and the very distinct natures of those rights, may result in difficulties in determining the place of establishment.

F. The Applicable Law of the Real Right in Foreign-Related Means of Transport

The law applicable to the real right in means of transport is not addressed in the Choice of Law Act 2010. The Maritime Law stipulates the law applicable to ship ownership, ship mortgages and maritime liens, while the Civil Aviation Law stipulates the law applicable to ownership, mortgages and maritime lien of civil aircraft.[62] It would be preferable for these positions to be contained in the Choice of Law Act 2010. The present dispersal of these provisions between multiple acts of legislation is detrimental to the systematisation and coordination of China's private international law.[63]

III. Expropriation

Expropriation and nationalisation are important parts of national economic sovereignty. The standard of compensation for the expropriation of foreign property is also one of the most controversial issues in international law. As for the compensation standard for nationalisation, there are three main viewpoints in the theory and practice of international investment: full compensation; appropriate compensation; and no compensation. Initially, China completely rejected full compensation (also called the Hull Principle), later insisting on adherence to the 'moderate principle' (appropriate compensation). However, China has now accepted the 'timeliness' and 'effectiveness' requirements of the Hull Principle.[64]

[59] J Huang, *Zhonghua Renmin Gongheguo Shewai Minshi Guanxi Falv Shiyong Fa Jianyigao Ji Shuoming* [*Draft and Explanation of the law of the People's Republic of China on the Application of Law in Foreign-related Civil relations*] (Renmin University of China Press, 2011) 81.

[60] ibid.

[61] The Civil Code of the People's Republic of China, Art 440.

[62] Maritime Law of the People's Republic of China, Arts 270–2; Civil Aviation Law of the People's Republic of China, Arts 185–7.

[63] HS Chun, 'Zhongguo Wuquan Chongtu Fa Tixi Zhi Chonggou' [Reconstruction of Real Right Conflict Law System in China] (2013) 4 *Journal of Henan University of Economics and Law* 53.

[64] As represented by China's 2003 model investment agreement, China has directly accepted the requirements of 'timeliness' and 'effectiveness' in the 'Hull Principles'. On the core issue of 'sufficiency', although it has not directly expressed 'sufficiency' or 'full amount', it has been in line with the model investment agreement of major Western countries and expressed as 'equal to the value of the expropriated investment'.

A. Expropriation and Nationalisation

At present, there is no unified definition of nationalisation in academic circles. It is generally believed that 'nationalisation' refers to mandatory measures taken by the state to, on the basis of the public interest, take property originally owned by private or foreign governments into state ownership.[65] As for expropriation, it is generally understood that there is no substantive difference between expropriation and nationalisation.[66] They are both coercive measures taken by the state and result in the taking of private property into state ownership. The two differences between expropriation and nationalisation is that expropriation means that the state uses the expropriated property for other purposes, while the purpose of nationalisation is to continue using the property for its original purpose. In addition, while expropriation affects only the rights and property of individuals, nationalisation is large-scale and reflects changes in the socio-economic structure of the country.[67]

B. Relevant Legislative Practice in China

i. Domestic Legislation

The legal basis for expropriation in China is found in the Constitution. The Constitution stipulates that the state may, for the benefit of the public interest, expropriate or take over the land and private property of citizens for public use, while paying compensation in accordance with the law.[68] Three main pieces of legislation elaborate the rules governing expropriation in succession: the Law of the People's Republic of China on Wholly Foreign-Owned Enterprises 1986 ('Foreign Investment Enterprise Law'); the Law of the People's Republic of China on Chinese-Foreign Equity Joint Ventures, revised in 1990 ('Chinese-Foreign Equity Joint Ventures Law'); and the Foreign Investment Law of the People's Republic of China ('Foreign Investment Law'), coming into force and implemented in 2020. Three points should be made. First, each piece of legislation stipulates the general rule that the state shall not nationalise or requisition any foreign-funded enterprise.[69] This is in order to dispel the doubts of foreign investors about nationalisation, so as not to discourage foreign investment in China. Second, each stipulates exceptions to the general rule, where expropriation can be implemented based on the needs of the public interest. Finally, each stipulates compensation to be paid to persons whose property is nationalised.[70] Expropriation and requisition must be conducted under statutory procedures, and fair and reasonable compensation must be made in a timely manner.[71]

In addition to these three pieces of legislation, there is legislation specifying rules applicable in the few cases of investments made by Taiwanese persons. The law of the People's Republic of China on the Protection of Investments by Taiwan Compatriots stipulates that:

> The state shall not nationalise or expropriate the investment of Taiwan investors. It is only in special circumstances, according to the need of public interest that the investments of Taiwan investors may be expropriated according to legal procedure with due remuneration.

[65] JS Yu, *Guoji Touzi Fa* [*International Investment Law*] 2nd edn (Law Press, China 2003) 278.
[66] ibid.
[67] YF Lv, *Guoji Touzi Fa* [*International Investment Law*] (Higher Education Press, 2005) 85.
[68] Constitution of the People's Republic of China (2018 Amendment), Arts 10, 13.
[69] Law of the People's Republic of China on Wholly Foreign-Owned Enterprises (expired), Art 4; Law of the People's Republic of China on Chinese-Foreign Equity Joint Ventures (expired), Art 2; Foreign Investment Law of the People's Republic of China, Art 20.
[70] ibid.
[71] Foreign Investment Law of the People's Republic of China, Art 20.

The Detailed Rules for the Implementation of the Law of the People's Republic of China on the Protection of Investments of Taiwan Compatriots further specify the standards and methods of compensation:

> Compensation shall be equivalent to the value of the investments at the moment just before the decision of requisition, including interest as calculated at a reasonable interest rate beginning on the day of requisition and ending on the day of payment, and may be converted into foreign exchange, or remitted back to Taiwan or out of the territory according to law.[72]

ii. International Treaties

Since China signed its first investment protection agreement with Sweden in 1982, more than 150 bilateral investment agreements have been signed which stipulate compensation arrangements for nationalisation. One example is in the 1988 Agreement between the People's Republic of China and Japan on Encouraging and Mutual Protection of Investment.[73] Per this agreement: expropriation and nationalisation measures, or other measures with similar effects, may only be taken for the benefit of the public interest; the measures must be carried out in a non-discriminatory manner; compensation must be given; and performance of the measures must comply with the laws and regulations. The agreement also stipulates the standards and methods of compensation.[74] Certain provisions on nationalisation and expropriation are generally present in the bilateral investment protection agreements signed between China and foreign countries. First, it is generally required that nationalisation and expropriation must: (a) be for the promotion of national security or the public interest; (b) follow procedures established by law; (c) be non-discriminatory; and (d) be accompanied by compensation. Second, in general the amount of compensation is the fair and reasonable market price of the expropriated property on the eve of nationalisation,[75] including interest calculated at a commercially reasonable rate and applied from the date of expropriation.

C. China's Compensation Standards for the Expropriation of Foreign Capital

Both the Foreign Investment Enterprise Law and the Chinese-Foreign Equity Joint Ventures Law stipulate 'corresponding compensation' as the compensation standard for the nationalisation or expropriation of foreign capital.[76] The Foreign Investment Law adopts 'fair and reasonable compensation' as the standard of compensation for the expropriation of foreign capital.[77] When examining all bilateral investment treaties between China and foreign countries, it will immediately be noticed that almost every treaty includes provisions such as 'compensation shall place the

[72] Law of the People's Republic of China on the Protection of Investments by Taiwan Compatriots, Art 4; Detailed Rules for the Implementation of the Law of the People's Republic of China on the Protection of Investments of Taiwan Compatriots, Art 24.

[73] Agreement between the People's Republic of China and Japan on Encouraging and Mutual Protection of Investment, Art 5.

[74] ibid.

[75] LH Chen, 'Lun Dui Waizi Guoyouhua De Buchang Biaozhun' [On the standard of compensation for nationalization of foreign capital] (2003) 4 *Journal of Graduate School of Chinese Academy of Social Sciences* 108.

[76] Law of the People's Republic of China on Wholly Foreign-Owned Enterprises (expired), Art 4; Law of the People's Republic of China on Chinese-Foreign Equity Joint Ventures (expired), Art 2.

[77] Foreign Investment Law of the People's Republic of China, Art 20.

investor in the same financial position as if there had been no expropriation' (the Sino-Japanese agreement and the Sino-Greek agreement) or 'compensation shall be equivalent to the actual value of the investment' (the Sino-French agreement). In addition, all agreements between China and foreign countries stipulate that compensation shall be in 'convertible currency' and shall be 'paid within a reasonable time'. These provisions are very similar to the 'full, timely, and effective' payment provisions of the US Model Bilateral Investment Treaty. Therefore, some scholars believe that 'corresponding compensation' can undoubtedly be understood to mean 'full compensation' when taken in conjunction with the relevant provisions of the Sino-foreign agreement.[78]

Conversely, some scholars argue that it is inappropriate to interpret 'corresponding compensation' as 'full compensation'.[79] The reason for this is that, on the premise that outbound investment has yet to become a major driver of China's economic development but the inflow of foreign capital remains a major driving force for China's economic development, and that most developing countries still adhere to their original positions and principles with regard to compensation for nationalisation and expropriation,[80] this change in China's position may detrimentally affect China's political cooperation and economic interactions with other developing countries. Against this, some scholars hold that conditions in China are sufficiently developed to justify the nationalisation compensation standard of 'full compensation is the basic principle, with appropriate compensation or no compensation being supplementary'.[81] Two features of this standard should be emphasised: (a) where no special treaty on nationalisation compensation has been signed between the countries concerned and the host country does not have sufficient grounds to demand that no, or only appropriate, compensation be paid for the nationalised property, the standard of full compensation shall be applied; (b) subject to the principles of fairness and mutual benefit, the host state has sufficient reasons not to provide full compensation for the nationalised property of the foreign person if the interests of the host state would be detrimentally affected by making full compensation. In such cases, appropriate or no compensation may be applied as a supplementary criterion.

To give full play to the benefits of foreign capital and ensure that foreign investors can carry out normal business activities in China and obtain reasonable profits under the country's current political and economic conditions, China has rightly taken various measures to protect the legitimate interests of foreign capital. As a result, foreigners' assets are generally not expropriated or nationalised on a large scale. Therefore, 'full compensation is the basic principle, with appropriate compensation or no compensation as a supplement' should be adopted in China.

IV. Succession to Property

Individuals are the main beneficiaries of private international law. Satisfying human needs is the most basic function, and value, of private international law.[82] Foreign jurisdiction-related inheritance law reflects an individual's property rights and is of far-reaching significance to descendants and heirs. This section focuses on the general considerations of succession, administration of a deceased's estate, intestacy and wills.

[78] CL Xu, 'Guoji Touzi Fa Zhong De Zhongda Zhengyi Wenti Yu Woguo De Duice' [The major controversial issues in international investment law and China's countermeasures] (1994) 1 *Social Sciences in China* 23–38.

[79] QJ He, 'Lun Guoji Touzi De Guoyouhua Buchang Biaozhun Zhi Chonggou' [On the reconstruction of international investment nationalization compensation standard] (2010) 9 *Reformation & Strategy* 165–7.

[80] The vast majority of developing countries advocate 'appropriate compensation' or' no compensation'.

[81] He, 'On the reconstruction' (n 80).

[82] DG Xu, *Guoji Sifa Qushi Lun* [*Trends in Private International Law*] (Peking University Press, 2005) 161.

A. General Considerations

Succession refers to the legal rules under which an heir inherits the legal private property and rights and interests left behind by a deceased person, in accordance with the deceased person's effective will or legal provisions applicable in the absence of an effective will. The modern inheritance system mainly centres around the inheritance of property.[83] As the basic method of transferring wealth after the death of a natural person, the core purpose of the inheritance system is the fair distribution of the inheritance among the heirs and between the heirs and other interested parties. In 1985, China's legislature passed the Succession Law. This legislation was necessitated by the fact that as living standards improved, individuals and families began to own an increasing amount of property, and disputes over inheritances therefore increased. China's Civil Code revised and improved the system of inheritance.[84] The 2010 Choice of Law Act adopts a parallel combination of statutory succession and testamentary succession. Intestate succession is the succession of property in accordance with general legal rules governing the scope, order of succession and individual shares of the inheritance in the absence of a will, as well as the manner in which property is distributed and acquired. Testamentary succession allows the deceased to change the scope, order or share of the legal succession before their death, so long as mandatory provisions of law are not violated. Testamentary succession has priority over legal succession.[85] In terms of applying foreign-related inheritance law, states historically tended to apply the law of the deceased's domicile and the law of the place of the estate.[86] However, with the increase of transnational succession cases and the concurrent increased complexity of succession, states have tended to adopt more flexible rules.[87]

B. Administration of a Deceased's Estate

The administration of an estate, whether distributed by testamentary of statutory succession, is dealt with by the heritage management system. This is a comprehensive system that attempts to ensure the integrity and fairness of the distribution, distribute the heritage in a fair and orderly way, and realise all rights related to the heritage. The system must be followed by the administrator for: the estate's custody, liquidation and preservation; preparation of the estate's inventory; the issuing of public notice; bankruptcy of the estate; estate distribution plans; and other measures.[88]

An estate is generally possessed by the deceased at the time of their death. Heirs do not acquire ownership of the estate until the division of the estate.[89] China's Civil Code establishes the administrator system. After succession begins, the executor becomes the administrator of the estate. If there is no executor, the successors must elect an administrator without delay. If the successors fail to elect an executor, the successors shall themselves collectively act as the administrator of

[83] WG Xu, *Shewai Minshi Guanxi Falv Shiyong Fa Shishi Yanjiu* [*A study on the Implementation of 2010 Choice of Law Act*] (Law Press, 2019) 382.

[84] Civil Code of the People's Republic of China, s 6.

[85] QS He, *Guoji Sifa Rumen Biji* [*Private International Law in a Nutshell*] (Law Press, 2019) 221. Also see The Civil Code of the People's Republic of China, Art 1133.

[86] 2010 Choice of Law Act, Art 31.

[87] FQ Yuan, *Renquan Baohu Yu Xiandai Jiating Guanxi Zhong De Guoji Sifa* [*Human Rights Protection and Modern Conflict of Family Laws*] (Peking University Press, 2010) 158.

[88] CY Fu, 'Yichan Guanli Zhidu De Sheli Jichu He Tixi Kuangjia' [Foundation and Architecture of Estate Management System] (2012) 8 *Journal of Law* 31.

[89] QP Tan, L Feng, 'Yichan Chuli Zhidu De Fansi Yu Chonggou' [Reflections and Reconstruction of The Estate Handling System] (2013) 4 *The Jurist* 124.

the estate. If there is no successor, or if all successors have given up their succession rights, the civil affairs department or the village committee in the place where the decedent resided before their death will act as administrator of the estate.[90] If there is any dispute over the administrator's election, interested parties may apply to the people's court for the appointment of a new administrator.[91] The previous Judicial Interpretation on the General Principles of the Civil Law addressed the case where a foreigner dies within the territory of China without heirs to inherit their property. Such a case will be dealt with in accordance with the laws of China, unless otherwise provided for by international treaties concluded or acceded to by the two relevant states (China and the nation of the deceased's nationality).[92]

In accordance with the 2010 Choice of Law Act, the administration of an estate is governed by law at the locality of the estate.[93] Regarding the attribution and distribution of an uninherited estate, the laws at the locality of the estate at the time of death of the deceased will apply.[94] It can be seen that the application of laws on estate management take into greater consideration the close connection between the location of the estate and the inheritance of the estate.[95] As an integral part of China's inheritance legal system, the establishment of the estate management system highlights the legal values of freedom, equality, fairness and efficiency pursued by private law.[96]

C. Intestacy

Where the deceased dies intestate, the General Principles of Civil Law once stipulated that '[movable property] shall be governed by the law of the place of domicile at the time of death of the deceased, and immovable property shall be governed by the law of the place where the immovable property is located'.[97] The 2010 Choice of Law Act similarly distinguishes between movable and immovable property, providing that in general the law of the deceased's habitual residence at the time of their death shall be applied to legal inheritance, but the law of the locality of the immovable property shall be applied to instances involving inheritance of immovable property.[98] That is, for immovable property the laws at the locality of property applies, while the deceased's personal law lex persona is applied to movable property.[99] This division of movable and immovable property is referred to as a 'scission' system. By contrast, a unitary system would treat both types of property in the same way. The advantage of adopting a unitary system of inheritance law is its simplicity and relative convenience in dealing with uniform, standard issues. However, the scission system is often more helpful in safeguarding the rights and interests of the parties in court and making the judgment easily recognisable and enforceable. However, it is unclear that this benefit outweighs the complexity introduced by treating movable and immovable property under different rules.[100] The 2010 Choice of Law Act complicates the situation yet

[90] Civil Code of the People's Republic of China, Art 1145.
[91] ibid, Art 1146.
[92] Opinions on General Principles of the Civil Law, Art 191.
[93] 2010 Choice of Law Act, Art 34.
[94] ibid, Art 35.
[95] ibid, Art 34,35.
[96] W Chen and T Shi, 'Woguo Sheli Yichan Guanli Zhidu De Shehui Jichu Jiqi Zhudu Goujian' [The Social Foundation and Institutional Construction of China's Establishment of Heritage Management System] (2013) 7 *Hebei Law Science* 19.
[97] General Principles of the Civil Law of the People's Republic of China, Art 149.
[98] 2010 Choice of Law Act, Art 31.
[99] T Du, *Guoji Sifa Yuanli* [*Principles of Private International Law*] (Fudan University Press, 2018) 171.
[100] NN Zhao, *Shewai Hunyin Jiating Anjian Lvshi Shiwu* [*Lawyers' Practice in Foreign-related Marriage and Family Cases*] (Law Press, 2015) 183.

further by distinguishing between statutory succession and testamentary succession, with the former adopting a scission system and the latter adopting a unitary system.[101]

D. Wills

Substantive legal requirements govern testators' abilities to make, revoke and amend their will, and the form in which wills may be expressed. The testamentary succession system in China is constructed around the principle of respecting the deceased's will, embodying the value of freedom.[102]

As regards the legal effect of a will, the 2010 Choice of Law Act stipulates that for judging the effect of a will, the laws at the place of the testator's habitual residence, or of the state of the testator's nationality, at the time when the testator makes their will or dies shall be applied.[103] In this respect, Chinese legislation adopts the unitary system, not distinguishing between movable and immovable property. Turning to the validity of the form of a will, the prevailing trend is *favour testamenti*.[104] The 2010 Choice of Law Act provides that a will is validly established if its form conforms to the laws of the place of the testator's habitual residence, state of nationality, or place of testamentary acts, at either the time when the testator makes the will or the time of death of the testator.[105] In respect of wills, the 2010 Choice of Law Act abandons the point of contact (*lian jie dian*) of 'residence',[106] grants increased importance to the contacting point of 'habitual residence' and abandons the contacting point[107] of 'location of immovable property'.[108] In practice, the provisions of different nations may overlap. Hence, in the case of *Lu, Liang v. Lu*, which concerned the substantive validity of a will, the court held that according to the 2010 Choice of Law Act, Lu's will was valid regardless of whether American law or Chinese law applied.[109]

[101] X Song, 'Tongyizhi Yu Qubiezhi De Duili Yu Jieshi', [Opposition and Interpretation between the Unitary system and the Scission System] (2011) *155 China Law 6*.

[102] Q Zheng, 'Ziyou Jiazhi Zai Woguo Yizhu Jicheng Zhong De Dingwei Yu Luoshi' [Positioning and Implementation of The Free Value in China's Testamentary Succession System] (2016) 2 *Research on Law and Commerce* 147–8.

[103] 2010 Choice of Law Act, Art 33.

[104] Du, *Principles of Private International Law* (n 100)175.

[105] 2010 Choice of Law Act, Art 32.

[106] 2010 Choice of Law Act do not follow General Principles of The Civil Law of The People's Republic of China, Art 149 and Succession Law, Art 36 where residence has been stipulated.

[107] For point of contact, please see ch 8.

[108] JZ Li, 'Lun Shewai Yizhu Falv Shiyong Zhidu De Fazhan Qushi–Jianlun Shewai Minshi Guanxi Shiyong Fa Di 32, 33 Tiao De Jieshi Yu Wanshan' [The Development Trend of the Legal Application System of Foreign-related Wills– also on the Interpretation and Improvement of Article 32 and 33 of the 2010 Choice of Law Act] (2014) 1 *Legal Science* 184.

[109] Guangdong Guangzhou Intermediate People's Court Decision *JerseyLuSHue v LeonaHsula etc* (2016) Yue-01 Min Zhong No 9704 (17 August 2017).

16

Jurisdiction and Applicable Law in Matters of Intellectual Property in China

YANG CAO

I. Introduction

Intellectual property (IP) refers to creations of the mind, such as inventions, literary and artistic works, designs, symbols and names, and images used in commerce.[1] Unlike traditional forms of property, such as real property and chattels, intellectual property is intangible. This intangibility permits intellectual property to easily cross borders and be exploited at the international level. Enforcing intellectual property rights (IPRs) in the context of alleged infringement, along with transferring or licensing IPRs to third parties in cross-border transactions, raises difficult jurisdictional issues.[2] Disputes concerning such transactions usually involve a two-factor process. First, it is necessary to decide which court has jurisdiction over cases which concern intellectual property infringement. In most cases, questions of infringement are closely related to issues of validity and ownership, which further complicates the jurisdictional issues. Second, once jurisdiction has been established, the court must determine the applicable law for establishing infringement and granting remedies. This chapter will discuss Chinese legislation and judicial practices in respect of this two-factor process, and the theoretical and practical issues raised by those practices.

II. Jurisdiction

Territoriality is the main principle of private international law. Its essential idea is that a country's laws are effective within the limits or boundaries of its territory. This principle has application in the domain of intellectual property.[3] For example, English and US courts have declined to exercise subject matter jurisdiction regarding infringement claims based on foreign IP rights, even if the parties both reside in the forum and the patents at stake concern the same invention, because

[1] 'What is Intellectual Property' (World Intellectual Property Organization) www.wipo.int/about-ip/en/ accessed 1 June 2020.

[2] TCJA van Engelen, 'Jurisdiction and Applicable Law in Matters of Intellectual Property' (2010) 14(3) *Electronic Journal of Comparative Law* www.ejcl.org/143/ art143-19.pdf accessed 8 July 2019.

[3] Hitsevich N, 'Intellectual property rights infringement on the internet: an analysis of private international law implications' (Unpublished Doctoral thesis, University of London, 2015).

of concerns relating to the interference with the sovereignty of other countries in the process of granting or denying IP protection.[4] Chinese courts also appear to exercise prudence when asserting jurisdiction over foreign IP related cases. Generally, Chinese courts decline to exercise jurisdiction over cases involving the infringement of foreign intellectual property rights. But some courts have recently begun to exercise such jurisdiction. In one case involving a Chinese citizen's infringement of a German copyright held by another Chinese citizen in Germany, a Chinese court applied substantive Chinese copyright law to determine the infringement of the German copyright.[5]

Courts mainly determine the jurisdiction of foreign-related intellectual property cases under the Civil Procedure Law, along with related judicial interpretations. The unique feature of IP related jurisdictional disputes is that validity issues are a precondition for deciding infringement. That is, the court has to decide in the first place whether the IP is valid. But whether the court has the jurisdiction to decide validity is often controversial in practice. Though the IP right itself is a private right, it bears on matters related to the public policy. Therefore, the issue is often the degree to which the court should intervene with a contractual determination of jurisdictional issues on the basis that the parties' autonomy to decide the issue for themselves is outweighed by matters of public policy. There are three main types of cases in which jurisdictional issues are controversial in practice: the validity of intellectual property rights; intellectual property infringement; and intellectual property related contracts.

A. Infringement

China's provisions on jurisdiction in intellectual property infringement cases are mainly found in Article 28 of the Civil Procedure Law. This Article stipulates that an action instituted for infringement shall fall under the jurisdiction of the people's court at the place where the infringement occurs, or at the domicile of the defendant.[6] Additionally, the Copyright Law, Trademark Law, Patent Law, and the Several Provisions of the Supreme People's Court on the Application of Legal Issues in the Trial of Patent Dispute Cases stipulate ancillary jurisdictional rules. Chinese courts have applied the principle of absolute territorial jurisdiction in cases involving violations of Chinese intellectual property rights, bringing cases of this nature under the exclusive jurisdiction of the Chinese courts. There are no clear legislative provisions addressing cases of infringement of foreign intellectual property rights. Traditionally, Chinese courts have refused to exercise jurisdiction over cases that purely involve the infringement of foreign intellectual property rights. However, there are signs that the tide is turning, with the courts taking the bold move of exercising jurisdiction in recent cases.[7] This advance, however, is marred by the lack of clear rules and standards governing the circumstances under which Chinese courts can take jurisdiction over

[4] A Peukert, 'Territoriality, and Extraterritoriality in Intellectual Property Law' (2010) in G Handl, J Zekoll and P Zumbansen (eds), *Beyond Territoriality: Transnational Legal Authority in an Age of Globalization* (Queen Mary Studies in International Law, Brill Academic Publishing, 2012) 189–228.

[5] Beijing IP Court Decision *Xiang Wei Ren v Peng Li Chong* (2015) Jing Zhi Min Zhong Zi No 1814.

[6] Civil Procedure Law of the People's Republic of China, most recently amended at the 28th session of the Standing Committee of the 12th National People's Congress on 27 June 2017, Art 28.

[7] For example, all the courts have exercised jurisdiction over foreign-related IP cases in the Beijing Municipality Intermediate People's Court No 1 Decision *Beiying Audio Visual Corp v Beijing Film Academy* (1996) 1 Supreme People's Court Gazette; Shanghai Intermediate People's Court No 2 Decision *Wu Guangzhong v Shanghai Duoyunxuan* (1996) 2 Supreme People's Court Gazette; Beijing IP Court Decision *Xiang Wei Ren v Peng Li Chong* (2015) Jing Zhi Min Zhong Zi No 1814.

foreign intellectual property cases. Notably, the Model Law of the People's Republic of China on Private International Law drafted by the China Institute of Private International Law fails to provide rules for jurisdiction over foreign-related intellectual property infringements.[8]

B. Matters Relating to a Contract

In determining their jurisdiction over foreign-related intellectual property contract disputes, Chinese courts borrow from general contract doctrine, contained in Articles 23, 265 and 266 of the Civil Procedure Law.[9] The people's court has jurisdiction in all cases in which China is: (i) the place where the defendant resides; (ii) the place where the contract is signed; (iii) the place where the contract is performed; (iv) the place where the subject matter of the litigation is located; (v) the place where the property can be seized; and (vi) the place of the infringement or the location of the representative office. If any of these connecting factors are found, the parties have the right to file their case in the people's court, which will have jurisdiction, except for cases involving the validity of intellectual property rights, which are subject to the exclusive jurisdiction of the country where the right is held. Though stating that the presence of one connecting factor is sufficient to ground Chinese jurisdiction, Chinese law is silent on whether there are circumstances where the absence of one or more conditions may negate this jurisdiction. Engaging with this hypothetical, one possibility is to have recourse to the principle of inconvenient courts, whereby the courts should refuse jurisdiction even when legally permissible if the absence of one or more of the connecting factors makes the case unsuitable for Chinese jurisdiction. This option has the advantage of avoiding pressure from foreign sovereign countries, better protecting the national interest.[10]

Article 242 of the Civil Procedure Law of 2007 provided rules for party autonomy over jurisdiction. However, Article 242 was deleted in the 2012 amendment of the Civil Procedure Law. Presently, Article 34 of the Civil Procedure Law is applied to decide the validity of a party-agreed jurisdiction. According to Article 34, the parties have limited discretion in choosing the jurisdiction to govern their contract. Parties may choose between courts in the following places: (i) the domicile of defendant; (ii) the place of performance of the contract; (iii) the place of signing of the contract; (iv) the domicile of the plaintiff; or (v) the place of the contract's subject matter. Article 34 additionally stipulates that the court chosen by the parties should be located in a place that has an actual connection with the contract. Generally, the Chinese courts follow the parties' choice of jurisdiction. In exceptional cases, however, the courts will consider whether a foreign judgment can be easily enforced. In one case concerning the assignment of a Chinese patent between two foreign companies, the parties agreed to Korean jurisdiction over issues regarding a Chinese patent assignment.[11] The Beijing IP Court held that the issue of enforceability plays a key role in considering the validity of an agreement regarding choice of law. The legal rights of the concerned party cannot be effectively protected if the verdict cannot be effectively enforced. In this case, there was no agreement between China and Korea to recognise and enforce the

[8] Chinese Society of Private International Law, 'Model Law of Private International Law of the People's Republic of China', in P Sarczvic and P Volken (eds), *Yearbook of Private International Law* vol 3 (Sellier de Gruyter, 2001) 349.

[9] Civil Procedure Law of the People's Republic of China, most recently amended at the 28th session of the Standing Committee of the 12th National People's Congress on 27 June 2017, Arts 23, 265, 266.

[10] L Xue, Y Li, 'Lun zhong guo she wai zhi shi chan quan an jian guan xia quan de xian zhuang ji wan shan' [On the jurisdiction of China's Foreign-related Intellectual Property cases: Current State and Improvements] (Zhengzhou Intermediate People's Court Blog, 10 July 2012) http://zzfy.hncourt.gov.cn/public/detail.php?id=19458 accessed 31 August 2020.

[11] Beijing Intellectual Property Court Decision *LG Xian Shi You Xian Gong Si v Da Lin Jing Gong Zhu Shi Hui She* (2016) Jing-73 Min Chu No 1155.

judgments of Korean courts in China, so the Korean decision could not be enforced. This led the Chinese court to declare the agreement invalid. The court established a new factor in this case for considering the validity of the party's choice of law in IP cases: whether the judgment by a foreign court can be effectively enforced in China. This requires the parties to consider enforceability before agreeing on jurisdiction issues.

C. Validity

Can a court adjudicate the validity of foreign-related IP? Given that the defendant is likely to invoke the invalidity defence in an IP infringement case, the determination of validity is a precondition for these cases. Under the principle of territoriality of intellectual property rights, an intellectual property right is valid only in the territory in which it is granted or registered. Thus validity issues should generally be decided by the court of the country in which the intellectual property is granted or registered. According to Article 6 of the 2018 Draft Convention on the Recognition and Enforcement of Foreign Judgments, a judgment that rules on the registration or validity of an intellectual property right to be granted or registered shall be recognised and enforced only if the state of origin is the state in which grant or registration has taken place, or, under the terms of an international or regional instrument, is deemed to have taken place. This Draft Convention grants exclusive jurisdiction over issues involving the validity of intellectual property rights to the state in which the application for grant or registration is made. In line with this principle, no Chinese courts have exercised jurisdiction over cases involving validity issues of foreign intellectual property rights.

China adopts a unique bifurcated system to determine the validity of intellectual property rights. Although Chinese courts can assert jurisdiction over the issue of the validity of Chinese intellectual property rights, they cannot decide the validity of such rights in the first instance.[12] Rather, validity is determined by administrative organs, with the courts having an appellate jurisdiction. That is, courts can only decide the question of validity in the context of an appeal against an administrative decision. Additionally, litigation over validity of intellectual property rights is classified as administrative litigation. Some jurisdictions empower their courts to directly decide whether a patent or trademark is valid. This raises the question of whether a Chinese court can enforce such a judgment, given that it lacks the decisional power of the foreign court. This is a serious issue, because enforcing a judgment implies that the court has jurisdiction over the underlying decision regarding validity; but Chinese patent and trademark laws explicitly prohibit courts from making such decisions.

III. Applicable Law

The Law of the People's Republic of China on the Laws Applicable to Foreign-related Civil Relations (2010 Choice of Law Act) contains three articles regulating intellectual property rights. Article 48 is concerned with what law should be applied in dealing with the proprietorship and

[12] T Dong, TX Wang, 'Zheng Que Ren Shi Zhuan Li Quan Xiao li Ren Ding Zhong de Xin Zheng Si Fa Zhi Quan Er Fen Fa' [Correct Understanding of the "Administrative/Judicial" Dichotomy in the Determination of the Validity of Patent Rights] (2019) 3 *Intellectual Property*.

content of intellectual property rights.[13] It provides that the ownership and content of intellectual property rights should be governed by the law of the place where protection is sought. Article 49 states that the parties may choose the law applicable to the transfer and licence of intellectual property rights. Absent any choice by the parties, the relevant provisions of the 2010 Choice of Law Act on general contracts will apply. Article 50 provides that liability for infringement is governed by the law of the place where protection is sought. The parties may also choose to apply the law of the forum after the infringement occurs. There seems to be no consensus in theory and practice as to the determination of 'the place where protection is sought'. In practice, some courts apply the law of the place where the infringement occurred.[14] The Beijing High Court has held that Chinese law should be applied in cases in which foreigners ask for the protection of valid Chinese intellectual property rights and foreign law should not be considered.[15] The Beijing High Court has also held that if a case involves Chinese domiciled natural persons or entities, the court can apply Chinese laws even if the infringement occurs outside of China.[16] It therefore seems that Chinese courts treat the location of the court as the place where protection is sought. One study shows that in 26 cases involving the application of Article 48 of the Laws on Applicable Laws from 2011–2018, almost all directly applied Chinese laws without explaining why the place of the court was the place of the protection sought.[17] However, this approach is not sustainable as a matter of legislative interpretation. Presumably, a term used more than once in the same statute or treaty has the same meaning wherever it appears. And by the same token, different terms are generally presumed to have different meaning. In consequence, as analysed below, the 'place of the protection' cannot be synonymous with 'the place of the court'.

A. The Place Where Protection is Sought (Claimed)

There is substantial variation across Chinese courts in the interpretation of 'The place where the protection is sought.' The place of the court,[18] the place of infringement,[19] and the place where the IP rights originated[20] are respectively regarded as 'The place where the protection is sought' by different courts. Three points can be made. First, the place where protection is sought cannot be same as the place of the court. Article 50 of the Law on Applicable Laws stipulates that liability for infringing intellectual property rights is governed by the law of the place where protection is sought, and the parties may also choose to apply the law of the forum after the infringement occurs.[21] Article 50 hence differentiates the place where the protection is sought

[13] The Law of the People's Republic of China on Choice of Law for Foreign-related Civil Relationships, adopted at the Seventeenth Session of the Eleventh Standing Committee of the National People's Congress of the People's Republic of China on 28 October 2010, and took effect on 1 April 2011.

[14] Hangzhou Bingjiang District Court Decision *Ri Ben Ban Ma Zhu Shi Hui She v Qiu Ting Xi* (2012) Hang Bing Zhi Chu Zi No 185.

[15] Answers by Beijing Municipal Higher People's Court of Several Questions Relating to Application of Law to Foreign-related Civil IP Cases (Higher People's Court, Fa Fa (2004) 49 Hao, 18 February 2004), Art 11.

[16] ibid, Art 18.

[17] XY Yuan, 'Wo Guo She Wai Zhi Shi Chan Quan Jiu Fen Fa Lu Shi Yong di Wen Ti Ji Wan Shan' [The Problems and Solutions to Applicable Laws in Foreign-Related IP Cases] (2018) 4 *Journal of East China University of Political Science and Law.*

[18] Hangzhou Intermediate Court Decision *Mei Guo Hua Er Tui JIan Gong Si v Yi Wu Shi Ke Mei Jia Yong Dian Qi You Xian Gong Si* (2017) Zhe-01 Min Chu No 1554.

[19] Guangzhou IP Court: No 50, (2015) Yue Zhi Fa Min Zhu.

[20] Shanghai Pudong District Court Decision *Ai Mo Sheng Dian Qi Gong Si v Shang Hai Zhen Hang Zhi Leng She Bei You Xiang Gong Si* (2017) Hu-0115 Min Chu No 65069.

[21] Article 50 of The Law of the People's Republic of China on Choice of Law for Foreign-related Civil Relationships, adopted at the Seventeenth Session of the Eleventh Standing Committee of the National People's Congress of the People's Republic of China on 28 October 2010, and took effect on 1 April 2011.

from the location of the court. Second, the place where protection is claimed is different from the place where protection is requested. Many countries refuse to protect foreign intellectual property for reasons of public order or inconvenient court principles of international comity. The concern here is that intellectual property cases that occur abroad or cases involving foreign intellectual property rights should be exclusively administered by foreign courts.[22] However, with the increase of the cross-border use of intellectual property rights, the rapid growth of transnational intellectual property cases, and the complexity of transnational intellectual property issues, some countries have gradually begun to assert jurisdiction over intellectual property cases arising in foreign countries or cases involving foreign intellectual property rights. The jurisdiction of foreign-related civil cases can be based on multiple criteria, such as personal jurisdiction (where the defendant resides), international jurisdiction rules (where the infringer's property is located), and legal jurisdiction rules (for example, the place where the contract is performed, the place of the infringement, etc). The provisions of Article 241 of the Civil Procedure Law of China on the jurisdiction of foreign-related civil cases also clearly enumerate multiple connecting elements to be considered in exercising jurisdiction.[23]

Chinese courts have no consensus on what is 'the place where the protection is sought'. Literally, 'the place where the protection is sought' should be the place where the rights holders seek to protect their intellectual property rights. Generally, the rights holders will seek to protect their intellectual property rights in the place where the rights are registered or granted. So, the place of the protection will be the place where the rights are granted or registered. It would be irrational for a rights holder to seek the protection of his/her rights in a place where the rights do not exist or are invalid.

B. Ownership and Content

Article 48 of the Laws on Applicable Law provides that the ownership and content of intellectual property rights should be governed by the law of the place where protection is sought. Intellectual property's definition of ownership and content differs from that of real property. Different countries have different intellectual property systems, so definitions of the ownership and content of intellectual property exhibit significant variance. Indeed, the umbrella concept of intellectual property conceals significant differences in the varieties of intellectual property which exist beneath the surface. Trademark, copyright, and patent laws each provide a different way of defining ownership, and the content of these laws are different. Careful exegesis of the different types of intellectual property must be conducted in order to clarify the applicable law.

i. Copyright

The term 'copyright' describes the rights that creators have over their literary and artistic works.[24] In contradistinction with patents and trademarks, literary and artistic works are under copyright protection from the moment they are created and fixed in a tangible form that is perceptible either

[22] L Zhong, 'She wai zhi chan qin quan su song zhong de guan xia quan he fa lu shi yong' [Foreign-related Intellectual Property Litigation: Jurisdiction and Legal Applicability] (*Ren Min Fa Yuan Bao*, 31 December 2009) http://rmfyb.chinacourt.org/paper/html/2009-12/31/content_1123.htm accessed 31 August 2020.

[23] Civil Procedure Law of the People's Republic of China, Art 241.

[24] 'What is Copyright?' (*World Intellectual Property Organization*) www.wipo.int/copyright/en/ accessed 7 July 2019.

directly or with the aid of a machine or device. That is, copyright arises automatically, with no requirements for registration or other formalities. While territorial in nature, foreign copyrights are easily protected due to the lack of formality requirements. Both the Berne Convention and the Agreement on Trade-Related Aspects of Intellectual Property Rights (TRIPs) require the protection of their members' copyrights and specify a lack of formality requirements for protection.[25] Therefore, foreign copyrights that are not registered in China can still be easily protected locally as Chinese copyrights. If the above theory is followed, not all foreign-related copyright disputes will raise questions of applicable law. However, the theory clearly conflicts with the statutory language of the 2010 Choice of Law Act, which stipulates that the ownership and content of intellectual property rights should be governed by the law of the place where protection is sought. Therefore, the Beijing High Court has decided that the law of the place in which the work subsists should be applied for the protection of a foreigner's copyright, but the ownership and content of the copyright of a work should be decided under Chinese Copyright Law if a foreigner asks for Chinese copyright protection of foreign published work.[26] In practice, most Chinese courts treat foreign published works as having automatic Chinese copyright protection, applying Chinese copyright law to protect the works published abroad.

There are two different copyright systems in the international arena: the authorship right system and the copyright system. The authorship system emphasises the protection of authors' rights, generally conferring ownership on creators, while the copyright system focuses on the exploitation of the economic value of the works, conferring ownership on investors. Almost every country has its unique way of defining copyright ownership. Even similar concepts may be defined in different ways. For ownership of intellectual property, the place where the protection is sought can be the place in which the work is first published, the place in which the court is asked for protection, or the place in which the author is domiciled. However, for the content of copyright, there is greater consensus by virtue of the Berne Convention and TRIPs Agreement and the difference in content of copyright rules is becoming very small. Accordingly, the choice of law issue in copyright content has no substantial effect on copyright protection.

ii. Trademark and Patent

Unlike copyright, the protection of trademarks and patents involves compliance with a series of formal requirements. Trademarks have to be registered, and inventions must be protected by patents granted by competent authorities. The corollary of these requirements is that Chinese patents and trademarks are only valid in China, with the ownership of trademark and patents written in the aforementioned documents. Article 93 of the 2000 Model Law on International Private Law (sixth draft) stipulates that the validity, content, and effect of patent rights rests on the law of the place at which the patent application is filed.[27] Similarly, Article 94 of the 2000 Model Law stipulates that the validity, content, and effect of trademark rights rest on the law of the place in which the trademark is registered. The principle that ownership and content of trademarks and patents should be decided by the law of the place in which they are registered or granted is widely accepted. Normatively, this principle is the best choice for the regulation of ownership and

[25] Berne Convention for the Protection of Literary and Artistic Works 1886; Agreement on Trade-Related Aspects of Intellectual Property Rights, 1869 UNTS 299, 33 ILM 1197 (1994) ('TRIPS Agreement').

[26] Answers by Beijing Municipal Higher People's Court of Several Questions Relating to Application of Law to Foreign-related Civil IP Cases (Higher People's Court, Fa Fa (2004) 49 Hao, 18 February 2004) Art 10.

[27] China Society of Private Law, 'Model Law on International Private Law (sixth draft)' (*China Society of Private Law*, 2000) www.cspil.org/Plus/m_default/Cms/docDetail.php?ID=208 accessed 31 August 2020.

content of trademarks and patents, for two reasons. First, ownership rules concerning patents and trademarks vary significantly from country to country, given that these are unique rights granted by sovereign states. Consequently, this creates conflict. For instance, in the case where a registered document in the country of origin explicitly states that one party is the owner of the patent or trademark, applying the different rules of another country may identify a different owner. This conflict would harm the sovereign rights of states, and create forum shopping problems. Second, a party who is not the owner in the country of origin may become the owner in another country if the law of that other country is applied. This would mitigate against legal certainty in the international patent and trademark system.

Owing to the variance in protection provided to patents and trademarks from country to country, intellectual property is excluded from the Convention on the Recognition and Enforcement of Foreign Judgments in Civil or Commercial Matters. For example, Chinese patent law has rules governing private use, while such rules are not present in US patent law.[28] Therefore, the determination of the content of a patent or trademark may be best decided by the law of the country of origin, where the patent was registered or granted. On the other hand, where the ownership or content of the patent and trademark is concerned, the place where the protection is sought should be the place where the patent or trademark is granted.

C. Transfer and Licensing

Article 49 of the 2010 Choice of Law Act stipulates that parties may by agreement choose the law applicable to the transfer and licensing of intellectual property rights. Absent any choice by the parties, the relevant provisions of the 2010 Choice of Law Act on contract are applicable.

i. Party Autonomy

Article 49 of the 2010 Choice of Law Act gives the parties limited autonomy over the choice of applicable law, restricted to the choice of law for intellectual property transfer and licensing.[29] According to Article 48, the law of the place where protection is sought shall apply where the ownership and content of the rights of the intellectual property are concerned. Generally speaking, intellectual property transfer and licensing engage contractual issues.[30] Hence the applicable laws governing intellectual property transfer and licensing largely derive from contract law. This is made explicit by the 2010 Choice of Law Act, which points out that contract rules should apply to intellectual property transfer and licensing in the absence of party choice. The licensing and transfer of intellectual property rights involve a number of contractual issues – such as contract formation, contractual obligations, contract interpretation, and payment methods – and

[28] Article 11 of Patent Law of People's Republic of China. Adopted at the 4th Meeting of the Standing Committee of the Sixth National People's Congress on 12 March 1984. Amended in accordance with the Decision of the Standing Committee of the Seventh National People's Congress on Amending the Patent Law of the People's Republic of China at its 27th Meeting on 4 September 1992. Amended again in accordance with the Decision of the Standing Committee of the Ninth National People's Congress on Amending the Patent Law of the People's Republic of China adopted at its 17th Meeting on 25 August 2000.

[29] Article 49 of The Law of the People's Republic of China on Choice of Law for Foreign-related Civil Relationships, adopted at the Seventeenth Session of the Eleventh Standing Committee of the National People's Congress of the People's Republic of China on 28 October 2010, and took effect on 1 April 2011.

[30] ibid, Art 48.

raise the question of whether those issues can be governed by the laws chosen by the parties. Article 4 of the 2010 Choice of Law Act provides for the direct application of Chinese mandatory laws, regardless of the parties' choice.[31] Intellectual property is highly related to public policy and almost every country has compulsory mechanisms which restrict the licence and transfer of intellectual property. These mandatory laws are therefore particularly important in the intellectual property field.

Examples of mandatory laws are Article 16 of the Foreign Trade Law and Articles 8, 9, 10, 32, 32 and 33 of the Regulations on Technology Import and Export Administration of the People's Republic of China, which clearly state that certain technologies are prohibited from export or import.[32] In addition, Chinese intellectual property laws impose certain restrictions on the transferability of specific intellectual property rights. Article 42 of the Trademark Law requires the simultaneous transfer of the same or similar trademarks, prohibiting their separate transfer to different parties.[33] This position is supported by the Paris Convention. Article 6 of the Paris Convention states:[34]

> When, in accordance with the law of a country of the Union, the assignment of a mark is valid only if it takes place at the same time as the transfer of the business or goodwill to which the mark belongs, it shall suffice for the recognition of such validity that the portion of the business or goodwill located in that country be transferred to the assignee, together with the exclusive right to manufacture in the said country or to sell therein, the goods bearing the mark assigned.

This paragraph implies that the transferability of the mark should be governed by the law of the country where protection is sought. In addition, the mandatory provisions governing the form and effect of intellectual property contracts preclude parties' freedom of choice. Some countries set mandatory formal requirements for intellectual property contracts. These requirements may affect the validity or the effectiveness of the contract. For example, Article 10 of the Patent Law, Article 42 and 43 of the Trademark Law, and Article 26 of the Copyright Law clearly govern the registration of relevant intellectual property contracts. Article 5 of the Patent Law states that Chinese law shall be applied where the application of foreign law would be prejudicial to the social and public interest of China. If the application of the law chosen conflicts with the public interests of China, the law chosen by the parties may be excluded. In one case,[35] the Beijing Intellectual Property Court held that:

> According to the first paragraph of Article 145 of the General Principles of the Civil Law of China, the parties to a foreign-related contract may choose to apply the law applicable to the contractual dispute. Article 49 of the Law on Applicable Laws clearly holds that the parties may agree to choose the

[31] ibid, Art 4.

[32] Foreign Trade Law of the People's Republic of China, adopted at the Seventh Meeting of the Standing Committee of the Eighth National People's Congress on 12 May 1994, promulgated by Order No 22 of the President of the People's Republic of China on 12 May 1994, and effective as of 1 July 1994; Regulations on Technology Import and Export Administration of the People's Republic of China (Order of the State Council No 331, issued 10 December 2001, effective 1 January 2002, amended 8 January 2011, in Order of the State Council No 588).

[33] Adopted at the 24th Session of the Standing Committee of the Fifth National People's Congress on 23 August 1982, revised for the first time according to the Decision on the Amendment of the Trademark Law of the People's Republic of China adopted at the 30th Session of the Standing Committee of the Seventh National People's Congress, on 22 February 1993, and revised for the second time according to the Decision on the Amendment of the Trademark Law of the People's Republic of China adopted at the 24th Session of the Standing Committee of the Ninth National People's Congress on 27 October 2001.

[34] Paris Convention for the Protection of Industrial Property (20 March 1883, revised at Brussels on 14 December 1900, at Washington on 2 June 1911, at the Hague on 6 November 1925, at London on 2 June 1934, at Lisbon on 31 October 1958, and at Stockholm on 14 July 1967) Geneva: United International Bureaux for the Protection of Intellectual Property 1968.

[35] Beijing Intellectual Property Court Decision (2016) Jing 73 Min Chu No 1155.

applicable law for the transfer and licensing of intellectual property rights. It can be seen that China's conflict of laws rules allow parties to agree on the application of laws other than the law of the courts for the contract of transfer of intellectual property rights. In this case, although the court found that the applicable law for jurisdiction chosen by the parties was void in respect of the Chinese patent, the agreement on the applicable law of the transfer contract did not violate the mandatory provisions of the Chinese law. The agreed applicable law in this case is Korean law.

ii. Applicable Laws When Parties Fail to Choose

Absent any contractual choice of law by the parties, the relevant provisions of the 2010 Choice of Law Act on contract apply. Accordingly, in the absence of any choice by the parties, the law of the habitual residence of the party whose performance of the obligation is most characteristic of the contract or the law that is most closely connected with the contract shall be applied. When it comes to defining the most characteristic performance, intellectual property transfer and licensing contracts are more complicated than ordinary contracts because they contain substantial multi-obligations. For example, in a patent transfer and licensing contract, the assignor or licensor is responsible for delivering technical information related to the implementation of the patent, providing necessary technical guidance, ensuring that it is the legal owner of the patent, and ensuring the integrity and validity of the patented technology. The assignee or the licensee usually must pay the transfer fee or royalties according to the agreement and implement the patent according to the agreed scope and time limit. If the licence fee is determined by the sales volume of the product, the profit rate or the proportion of the business amount, the rights and obligations of both parties will be complicated further.

It has been argued that the obligation which is most characteristic of the contract should be presumed to be that carried out by the assignee or licensee who is obligated to perform the contract, or by the rights holder when such an obligation does not exist. Some authors argue instead that the obligation which is most characteristic of contract should be determined according to the nature of the rights granted by the transaction.[36] Without rights, any use is impossible, and the characteristic performance cannot be determined according to the effect of the transfer. These writers argue that it is natural to focus on the obligations of the assignor of the right. There is also a third view, that the performance of either party seems to be equally characteristic when a patent cross-licensing contract is agreed.[37] It seems likely that each view has merit but goes wrong in attempting to generalise across all cross-border intellectual property contracts. After all, no simple rule can be applied in all situations for a contract that contains plural rights and obligations. In intellectual property transfer or licensing contracts, the obligation which is most characteristic of the contract may not necessarily be determined according to some abstract and objective standards but must be determined according to the specific circumstances of the case through the closest connection standard. When the performance of the contractor or the licensor is more representative of the characteristics of the contract, that performance may be considered to be characteristic performance, in which case the law of the assignor or the licensor's habitual residence shall apply.

[36] L Zhu, 'She Wai Zhi Shi Chan Quan Guan Xi di Fa Lu Shi Yong' [The Applicable Law of Foreign-Related IP Cases] (2012) 9 *Journal of People's Judiciary*.

[37] ibid.

D. Infringement

Article 50 of the 2010 Choice of Law Act stipulates that liability for infringing intellectual property rights is governed by the law of the place where protection is sought. The parties may also choose to apply the law of the forum after the infringement occurs.

i. The Law of the Place Where Protection is Sought

Lex loci protectionis, as does any applicable law rule that mirrors the territoriality principle, demands that the infringement of an intellectual property right be adjudicated by the law of the country that grants that right. If the right is infringed in several states, the law of each state would apply with respect to the part of the infringement occurring in that state. The territoriality approach and *lex loci protectionis* rule have traditionally been justified by the need for states to maintain sovereignty over their national copyright laws as a part of national cultural policies.[38] The *lex loci protectionis* rule is implemented by Article 8(1) of the European Union's Rome II Regulation and requires each intellectual property infringement to be subject to the law of the country in which protection is sought.[39] The law of the place where protection is sought can be the place in which infringement occurs. Generally, holders of intellectual property rights will seek protection in the place where infringement occurs because it is relatively easy to find evidence and receive damages from the infringing party. It is also best for the rightsholder to seek protection in the infringing place due to the principle of territoriality and the independent protection of intellectual property rights. For these reasons, protection is in practice typically sought in the place of infringement.

For example, a patent holder files a complaint in a Chinese court for patent infringement, though the patent was granted in the US and the infringement occurred in the US. The place in which protection is sought is the US and the applicable law for this case should be US patent law. Section 271(f)(1) of the US Patent Law provides that whoever without authority supplies or causes to be supplied in or from the US all or a substantial portion of the components of a patented invention, where such components are uncombined in whole or in part, in such manner as to actively induce the combination of such components outside of the US in a manner that would infringe the patent if such combination occurred within the US, shall be liable as an infringer.[40] Hence, for example, a Chinese company infringes US patent rights if it imports all of the parts of a US patented invention from the US, and assembles all of the parts in China into a product that comes within the protection scope of the corresponding patents in the US. If a US patentee sues the Chinese company in China for infringement of its patent rights, the place where protection is sought is the US, even though some or all of the alleged infringements occurred in China. Accordingly, the Chinese courts should apply US law. The place of infringement includes both the place where the infringement is committed and the place where the result of infringement is felt. When the place where the infringement is committed and the place where the result of infringement is located are in different jurisdictions, there will be more than one place of infringement. Therefore, greater certainty is achieved by applying the law of the place where protection is sought, rather than the law of the place of infringement. If infringing actions happen

[38] R Matulionyte, 'Enforcing Copyright Infringements Online: In Search of Balanced Private International Law Rules' (2015) 6 *Journal of Intellectual Property, Information Technology and Electronic Commerce Law* 132.

[39] ibid.

[40] 35 USC § 271 (2012).

in different jurisdictions simultaneously, they should all be considered independent infringements and should be governed separately by the law of the place in which protection is sought.

Another issue worth discussion is cyber-related infringing activity. The 2010 Choice of Law Act contains no clear rules on cyber-related infringing activity. Article 3:603 of the European Max Planck Group on Conflict of Laws in Intellectual Property's 'Principles on Conflict of Laws in Intellectual Property' (CLIP Principles) covers ubiquitous infringement.[41] It states:

1. In disputes concerned with infringement carried out through ubiquitous media such as the Internet, the court may apply the law or the laws of the State or the States having the closest connection with the infringement, if the infringement arguably takes place in every State in which the signals can be received.
2. In determining which State has the closest connection with the infringement, the court shall take all the relevant factors into account, in particular, the following:
   a. the infringer's habitual residence;
   b. the infringer's principal place of business;
   c. the place where substantial activities in furtherance of the infringement in its entirety have been carried out;
   d. the place where the harm caused by the infringement is substantial concerning the infringement in its entirety;
3. Notwithstanding the law applicable according to paragraph 2, any party may prove that the rules applying in a State or States covered by the dispute differ from the law applicable to the dispute in aspects that are essential for the decision. The court shall apply the different national laws unless this leads to inconsistent judgments, in which case the differences shall be taken into account in fashioning the remedy.

The rule means that in the case of ubiquitous (online) infringements of intellectual property rights, the court may apply to the entire cross-border dispute the single law that has the closest connection with the dispute.

ii. Party Autonomy

The question of whether the principle of party autonomy can be applied to cases of intellectual property infringement is controversial.[42] Intellectual property is highly related to public policy and can therefore never be a purely economic issue. Party autonomy in infringement cases may undermine the public policy of the granting country. For example, some countries have lax protection for patent rights because this suits the country's economic and cultural development. Respect for party autonomy would be detrimental to the economic development of such a country because its lax protection could be easily avoided by the party choosing a more stringent law. Another reason for the limited utility of party autonomy in this context is that the infringement of intellectual property is highly related to the content of intellectual property. In this respect, intellectual property differs from moveable property. The court cannot decide whether a patent is infringed before the content of the patent is clearly defined and determined. Intellectual property rights are a kind of exclusive right. Any party's use of the content of intellectual property without the authority of the rights holder is an infringement of the rights holder's intellectual property

[41] European Max Planck Group on Conflict of Laws and intellectual Property, *Conflict of laws in intellectual property: the CLIP principles and commentary* (OUP, 2013).

[42] L Zhu, 'She Wai Zhi Shi Chan Quan Guan Xi di Fa Lu Shi Yong' [The Applicable Law of Foreign-Related IP Cases] (2012) 9 *Journal of People's Judiciary*.

rights. So the content of the intellectual property determines what kind of activity constitutes infringement. According to the 2010 Choice of Law Act, the content of intellectual property is decided by the law of the place where protection is sought. The content of intellectual property cannot be decided by the law chosen by the parties. If the applicable law governing the content of intellectual property cannot be chosen by the parties, then the applicable law governing infringement, which depends on the determination of the content of the intellectual property, should similarly not be chosen by the party.

To summarise, party autonomy in the regulation of infringement has to be limited. First, the applicable law chosen by the rights holder cannot threaten the public policy of the country of the forum and the granting or registering country. Each country has the sovereign right to protect its public interest using intellectual property laws. Second, the parties to a dispute cannot choose the law governing the content of intellectual property and the rules governing infringement. The parties can only choose the law governing liability for infringement. Subject to these significant constraints, Chinese law will respect parties' autonomy in choosing the applicable law.

IV. Conclusion

In closing, intellectual property protection is a highly sensitive public policy issue. Currently, Chinese courts take a prudential attitude toward exercising jurisdiction over foreign-related cases, which manifests itself in the general rule that Chinese courts refuse to exercise jurisdiction in cases that are completely foreign, without connecting Chinese factors being engaged. Recently, however, Chinese courts have begun to take jurisdiction over purely foreign cases. While Chinese law has clear rules that apply to intellectual property issues, Chinese courts seem to apply a simplified method to deal with intellectual property cases, which leads to a number of contradictions with the statutory language of the 2010 Choice of Law Act. Two are particularly significant. First, Chinese courts usually regard the place where protection is claimed as the appropriate forum. This is clearly contradictory to the plain language of the 2010 Choice of Law Act. Second, where the parties have made a choice of law, Chinese courts generally use Chinese intellectual property law to decide infringement issues. This is also contradictory to the plain language of the 2010 Choice of Law Act, which explicitly stipulates that the parties can choose the law applicable to infringement liability. Mistaken understanding of the 2010 Choice of Law Act is unfortunately common in judicial practice, and it is to be hoped that corrections will be made in the future.

17

Family Law

ZHENGYI ZHANG, JINGNING ZHANG

I. Marriage

Chinese law does not provide a specific definition for the term marriage. However, 'marriage' is generally understood as a relationship through which a male and a female are legally recognised as husband and wife after completing certain preliminary formalities. Marriage is one of the fields where conflict of laws rules have been the most varied.[1] Key issues are the determination of the applicable law for the formal and substantive requisites for marriage.

It is worth noting that, with changes in social thinking and the progress of the social welfare system, people's conceptions of marriage and family in western states have changed greatly. The most obvious phenomenon is the decline in marriage rates and the rise in divorce rates, as well as the rise in non-marital cohabitation. In China, the phenomenon of cohabitation without marriage has also emerged in large numbers in recent years,[2] prompting a large number of related disputes. Scholars have begun to discuss how to define non-marital cohabitation legally.[3] According to the relevant judicial interpretations of the Supreme People's Court of China, Chinese law has gradually shifted from a completely negative attitude towards non-marital cohabitation to a neutral attitude.[4]

A. Formal Validity

The formal requirements for marriage are the rules governing the ways in which a legal marriage may be concluded. Marriages may be formed through civil registration or through religious means. Marriage by civil registration requires both parties to undergo registration procedures at registration offices authorised by the law. A marriage is formed only after specific certificates are issued. Marriage through religious means requires both parties to the marriage to hold a certain

[1] G Cuniberti, *Conflict of Laws: A Comparative Approach* (Edward Elgar, 2017) 443–444.

[2] J Yu, 'Research on property Rights Protection of Unmarried Cohabitation of young people' (2019) 12 *China Youth Study* 36.

[3] Related discussion could be found in the following: D Xu, 'A historical view of Actual Marriage between non-marriage and marriage' (2016) 3 *Law Review* 185, D Xiang, N Zhao, 'The Reconstruction of Family System by the Relational Contract Theory' (2017) 2 *Hebei Law Science* 103.

[4] SY Li and FY Ou, *Guo Ji Si Fa* [*Private International Law*] (Peking University Press, 2018) 169.

religious ceremony in accordance with the provisions of their own religion before the marriage is formed.[5] China currently adopts marriage by civil registration.

The General Principles of the Civil Law of the People's Republic of China ('General Principles') provide that the marriage of a citizen of the People's Republic of China (PRC) to an alien is governed by the law of the place of the marriage.[6] Hence, for example, Chinese law will apply where a marriage between a Chinese citizen and an alien takes place within Chinese territory; but where a Chinese citizen and an alien marry outside the territory of China, the law of the country where the marriage takes place will apply. This provision does not distinguish between the substantial and formal requirements for marriage. The Law of the People's Republic of China on Choice of Law for Foreign-Related Civil Relationships promulgated in 2010 ('2010 Choice of Law Act') stipulates that marriage procedures shall be valid provided they conform to any one of: the law of the place where the marriage is formed; the law of the habitual residence of one party; or the law of the state of nationality of one party.[7] This renders marriage procedures more convenient for the parties and facilitates the successful formation of marriages. These legal norms apply to all marriages, whatever the nationalities of the parties and wherever in the world the marriage takes place. However, with regard to marriages between Chinese people abroad, another system may apply. This is consular marriage, in which a country authorises its consular or diplomatic representatives to marry its nationals in accordance with the country's domestic laws, provided that the host country does not object. The Regulations on Marriage Registration stipulate that embassies and consulates of the PRC stationed abroad may manage registrations for marriages where both parties are Chinese citizens residing in the host country.[8]

As different states or regions adopt varying standards for the formal and substantial requirements for marriage, it is possible for a marriage to be valid in one country or region but invalid in another country or region. This is called a 'limping marriage'.[9] China has not yet developed specific legal norms for resolving 'limping marriages'.

B. Capacity

The substantial requirements of the formation of marriage include both positive conditions that the parties must have satisfied and negative conditions that the parties must not violate. Generally, key requirements are that both parties must have reached the age of marriage, that there should be no bigamy, that the two parties must not be immediate family members, that the marriage is voluntary, that the two parties are not blood relatives who are prohibited from marrying, and that neither party has an existing illness that bars marriage.[10] In China, in accordance with the Civil Code of the People's Republic of China, the following conditions must be satisfied in order for a marriage to be formed. First, the marriage must be a completely voluntary decision made by both

[5] XW Zhao and HF Du, *Guo Ji Si Fa Xue Yuan Li Yu An Li Jiao Cheng* [*Principles and Case Studies of Private International Law*] (China Renmin University Press, 2016) 244.

[6] General Principles of the Civil Law of the People's Republic of China 1987 (revised by Decision of the Standing Committee of the National People's Congress on Amending Some Laws 2009, invalidated by Civil Code of the People's Republic of China 2021), Art 147; Notice of the Supreme People's Court on Issuing the Opinions on Several Issues concerning the Implementation of the General Principles of the Civil Law of the People's Republic of China (For Trial Implementation) 1988, Art 188.

[7] Law of the People's Republic of China on Choice of Law for Foreign-related Civil Relationships 2010, Art 22.

[8] Regulations on Marriage Registration of People's Republic of China 2003, Art 19.

[9] T Du, *Guo Ji Si Fa Yuan Li* [*Principles of Private International Law*] (Fudan University Press, 2018) 157.

[10] DG Xu, *Guo Ji Si Fa (Mu Ke Ban)* [*Private International Law (MOOC)*] (Peking University Press, 2016) 140.

parties. Second, the man should not be younger than 22 years old and the woman should be no younger than 20 years old.[11] Third, the man and the woman wishing to get married must apply by themselves for their marriage registration in person at a marriage registration office.[12] Fourth, the prospective spouses may not be direct blood relatives or collateral blood relatives within three generations.[13]

Pursuant to the General Principles, as discussed in A above, if an alien and a Chinese citizen apply for marriage in China, the substantial requirements including the legal age of marriage will be governed by Chinese law. If the foreigner has not reached the age of marriage prescribed by Chinese law, the marriage registration authority shall not register the marriage. Invalid marriages are those that involve bigamy, a blood relationship between the parties that prohibits marriage, and underage marriage.[14] The circumstances under which a party may request the court to revoke the marriage are where a marriage has been consented to under duress[15] and where one party suffers from a serious illness but has failed to truthfully inform the other party prior to marriage registration.[16] An invalid or voided marriage is retrospectively null; that is, it has no legal binding force since its purported beginning. In such cases, the innocent party is entitled to the right to claim damages.[17]

The 2010 Choice of Law Act stipulates that the law at the mutual habitual residence of the parties shall apply in identifying the substantial requirements for marriage.[18] In the absence of a mutual habitual residence, the law of the state of the parties' mutual nationality shall apply. If the marriage is formed at the habitual residence or the state of nationality of one of the parties, in the absence of a mutual nationality, the law of the place where the marriage is formed shall apply.[19] This legislation abolishes the previous practice of the single application of the law of the place where the marriage is established, reflecting a trend towards greater flexibility in order to promote the effectiveness of more marriages. The 2010 Choice of Law Act adopts on a massive scale the conditional, successive and selective application of law in conflict resolution, mainly to enhance legitimacy and reasonableness in the application of law.[20]

C. Consent of the Parties

The decision to enter into marriage must be a completely voluntary one made by the two parties. Coercion of one party by the other, or any other organisation or individual, is prohibited.[21] The common practice in most countries is to directly stipulate for consent as an essential requirement for the validity of a marriage.[22] In line with this common international practice, China

[11] Civil Code of the People's Republic of China 2020, Art 1047.
[12] ibid, Art 1049.
[13] ibid, Art 1048.
[14] ibid, Art 1051.
[15] ibid, Art 1052.
[16] ibid, Art 1053.
[17] ibid, Art 1054.
[18] Law of the People's Republic of China on Choice of Law for Foreign-related Civil Relationships 2010, Art 21.
[19] ibid.
[20] WG Xu, *She Wai Min Shi Guan Xi Fa Lv Shi Yong Fa* [*A study on the Implementation of Law of the People's Republic of China on Choice of Law for Foreign-related Civil Relationships*] (Fa Lv Chu Ban She, 2019) 337.
[21] Civil Code of the People's Republic of China 2020, Art 1046.
[22] FQ Yuan, *Ren Qun Bao Hu Yu Xian Dai Jia Ting Guan Xi Zhong De Guo Ji Si Fa* [*Human Rights Protection and Modern Conflict of Family Laws*] (Peking University Press, 2010) 81.

implements a marriage system underpinned by freedom, monogamy and equality between men and women. Marriage and family are protected by the state.[23] The early marriage law prohibited arranged marriages, mercenary marriages and other acts of interference with freedom of marriage.[24]

D. Public Policy

Recognition of the locality where the marriage is established as a connecting point might be easily exploited by people to evade the law. Those with such intentions are likely to choose a region with looser marriage provisions in which to form their marriage. This is harmful to the maintenance of the marital system as well as to the ethical and moral ideologies of the states where the parties belong. The legal effect of marriage should come from the consent of the parties, but this consent cannot outweigh important public interests. The behaviour theory of German Civil Law could clarify the role of autonomy in marriage, namely that as long as the marriage does not violate the prohibitive norms of the parties' nationalities, parties should be entitled to decide whether to get married and who to marry, so as to realise the freedom to marry through their own intentions. However, the prohibitive norms of marriage may differ greatly across states and regions. Polygamy is permitted in certain states and regions but not others. Same-sex marriage is increasingly recognised, but still prohibited in much of the world. As a result of these significant differences, the application of the law where the marriage was formed as the only connecting factor gives rise to issues of recognition of foreign marriages.

E. Polygamous Marriages

Polygamy was a common phenomenon in ancient societies and was later found mostly in Asia and Africa.[25] In modern society, polygamy not only violates Chinese legal provisions requiring monogamy,[26] but also violates customs of kindness and endangers the public interest of China.[27] The courts therefore reject claims for recognition of polygamous marriages. The courts reject separate claims for recognition of same-sex marriages or partnerships established outside Chinese jurisdiction on the ground that they are contrary to the public interest of China.[28] In judicial practice, a public order reservation system is usually applied to invalidate it. For example, in the succession dispute between Fan Huanming, Fan Shuzhao and Ling Zhiqing and Fan Rongfu, the court was first confronted with the issue of whether Fan Huanlun's marriage to Zheng in Hong Kong was valid. The court at the first instance recognised Fan's double marriage, while the court at the second instance rejected it.[29]

[23] Civil Code of Peoples' Republic of China 2020, Art 1041.

[24] Marriage Law of People's Republic of China, Arts 2, 5.

[25] AG Xu, 'The Ancient Tradition of Polygamy and the Response to Modern Law' *People's Court Daily* (Beijing, 11 May 2012) 005.

[26] Civil Code of Peoples' Republic of China 2020, Art 1041.

[27] The good custom in marriage mainly refers to maintaining the stability of marriage and monogamy.

[28] D Pan, 'The Status of Foreign-related Gay marriage in Chinese Law' (2012) 1 *Yunnan University Law Journal* 192.

[29] Shanghai Intermediate People's Court No 1 Decision (1999) No 393.

F. Same-sex Marriages and Civil Unions

In recent years, some states and regions have extended the availability of the institution of marriage to same-sex couples. Others, while not recognising same-sex marriages, have created legal relationships similar to marriage but available to same-sex couples, often called 'civil unions'. Though the trend in recent years is for increasing recognition of same-sex marriage, the institution of marriage is still only available to same-sex couples in a relatively small number of states: 29 at the time of writing. Chinese law does not recognise same-sex marriage. In the marriage registration case between Sun Wenlin and Hu Wenliang in 2016, the court ruled against the plaintiff, who sought recognition of a same-sex marriage. The court held that monogamy requires that the two people who enter into a marital relationship be a man and a woman. Chinese law has no provisions on the registration of homosexual marriage. Hence, the administrative behaviour by the Furong District Civil Affairs Bureau in declining to recognise the same-sex marriage in this case was legal.[30] The case has been dubbed the 'first case of same-sex marriage registration' by the public.[31]

Chinese law contains no explicit provision on the recognition of foreign same-sex marriages. In this regard, the courts at the very beginning of a case in which the issue arises must characterise foreign-related same-sex marriage. In doing so, courts must determine how to resolve the legal conflict between Chinese law, which does not recognise same-sex unions, and the relevant law which does in other states or regions.[32] According to the Law of the People's Republic of China on Choice of Law for Foreign-related Civil Relationships, the nature of foreign-related same-sex marriages must be determined in accordance with Chinese law.[33] In mainland China, same-sex civil unions are a recognised kind of civil relationship.[34] Some scholars believe that if court disputes are over substantive issues such as property inheritance involving a same-sex marriage or same-sex partnership, and the consequences of these issues do not directly impact the social and public interests of the state, then the effectiveness of the marriage or partnership can be recognised as a preliminary question.[35]

Upon invoking the need for the preservation of public order, Chinese courts are likely to refuse to recognise the application of foreign laws on same-sex marriage and will apply Chinese law to manage homosexual marriages involving non-Chinese nationals.[36] However, in the context of globalisation, acceptance of homosexual relationships and demand for the legalisation of homosexual marriage are increasing every day. For example, Brian Davidson, the British Consulate General in Shanghai, married his Chinese boyfriend at the British Ambassador's Residence in 2014. In this special situation, the same-sex marriage was recognised.[37] In the future, China may have to consider again the question of the recognition of foreign-related same-sex marriages. For this reason, some scholars propose that China should prioritise reforming the law

[30] The sixth of the top ten influential Lawsuits in China in 2016: Administrative dispute case of marriage Registration between Sun Wenlin et al and Civil Affairs Bureau of Furong District, Changsha, Same-sex marriage registration case.

[31] Eastday, 'The Civil Affairs Bureau's Refusal to Register a Gay Marriage' (Eastday, 13 April 2016) http://news.eastday.com/eastday/13news/auto/news/china/20160413/u7ai5526684.html accessed 22 Oct 2020.

[32] DP He, 'Difficulties and Solutions in the Application of Laws concerning Foreign-related Same-sex Unions in China' (2013) 12 *Fujian Forum* (Humanities and Social Sciences Edition) 198.

[33] Law of the People's Republic of China on Choice of Law for Foreign-related Civil Relationships 2010, Art 8.

[34] Q He, 'A Study on the Application of Foreign Same-sex Marriage Law' (2012) 10 *Hebei Legal Science* 137.

[35] D Pan, 'The Status of Foreign-related Gay marriage in Chinese Law' (2012) 1 *Yunnan University Law Journal* 192.

[36] FQ Yuan and CG Sun, 'Legal Symposium on the Family Affairs Concerning Foreign Elements' (2017) 1 *Law Press* 38.

[37] Xinhua News, 'The British Consul General in Shanghai has married her Chinese Boyfriend' (Xinhua News, 6 Sept 2014) www.xinhuanet.com//photo/2014-09/06/c_126961740.htm accessed 22 Oct 2020.

on the identification of same sex marriages, or alternatively formulate conflict rules specifically targeting same sex marriages. The latter is to analogise the marital conflict rules of heterosexual marriage to same-sex marriage, aiming for a means of transition to effectively protect the rights and obligations of same-sex spouses in the current legal blank state.[38]

II. Matrimonial Causes

Divorce is the legal means by which spouses dissolve their marriage while they are alive. In addition to the direct consequences of the dissolution, divorce involves a series of changes in complex personal and property relationships, such as changes in family relationships, issues of parental responsibility for children and the division of joint property ownership.[39] Due to the exceptional nature of foreign-related matrimonial cases, their litigation process differs from domestic divorce cases. Amongst other factors, such litigation encompasses different means of divorce and more cases concerning cross-domain property, and have a relatively long processing cycle.[40] Matrimonial proceedings mainly include divorce, nullity and separation, presumption of death, and financial relief.

A. Divorce, Nullity and Separation

As society develops, the divorce rate across the world has been on the rise. Transnational divorce proceedings are therefore increasingly frequent. The application of foreign-related divorce law mainly involves two aspects: first, the conditions of foreign-related divorce, ie the standards or causes for foreign-related divorce; second, the validity of foreign-related divorces.[41] The application of divorce law in China has also undergone changes as stipulated by legislation, from the General Principles of the Civil Law and its judicial interpretation to the 2010 Choice of Law Act. The General Principles stipulate that the law where the court entertaining the case is situated shall be applied to the divorce between a Chinese citizen and an alien.[42] Supplementary provisions in the Opinions of the Supreme People's Court of China on the General Principles of the Civil Law state that where a Chinese court is processing a foreign-related divorce case and a division of property is caused by the divorce, Chinese law shall be applied, while the law where the marriage is formed shall be applied to determine whether the marriage is valid.[43] The 2010 Choice of Law Act classifies divorce with foreign elements into divorce by litigation, initiated by one or both spouses as litigants, and divorce by agreement, where both spouses voluntarily agree to dissolve their marriage.[44] The freedom to divorce means that a spouse has the freedom to dissolve

[38] XY Long, 'Legal Application of Foreign Same Sex Marriage in China' (2012) 6 *Journal of Central South University* (Social Science edition) 102A.

[39] W Ding, *Zhong Guo Guo Ji Si Fa He Xie Fa Zhan Yan Jiu* [*A study on the harmonious Development of Private International Law in China*] (Shanghai Academy of Social Sciences Press, 2009) 207.

[40] NN Zhao, *She Wai Hun Yin Jia Ting An Jian Lv Shi Shi Wu* [*Lawyers' Practice in Foreign-related Marriage and Family Cases*] (Law Press, 2015) 13–14.

[41] JL Wang, 'Discussion on the Application of Law in Foreign-related Marriage and Family Relations' (2010) 4 *Modern Law* 165.

[42] General Principles of the Civil Law of the People's Republic of China 1987, Art 147.

[43] Notice of the Supreme People's Court on Issuing the Opinions on Several Issues concerning the Implementation of the General Principles of the Civil Law of the People's Republic of China (For Trial Implementation), Art 188.

[44] QS He, *Guo Ji Si Fa Ru Men Bi Ji* [*Private International Law in a Nutshell*] (Law Press, 2019) 204.

their marital relationship in accordance with the law, which further means that the parties to a marriage enjoy the right to decide whether to maintain their marital relationship or not.[45] The divorce agreement is a 'package' agreement reached by the husband and wife after weighing their interests and considering the advantages and disadvantages, including the dissolution of their marital relationship, the maintenance of their children, the division of joint property, respective commitments to the husband and wife's debts, compensation for divorce, and so on. This demonstrates the dual aspects of the agreement – the personal and the proprietary.[46]

According to the Regulations on Marriage Registration, where Chinese citizens married to foreigners voluntarily divorce in mainland China, or where mainland residents married to overseas Chinese or to Hong Kong, Macau, or Taiwan residents voluntarily divorce in mainland China, both parties must jointly go to the marriage registration institution at the mainland resident's permanent registered residence for divorce registration.[47] The 2010 Choice of Law Act stipulates that the law where the court processing the case is situated shall be applied to divorce by litigation.[48] In a divorce by agreement, the parties may choose to apply the law of the habitual residence or state of nationality of one of the parties. If the parties make no such choice, the laws of their mutual habitual residence will apply. If there is no mutual habitual residence, the laws of the parties' mutual state of nationality will apply. If there is no mutual nationality, the laws of the place of the institution managing the divorce formalities will apply.[49] This approach adopts the principle of limited autonomy for divorce by agreement, allowing the parties a limited choice of law, but in the case of divorce by litigation adopting the single law centred around the court's location. The 2010 Choice of Law Act sets forth clear provisions applicable to divorce by agreement, thus making up for deficiencies left by the General Principles of the Civil Law, refining regulations on foreign-related divorce, with habitual residence as a connecting point in divorce by agreement. This both increases flexibility in the application of law and guarantees that there will be sufficient connection between the law chosen by the parties and facts of the case.[50]

The courts have further clarified the application of law in foreign-related divorce by litigation. For example, in the divorce case between the South Korean citizen Kwon and the Chinese citizen Kim, the Chinese court made clear that it had jurisdiction over the foreign-related divorce dispute. Kwon's claim for divorce was to be governed by the law of the place where the court entertaining the case was located, namely the law of China.[51] In the divorce dispute between Lian, a Chinese citizen, and Bei, an Australian citizen, the plaintiff claimed that, due to emotional discord between the parties, the defendant had returned to Australia to live, as a result of which the plaintiff and the defendant could not continue their married life. Accordingly, both parties agreed to divorce, and requested the court to grant their divorce. The court held that the law of the People's Republic of China should be applied in accordance with the 2010 Choice of Law Act. In the eye of the court, the essential criterion for deciding whether divorce could be granted was whether the emotional foundation for the marriage still subsisted. Marriage should be based on

[45] F Yu, 'Application of The Principle of Autonomy in Foreign-related Divorce' (2011) 1 *Journal of Xiamen University* (Philosophy and Social Science edition) 47.

[46] L Wang, On the Reference and Application of Identity Relationship Agreement to Civil Code Contract, *Jurist* (2020), Vol 1, 36.

[47] Regulations on Marriage Registration of People's Republic of China 2003, Art 10.

[48] Law of the People's Republic of China on Choice of Law for Foreign-related Civil Relationships 2010, art 27.

[49] Law of the People's Republic of China on Choice of Law for Foreign-related Civil Relationships 2010, ibid, Art 26.

[50] XB Qiao, 'Applicable Laws of Foreign-related Divorce: Tradition, Reform and Development – a Concurrent Review of relevant provisions of Law of the People's Republic of China on Choice of Law for Foreign-related Civil Relationships' (2013) 6 *Jianghan Academics* 46.

[51] Intermediate People's Court of Yanbian Korean Autonomous Prefecture Decision (2016) 24 No 95.

affection. The plaintiff and the defendant had agreed to divorce, so it could be concluded that the affection they had had for each other had substantially broken down, and thus the divorce should be granted.[52] When applying Chinese law, separation is a crucial factor to be considered in divorce cases. In the case concerning the divorce between Hong Kong resident Chen and mainland Chinese resident Lin, although the couple had been married for many years and had a son, the couple confirmed that they had lived apart for 17 years since their separation in 1999.[53]

The situation showed the depth of the antagonism between them, and became one of the main factors considered in the granting of their divorce. In the case concerning the divorce between Canadian citizen Ou and Chinese citizen Jiang, the two parties lived in different countries after marriage and were unable to cultivate spousal affection due to their long-term separation.[54] In the course of the trial, the court applied the law of the place where the divorce was litigated, that is, Chinese law, and confirmed that the relationship between the husband and the wife was discordant and their affections had indeed broken down. Finally, some divorce cases will raise issues as to the validity of the marriage. These issues are dealt with under the principles and provisions outlined in section I.

It is worth noting that China's Civil Code has created a 'cooling off period' for applicants for the registration of divorce, namely, that within 30 days starting from the date of receipt of the application by the marriage registration authority, any party unwilling to divorce may withdraw the application. After these 30 days, the parties have another 30 days to apply in person to the marriage registration authority for the issue of a divorce certificate. If no application is made within that period, the application for their registration of divorce shall be deemed to have been withdrawn.[55]

B. Presumption of Death

The Chinese Civil Code grants interested parties the right to declare the death of a natural person to the court, subject to one of two conditions being satisfied: that the person has disappeared for four years; or that they have disappeared for two years following an accident. Where a natural person has disappeared due to an accident and it is proved by the relevant authorities that it is impossible for a natural person to have survived that accident, the application for a declaration of the presumption of death is not subject to the limitation of two years.[56] In cases of husband-wife relationships, the marital relationship of the person presumed dead ends at the date of death. If the declaration is revoked, the marital relationship recovers as of the date of that revocation, except where the remaining spouse has remarried or declares in writing to the marriage registration authority that they are not willing to resume the marriage.[57] In accordance with the Law of the People's Republic of China on Choice of Law for Foreign-related Civil Relationships, the law at the habitual residence of a natural person shall apply to the declaration of presumed death.[58]

[52] Civil Judgment of Tonglu County People's Court (Zhejiang Province) Decision (2014) No 1083.
[53] Foshan Intermediate People's Court (Guangdong Province) Decision (2014) No 1221.
[54] Intermediate People's Court of Yanbian Korean Autonomous Prefecture Decision (2014) 24 No 56.
[55] Civil Code of the People's Republic of China 2020, Art 1077.
[56] ibid, Art 46.
[57] ibid, Art 51.
[58] Law of the People's Republic of China on Choice of Law for Foreign-related Civil Relationships 2010, Art 13.

C. Financial Relief

Marital property relationships mainly involve the rights and obligations of the husband and wife regarding family property. The 2010 Choice of Law Act stipulates the following laws governing husband-wife property relationships. The parties concerned may, by agreement, choose the law of the habitual residence or state of nationality of one of the parties, or the law of the area where the main property of one of the parties is situated. If the parties have made no such choice, the laws at the mutual habitual residence shall be applied; if there is no mutual habitual residence, the law of the parties' mutual state of nationality shall be applied.[59] The application of the law that the parties autonomously choose or the law of the parties' mutual habitual residence emphasises the protection of equal rights between husband and wife, while the application of the law where the real estate is situated protects third-party creditors through the registration of real estate.[60] In the divorce property dispute case between US citizen Da and Chinese citizen Zheng, the court reaffirmed the autonomy of both parties. The plaintiff chose the law of the state of the defendant's nationality, China, as the applicable law, and the defendant agreed to this choice during the trial. Accordingly, Chinese law was applied in the case.[61] In a divorce case involving a property dispute between Singapore citizen Zhang and Chinese citizen Shi, the court adopted the principle of the most significant connection, holding that the case should be categorised as a post-divorce property dispute. The disputed property lay within the territory of the People's Republic of China, so it was correct for the court at the first instance to apply Chinse law, which had the most significant connection with the property relationship between the husband and the wife.[62]

III. Children

The primary bond in social relations is that between husband and wife, followed by that between parents and children, and finally other familial bonds.[63] Family relationships are a network of warp and weft. The weft is the horizontal marital relationship between the man and the woman through marriage, while the warp is the vertical parent-child relationship. Family legal relationships include not only the rights and obligations between husband and wife, but also the rights and obligations between the parents and their children.[64] This section discusses parental responsibility, guardianship, maintenance, legitimation and adoption, and abandonment of children.

A. Parental Responsibility

Legislation on parent-child relationships across the world currently tend to emphasise the protection of children's interests.[65] In accordance with the 2010 Choice of Law Act, the law of the mutual

[59] ibid, art 24.

[60] Q Hua, 'Application of Marriage Real Estate Law from the Perspective of Gender, Learning and Practice' (2015) 10 *Learning and Practice* 83.

[61] Xiacheng District People's Court (Hangzhou City, Zhejiang Province) Decision (2016) 0103 No 8721.

[62] The Intermediate People's Court of Zhuhai City, Guangdong Province Decision (2016) 4 No 2814.

[63] Y Zhao, 'Value Shift of Marital Property System from the Perspective of Justice' (2016) 1 *China Law* 227.

[64] FQ Yuan, *Ren Quan Bao Hu Yu Xian Dai Jia Ting Guan Xi Zhong De Guo Ji Si Fa* [*Human Rights Protection and Private International Law in Modern Family Relations*] (Peking University Press, 2010) 111.

[65] T Du, *Guo Ji Si Fa Yuan Li* [*Principles of Private International Law*] (Fudan University Press, 2018) 165.

habitual residence should be applied to the personal and property relations between parents and children. If there is no mutual habitual residence, the courts must apply the law that better protects the rights and interests of the weak, choosing between the law at any party's habitual residence or state of nationality.[66] In family relationships, children are weaker than their parents in terms of physical ability, economy capacity and life experience, and when transnational legal disputes occur between them, it is urgent to take this into account when balancing their interests in law.[67] In the context of private international law, the weaker party is the party who is at a disadvantage in making a choice of law or of the means of dispute settlement, and in making a choice of the location for the settlement. Private international law protects the weaker party in order to prevent the stronger party's choice of law from curtailing the level of protection of the weaker party's rights.[68] The 2010 Choice of Law Act does not provide a comprehensive definition of 'the weaker party'. The term appears only once in the legislation.[69] However, Fang Luo, by examining a range of rules, has identified three main kinds of objects for protection.[70] First, the party who is weak physically and psychologically, with obvious emotional and economic dependence on others to satisfy their basic needs. Second, the contracting party that is relatively weak in terms of negotiation capability, skills, and the acquisition of information. Third, the party with obvious weakness or special difficulties in their economic strength and ability to protect their rights.[71] The protection of children falls into the first category.

B. Guardianship

Guardianship refers to the traditional family law system mainly applicable to the protection of minors or persons with intellectual disabilities. The substantive rules of China's guardianship system are mainly found in the Civil Code, and the provisions on guardianship mainly involve the scope and designation of guardians, guardianship duties, and the termination of guardianship. A guardian should perform their duties of guardianship in accordance with the principle that most benefits the ward.[72] As for the application of law, the Judicial Interpretation of The General Principles of the Civil Law of China stipulates that the establishment, alteration and termination of guardianship shall be governed by the laws of the ward's country; if the ward has residence within Chinese territory, the laws of China shall apply.[73] According to the 2010 Choice of Law Act, the courts shall apply the law that best protects the rights and interests of the persons under guardianship, between the law of either party's habitual residence or state of nationality.[74] The same article stipulates that the law in favour of the guardian shall be selected from the law of the state of nationality or the law of habitual residence of the party concerned.

[66] Law of the People's Republic of China on Choice of Law for Foreign-related Civil Relationships 2010, Art 25.

[67] DG Xu, 'Humane Care and the Protection of the Interests of the Weak in Private International Law' (2004) 5 *Journal of Contemporary Law* 20.

[68] FQ Yuan, 'Reflections and Reconstruction of the Protection System of the Weak in China's Private International Law' (2014) 6 *Law and Commercial Studies* 105.

[69] Law of the People's Republic of China on Choice of Law for Foreign-related Civil Relationships 2010, Art 25.

[70] F Luo, 'Protection of the Interests of the Weak in the Law of the People's Republic of China on Choice of Law for Foreign-related Civil Relationships' (2019) 4 *Chinese Academy of Social Sciences Graduate Journal* 51–52.

[71] In terms of product tort liability, compared with the operators with strong economic strength and worldwide business services, the infringed is obviously in a weak position.

[72] Civil Code of the People's Republic of China 2020, Art 35.

[73] Notice of the Supreme People's Court on Issuing the Opinions on Several Issues concerning the Implementation of the General Principles of the Civil Law of the People's Republic of China (For Trial Implementation), Art 190.

[74] Law of the People's Republic of China on Choice of Law for Foreign-related Civil Relationships 2010, Art 30.

This practice, an example of the private international law principle that the interests of the weak are to be protected, accords with the pursuit of substantive justice in contemporary private international law.[75]

In the guardianship of minors, the most direct embodiment of the 'most beneficial to the ward' principle is in the achievement of the 'best interests of minors'. That is, the guardian is required, before resolving issues on the disposal of minors, to satisfy the ward's interests rather than the guardian's own interests, whilst gradually engaging the minor with decision-making according to the minor's psychological maturity. In the field of adult guardianship, in order to best benefit the person under guardianship, it is generally necessary for the court to support the ward's own decision. This ensures the ward is restrained only to the minimum necessary extent, supporting them to claim their own best interests.[76] In the case where Hu and Yu applied for the revocation of their guardianship, the court recognised that the case was a foreign-related dispute over guardianship as the applicant Hu was a Canadian citizen. Hu and Yu were grandparents to a child, Zheng. Zheng had lived from birth with his parents in Shanghai. While Zheng was still a child, his parents died, and his grandparents took responsibility for his daily life and studies. Eventually, Hu and Yu reached a mediation agreement where each agreed that Yu would temporarily act as Zheng's guardian, while Hu would have the right to visit Zheng once every 2-3 weeks when Hu was in Shanghai. Both Yu and Hu were entitled to visit Zheng's school to learn about the progress of his education. The court decided that the application of Chinese law was more conducive to the protection of Zheng's rights and interests.[77]

C. Maintenance

Maintenance refers to a legal system in which a person with greater economic capacity provides financial assistance to a relative, to enable that relative to maintain their life and wellbeing. Maintenance may be between husband and wife, between parents and children, and between other relatives.[78] China's General Principles of the Civil Law stipulates that maintenance shall be governed by the laws of the state with which the person to be maintained has the closest connections.[79] The Judicial Interpretation of the General Principles of the Civil Law further clarifies that the law of the country most closely related to the persons being maintained shall apply to the maintenance between parents and children, husbands and wives, and other persons of suitable familial relationship.[80] The 2010 Choice of Law Act fully takes into account the protection of the interests of the persons being maintained and stipulates that the law in favour of the protection of the rights and interests of the persons being maintained, amongst the law of the habitual residence of one party, the law of the state of nationality of one party or the law where the main property of one party is located, shall be applied to maintenance.[81]

[75] F Yu, 'Definition of "Principle of In Favour of" in Private International Law – Comments on the Law of the People's Republic of China on Choice of Law for Foreign-related Civil Relationships' (2012) 15 *China Annual Journal of Private International Law and Comparative Law* 67.

[76] HM Qin, 'Development, Problems and Suggestions for the Improvement of China's guardianship System' (2020) 3 *Journal of Zhejiang University of Science and Technology* (Social Science edition) 314.

[77] Minhang District People's Court of Shanghai Decision (2015) No 39.

[78] LZ Gao, *Fu Yang Zhi Du Yan Jiu* [*Research on the Maintenance System*] (Law Press, 2006) 1.

[79] The General Principles of the Civil Law of China 1987, Art 148.

[80] Notice of the Supreme People's Court on Issuing the Opinions on Several Issues concerning the Implementation of the General Principles of the Civil Law of the People's Republic of China (For Trial Implementation), Art 189.

[81] Law of the People's Republic of China on Choice of Law for Foreign-related Civil Relationships 2010, Art 29.

In November 2007, the Hague Conference on Private International Law meeting of the twenty-first diplomatic conference passed the Protocol on the Law Applicable to Maintenance Obligations by negotiations and consensus. The protocol specified the types of maintenance relationships where a debtor can raise defences.[82] 71 states, including China, signed on the final document to promote the birth of the protocol.[83]

D. Legitimacy, Legitimation and Adoption

The legitimation of children born outside marriage refers to the system whereby such children obtain the same rights as children born within marriage. Legitimation may occur as a result of the marriage of the child's biological parents, adoption of the child, or by administrative or judicial declaration. At present, China has no specific legislation on legitimation. It may be said that such legislation is not necessary, as the Civil Code clearly provides that children born outside marriage are entitled to the same rights as children born within marriage.[84] The development of private international law has seen states gradually adopting a more relaxed and flexible approach to choosing the law applicable to the legitimation of foreign-related children born out of wedlock. Increasing attention is paid to the need to protect illegitimate children, who are in a weaker position. Some scholars believe that regardless of the method of legitimation, the legitimation of the child should be ensured.[85] That is, if there is a choice of law, and an illegitimate child is not eligible for any method of legitimation in one legal regime, the law most conducive to the establishment of legitimation should be applied.

Legislation on foreign-related adoptions in China developed from scratch in the 1990s and is likely to develop further in the twenty-first century.[86] As international adoption is a very complex process, it is necessary to have certain legal rules to coordinate and regulate relevant conduct, adjust relevant relationships, and prevent the abuse of international adoptive rights and international child trafficking. The relevant legal norms of international adoption should generally include substantial requirements as well as formal requirements for the formation of such relationships, as well as rules on jurisdiction, recognition and enforcement, application of law and conflict of laws.[87]

Chinese legislation on international adoption has long required that all foreign-related adoptions occurring in China should be handled in accordance with Chinese law. This is not because China does not recognise the extraterritorial effect of other countries' legislation on international adoption, but because Chinese law seeks to protect Chinese children adopted by foreigners.[88] However, with the increasingly frequent and close exchanges between countries, adoption has begun to more frequently cross national borders, and transnational adoption has become

[82] A Bonomi, 'Preliminary Draft Protocol on the Law Applicable to Maintenance Obligations Explanatory Report' (*Hague Conference on Private International Law*, 33 August 2007) www.hcch.net/en/publications-and-studies/details4/?pid=4140&dtid=35 accessed 27 July 2020.

[83] Now only Brazil, EU, Kazakstan, Serbia has ratified the Protocol. HCCH, 'Protocol of 23 November 2007 on the Law Applicable to Maintenance Obligations Status Table' (HCCH, 9 Dec 2019) www.hcch.net/en/instruments/conventions/status-table/?cid=133 accessed 22 Oct 2020.

[84] Civil Code of the People's Republic of China 2020, Art 1071.

[85] Y Lin, 'Research on Legitimation of Illegitimate Children Concerning Foreign Elements and Relative Law Applications' (2006) 11 *Law Science Magazine* 48.

[86] XM Jiang, 'Application of foreign-related adoption law in China' (2006) 6 *Global Law Review* 738.

[87] XM Jiang, 'The Concept and Origin of International Adoption Law' (2000) 2 *Law Journal* 136.

[88] LN Zhu, 'Legal Analysis of Conflicts of International Adoption Laws' (2011) 18 *Frontiers* 18.

a universal and high-profile international civil exchange. As a result, relevant legal conflicts in various states have also intensified. The General Principles of the Civil Law in the early period did not expressly provide for the application of law on foreign-related adoptions, and so provisions on the application of law on foreign-related child support were applied by way of analogy. The Adoption Law of China provides only in general terms that aliens may adopt children in the PRC.[89] The Adoption Law of The People's Republic of China does not define the concept of 'children' in any way, which can be understood either as referring only to the children of Chinese citizens or as including the children of foreigners in addition to the children of Chinese citizens. The Adoption Law and relevant regulations, adhering to the one-way foreign-related adoption model, have great limitations. They only provide relevant rules on the adoption of Chinese children by foreigners, but do not provide for the adoption of foreign children by Chinese citizens.[90] Foreigners who adopt children in China have to undergo relevant procedures at the China Child Welfare and Adoption Centre.[91]

The 2010 Choice of Law Act stipulates that the laws of the respective habitual residences of the adopter and the adoptee shall be applied to determine the qualifications for, and procedures of, adoption. The law of the habitual residence of the adopter at the time of adoption determines the validity of the adoption. The law of the habitual residence of the adoptee at the time of adoption or the law where the court is situated will apply to the termination of the adoptive relationship.[92] The current rule adopts the principle of uniform application of law and does not distinguish between substantial and formal requirements.[93] In general, this simplifies the legal situation and thus beneficially encourages cross-border adoption. In addition, relevant Judicial Interpretations have clarified how the 'habitual residence' of natural persons is to be defined, including time cut-offs, key considerations in judicial decisions, and exceptional circumstances.[94]

In 2005, the Standing Committee of the National People's Congress of China approved the Convention on The Protection of Children and Cooperation in Respect of Inter-country Adoptions, making it clear that the Ministry of Civil Affairs is the central organ in China to fulfil the duties entrusted under the Convention and the sole provider of information of the state regarding inter-country adoptions.[95] The functions of the central organs provided for in Articles 15 to 21 of the Convention are performed by the China Adoption Centre. A foreign adopter may not adopt Chinese children who have habitually resided in China unless the government of the country of which the adopter is a citizen, or government-authorised organisations in that country, properly performs the duties required of central governing organs by the Convention. The certificate of adoption involving Chinese and foreign nationals shall be issued by the civil affairs department of the people's government of the province, autonomous region or municipality directly under the central government where the adoptee's permanent residence is located, and the adoption registration certificate issued by the department shall be the adoption certificate.

[89] Adoption Law of People's Republic of China 1991, Art 21.

[90] XM Jiang, 'The Reconstruction of the Applicable Law Concerning the Substantial Requirements for Establishment of the Foreign Related to Adoption in China' (2019) 6 *Present Day Law Science* 8.

[91] Measures for Registration of Adoption of Children by aliens in the People's Republic of China 1999, Art 8.

[92] Law of the People's Republic of China on Choice of Law for Foreign-related Civil Relationships 2010, Art 28.

[93] XM Jiang, 'Reconstruction of the Applicable Norm of substantial Elements of the Establishment of Foreign-related adoption Relations in China' (2019) 6 *Presentday Law Science* 7.

[94] Judicial Interpretation I on Law of the People's Republic of China on Choice of Law for Foreign-related Civil Relationships, Art 15.

[95] ZS Zhu, 'Comments on the Protection of Children and Cooperation in International Adoption' (2000) 4 *Politics and Law* 76.

China is not obliged to recognise adoptions pursuant to an agreement reached under Article 39, Paragraph 2, of the Convention.[96]

E. Wrongful Abandonment of a Child

In the field of criminal justice in China, a person who refuses to support a child for whom they have responsibility and who is incapable of living independently commits, if the circumstances are abominable, the crime of desertion.[97] In the field of foreign-related civil affairs, such acts fall within the scope of adjustments of parent-child relationships and are to be regulated in accordance with the law on parent-child relationships. Hence, the law of the mutual habitual residence will be applied to the personal and proprietary relations between parents and children. If there is no mutual habitual residence, the courts should apply the law that better protects the rights and interests of the weaker party, choosing between the law at any party's habitual residence or state of nationality.[98] In addition, the analogical approach to the application of foreign-related laws can be used to supplement for deficiencies in the law on foreign-related abandoned children. This means that the rights and interests of the persons to be maintained are to be adequately taken account of, and that from the law that most benefits the person to be maintained shall be applied, choosing between the law of any party's habitual residence, state of nationality of one party, or the law where the main property of one party is located.[99]

IV. Mental Incapacity

A natural person's capacity includes both legal and behavioural capacity. Legal capacity of a natural person is the qualification for a natural person to enjoy civil rights and be subject to civil obligations, as well as the prerequisite for a natural person to be the subject of private international law. A natural person enjoys civil capacity from the time of their birth to the time of their death.[100] The behavioural capacity of a natural person is the qualification for a natural person to acquire new civil rights and undertake new civil obligations through their own conduct. The acquisition of a natural person's behavioural capacity requires a certain age and a certain level of intellect. According to Chinese law, natural persons over the age of 18 are adults and may independently enjoy civil capacity. A minor who has reached the age of 16 and whose main source of income is his own labour is to be regarded as a person with full behavioural capacity.[101] Minors over the age of eight have limited capacity,[102] and minors under the age of eight are persons without civil capacity.[103] The requirement of intellectual capability is primarily intended to protect the interests of persons who have reached the age of adulthood but are mentally restricted by nature or nurture, especially those with certain intellectual disabilities.[104] According to Chinese law, an

[96] SY Li and FY Ou, *Guo Ji Si Fa* [*Private International Law*] (Peking University Press, 2018) 174–175.
[97] Criminal Law of People's Republic of China 1997, Art 261.
[98] Law of the People's Republic of China on Choice of Law for Foreign-related Civil Relationships 2010, Art 25.
[99] ibid, Art 29.
[100] Civil Code of the People's Republic of China 2020, Art 13.
[101] ibid, Art 18.
[102] ibid, Art 19.
[103] ibid, Art 20.
[104] WG Xu, *She Wai Min Shi Guan Xi Fa Lv Shi Yong Fa* [*A study on Law of the People's Republic of China on Choice of Law for Foreign-related Civil Relationships*] (Law Press, 2019) 366.

adult who is unable to fully recognise their own conduct is a person with limited capacity for civil conduct, and their civil acts shall be conducted by an agent or conducted with the approval and ratification of the agent. However, such adults may independently perform civil acts for pure profit, and civil acts appropriate for the particular adult's level of intellect and condition of mental health.[105]

The law of the natural person's habitual residence is applied in identifying the person's civil capacity and behavioural capacity.[106] If a natural person, however, is engaged in civil activities and has no behavioural capacity according to the laws of that person's habitual residence, but is confirmed as competent for civil acts in accordance with the law where the acts are performed, the latter law shall be applied, except in cases involving marriage, family or inheritance.[107] These provisions, especially those concerning the behavioural capacity of natural persons, show that the habitual residence of a person is the basic connecting point for determining the civil capacity and behavioural capacity of natural persons. However, in order to protect the interests and stability of commercial transactions, it has been confirmed that in cases of conflicts, the behavioural capacity of a natural person would be determined according to the law where the act is performed, thus maintaining the safety of civil transactions. Nevertheless, due to their exceptional nature, the application of laws involving marriage, family and inheritance follows specific rules.

[105] Civil Code of the People's Republic of China 2020, Art 22.
[106] Law of the People's Republic of China on Choice of Law for Foreign-related Civil Relationships 2010, Art 11.
[107] ibid, Art 12.

18

Law of Corporations and Insolvency

XIAOLIN LI

I. Capacity, Agency, and Internal Management

A. Introduction

In order for a person to have legal rights, they must be recognised in law to be a 'person'. It is almost a universal choice-of-law rule that the personal law of a person's domicile determines the most essential qualities of legal personhood – such as birth, continuance, and demise, as well as status, capacity, constitution, and management.[1] In the field of cross-border insolvency law,[2] this rule has been overshadowed by modern legislative instruments such as the UNCITRAL Model Law on Cross-Border Insolvency ('UNCITRAL Model Law') and the European Insolvency Regulation ('EIR'), which grant insolvency representatives direct access to foreign courts and provide expedited and standardised recognition in foreign insolvency proceedings. Nevertheless, the domicile rule is still frequently resorted to in an effort to recognise the vesting effect of insolvency proceedings initiated in the debtor's domicile, or from another perspective, to recognise the representative powers of the foreign representative appointed therein in jurisdictions that do not follow the aforesaid modern instruments. China is among these jurisdictions.

According to this long-established choice-of-law rule concerning the internal affairs of a legal person, if foreign insolvency proceedings are commenced at the place where the debtor's domicile is located, certain aspects of the proceedings may be given effect by local courts provided that they can be deemed as matters concerning essential qualities of the debtor and are thus subject to the debtor's personal law. The foreign administrator may thus exercise certain rights and duties under the personal law of the debtor. For example, the administrator may have the power to act

[1] I Fletcher, *Insolvency in Private International Law* 2nd edn (OUP, 2005) 2001–02; L Collins, *Dicey & Morris on the Conflict of Laws* 15th edn (Sweet & Maxwell, 2012), Rule 156 (2).

[2] The term 'Insolvency' is commonly used to describe all types of collective court-supervised proceedings against both legal entities – either incorporated or non-incorporated – and individuals. The definition of 'Bankruptcy', to the contrary, may diverge among jurisdictions. For instance, it encompasses the default of both natural person and legal person in the US, and yet only includes natural person in English commonwealth jurisdictions. Nevertheless, in order to distinguish between the general default of legal persons and individuals, the term 'Insolvency' in this book mainly refers to the default of legal persons, while 'Bankruptcy' is used in the cases of natural persons in the next chapter. However, considering the overlapping of the private international law concerning the two kinds of proceedings, in some places, the usage of one of the terms does not necessarily exclude its applicability of the other.

on behalf of the debtor, either as a representative[3] or in their own name,[4] as long as this power falls into the capacity of the debtor before the debtor enters into insolvency proceedings. This power may include the foreign administrator's standing to sue[5] and to request local entities such as banks and accountants to act in accordance with the administrator's instructions if they would have complied with such requests had they come from the debtor's board of directors.[6] The representative may also be vested with, or be entitled to take over, the debtor's assets, and therefore can protect the insolvency assets from malicious transfer and disposal by the debtor who has been deprived of such power under the *lex fori concursus* ie the law of the Member State where such proceedings are opened.[7] However, the administrator may not be able to invoke the powers that are aimed at preventing individual actions of the creditors, such as seeking a stay of proceedings, or other protective provisions such as avoidance rules under insolvency law.[8]

This 'bypass' of formal court recognition procedures has, in fact, already been conducted in states which adopt a territorialism approach and states which were at the beginning stage of reforming their cross-border insolvency laws before a modified universalism approach was formally accepted.[9] It also serves as an alternative for jurisdictions that have already adopted modified universalism in the insolvency field. For example, in England, foreign liquidations commenced in the debtor's place of incorporation and liquidators appointed therein are recognised without any difficulty.[10] The effect of this recognition is that the foreign representatives will locally be accepted as persons with standing to represent the collective interests of creditors and to invoke the assistance of the local courts under English law.[11] These effects are automatically recognised, mostly without having to go through formal court procedures.[12]

B. The Situation in PRC

The choice of law rule that a legal person's internal affairs shall be governed by the personal law of its place of domicile, ie *lex domicilii*, is important for jurisdictions that have not adopted any

[3] See, eg, Supreme People's Court Fourth Civil Division Decision *Thumb Environmental Technology Group v Sino-Environment Technology Group* (2014) Min Si Zhong Zi No 20.

[4] See, eg, *The Joint Official Liquidators of A Company v B and Another* [2014] 4 HKLRD 374 *(Re A Company)*.

[5] See, eg, *Sino-Environment* (n 3).

[6] See, eg, *Re A Company* (n 4) [4].

[7] See, eg, GJ Tu and XL Li, 'The Chinese Approach Toward Cross-Border Bankruptcy Proceedings: One Progressive Step Ahead' (2015) 24 *INSOL International Insolvency Review* 57, 63–64 (discussing Chinese Supreme Court decision of *Sino-Environment*); *Singularis Holdings Limited v PricewaterhouseCoopers* [2014] UKPC 36 [12] (mentioning that English courts could on ordinary principles of private international law recognise the vesting power of a foreign liquidator appointed or recognised under the law of its incorporation). See also P Omar, 'The Universe of Insolvency Cooperation and the Primeo Directive' (2015) 12 *International Corporate Rescue* 32, 32.

[8] Tu and Li, 'The Chinese Approach' (n 7) 65, 66.

[9] Two good examples are Sweden and The Netherlands, both of which are almost closed to foreign bankruptcy proceedings in the absence of international treaties or regional regulation. However, both of the two states allow foreign bankruptcy administrators to represent and claim for the bankrupt assets located in their territories. See AJ Berends, 'The UNCITRAL Model Law on Cross-Border Insolvency: A Comprehensive Overview' (1998) 6 *Tulane Journal of International and Comparative Law* 309, 397–398; M Bogdan, 'International Bankruptcy Law in Scandinavia' (1985) 34 *International and Comparative Law Quarterly* 49, 69–74; M Bogdan, 'Security Interests in International Bankruptcies in Sweden' (1998) 67 *Nordic Journal of International Law* 289, 291; PR Wood, *Principles of International Insolvency* 2nd edn (Sweet & Maxwell 2007) 841, 851.

[10] In England, the domicile of a corporation is deemed as located almost 'immutably' in its country of formation. See Fletcher, *Insolvency* (n 1) 201.

[11] ibid.

[12] For a comparative study on the powers of foreign representatives at the early stage of the development of cross-border insolvency law, see SA Riesenfeld, 'The Status of Foreign Administrators of Insolvent Estates: A Comparative Survey' (1976) 24 *American Journal of Comparative Law* 288.

modern cross-border insolvency legislation based on modified universalism. China has adopted a similar choice of law rule with respect to the 'internal matters' of a legal person.[13] According to the Application Law:

> the law where the legal person and its branch is registered shall govern its civil rights capacities, civil acts capacities, organisational institutions, rights and obligations of shareholders, etc. If the main place of operation of a legal person is inconsistent with the place of registration, the law of the main place of operation may apply.[14]

This provision was used by the Supreme People's Court ('SPC') to recognise the representative power of foreign representatives appointed according to the *lex domicilii* of the debtor. Compared with jurisdictions such as England and Hong Kong, the personal-law alternative is particularly important for China because of the rigorousness and vagueness of Article 5 of the Enterprise Bankruptcy Law of China ('Enterprise Bankruptcy Law'), which does not give foreign insolvency representatives direct access to local courts, or provide any easily accessible remedy for foreign insolvency representatives.[15] As a matter of fact, Article 5 has never been successfully invoked to recognise a foreign insolvency judgment or in any other way assisted a foreign insolvency proceeding.[16] Therefore, pragmatic solutions have emerged to mitigate this deficiency. These solutions were originally developed from cross-border bankruptcy cases between the mainland of China and Hong Kong relating to enterprise groups. In a number of reported cases, Hong Kong liquidators or provisional liquidators were successfully appointed as directors, presidents, or even attorneys of foreign debtors and their Chinese subsidiaries through board resolutions, in order to gain control over the mainland subsidiaries of debtors that had entered into (provisional) winding up proceedings in Hong Kong.[17] The legitimacy of this bypass of Article 5 was confirmed and further developed by the SPC's judgment in *Thumb Environmental Technology Group v Sino-Environment Technology Group* ('*Sino-Environment*'), where the SPC allowed Singapore judicial managers to act as an internal institution of the debtor company even if the foreign proceeding could not be recognised under Article 5 of the Enterprise Bankruptcy Law.[18]

[13] A more detailed discussion of the interaction of this choice of law rule and special jurisdiction of Chinese court upon internal matters of a legal person can be found at GJ Tu and XL Li, 'The Second Amendment to PRC Civil Procedure Law: An International Civil Litigation Perspective' (2013) 43 *Hong Kong Law Journal* 633 at 639–42.

[14] See Art 14 of the Law on the 'Zhonghua Renmin Gonghe Guo Shewai Minshi Falv Guanxi Shiyong Fa' [Application of Law for Foreign-Related Civil Legal Relationships of the People's Republic of China] adopted on 28 October 2010.

[15] See generally Tu and Li, 'The Chinese Approach' (n 7).

[16] Prior to the enactment of the EBL, Chinese courts had granted recognition to two bankruptcy judgments respectively rendered in Italy and France according to the bilateral treaties that were signed with the two countries. See Foshan Intermediate People's Court Decision *B&T Ceramic Group s.r.l.* (Applying for the Recognition and Enforcement of an Italian Bankruptcy Judgment) (2000) Fo Zhong Fa Jing Chu Zi No 633; Guangzhou Intermediate People's Court Decision *Antoine Montier* (Applying for the Recognition and Enforcement of a French Bankruptcy Judgment) (2005) available at old.ccmt.org.cn/shownews.php?id=8413 (accessed 13 March 2019). In Wuhan Intermediate People's Court Decision *Sascha Rudolf Seehaus* (Applying for the Recognition and Enforcement of a German Bankruptcy Judgment) (2012) E Wuhan Zhong Minshang Wai Chuzi No 16, the German bankruptcy judgment was recognised but was not based on the EBL.

[17] See, eg, Guangzhou Municipal Intermediate People's Court Decision *Gu Laiyun v Nardu Company Ltd* (2007) Sui Zhong Fa Min Si Zhong Zi No 7 (where one of the liquidators of the defendant was elected as the vice president of a Mainland joint venture in order to take over the business licence, seals, accounting records and properties of the joint venture); *Casey Mcdonald and another v Golden Dynasty Enterprises Ltd and Others* [2008] HKC 881 (where the BVI receivers were authorised in a board resolution and a power of attorney to take actions for and on behalf of the insolvent parent, in order to obtain the power to take over the assets owned by the Mainland subsidiaries).

[18] *Sino-Environment* (n 3).

i. Sino-Environment: *The SPC-Endorsed Bypass*

The appellant, Sino-Environment Technology Group Limited ('the parent'), was a Singapore company under the judicial management of the High Court of the Republic of Singapore. The respondent, Thumb Environmental Technology Group ('the subsidiary'), was one of the appellant's wholly-owned Chinese subsidiaries. The judicial manager of the appellant suspended a scheduled capital increase to the subsidiary and attempted to take over the subsidiary by replacing its directors and legal representatives following the insolvency of the parent. However, the de facto controllers of the subsidiary refused to cooperate. The Chinese SPC had to answer, inter alia, whether the judicial manager (who later became the liquidator of the parent) had the right to represent the parent in legal proceedings in China, and whether the shareholder resolution concerning the appointment of new directors and legal representatives during the judicial management proceedings was effective in China.[19]

The answer would have been simple if China had been equipped with any modern cooperative mechanisms on cross-border insolvency matters similar to the UNCITRAL Model Law[20] or European Insolvency Regulation. Yet in this case, the SPC did not examine whether the Singapore judgments could satisfy the requirements for recognition under the Enterprise Bankruptcy Law, which, according to Article 5, they clearly could not. As a matter of fact, the judicial manager had already tried to obtain a stay from the lower courts in Fujian Province of Chinese proceedings initiated by the subsidiary against the parent requesting the payment of the rest of capital increase, which ought to have been paid by the parent prior to its insolvency. The application was eventually rejected because the Singapore proceedings were held to 'have no legal effect without going through a formal recognition proceeding in China'.[21] The Supreme Court took an alternative approach and relied on the traditional principles of private international law. Rather than resorting to Article 5 of the Chinese Enterprise Bankruptcy Law, it cited Article 14 of the Application Law, which stipulates that the internal affairs of a legal person and its branches shall be governed by the law of the place where such entity is registered.[22] The Court then decided that the civil rights and capacity of the judicial manager and liquidator of the parent should be governed by the law of Singapore, where it was registered. Although the Court did not specify its reason for characterising the power of the bankruptcy administrator as the internal affairs of the company, it seems that the bankruptcy administrator was deemed to be an internal organisation of the company, and thus fell within the scope of Article 14 of the Application Law. Consequently, the Court confirmed the validity of the liquidator's representative's power based on Sections 227G(2) and 272(2)(a) of the Companies Act of Singapore. The shareholder resolution of the Chinese subsidiary made by the judicial manager was confirmed as effective by similar logic. First, the Court held that since the subsidiary was a wholly-foreign-owned company incorporated in China, its appointment of directors and legal representative should be governed by Chinese law and thus be determined by its sole shareholder ie the Singapore parent. The Court then decided that the issue of which entity would be eligible to make the decision for the parent,

[19] ibid.

[20] UNCITRAL Model Law on Cross-Border Insolvency (United Nations, New York 1997).

[21] *Sino-Environment* (n 3).

[22] However, if the place of registration is different from the place where the legal person's principal business is located, the internal affairs may be governed by the law of the place of principal business. See Art 14 of The Law of the People's Republic of China on Choice of Law for Foreign-related Civil Relationships, adopted at the Seventeenth Session of the Eleventh Standing Committee of the National People's Congress of the People's Republic of China on 28 October 2010, and took effect on 1 April 2011.

as an internal affair of the company, should also be determined by Singapore law. Singapore law provided that a judicial manager can exercise all the powers and duties of the bankrupt debtor's directors, including, among others, removing the board members and management of the debtor's wholly-owned-subsidiaries.[23]

In *Sino-environment*, the judicial managers were permitted to represent the debtor in pending lawsuits, remove uncooperative board members and management of the debtor's solvent subsidiaries in China, and take control of the subsidiary's assets by appointing new board members, after the SPC confirmed that the managers were empowered to do so under Sections 227G(2) and 272(2)(a) of the Singapore Companies Act, that is, the law of the debtor's domicile.[24] Here, what was recognised was the managers' representative power which, theoretically, should be wide enough to encompass the power to carry out any activities that can be conducted by the bankrupt debtor.[25] However, it is unlikely that some types of typical relief under bankruptcy law, such as a stay of proceedings, avoidance of fraudulent trading, and unfair preference could be granted by resorting to this bypass, because there is no way for them to be deemed to be the 'internal affairs' of the debtor company.[26] Additionally, it must be noted that here the jurisdictional ground of the commencement of the foreign bankruptcy proceeding was crucial. The foreign proceedings must be initiated in the debtor's place of incorporation or the place of principal business where the latter is not in the place of incorporation, so that the *lex fori concursus* can be applied as the personal law of the debtor.

ii. Asia Steel: *The Limitation of the Bypass*

The bypass, which was invested with much hope as a breakthrough in Chinese cross-border insolvency law,[27] was soon proved to be fragile and unstable in the saga of *China Metal Recycling Group*, the notorious metal recycler 'giant' based in mainland China, which turned out to involve a massive accounting fraud 'on an industrial scale.'[28] The holding company of the group, China Metal Recycling (Holdings) Ltd, which was listed on the Main Board of the Stock Exchange of Hong Kong Ltd, was eventually delisted and wound up on public interest grounds by the Hong Kong High Court.[29] Prior to the winding up, however, the provisional liquidators ('PLs')

[23] According to SET Group's attorney's arguments during the investigation process of the court trial, the directors and legal representative of TET Group should be appointed by its shareholder as stipulated in TET Group's bylaw. See the video recording of the hearing of *TETG* from 1:16:01-1:16:39 (file with author).

[24] See *Sino-Environment* (n 3). For a detailed discussion of the case, see Tu and Li, 'The Chinese Approach' (n 7).

[25] See Tu and Li, 'The Chinese Approach' (n 7) 64–65. For example, in Hong Kong, even without going through a formal recognition procedure, foreign liquidators appointed in the debtor's place of incorporation are allowed to request local entities such as banks and accountants to provide information as long as these entities would have complied with such request had it come from the board of directors of the debtor. See *Re A Company* (n 4); *Bay Capital Asia Fund, LP (In Official Liquidation) v DBS Bank (Hong Kong) Ltd* [2016] HKEC 2377. See also Tu and Li, 'The Second Amendment' (n 13) 34–39.

[26] Tu and Li, 'The Chinese Approach' (n 7) 65–66.

[27] ibid (describing the bypass as a 'progressive step forward'). In fact, the SPC was so confident of the social effect to be produced by the judgment, that for the first time in history, it invited foreign diplomats and reporters to attend the hearing and broadcasted live the trial online. See 'The Supreme People's Court Invited Foreign Diplomats to Attend Its Court Trial for the First Time: A Case of Appeal Concerning Capital Contribution by Foreign Shareholder was instantly adjudged in the Court (12 June 2014) www.chinacourt.org/article/detail/2014/06/id/1313736.shtml accessed 3 June 2014. *Sino-environment* was also selected as one of the representative cases demonstrating the services and guarantee provided by the peoples' court for the BRI Construction. See Typical Cases Providing Judiciary Service and Guarantee for the 'Belt and Road' Construction (Supreme People's Court, 7 July 2015).

[28] In *re China Metal Recycling (Holdings) Ltd* [2015] 2 HKLRD 415 (HC) [81].

[29] ibid.

attempted to achieve the voluntary cooperation of the Chinese subsidiaries, but eventually failed. They then resorted to the bypass established in *Sino-Environment*, and exercised their power as provisional liquidators, appointing themselves as the directors and legal representatives of these subsidiaries through shareholder resolutions of the mainland based subsidiaries.[30] However, the local governments where the companies were registered refused to change the registered information without receiving the subsidiaries' business licences and seals, which were kept by the senior management and were meant to be replaced by the PLs. The PLs immediately initiated a series of court proceedings where the subsidiaries were registered, seeking an order to compel the change of registration information and handing over of the business licences and company seals, so that they could take control of the subsidiaries.[31]

The SPC's decision in *Sino-environment* was well observed by the lower courts. In all four cases, the effectiveness of the shareholder resolution was confirmed, and the management were held to have an obligation to cooperate with the PLs. However, the PLs experienced unreasonably long court procedures, which ultimately made the enforcement of the favourable judgments impossible. For example, in the proceedings initiated for Zhongshan Asia Copper Metal Material Ltd, the management objected to the jurisdiction of Zhongshan Intermediate People's Court, and then appealed the decision dismissing their objection.[32] A hearing on substantive matters was not held until eight months after the PLs submitted their petition. It then took 18 months more for the Court to deliver a judgment. By then, a local reorganisation proceeding against this subsidiary was already completed before the same court and the Hong Kong parent company was no longer the shareholder according to the reorganisation plan.[33] Therefore the judgment confirming the effectiveness of the shareholder resolution was rendered nugatory. In another case for a Zhenjiang subsidiary, three years lapsed before the appeal process was finally completed. Similarly, a local reorganisation was completed by then, and the Hong Kong parent was held to 'have no legal basis to claim a shareholder's right' because it had lost its equity in the subsidiary during the reorganisation.[34] The situation should largely be the same if the assets and operations that the foreign representatives sought to take over were directly held by the debtor, rather than through a locally incorporated subsidiary. Here the appeal system and procedure concerning jurisdiction disputes were legally used, but in bad faith. Recognition delayed was recognition denied. It is obvious that the bypass cannot guarantee the timely and effective protection of the bankruptcy assets from the hands of creditors and debtors. However, in the absence of a modern cross-border insolvency law which would grant direct access to foreign representatives and standardised and expedited recognition and relief to foreign proceedings, the choice-of-law rule concerning internal affairs of legal persons could at least solve part of the problems.

[30] ibid [31].

[31] *Asia Steel (Investment) Co Ltd v Zhongshan Asia Copper Metal and Material Co Ltd* [2013] Zhong Zhong Fa Min Si Chu Zi No 15, [2016] Yue Min Zhong No 693, [2017] Yue 20 Min Chu No 17; *Asia Steel (Development) Co Ltd v Guangzhou Asia Copper Metal Co Ltd and Others* [2013] Sui Huang Fa Min Er Chu Zi No. 589, [2015] Sui Zhong Fa Min Si Zhong Zi No. 89; *Asia Steel (Hong Kong) Co Ltd v Guangzhou Asia Steel Metal Co Ltd and Others* [2015] Sui Zhong Fa Min Si Zhong Zi No 90; *Asia Steel (Investment) Co Ltd v Yangzhong Asia Steel Metal Co Ltd* [2013] Zhen Shang Wai Chu Zi No 13, [2015] Su Shang Wai Zhong Zi No 00048; *Asia Steel (Development) Co Ltd v Wuhan Asia Steel Metal Co Ltd* [2013] E Wuhan Zhong Minshang Wai Chu Zi No 00025, [2016] E 01 Min Chu No 6419.

[32] See *Asia Steel (Investment) Co Ltd v Zhongshan Asia Copper Metal and Material Co Ltd* (n 31).

[33] ibid.

[34] See *Asia Steel (Investment) Co Ltd v Yangzhong Asia Steel Metal Co Ltd* (n 31).

II. Choice of Law in Insolvency Cases

A. The Arising of Choice of Law Issues in Insolvency

Early works regarding cross-border insolvency law focused purely on choice of forum and did not place much emphasis on the issue of choice of law.[35] It seems to have been a common assumption for most scholars at that time that *lex fori concursus*, ie law of the jurisdiction in which insolvency proceedings are commenced, should govern all, or at least the most essential aspects, of insolvency proceedings.[36] This is partly due to the traditional view that insolvency law is purely procedural law.[37] The general principle in private international law is that the *lex causae* or *lex situs* determines substantive laws which govern the creation, contents, and termination of rights and duties, while procedural laws, which determine the implementation of such rights and duties, are determined by *lex fori*.[38] For this reason, courts used to apply local law to insolvency cases, because it is self-evident that a court should always apply its own procedural law.[39] Today, insolvency laws are no longer considered to be purely procedural. One typical illustration is the commonly seen substantial alteration of secured claims. With the rise of reorganisation as a preferable solution to debtor's default, and increased awareness of the need to protect the going concern value of a business as a whole, secured creditors' claims are often subject to suspension, or derogation in other forms.[40]

Another similarly convincing explanation is that insolvency law – especially those substantive rules concerning 'avoidance, set off, and priority and ranking of claims'[41] – serves as a type of 'meta-law' that 'swoops in and trumps baseline legal relationships in cases where the debtor commits general default on its financial obligations' and usually reflects local policy and legal culture.[42] It might be much easier to persuade jurisdictions having similar insolvency laws to apply each other's laws since the 'outcome difference' brought about by this recognition may be relatively insignificant.[43] However, some countries may object to these differences even where

[35] See JL Westbrook, 'The Lessons of Maxwell Communication' (1996) 64 *Fordham Law Review* 2531, 2533–35; LM LoPucki, *Courting Failure* (University of Michigan Press, 2005) 232; JL Westbrook, 'Locating the Eye of the Financial Storm' (2007) 32 *Brooklyn Journal of International Law* 1019.

[36] ibid.

[37] It had been argued that bankruptcy law was merely a procedure for giving effect to entitlements that are granted under non-bankruptcy laws. See, eg, J Baird, 'A World Without Bankruptcy' (1987) 50 *Law & Contemporary Problems* 173; CW Mooney, Jr., 'A Normative Theory of Bankruptcy Law: Bankruptcy As (Is) Civil Procedure' (2004) 61 *Washington & Lee Law Review* 931.

[38] See generally, E Spiro, 'Forum Regit Processum (Procedure Is Governed by the Lex Fori)' (1969) 18 *The International and Comparative Law Quarterly* 949. See also R Garnett, *Substance and procedure in private international law* (Oxford University Press, 2012) 2.01–2.03.

[39] EJ Janger, 'Silos: Establishing the Distributional Baseline in Cross-Border Bankruptcies' (2014) 9 *Brooklyn Journal of Corporate, Financial & Commercial Law* 180, 185.

[40] UNCITRAL Legislative Guide on Insolvency Law, Parts I-II (United Nations 2005) 207 (UNCITRAL Legislative Guide); EJ Janger, 'Virtual Territoriality' (2010) 48 *Columbia Journal of Transnational Law* 401, 413.

[41] ibid.

[42] See JAE Pottow, 'Greed and Pride in International Bankruptcy: The Problems of and Proposed Solutions to 'Local Interests' (2006) 8 *Michigan Law Review* 1899, 1902; F Tung, 'Fear of Commitment in International Bankruptcy' (2001) 33 *The George Washington International Law Review* 555, 559.

[43] JL Westbrook, 'Theory and Pragmatism in Global Insolvencies: Choice of Law and Choice of Forum' (1991) 65 *American Bankruptcy Law Journal* 457, 467, 468 (illustrating a hypothetical cross-border insolvency case between the UK and one of its former colonies having similar insolvency laws) (Westbrook, 'Theory and Pragmatism'). A reduced outcome difference may also occur where a unified set of choice of law rules is accepted by the jurisdictions involved. See Janger, 'Virtual Territoriality' (n 40); J Pottow, 'Beyond Carve-outs and Toward Reliance: A Normative Framework for Cross-Border Insolvency Choice of Law' (2014) 9 *Brooklyn Journal of Corporate, Financial, and Commercial Law* 197.

there is only minimal divergence in details.[44] It is thus understandable that many jurisdictions refuse to apply foreign substantive insolvency law.[45] Nevertheless, the fear of outcome difference might be exaggerated by legislators. Universalists argue that the legal certainty brought about by a set of unified and predictable laws, and the rough balance of benefits and losses for local creditors in the long term, could justify the differences in outcome in individual cases caused by the application of foreign laws.[46]

The reluctance to apply foreign law in insolvency proceedings is compounded by the sovereign concerns of legislators. Historically, the court's insolvency jurisdiction was territorially based on a state's *in rem* control over assets within its borders.[47] Courts adhered to the 'Grab Rule' and would normally apply *lex fori concursus* to the assets that had been 'grabbed'.[48] Against this background, it was unnecessary to apply foreign law in bankruptcy proceedings. Local procedures controlled without regard to any reasoned choice of law analysis.[49] Choice-of-law only became an important issue in cross-border insolvency law with the globalisation of business and investment and the emergence of the theory of universalism which, in its pure form, requires the application of the law of the debtor's home state with respect to all of the debtor's interests and all of its assets, wherever they are located.[50] While universalism is obviously too ideal to be implemented in practice,[51] a concept of modified universalism has been adopted in modern cross-border insolvency instruments governed by the UNCITRAL Model Law and the European Insolvency Regulation. Modified Universalism accepts the central premise of universalism and yet is qualified by pragmatic exceptions.[52] In particular, it allows the law of the states where the debtors' overseas assets are located to govern the administration and distribution of these assets to protect creditor's expectations and to limit the differences in outcome caused by deference to the main proceeding to an acceptable extent.[53]

B. Complexity of Choice of Law Rules in Insolvency Cases

Our discussion of choice-of-law rules in insolvency cases will start with a hypothetical scenario that demonstrates the complexity of the issue. The debtor, A, is a multinational company incorporated in state U. Insolvency proceedings against A are commenced in state V, where A's real

[44] For instance, *Singularis* involves the divergence of liquidator's powers between Bermuda and Cayman Island, both of which are essentially based on and deeply influenced by English insolvency law.

[45] Scholars considered the holding in *Singularis* implied a denial of future possibility of applying foreign law. See, eg, G McCormack and A Hargovan, 'Australia and the International Insolvency Paradigm' (2015) 37 *Sydney Law Review* 389, 402.

[46] Westbrook, 'Theory and Pragmatism' (n 43) 464–466.

[47] Even today, the 'grab rule' still governs in a considerable number of jurisdictions in the world. See, eg, J Greene, 'Bankruptcy Beyond Borders: Recognizing Foreign Proceedings in Cross-Border Insolvencies' (2005) 30 *Brooklyn Journal of International Law* 685, 704–05.

[48] See AL Gropper, 'The Curious Disappearance of Choice of Law as an Issue in Chapter 15 Cases' (2014) 9 *Brooklyn Journal of Corporate, Financial & Commercial Law* 152, 154.

[49] Westbrook, 'Theory and Pragmatism' (n 43) 460.

[50] See generally, L LoPucki, 'Cooperation in International Bankruptcy: 'A Post-Universalist Approach' (1999) 84 *Cornell Law Review* 696 (LoPucki, 'Cooperation in International Bankruptcy'); JL Westbrook, 'A Global Solution to Multinational Default' (2000) 98 *Michigan Law Review* 2276; A Guzman, 'International Insolvency: 'In Defense of Universalism' (2000) 98 *Michigan Law Review* 2177.

[51] See, eg, LoPucki, 'Cooperation in International Bankruptcy' (n 50); F Tung, 'Fear of Commitment in International Bankruptcy' (2001) 33 *The George Washington International Law Review* 555.

[52] For the different features of universalism and its contra-theory, territorialism, and their respective variations ie modified universalism and cooperative territorialism, see ibid.

[53] ibid.

seat is located. One creditor, B, a multinational company incorporated in state X, enters into a contract with A to secure a loan granted by B shortly before B files for bankruptcy. The original loan agreement and the subsequent guarantee are both governed by the law of state X, the home state of B. This is a typical scenario where an unfair preference is suspected. The routine questions to be answered for the purpose of determining the establishment and ranking of the creditor's claims are as follows. (1) Is the original loan agreement effective or not (ie the existence of the creditor's claim)? (2) Does the subsequent transaction constitute an preferential payment or make A a secured creditor? (3) Is the relevant transaction avoidable or not? Each question needs to undergo a choice-of-law analysis. For each question, legislators may choose among: the law of the debtor's home state, ie, where the debtor possesses its real seat or statutory seat; *lex fori concursus*, ie, the law of the insolvency forum; the law applicable to each of transactions calculated according to ordinary choice of law rules, ie either *lex situs* or the law chosen by parties. Under some circumstances, notably where avoidance is involved, some states may even choose a more complex approach, such as deeming the transaction avoidable as long as it is avoidable under either of the aforesaid laws, or only if it is avoidable under two or more of the aforesaid laws.[54]

The reality, which may involve hundreds of transactions and claims in one insolvency proceeding, is usually even more complex than the hypothetical scenario. As summarised by Fletcher, choice-of-law rules may have a direct influence on numerous aspects of insolvency law, including but not limited to:

a. The effect of the insolvency proceedings upon current contracts to which the debtor is a party and the validity of any claims arising out of such contracts;
b. the question of the avoidance law to be applied in relation to antecedent transactions entered into with the debtor;
c. the impact upon any type of security, or quasi-security, arrangement of which the creditor seeks to avail himself; and
d. the availability of any right of set-off in the case of any creditor who is also a debtor to the insolvent entity.[55]

States may diverge significantly with regard to both the relevant substantive laws and the choice-of-law rules that clarify the governing law of these issues. To increase certainty and reduce complexity regarding the applicable laws, various innovations have appeared, mainly through a process of unification and harmonisation.

C. Classification

i. Insolvency Law verses Non-Insolvency Law: Delimiting the Scope

As illustrated by the hypothetical case, both insolvency law and non-insolvency law will be applied in insolvency proceedings. As a result, in each cross-border insolvency case, the court must perform a choice-of-law analysis and determine whether the issue falls in or out of the realm of insolvency law.[56] Generally speaking, laws creating rights or claims against the debtor,

[54] See JL Westbrook, 'Choice of Avoidance Law in Global Insolvencies' (1991) 17 *Brooklyn Journal of International Law* 499, 513–14 (listing five options for choice of avoidance laws for American courts).

[55] Fletcher, *Insolvency* (n 1) 89.

[56] JL Westbrook, 'Universalism and Choice of Law' (2005) 23 *Penn State International Law Review* 625, 626; JL Westbrook, 'Avoidance of Pre-Bankruptcy Transactions in Multinational Bankruptcy Cases' (2007) 42 *Texas International Law Journal* 899, 900; JL Westbrook, 'A Comment to Universal Proceduralism' (2009-2010) 48 *Columbia Journal of Transnational Law* 503, 508.

such as civil, commercial, or public laws, are classified as non-insolvency law.[57] Non-insolvency laws govern the validity and value of the relevant right and associated legal claim and should be decided by applying the common choice-of-law rules of the forum.[58] By contrast, the role of insolvency law is to determine the effect of insolvency proceedings upon the rights and claims of creditors and insolvent debtors, and confirm, restrict or modify them where appropriate.[59] For example, in Question 1 of the hypothetical scenario (section II.B), the existence of the creditor's claim is a non-insolvency issue governed by contract law. Questions 2 and 3 are insolvency issues governed by the avoidance rules and priority rules. Again, presuming that A has breached a contract with a second claimant, C, the court must decide upon non-insolvency issues such as whether the contract was breached and the availability and quantification of damages, and insolvency issues such as the amount of the distribution B may receive in the bankruptcy proceedings of A.[60] If a third claimant, D, filed a tort claim against A, the court would have to decide upon non-insolvency issues such as whether or not A's act or omission has given rise to a right of action or civil liability for tort and the extent of the remedy, and insolvency issues such as the amount of the distribution D may receive in the insolvency proceeding of A. In both cases, the choice of the non-insolvency laws is normally decided by applying ordinary choice-of-law rules. For the contract claim, it may be *lex domicilii, lex loci contractus*, or the law chosen by the parties. For the tort claim, it may be the *lex loci delicti* or the law of the place, which has the most significant relationship with the occurrence and the parties. The question to be solved in cross-border insolvency law is to find the appropriate applicable law for the distributional priority of the claims.

This chapter deals only with the applicable laws for insolvency issues. Choice of laws rules concerning non-insolvency issues – which are often unavoidable in insolvency proceedings – are discussed in other chapters of this book.

ii. Procedural verses Substantive: Potentially Greater Diversity Caused by Inconsistent Classification

Courts do not hesitate to apply their own procedural laws.[61] Therefore, the application of foreign law only becomes an option where the issue before the court is classified as a substantive matter. The distinction between procedural and substantive insolvency law is one major aspect where states diverge considerably. According to Fletcher, the lack of a standardised approach to the classification of legal rules into these two broad categories generated a 'fresh wave of diversity'.[62] Fletcher suggested that procedural rules governed by *lex fori concursus* should include steps taken to commence insolvency proceedings by the presentation of a petition, the conduct of hearings, meetings, processing of claims, and the declaration and payment of dividends to creditors. Some vital issues such as the types of claims that qualify as provable debts and the ranking of different types of debt in terms of priority of payment are also deemed to be procedural laws in some states. Substantive insolvency laws include the above-mentioned rules that may have significant effects upon the outcome of the insolvency proceeding, including rules concerning avoidance, security, contract, and set-off.[63]

[57] UNCITRAL Legislative Guide (n 40) 68.
[58] ibid, 69.
[59] ibid.
[60] A similar example was given in Westbrook, 'A Comment on Universal Proceduralism' (n 56) 508.
[61] See text to nn 42–43.
[62] Fletcher, *Insolvency* (n 1) 87.
[63] ibid, 88.

iii. Substantive Insolvency Law

There are basically two options available for choosing substantive insolvency laws. They can be governed by *lex fori concursus* for the purpose of simplifying the choice-of-law process and enhancing the efficiency of insolvency administration. They can also be governed by the applicable law expected by local creditors according to ordinary choice-of-law rules and principles.

iv. Lex Fori Concursus: *The Ideal and (Probably) Future Trend*

Advocates of universalism, led by Westbrook, insist that the *lex fori concursus* of the main proceeding should ideally govern all the issues arising out of a cross-border insolvency case, wherever the debtor's assets are located.[64] Westbrook suggests that, in addition to procedural rules, the law of the main forum should decide the 'big four' substantive issues that are directly linked to local policies: (a) control; (b) liquidation or reorganisation of the debtor; (c) distribution of benefits, mainly focusing on priority rules; and (d) avoidance of transactions.[65] In modern times, cross-border insolvency mechanisms adopting modified universalism declare the universal effect of main insolvency proceedings opened against debtors that have centres of main interests in their territory. The UNCITRAL Legislative Guide on Insolvency Law expressly stipulates, at Part Two, Section I-C, that insolvency effects, ie, the limits and restrictions imposed by insolvency proceeding upon the rights and claims established based on applicable laws of other fields, are typically governed by *lex fori concursus*.[66] According to the Legislative Guide, *lex fori concursus* will generally govern: 'the commencement, conduct, administration and conclusion of those proceedings'.[67] A list given in Recommendation 31 of the Guide includes virtually all matters that could be governed by *lex fori concursus*.[68] So far, the European Insolvency Regulation is the only legislative work in force that addresses choice-of-law issues in cross-border insolvencies. As a typical representation of the modified universalist approach, the choice of law is closely tied to the choice of forum.[69] Subject to a few exceptions, the law applicable to insolvency proceedings and their effects shall be *lex fori concursus*.[70] The *lex fori concursus* shall determine the conditions for the opening of those proceedings, their conduct, and their closure, both procedural

[64] See, eg, Westbrook, 'Theory and Pragmatism' (n 43) 460. Also see Westbrook, 'Locating the Eye' (n 35) 1019.

[65] ibid.

[66] UNCITRAL Legislative Guide (n 40) 68–69.

[67] ibid.

[68] See Recommendation 31: '(a) Identification of the debtors that may be subject to insolvency proceedings; (b) Determination of when insolvency proceedings can be commenced and the type of proceeding that can be commenced, the party that can apply for commencement and whether the commencement criteria should differ depending upon the party applying for commencement; (c) Constitution and scope of the insolvency estate; (d) Protection and preservation of the insolvency estate; (e) Use or disposal of assets; (f) Proposal, approval, confirmation and implementation of a plan of reorganisation; (g) Avoidance of certain transactions that could be prejudicial to certain parties; (h) Treatment of contracts; (i) Set-off; (j) Treatment of secured creditors; (k) Rights and obligations of the debtor; (l) Duties and functions of the insolvency representative; (m) Functions of the creditors and creditor committee; (n) Treatment of claims; (o) Ranking of claims; (p) Costs and expenses relating to the insolvency proceedings; (q) Distribution of proceeds; (r) Conclusion of the proceedings; and (s) Discharge.' See UNCITRAL Legislative Guide (n 40) 73.

[69] Arts 4–15 of Council Regulation (EC) 1346/2000 of 29 May 2000 on insolvency proceedings (EIR 2000); Arts 7–18 of Regulation (EU) 2015/848 of the European Parliament and of the Council of 20 May 2015 on Insolvency Proceedings (EIR Recast).

[70] Art 4 of EIR 2000; Art 7 of EIR Recast (n 69).

and substantive.[71] Similar clauses can also be found in the ALI Global Rules on Conflict-of-Laws Matters in International Insolvency Cases ('ALI Global Rules').[72]

v. Ordinary Choice of Law Analysis: The Reality

Other legislation allows exceptions to be made to the application of *lex fori concursus*, especially with regard to substantive insolvency laws. In the US, for instance, the choice of law in bankruptcy cases has followed the 'Centre of Gravity'[73] or 'interest analysis'[74] approach. Both approaches require the application of the law of the jurisdiction with the most substantial interest in the matter in dispute.[75] A pre-insolvency transaction is avoidable if it is voidable under the avoidance law *that is applicable under given circumstances* by a creditor holding an unsecured claim.[76] In France, avoidable transactions are governed by *lex fori concursus*, and yet the conditions for the existence and maintenance of a security granted in favour of a creditor over immovable and over property collected or realised in another country is governed by *lex situs*.[77] Even these adoptions of universalism leave room to apply *lex situs* or *lex causae* as exceptions to the routine application of *lex fori concursus*. For example, the UNCITRAL Legislative Guide specifies two exceptions to the application of *lex fori concursus*: the rights and obligations of the participants in a payment or settlement system or in a regulated financial market (governed solely by the law applicable to

[71] These matters include: (a) the debtors against which insolvency proceedings may be brought on account of their capacity; (b) the assets which form part of the insolvency estate and the treatment of assets acquired by or devolving on the debtor after the opening of the insolvency proceedings; (c) the respective powers of the debtor and the insolvency practitioner; (d) the conditions under which set-offs may be invoked; (e) the effects of insolvency proceedings on current contracts to which the debtor is party; (f) the effects of the insolvency proceedings on proceedings brought by individual creditors, with the exception of pending lawsuits; (g) the claims which are to be lodged against the debtor's insolvency estate and the treatment of claims arising after the opening of insolvency proceedings; (h) the rules governing the lodging, verification and admission of claims; (i) the rules governing the distribution of proceeds from the realisation of assets, the ranking of claims and the rights of creditors who have obtained partial satisfaction after the opening of insolvency proceedings by virtue of a right *in rem* or through a set-off; (j) the conditions for, and the effects of closure of, insolvency proceedings, in particular by composition; (k) creditors' rights after the closure of insolvency proceedings; (l) who is to bear the costs and expenses incurred in the insolvency proceedings; (m) the rules relating to the voidness, voidability or unenforceability of legal acts detrimental to the general body of creditors. See Art 4(2) of EIR 2000; Art 7(2) of EIR Recast (n 69).

[72] See Rule 12 of Global Rules on Conflict-of-Laws Matters in International Insolvency Cases, in *Transnational Insolvency: Global Principles for Cooperation in International Insolvency Cases*, reported by Ian Fletcher and Bob Wessels (The American Law Institute, 2012):

> '12.1. Save as otherwise provided in [this Act/these Rules], the law applicable to insolvency proceedings and their effects shall be that of the state within the territory of which such proceedings are opened, hereafter referred to as 'the state of the opening of proceedings.
>
> 12.2. The law of the state of the opening of proceedings shall determine the conditions for the opening of those proceedings, their conduct, administration, conversion, and their closure.'

[73] See, eg, *re Int'l Admin. Servs Inc* 211 B.R. 88, 95 (Bankr. M.D. Fla. 1997). Nevertheless, the most well-known example of the Center of Gravity approach might be *Maxwell Commc'n Corp v Barclays Bank plc* 170 B.R (Bankr. S.D.N.Y. 1994) (hereinafter, '*in re Maxwell Commc'n Corp plc*'), in which the US courts almost held in consensus that the UK laws should govern in deciding some disputes related to avoidance in the US proceeding, because the UK has a much closer connection with these disputes than the US does. Consequently, the US proceeding was dismissed.

[74] One example is *re Koreag, Controle et Revision S.A.*, 961 F.2d 341 (2d Cir. 1992).

[75] See, eg, in *Hong Kong and Shanghai Banking Corp Ltd v Simon*, the court concluded: 'In most cases, the court will defer to where the 'center of gravity' of multiple proceedings exists, if one can be ascertained.' *Hong Kong and Shanghai Banking Corp Ltd v Simon*, 153 F.3d 991 (9th Cir. 1998); in *re Maxwell*, Chief Judge Brozman found that 'the traditional federal choice-of-law rule is to apply the law of the jurisdiction having the greatest interest in the controversy … The court is required to evaluate all of the various contacts each jurisdiction has with the controversy in terms of their relative importance with respect to a particular issue and make a reasoned determination as to which jurisdiction's laws and policies are implicated to the greatest extent.' *Re Maxwell Commc'n Corp plc* 170 B.R at 816 (Bankr. S.D.N.Y. 1994).

[76] Fletcher, *Insolvency* (n 1) 100.

[77] ibid.

that system or market),[78] and the rejection, continuation, and modification of labour contracts (governed by the law applicable to the contract).[79] In order to increase certainty and diminish commercial risk, the Legislative Guide also suggests that rights *in rem* (governed by the law applicable to security interests)[80] and avoidance provisions (the law governing the transaction, or its combination with *lex fori concursus*)[81] may also be excluded from the applicable scope of *lex fori concursus*.

Similarly, while some substantive issues such as distribution and avoidance rules are governed by *lex fori concursus* under the EIR, the EIR also makes considerable concessions and contains special choice-of-law rules concerning third parties' rights *in rem* (governed by *lex situs*),[82] payment systems and financial markets (governed solely be the law of the state applicable to the system or market),[83] contracts of employment (governed by the law of the state applicable to the contract of employment),[84] as well as set-off (governed by the law applicable to the insolvent debtor's claim),[85] reservation of title (governed by *lex situs* at the time of the opening of the insolvency proceeding),[86] contracts relating to immoveable property (governed by *lex situs*)[87] and to rights subject to registration (governed by the law of the state under the authority of which the register is kept),[88] community patents and trademarks (probably the *lex fori concursus*),[89] detrimental acts (applicable law of the act),[90] protection of third-party purchasers (*lex situs* of the immoveable, or the law of the state where the register is kept),[91] and the effects of insolvency proceedings on pending lawsuits (governed solely by the law of the Member State in which that lawsuit is pending or in which the arbitral tribunal has its seat).[92] The ALI Global Rules adopt a similar list and specify special choice of law rules for rights of secured creditors (*lex situs*),[93] set-off (law applicable to the claim),[94] labour contracts (law of the state applicable to the contract of employment),[95] and defences to avoidance (applicable law of the act).[96]

Choice-of-law rules in Chinese insolvency cases are severely under-developed compared with the European Union and the enacting states of the UNCITRAL Model Law. The only legislative authority relating to choice-of-law issues in insolvency is Article 14 of the Application Law, as discussed in section I.B. Other legislation on insolvency is silent on choice-of-law issues, for example in local insolvency proceedings opened under the Enterprise Bankruptcy Law, or

[78] See Recommendation 32, UNCITRAL Legislative Guide (n 40) 74. EIR has the similar exception with regard to payment systems and financial markets. See Art 9 of EIR 2000 (n 69).

[79] See Recommendation 33, UNCITRAL Legislative Guide (n 40) 74.

[80] UNCITRAL Legislative Guide (n 40) 71.

[81] ibid.

[82] Art 5 of EIR 2000; Art 8 of EIR Recast (n 69).

[83] Art 9 of EIR 2000; Art 12 of EIR Recast (n 69).

[84] Art 10 of EIR 2000; Art 13 of EIR Recast (n 69).

[85] Art 6 of EIR 2000; Art 9 of EIR Recast (n 69).

[86] Art 7 of EIR 2000; Art 10 of EIR Recast (n 69).

[87] Art 8 of EIR 2000; Art 11 of EIR Recast (n 69).

[88] Art 11 of EIR 2000; Art 14 of EIR Recast (n 69).

[89] Art 12 of EIR 2000; Art 15 of EIR Recast (n 69). See also 'The Protection of Intellectual Property Rights in Insolvency Proceedings INSOL International – Special Report (November 2017)', presented by Richard Chesley, Oksana Rosaluk, and Joe Riches, at 10 <available at: www.insol.org/_files/TechnicalSeries/Special%20Reports/Protection%20of%20Intellectual%20Property%20Rights%20-%208%20November%202017.pdf accessed 5 August 2018.

[90] Art 13 of EIR 2000; Art 16 of EIR Recast (n 69).

[91] Art 14 of EIR 2000; Art 17 of EIR Recast (n 69).

[92] Art 15 of EIR 2000; Art 18 of EIR Recast (n 69).

[93] Rules 15–16 of ALI Global Rules (n 72).

[94] Rules 17–18 of ALI Global Rules (n 72).

[95] Rules 20–21 of ALI Global Rules (n 72).

[96] Rules 22–23 of ALI Global Rules (n 72).

ancillary proceedings opened under Article 5 of Enterprise Bankruptcy Law for the purposes of recognising and enforcing a foreign insolvency judgment. However, a somewhat related provision is Article 50 of the Minutes of the National Courts' Meeting on Bankruptcy Adjudication, which stipulates that local assets of the foreign debtor must be used to satisfy local secured and priority claims before being turned over to the foreign insolvency representatives, and be distributed according to the decision of the foreign court.[97] Accordingly, Chinese courts might indirectly apply the foreign insolvency law that was applied by the foreign court in reaching its decision.

D. Effect of Insolvency on Assignments of Property

Insolvency proceedings are collective, court-supervised proceedings having expansive reach.[98] To ensure their efficiency, specific powers are usually entrusted to insolvency practitioners (liquidators, bankruptcy administrators, insolvency representatives, judicial managers, trustees, etc) who generally have more specific knowledge and experience to administer insolvency proceedings.[99] Where an insolvency representative is appointed, a general assignment for the benefit of creditors will be made, which vests the representative with powers to manage and dispose of the debtor's assets, act on behalf of the debtor, and conduct investigation and preservation activities for the benefit of the creditors.[100] There are two typical choice-of-law scenarios in this aspect. The first, as called by LoPucki, is the agency problem. Jurisdictions may diverge in their recognition of the entity that is eligible to control the insolvency process.[101] Some jurisdictions adopt a creditor-friendly regime by giving creditors and their representatives more control than the debtor over insolvency proceedings.[102] Some others adopt a debtor-friendly regime by granting debtors the power to control the insolvency process under certain circumstances.[103] Others seek to strike a balance.[104] Case placers, who are referred to as an alliance between incumbent management, lawyers, and bankers, are generally more attracted to the laws of jurisdictions that are willing to allow management to retain control of the bankruptcy proceeding.[105] LoPucki gives the example of domestic forum shopping within the US, where case placers demonstrate their preference for states willing to leave management in control of the bankruptcy case.[106]

The second scenario concerns the governing law of the scope of powers of the controlling entity of the insolvency proceeding – no matter whether it is a debtor in possession or an insolvency

[97] See Art 50 of Minutes of the National Courts' Meeting on Bankruptcy Adjudication [Fa (2018) 53]: 'Rights Protection and Interests Balancing in Cross-border Insolvency Cases. Cooperation should be carried out based on art 5 of Enterprise Bankruptcy Law. Upon recognizing a foreign judgment or decision, the residual assets of the debtor within the border of the People's Republic of China may be distributed according to the law of the foreign court, provided that local secured creditors, and local priority claims including employee credits, social insurance fees, and taxes are paid in full.'

[98] See Fletcher, *Insolvency* (n 1) 1.07–1.10; JL Westbrook, 'The Control of Wealth in Bankruptcy' (2004) 82 *Texas Law Review* 796, 821; Pottow, 'Greed and Pride' (n 42) 1902; JL Westbrook, C Booth, C Paulus, and H Rajak, *A Global View of Business Insolvency Systems* (Martinus Nijhoff Publishers, 2010) 74–78.

[99] See UNCITRAL Legislative Guide (n 40) 33–34, 174–187.

[100] ibid, 174–189. See also Westbrook et al, *A Global View of Business Insolvency Systems* (n 98) 74–78.

[101] LoPucki, *Courting Failure* (n 35) 221–226.

[102] For instance, the insolvency cases in the UK used to be administered for the benefit of the secured creditors until the enactment of the UK Enterprise Act 2002, which limits the power of secured creditors in insolvency. See V Finch, *Corporate Insolvency Law: Perspectives and Principles* (Cambridge University Press, 2012) 21.

[103] See, eg, insolvency proceedings could be administered by a debtor in possession in US. See 11 U.S.C. § 1106-07 (2018).

[104] UNCITRAL Legislative Guide (n 40) 15.

[105] LoPucki, *Courting Failure* (n 35) 225.

[106] ibid.

practitioner. Assume that the debtor goes into insolvency proceedings in its domicile, state A, and that all of the debtor's assets, local and global, were assigned to the insolvency practitioner in state B where the debtor possesses significant amount of assets. In these circumstances, should the court in state B turn over these assets to the liquidator? As early as the 1800s, English law had established the rule that the personal property of the bankruptcy debtor, wherever situated, passes to the assignee in bankruptcy, whether he/she is appointed in England or elsewhere.[107] Similarly, in continental Europe, it was common practice for courts to order payment or delivery of a foreign debtor's property to the assignee appointed in the bankruptcy proceedings opened in the debtor's domicile.[108] American courts provided a very different answer. For example, in *re Accounting of Waite*, the New York court ordered a turnover of funds from a US citizen to the British trustee who was appointed in London for a partnership in which the US citizen had been involved. Yet the court stated that the turnover was made only on the basis of international comity, 'and not as a concession that the assignment under which the assignees claim has under our laws any force or validity in this State'.[109]

Nowadays, the choice of appropriate law on the vesting effect of foreign insolvency proceeding seems to be the choice between universalism and territorialism. The historical approach, territorialism, suggests that insolvency administration should be based on the location of the debtor's assets. States adopting this approach generally do not assert any extraterritorial effects of insolvency proceedings commenced by its own courts and will not recognise the extraterritorial effect of proceedings in foreign states. As a result, foreign insolvency proceedings have no effect over local assets at all. The choice-of-law issue can only arise under systems adopting universalism or its modified versions. Universalism is the principle that insolvency proceedings opened in the home state of the debtor shall have 'universal' effect over all the assets and interests of the debtor wherever they are located.[110] Consequently, under an ideal universalism system, all the debtor's properties, local or foreign, pass to the insolvency representative appointed in the main proceedings. The law of the debtor's home state govern everything.[111] However, different versions of modified universalism may suggest different approaches to the determination of the laws applicable to the assignment of properties in insolvency proceedings. For example, under the EIR, the insolvency practitioner appointed in a main proceeding may exercise all the powers conferred on it by the law of the main forum in another Member State, as long as there is no other insolvency proceeding pending or contrasting preservation measure following a request for the opening of insolvency proceedings in that state.[112] Apparently, the *lex fori concursus* applies here.

In contrast, the UNCITRAL Model Law provides that courts should apply local law, ie the local statute enacting the Model Law. An enacting state is permitted to allow domestic courts to grant any appropriate relief that may be available to an insolvency representative appointed under

[107] S Williston, 'The Validity of Attachments Made Abroad by Creditors of an Insolvent Debtor' (1891) 5 *Harvard Law Review* 211, 211–213; HR Bailey, 'An Assignment in Insolvency, and Its Effect upon Property and Persons out of the State' (1893) 7 *Harvard Law Review* 281, 282.

[108] ibid.

[109] *Re Accounting of Waite*, 99 N.Y. (1885) 439, 448–450.

[110] See Westbrook, 'A Global Solution' (n 50) 2300; Westbrook, 'Theory and Pragmatism' (n 43); Guzman, 'International Bankruptcy' (n 50); IF Fletcher, 'Maintaining the Momentum: The Continuing Quest for Global Standards and Principles to Govern Cross-Border Insolvencies' (2007) 32 *Brooklyn Journal of International Law* 767; J Pottow, 'The Myth (and Realities) of Forum Shopping in Transnational Insolvency' (2007) 32 *Brooklyn Journal of International Law* 785; IF Fletcher and B Wessels, 'Shaping Rules for Cooperation in International Corporate Insolvency Cases through Dialogue' (2010) 7 *European Company Law* 149.

[111] SK Harding, 'Re Sefel Geophysical LTD: A Canadian Approach to Some Specific Problems in the Adjudication of International Insolvencies' (1990) 12 *Dalhousie Law Journal* 412, 419.

[112] Art 21(1) of EIR Recast (n 69).

local laws, whether the foreign proceeding is main or non-main.[113] The courts may, among other things, entrust the administration, realisation, or even the distribution of all or part of the debtor's assets to the foreign representative or another person, provided that the interests of local creditors are adequately protected.[114] At the same time, the rights to transfer, encumber, or otherwise dispose of any assets of the debtor are automatically suspended upon the recognition of a foreign main proceeding.[115] In addition, the extraterritorial effect of a foreign main proceeding can basically be blocked or weakened by the commencement of a local full insolvency proceeding.[116] Nevertheless, it is the local law incorporating the UNCITRAL Model Law that is applied here.

Chinese law does not contain any explicit provision specifying the effect of insolvency on assignments of property in local bankruptcy proceedings or in an ancillary proceeding initiated under Article 5. Article 5 of the Enterprise Bankruptcy Law stipulates that local *insolvency proceedings* commenced before Chinese courts shall have universal effects upon the bankruptcy assets, wherever they are located.[117] Yet the law is silent on what law applies to these assets. For ancillary proceedings, the Bankruptcy Minutes clarifies the effect of the recognition of a foreign judgment or court order, but requires that local assets be used to satisfy local secured and priority claims.[118] This is, essentially, the application of the law concerning the ranking of claims under the Enterprise Bankruptcy Law. Besides, choice-of-law issues concerning the assignment effect could also arise without invoking full or ancillary proceedings. It is also possible that recognition is not required if the assignment is deemed to be an internal affair of the debtor and thus governed by the law of the place where the debtor's domicile is located. It is possible that the insolvency effects upon the assignment of properties may be characterised as matters relating to properties and thus governed by the law where the properties are situated.[119] Yet it is also possible that the effect of the assignment is governed by the law of the forum, ie the Enterprise Bankruptcy Law.

E. Effect of Insolvency on the Discharge of Debts

The discharge of debts of legal persons only occurs in cases of reorganisation. This is because, in liquidation proceedings, the debtor will either be de-registered or become a shell after the closure of the proceedings and thus the discharge issue does not arise. Permitting the debtor to discharge debts and claims may ensure the success of the reorganisation and promote commercial certainty by giving binding effect to the reorganisation plan.[120] Discharge rules in different jurisdictions may vary, for example, with regard to the time that the discharge becomes effective[121] and with

[113] Art 21(1) of UNCITRAL Model Law.

[114] Art 21(2) of UNCITRAL Model Law.

[115] Art 20(1)(c) of UNCITRAL Model Law.

[116] See, eg, once a local proceeding is opened, all the reliefs, either mandatory or discretionary, should be made or modified or terminated to ensure that they are in consistence with the local proceeding. If there is already pending a local proceeding, the recognition of a foreign main proceeding does not even trigger the automatic reliefs under Art 20. See Art 29 (a)(i)(ii), (b)(i)(ii) of UNCITRAL Model Law.

[117] See Art 5 of EBL: 'A bankruptcy proceeding commenced under this law shall have effect upon the debtor's assets located outside of China ….'

[118] See Art 50 of Minutes of the National Courts' Meeting on Bankruptcy Adjudication [Fa (2018) 53]: 'Rights Protection and Interests Balancing in Cross-border Insolvency Cases. Cooperation should be carried out based on art 5 of Enterprise Bankruptcy Law. Upon recognizing a foreign judgment or decision, the residual assets of the debtor within the border of the People's Republic of China may be distributed according to the law of the foreign court, provided that local secured creditors, and local priority claims including employee credits, social insurance fees, and taxes are paid in full.'

[119] Arts 36–40 of the Application Law.

[120] UNCITRAL Legislative Guide (n 40) 284.

[121] ibid.

regard to restrictions on the claims that are 'dischargeable'.[122] Therefore, it is important to clarify the applicable laws governing discharge. Under English common law, '[i]n principle, it would seem that a foreign composition with creditors, like a discharge in a foreign bankruptcy, is not regarded as effective in England unless it operates as a discharge according to the law applicable to the contract'.[123] This principle, which was established in the English Court of Appeal's decision *Antony Gibbs & Sons v Société Industrielle et Commerciale des Métaux* ('*Gibbs*'),[124] still applies in English commonwealth jurisdictions today.[125] However, modern insolvency laws in other jurisdictions based on the principle of universalism require that the discharge of debt be governed by *lex fori concursus*. For example, American courts recognise the effect of a foreign discharge made in the debtor's COMI based on international comity even though Chapter 15 of the US Code does not expressly address the issue of discharge.[126] This is also the case in Canada, which inherited English insolvency traditions and customs, has nevertheless abandoned the traditional *Gibbs* principle.[127] The *Gibbs* rule has also been frequently contested in other English commonwealth jurisdictions, in particular by insolvency practitioners seeking the implementation of a reorganisation plan or procedures of a similar nature that were binding upon all creditors globally.[128] Hong Kong, for instance, is one jurisdiction that follows the *Gibbs* principle in a pragmatic, or even reluctant, way.[129]

Neither the Enterprise Bankruptcy Law nor the Minutes of the National Courts' Meeting on Bankruptcy Adjudication (Bankruptcy Minutes) specify the applicable law governing the discharge of debts in insolvency matters. Nevertheless, it is worth noting that Article 5 of the Enterprise Bankruptcy Law provides recognition rules for foreign insolvency 'judgments' and 'orders' in general, without distinguishing judgments concerning procedural matters (for example, those opening insolvency proceedings and appointing insolvency representatives), and those concerning substantive matters, such as judgments concerning distribution and discharge.[130] Therefore, Chinese courts will recognise a discharge made under a foreign law as long as the requirements of Article 5 are satisfied. Nevertheless, it is still uncertain which law will govern the discharge. I suggest that *lex fori concursus* is the best candidate to be the default choice-of-law rule in insolvency law. The *Gibbs* rule is gradually becoming unpopular and should not be adopted in China. The approach to be taken by Chinese courts is yet to be determined in light of the vagueness of Article 5 and the above-mentioned fact that a Chinese court has never successfully recognised a foreign insolvency judgment or order based on Article 5.

[122] The US, for example, does not discharge certain tax debts and customs duty. See 11 U.S.C. § 1141(d)(6) (2018): 'The confirmation of a plan does not discharge of debtor that is a corporation from … a tax or customs duty to which the debtor made a fraudulent return … [or] willfully attempted in any manner to evade or to defeat such tax or customs duty.' Also see JL Westbrook, 'Chapter 15 and discharge' (2005) 13 *American Bankruptcy Institute Law Review* 503, 506.

[123] Collins, *Dicey & Morris* (n 1) 31-096.

[124] (1890) LR 25 QBD 399.

[125] *Global Distressed Alpha Fund 1 Limited Partnership v PT Bakrie Investindo* [2011] EWHC 256 (Comm); *WB Geneva SA v North America Steamships Ltd* [2007] EWHC 1167 (Comm).

[126] See, eg, *Canada Southern Ry Co v Gebhard* 109 U.S. 527 (1883); *Allstate Insurance Co v Hughes*, 174 B.R. 884 (S.D.N.Y. 1994); *re Board of Directors of Hopewell International Insurance Ltd*, 238 B.R. 25 (Bankr. S.D.N.Y. 1999), affd, 275 B.R. 699 (S.D.N.Y. 2002); *Oui Financing LLC v Steven Dellar and Oui Management SAS*, 2013 US Dist LEXIS 146214. Also see generally Westbrook, 'Chapter 15' (n 122).

[127] Westbrook, 'Chapter 15' (n 122) 506–07.

[128] See generally, K Ramesh, 'The Gibbs Principle: A Tether on the Feet of Good Forum Shopping' (2017) 29 *Singapore Academy of Law Journal* 42.

[129] This principle has made the place whose law governs the essential contracts entered into by the debtor as an independent jurisdictional ground for sanctioning parallel scheme of arrangement. See *re LDK Solar Co Ltd (in provisional liquidation)*, HCMP 2215/2014 at 49-52. But see *Hong Kong Institute of Education v Aoki Group (No 2)* [2004] 2 HKC 397.

[130] See Art 5 of EBL.

F. Rules Relating to Distribution and Priority

Distribution and priority rules in insolvency law are directly related to the local policies of each state, and thus one realm where states diverge significantly. For example, some jurisdictions recognise the rights of secured creditors to have first priority, while some others subordinate secured creditors' claims to the administration cost of insolvency proceedings.[131] In some jurisdictions, tax claims are deemed to be priority claims, while in others they are not.[132] In some jurisdictions, employee claims rank higher than other priority claims such as tax and social security claims, and sometimes even above secured claims.[133] In other jurisdictions, they rank equally with other priority claims and below secured claims. Some jurisdictions do not even deem employee claims as priority claims.[134] Different ranking lists directly reflect a state's attitude towards different groups of creditors and the social value represented by them. Although scholars strongly recommend that distribution and priority rules should be classified as procedural issues in insolvency proceeding, and thus be governed by *lex fori concursus*, their vital and direct influence upon creditors' interests and their close connection to local policies have given rise to fierce debate.[135]

The earliest proposal that provided an alternative for choice-of-law rules for distribution is the theory of 'Neuorientierung (New Orientation)' proposed by a German professor, Wilmowsky, in 1997.[136] Wilmowsky agrees with the universalism approach that the *lex fori concursus* should determine the question of 'asset deployment', that is, the question of whether the debtor should be restructured or liquidated.[137] However, he argues that questions of 'asset distribution', that is, distribution rules including the ranking and preferences of a claim, should be decided by the insolvency laws of the state which is in charge of protecting debtors who have intervened to protect their interests under non-insolvency laws.[138] Employees and tort victims are two illustrations given by the author.[139] A better-known theory advocating for the reform of choice-of-law rules in cross-border insolvency law is the virtual territorialism proposed by the American scholar, Edward J Janger.[140] According to Janger, the application of *lex fori concursus* in the distribution of the debtor's assets would lead to jurisdictional competition that 'races to the bottom'.[141]

However, centralisation of pure procedural rules can avoid such jurisdictional competition.[142] Therefore, Janger suggests that the main court should administer all the assets of the debtor according to local procedural law; but for substantive matters that affect the outcome of *distribution*, the court would not necessarily apply *lex fori concursus*. Instead, the choice of substantive insolvency laws should be determined by ordinary choice-of-law principles. Janger therefore

[131] The Bahamas is one such example. See s 267(1) of The Bahamas Companies Act (1992).

[132] UNCITRAL Legislative Guide (n 40) 271.

[133] ibid, 272.

[134] ibid.

[135] See, eg, Westbrook, 'Theory and Pragmatism' (n 43) 459.

[136] See P von Wilmowsky, 'Choice of Law in International Insolvencies – A Proposal For Reform', in J Basedow and T Kono (eds), *Legal Aspects of Globalisation: Conflict of Laws, Internet, Capital Markets and Insolvency in A Global Economy* (Kluwer Law International, 2000) 203; B Wessels, 'Contracting Out of Secondary Insolvency Proceedings: The Main Liquidator's Undertaking in the Meaning of art 18 in the Proposal to Amend the EU Insolvency Regulation' (2014) 9 *Brooklyn Journal of Corporate, Financial and Commercial Law* 63, 82–83.

[137] ibid, 203, 205–206.

[138] ibid.

[139] ibid, 211.

[140] See EJ Janger, 'Universal Proceduralism' (2007) 32 *Brooklyn Journal of International Law* 819; Westbrook, 'A Comment on Universal Proceduralism' (n 60); Janger, 'Virtual Territoriality' (n 40).

[141] Janger, 'Virtual Territoriality' (n 40) 429.

[142] ibid.

suggests the harmonisation of the 'few procedural rules necessary to administer a case comprising all of the debtor's assets and operations and a set of choice-of-law principles that would limit the effect of choice-of-forum on substantive entitlements'.[143]

The adoption of a set of dispersed choice-of-law rules where distribution is involved has also been supported by the emergence of synthetic secondary proceedings as an increasingly popular tool to avoid the opening of secondary proceedings and, at the same time, avoid applying the law of the main forum to matters that could have been governed in a local secondary proceeding.[144] This alternative recently made its first formal appearance in the EIR Recast.[145] According to Article 36 of the EIR Recast, insolvency practitioners in main proceedings may, to avoid the opening of secondary proceedings, give a unilateral undertaking concerning assets located in the Member State where secondary proceedings could have been opened.[146] The insolvency practitioner may undertake that, when distributing these assets or the proceeds realised by the sale of these assets, the Member State's law governing distribution and priority rights will apply.[147] The undertaking must be approved by the known local creditors, creditors who, according to the Recast, have claims arising from or in connection with the operation of the related establishment.[148] The approval process shall follow local laws concerning qualified majority and voting procedures that apply to the approval of the restructuring plans.[149]

Neither the Enterprise Bankruptcy Law nor the Bankruptcy Minutes directly address the issue of the applicable law relating to distribution in insolvency. However, it is obvious that the recognition of a foreign bankruptcy proceeding does not affect the priority and secured rights of Chinese local creditors because, as aforementioned, local assets of the foreign debtor must first be used to satisfy local secured and priority claims.[150] The Bankruptcy Minutes do not expressly specify what law will apply to the unsecured claims and fails to provide other rules that may also influence the distribution outcome. However, Article 50 of the Bankruptcy Minutes specifies that the Chinese court will, after the full discharge of local secured and priority claims, distribute the debtor's local assets according to the decision made by the foreign court.[151] In such cases, the law applied by the foreign court is indirectly applied by the Chinese court.

III. Laws of Bankruptcy

Although the substantive laws governing the insolvency of legal persons and the bankruptcy of individuals in a given state may be very different, the choice-of-law rules applicable to insolvency

[143] ibid, 408–09.

[144] *Re MG Rover Belux SA/NV (In Administration)* [2006] (High Court of Justice Chancery); *re Collins & Aikman Europe SA* [2006] EWHC (Ch) 1343; *re Nortel Network* [2009] EWHC (Ch) 206.

[145] See Art 36 of EIR Recast.

[146] ibid.

[147] ibid.

[148] See Art 2(11) of EIR Recast. Local authorities that are established to guarantee the payment of employees' outstanding claims resulting from contracts of employment or employment relationships shall also be deemed as local creditors provided that national laws allows so. See Art 36(11) of EIR Recast.

[149] See Art 36(5) of EIR Recast.

[150] See Art 50 of Bankruptcy Minutes: 'Rights Protection and Interests Balancing in Cross-border Insolvency Cases. Cooperation should be carried out based on art 5 of Enterprise Bankruptcy Law. Upon recognizing a foreign judgment or decision, the residual assets of the debtor within the border of the People's Republic of China may be distributed according to the law of the foreign court, provided that local secured creditors, and local priority claims including employee credits, social insurance fees, and taxes are paid in full.'

[151] Art 50 of the Bankruptcy Minutes.

and bankruptcy are often the same.[152] Therefore, most of the discussion in Chapter 16 of this volume is applicable, *mutatis mutandis*, to the bankruptcy of individuals, especially to individual traders. For this reason, this section will only discuss situations where the two sets of choice-of-laws diverge. Another potential problem is that China has no personal bankruptcy law. There is no legislation and minimum bankruptcy practice reflecting the choice-of-law rules in personal bankruptcy cases.

A. Effect of Bankruptcy on Assignments of Property

The law governing the effect of bankruptcy on assignments of property in insolvency cases for legal persons has been discussed in section II.B. Under general principles and theories of private international law, the same rules apply in bankruptcy cases for individuals. However, one question is whether Chinese courts will recognise foreign judgments ordered in bankruptcy proceedings for individuals at all, as China has no bankruptcy law for individuals. This leaves Article 5 of the Enterprise Bankruptcy Law, which only addresses the insolvency of legal persons, as the only possible legal basis for Chinese recognition of foreign bankruptcy judgments. It is quite likely that neither Article 5 of the Enterprise Bankruptcy Law, nor Section 9 (Cross-border Insolvency) of the SPC Bankruptcy Minutes, which explains the implementation of Article 5, will apply to the recognition and choice-of-law issues in personal bankruptcy cases. However, the power of a foreign bankruptcy representative with regard to the assignment of assets and standing to sue might be classified as the capacity of this individual, and thus subject to their personal law, ie *lex domicilii*.

B. Effect of Bankruptcy as a Discharge of Debts

The choice of law issues regarding the effect of insolvency proceedings on discharge of debts for legal persons in reorganisation proceedings has been discussed in section II.E above. For individuals, the situation is quite different. Chinese courts may refuse to recognise a discharge of debts for individuals, because Chinese law contains no personal bankruptcy law. Unlike recognition with regard to the assignment of properties, no alternative is available for discharge because it can hardly be classified as the 'capacity' of an individual. Therefore, the recognition of a foreign bankruptcy discharge is essentially equivalent to the direct application of a foreign law that forms no part of the law of China, and thus may be intolerable due to a possible violation of Chinese public policy. This is a reasonable position where local law does not permit the insolvency of consumers or non-traders. For example, the Guide to Enactment and Interpretation of UNCITRAL Model Law suggests that enacting states that have not provided for the insolvency of consumers or whose insolvency law provides special treatment for the insolvency of non-traders may either exclude from the scope of application of the Model Law the insolvencies of non-traders, or insolvencies relating to natural persons residing in the enacting state whose debts have been incurred

[152] As a matter of fact, the universality of insolvency was adopted in personal bankruptcy cases even before being extended to winding-up cases for companies, because the principle can be traced back to the mid-18th century when English courts recognised the extraterritorial effect of foreign personal bankruptcies declared under the law of domicile in *Solomons v Ross*. See *Solomons v Ross* [1764] 1 H Bl 131n; *Galbraith v Grimshaw* [1910] AC 508. See also *Rubin v Eurofinance* [2012] UKSC 46 [11]–[20] (summarising the development of universalism in England and the US).

predominantly for personal or household purposes.[153] Therefore, it is submitted that Chinese courts are unlikely to recognise the foreign discharge of individuals or apply foreign law with regard to the discharge effect of foreign bankruptcy proceedings.

IV. Cross-border Insolvency

Choice-of-law issues in insolvency did not arise until the emergence and acceptance of universalism. Yet, ironically, it is precisely the universalists who advocate the elimination of the emerging choice-of-law issues. They envisage a future where there is one single international insolvency law administered by one single international court system in the world, similar to the US bankruptcy system where a federal bankruptcy code is applied in a federal bankruptcy court system across all American States.[154] However, it is very unlikely that this idea will become reality in the foreseeable future.[155] The US method works because of a strong central government exercising its constitutional authority. In the absence of such a structure, the unification of laws can only be achieved through a long and slow process of harmonisation and convergence, which requires close cooperation and practical demand.[156] Although a series of projects have already been launched to harmonise the scope of the exceptions and the applicable laws for certain rights and legal relations, it is more realistic to expect China to respect local interests and local policies, and to therefore apply the *lex situs* to certain substantive issues.[157]

[153] UNCITRAL on Cross-Border Insolvency with Guide to Enactment and Interpretation (United Nations 2013) 36–7.
[154] Westbrook, 'A Global Solution' (n 50) 2292–98.
[155] See Janger, 'Universal Proceduralism' (n 140), 834.
[156] It is even doubtful whether the unification of insolvency law would ever be realised in future, considering the important effect of international politics on international law. The effect on European Union law brought about by the UK's exit to European Union is one recent example. See also LG Zhong, *Romance of the Three Kingdoms*, Chapter One (first line after the opening poem): 'That which is long divided must unify; that which is long unified must divide. This is the basic law of the world.'
[157] See, eg, UNCITRAL Legislative Guide on Insolvency Law and ALI Global Principles.

19

Competition Law

MAOZHONG DING, DAN WANG

The effects of anti-competitive conduct by participants[1] in the global market are significantly greater than corresponding effects in the domestic market. Both public and private enforcement mechanisms may restrict anti-competitive conduct and provide remedies to eradicate illegal behaviour. With regard to public enforcement, domestic competition authorities exercise the power to launch investigations into transnational undertakings in line with the territorial principle. Long-arm jurisdiction, such as under the effects doctrine,[2] has been applied by a number of jurisdictions, including the US and Europe, in public enforcement cases where the domestic market has been or potentially will be impacted by foreign anti-competitive conduct. Private enforcement is more complex than public enforcement due to the diversity of competition law regimes across jurisdictions. Different jurisdictions tend to have different competition cultures and policies, making compromise a challenge for policymakers. Therefore, private international law, which seeks to respect the diversity of domestic competition law regimes while reducing competition law conflicts, is the primary tool of cross-border competition dispute resolution.[3] In China, the globalised environment has created enormous trade and investment opportunities. As a result, Chinese competition law will be under increasing global scrutiny, particularly following the Belt and Road Initiative ('BRI') proposed by China in 2013.

Divided into four sections, this chapter will primarily focus on the private enforcement of Chinese competition law against a global background. The first section will give a summary of the Chinese competition regime, introducing Chinese anti-monopoly and unfair competition law. The second will discuss general issues of jurisdiction of Chinese domestic courts and analyse the possibility of adopting the effects doctrine in China. The third will discuss the law to be applied by Chinese courts in cases of competition law infringement where the court's jurisdiction has been justified. The final section will focus on the recognition and enforcement of foreign competition judgments in China, especially the indirect jurisdiction of the requiring court and China's attitude towards punitive damages.

[1] Different jurisdictions adopted different words to describe these participants. For instance, the Anti-Monopoly Law of the People's Republic of China took the term 'business operator', and Arts 101 and 102 of the Treaty on the Functioning of the European Union ('TFEU') used the expression of 'undertakings'. Generally, it refers to any entity or person taking part in economic activities in a particular market regardless of its legal nature.

[2] In public enforcement, a state can grant its domestic competition law extraterritorial effect when the anti-competitive conducts occurred outside its territory have affected or are potentially felt to affect the domestic market.

[3] M Danov, 'Global competition law framework: A private international law solution needed' (2016) 12 *Journal of Private International Law* 77.

I. Overview of Chinese Competition Law

The legislative pattern of Chinese competition law tracks civil law jurisdictions such as Germany. However, anti-monopoly and anti-unfair competition laws are enforced in separate ways. Historically, the construction of the Chinese competition law system took a long path, during which the Chinese economy grew at a fast and unprecedented pace. Consequently, the Chinese Government became aware of the need to put in place a competitive legal system to support and maintain market order, while the debate amongst Chinese scholars has continued to rage for decades.[4] The PRC Anti-Unfair Competition Law (the 'AUCL') was implemented on 1 December 1993, and has been revised twice, first in 2017 and most recently in 2019. Subsequently, the anti-monopoly law was drafted. After more than ten years of development, the PRC Anti-Monopoly Law (the 'AML') was adopted at the 29th Meeting of the Standing Committee of the Tenth National People's Congress on 30 August 2007 and became effective on 1 August 2008. Interestingly, the AML and the AUCL neither marked a radical break with the basic patterns established by the US and Europe nor ignored the practicalities of China's political regime and its market demand for development.[5]

The AML follows the patterns of Europe and Germany by covering the regulation of cartel agreements, abuse of market dominance, and mergers.[6] Nevertheless, some provisions are specific to the Chinese market. For example, the rules relating to monopoly administration in the AML stipulate that local authorities shall be banned from restricting market competition through the abuse of governmental power. The AML is in essence a public law, and the responsibility for enforcing the law is placed on the relevant agencies: the Ministry of Commerce for mergers, the State Administration for Industry and Commerce for abuse of dominance, and the National Development and Reform Commission for other restrictive agreements.[7] Civic obligations are also applicable if infringement cases involving monopolistic conduct are taken to the court. The AUCL regulates unfair competition, such as obtaining competitive advantages by infringing on the others' registered trademarks, business corruption, invasion of business secrecy, false advertisement, collusion of bidding, low price dumping, and price discrimination. Liability for breaching the AUCL is similar to liability in the AML. In general, the AML focusses on the promotion of market competition while the AUCL targets the maintenance of fair market competition discipline. Additionally, relevant commercial laws, judicial interpretations, and international conventions play a significant role in the Chinese competition legal system as support or supplement to the AML and AUCL.

II. The Court's Jurisdiction Over International Competition Disputes

Generically, jurisdiction involves three aspects: jurisdiction to prescribe, jurisdiction to adjudicate, and jurisdiction to enforce. Jurisdiction to prescribe determines how and to what extent the competition law will be applied. Jurisdiction to adjudicate provides justification for the court's authority to hear the competition action before it. The jurisdiction to enforce means the power

[4] D Gerber, *Global Competition: Law, Markets, and Globalization* 1st edn (OUP, 2010) 225–226.
[5] ibid, 233.
[6] ibid.
[7] ibid.

to guarantee conformance to the judgment of infringement within a specific region. Jurisdiction to adjudicate in particular is a major issue in competition actions because it relates not only to the judicial sovereignty of a nation but also to the starting point of a competition case. Parallel proceedings and forum shopping (the self-interested evaluation of different jurisdictions) would take place if a number of different jurisdictions claimed legal dominion over an action, which would lead to inconsistent decisions as a result of the variation in domestic competition laws. Therefore, proper allocation of the jurisdiction to be applied is a significant preliminary issue to consider in cross-border competition disputes. For competition disputes occurring within Chinese territory, the Chinese courts apply the territorial principle to justify Chinese jurisdiction according to the statutory wording and judicial interpretation of the Civil Procedure Law.[8] The Civil Procedure Law gives Chinese courts jurisdiction over competition disputes, irrespective of the nationality of the parties, if the court is at the place: (1) where the tort is committed; (2) where the tortuous consequence happens; or (3) where the defendant's domicile is located.

To date, no rule has been established which explicitly describes how China will deal with foreign extraterritorial competition disputes that may have an impact on China's market. Judicial attempts to address the question have been controversial. The court in the case of *Huawei v InterDigital* attempted to adopt an objective territoriality principle to justify its jurisdiction.[9] This judgment faced criticism. What about the effects doctrine? Can the court justify its jurisdiction on the ground that the infringement happened abroad has been or will be a threat to the competition in the domestic market, and therefore hear the case which the court would not have jurisdiction if it applies territorial doctrine? The effects doctrine was initially adopted by the US to exercise long-arm jurisdiction over extraterritorial competition disputes and provides a possible path for China to follow in cross-border competition disputes. First, its successful application in other jurisdictions demonstrates its value in dealing with cross-border competition disputes. Second, considering the need of protecting the participants in the Chinese market is increasing and the number of transnational competition infringement cases is growing, it is possible for China to extend its jurisdiction over extraterritorial anti-competitive conduct in public enforcement to private enforcement in the future. The effects doctrine is not a concept newly introduced in China. Conversely, this doctrine has been involved in the AML.[10]

A. Effects Doctrine in the US and Europe

Initially, the territoriality doctrine was used by the US courts to justify jurisdiction in extraterritorial cases. The starting point was the *American Banana Co and United Fruits Co* (1909) case, where the court ruled that a statute will, as a generic rule, be meant to be confined in its operation and effect to the territorial boundaries within the jurisdiction of the lawmaker.[11] The effects doctrine provided a way to depart from this generic rule. In 1945, the effects doctrine

[8] Article 4 of Provisions of the Supreme People's Court on Several Issues concerning the Application of Law in the Trial of Civil Dispute Cases Arising from Monopolistic Conduct (Supreme People's Court, Fa Shi (2012) 5). It stipulates that the territorial jurisdiction over civil monopoly dispute cases shall be determined by taking into consideration the practicalities of a case and in line with the jurisdiction provisions of the Civil Procedure Law and relevant judicial interpretations with regard to torts, contract disputes, etc. Article 28 of Civil Procedure Law states that an action instituted for a tort shall be subject to the jurisdiction of the people's court at the place where the conduct of tort occurs or at the place of the defendant's domicile.

[9] Shenzhen Intermediate People's Court Decision *Huawei v InterDigital* (2011) Shen Zhong Fa Zhi Min Chu Zi No 858.

[10] Article 2 of the AML stipulates that the AML is applicable to monopolistic overseas conduct which plays a role in eliminating or restricting competition on the domestic market in China.

[11] *American Banana Co v United Fruit Co* 213 US 347 (1909).

was first raised in *United States v Aluminum Co of America*, where an international cartel agreement reached abroad was considered to have a negative impact in US territory as it restricted aluminium imports into the US.[12] Subsequently, the US court took jurisdiction over cross-border antitrust cases by adopting the effects doctrine.

In Europe, the effects doctrine is applied in the opposite way. Article 101 and 102 of the Treaty on the Functioning of the European Union ('TFEU') take a neutral stance on extraterritorial jurisdiction.[13] The Commission attempted to use an effects test to deal with subject-matter jurisdiction in the context of public enforcement of competition law, but the European Court of Justice ('ECJ') rejected this approach.[14] Instead, the court applied the 'single economic entity doctrine' and the 'implementation doctrine' to justify its jurisdiction. The ECJ first attempted to apply the single economy entity doctrine, which aims at multinational corporations. Under this doctrine, the Community has jurisdiction over a parent company which is beyond the Community's territory where that company takes control of subsidiaries within the Community. However, the 'single economy entity doctrine' does not cover the situation where the parent company simply supplies products to the Community, without having subsidiaries in the territory of the Community. The ECJ tried to resolve this problem by applying the 'implementation doctrine'. This doctrine distinguishes between the 'formation' and 'implementation' of a cartel agreement. A cartel agreement formed outside the Community will be subject to EU competition law as long as it is directly or indirectly implemented inside the Community. Eventually, the *Gencor*[15] and *Intel*[16] cases applied the effects doctrine.[17] In the meantime, the limitations of the effects doctrine were stressed by the General Court in the *Intel* case: the effect is required to be 'substantial, immediate, and foreseeable'.

B. Effects Doctrine in China

The effects doctrine is based on a principle that exists in the public enforcement of Chinese competition law. As stipulated in Article 2, the AML is also applicable to monopolistic overseas conduct that plays a role in eliminating or restricting competition in the Chinese domestic market. This provision is apparently the legal base on which Chinese competition authorities initiate investigations on anti-competitive conduct outside China that has adverse impacts on Chinese domestic markets. Nevertheless, the article is not the legal base of extraterritorial jurisdiction of the court in private enforcement proceeding. First, the AML is in the public law catalogue, which is primarily designed to address public enforcement rather than private enforcement. It is unlikely that the legislator would include a provision to justify a court's jurisdiction over civil cases in the public law catalogue. Second, the AML is classed as substantive law, whereas jurisdiction of the court is a procedural issue. It is doubtful that the AML would provide a provision of the court's jurisdiction which is usually included in a specific procedural law. Therefore, the effects doctrine in Article 2 only grants competition authorities the extraterritorial jurisdiction and is only applied in public enforcement cases. However, Article 2 of AML can still suggest the possibility of applying the effects doctrine in the private enforcement of cross-border competition cases in China.

[12] *United States v Aluminum Co of America* 148 F2d 416 (2d Cir 1945).

[13] A Jones, B Sufrin, N Dunne, *EU Competition Law: Text, Cases and Materials* 7th edn (OPU, 2019) 1197.

[14] ibid.

[15] Case T-102/96 *Gencor Ltd v Commission* [1999] ECR II-753.

[16] Case T-286/09 *Intel v Commission* [2014] OJ C245/8.

[17] ibid.

Extending the effects doctrine to private enforcement is inevitable, considering the tight economic connections between China and the rest of the world.

The problems of the territorial principle were revealed in *Huawei v InterDigital*.[18] In this case, the court justified its jurisdiction by determining China to be the place where the consequences of a tort occurred and applied the territorial principle in its judgment. However, the tortious conduct actually occurred in American territory. In this situation, applying the effects principle makes more sense than applying the territorial principle. This is because the plaintiff's competitors, Apple and Samsung, achieved better competitive conditions in the Chinese market, so China was the territory that was clearly affected by the tortious conduct.[19]

It should be noted that a unilateral declaration of extraterritorial jurisdiction premised on the effects doctrine may elicit hostile reactions from other jurisdictions, potentially leading to enforcement problems. The US court showed great sensitivity to the hostility of other states towards the effects doctrine by narrowing the conditions under which the doctrine could be applied, in *Foreign Trade Antitrust Improvements Act (FTAIA)* (1982).[20] Additionally, it showed respect for the notion of 'international comity,' despite controversy over the very notion of comity.[21] China should similarly take measures to reduce potential hostility. First, the use of the effects doctrine should be restricted in the manner adopted in the US and Europe. For instance, by making it a precondition that the effect be direct, substantial, and reasonably foreseeable. Establishing these restrictions sets a standard for application by the court, preventing randomness and unpredictability. In addition, it reduces conflicts of jurisdiction and thus mitigates the risk of rejection by foreign courts on the basis of indirect jurisdiction. Second, the courts should apply international comity. That is, courts should choose to decline jurisdiction when they believe that another state's interests outweigh the benefits to the Chinese market of applying the effects doctrine. Third, similar to international comity, the courts should apply the law of the state which is deemed to be more severely affected. States are unilaterally announcing their courts' jurisdiction over cross-border competition disputes in order to grant their domestic competition law extraterritorial effect.[22] Therefore, if Chinese courts, on a voluntary basis, apply the competition law of the state whose market has been subject to the most severe impact, the possibility of refusing the recognition and enforcement of foreign competition judgments can be decreased.

III. Choice of Law in International Competition Disputes

For the private enforcement of competition disputes, infringement and liability are crucial steps for the court to review the plaintiff's complaint. The two questions here are whether there was an infringement, and whether and how the defendant has incurred tortious liability. In international

[18] Shenzhen Intermediate People's Court Decision *Huawei v InterDigital* (2011) Shen Zhong Fa Zhi Min Chu Zi No 858.

[19] T Du, 'Lun Fanlongduan Kuaguo Minshi Susong Zhong Yuwai Guanxiaquan He Yuwai Shiyong Wenti De Qufen: Yi Zhongmei Xinjin Anli Wei Shijiao' [The distinction between extraterritorial jurisdiction and extraterritorial application in international antitrust litigations: A comparative analysis of recent Chinese and American cases] (2019) 1 *Journal of International Economic Law* 74.

[20] Article 1 of the FTAIA states that the Sherman Act 15 USC §§ 1-38 shall not be applicable to conduct involving trade or commerce with foreign nations, other than import transactions unless such conduct has a direct, substantial, and reasonably foreseeable effect on domestic or impact commerce or on the export business of a domestic person.

[21] Jones, Sufrin, Dunne, *EU Competition Law* (n 13) 1191.

[22] YP Lin, 'Chongtu Guifan Zai Jingzhenfa Yuwai Shiyong Zhong De Zuoyong Ji Tedian' [Effects and features of applying conflicts of rules to the extraterritoriality of competition law] (2010) 10 *Legal Science* 65.

competition disputes, the two questions may be determined by laws in different jurisdictions with the application of conflict rules.

To establish whether the plaintiff's right was infringed, the court must determine whether the defendant's conduct breached the AML or AUCL. In the assessment of anti-competitive conduct, Article 10 of the Interpretation of the Supreme People's Court on Several Issues Concerning the Application of the 'Law of the People's Republic of China on the Law Applicable to Foreign-Related Civil Relationships (Law on the Law Applicable to Foreign-Related Civil Relationships)' specifies that mandatory provisions set out in Article 4[23] of the Law on the Law Applicable to Foreign-Related Civil Relationships extend their application to foreign-related civil relationships including anti-monopoly issues. Therefore, the AML could be applied directly to assess monopolistic conduct. With regard to the unfair competition behaviour set out in AUCL, Article 2 of the Law on the Law Applicable to Foreign-Related Civil Relationships stipulates that in the absence of rules applying to foreign-related civil relations, the law having the closest relationship with this foreign-related civil relationship shall be deemed applicable. This provision grants judges the discretion to determine the applicable law when it comes to examining the unfair competition conduct. Second, liability for anti-competitive conduct is subject to the provisions of general infringement liability, as specified in Article 44 of the Law on the Law Applicable to Foreign-Related Civil Relationships. This provision states that if the parties reach consensus on applicable law after the occurrence of any tort, their agreement shall prevail. If the parties make no choice, the law at the mutual habitual residence of the parties shall apply. If the parties do not have a mutual habitual residence, the law at the place of the tort (place where the conduct occurred or the place where the consequence occurred) shall apply.

However, current Chinese laws regarding competition infringement liability fail to consider the particularity of competition law. Competition infringement may harm public interests more severely than other infringements. Competition law is particularly important in maintaining competition discipline and protecting customers' rights. Before the Law on the Law Applicable to Foreign-Related Civil Relationships was drafted, the Model Law on Private International Law of the PRC (6th draft, 2000) by the Chinese Society of Private International Law developed the applicable rule of competition infringement liability independently from general infringement liability.[24] However, this rule was not adopted in the Law Applicable to Foreign-Related Civil Relationships eventually. Nevertheless, the separate applicable rule on competition infringement liability deserves serious consideration in the context of the fast-paced development of the Chinese market. This is also the practice in some other jurisdictions.[25] For instance, Article 6 of the Regulation on the Law Applicable to Non-contractual Obligations[26] (Rome II) by the European Council specifies that the applicable law concerning non-contractual liability imposed by an act of unfair competition or limiting free competition is the law of the country where the impact on competitive relations or the collective interests of consumers has occurred or may occur. To engage in the global market, it is necessary for the Supreme Court to clarify the Law on the Law Applicable to Foreign-Related Civil Relationships, and adopt the effects doctrine in choice of law rules. Such a new applicable rule opens up the possibility for China's courts to apply

[23] If there are mandatory provisions on foreign-related civil relations in the laws of the PRC, these mandatory provisions shall directly apply.

[24] Article 122 of the Model Law on Private International Law of the PRC stipulates that the law of the place where the result of the tort occurs shall govern claims for damages arising from unfair competition. But this model law is academic in nature and is used only for reference by the legislative.

[25] Belgium, Switzerland, Australia, Romania, Liechtenstein, Austria, Russia.

[26] Regulation (EC) No 864/2007 of the European Parliament and of the Council of 11 July 2007 on the law applicable to non-contractual obligations (Rome II).

foreign competition law to determine liability, which would be effective in reducing the hostility of other states to the adoption of effects doctrine in exercising long-arm jurisdiction by the court.

IV. Recognition and Enforcement of Foreign Competition Judgments

A. General Rules on Recognition and Enforcement of Foreign Judgments

In order to enforce a foreign competition infringement judgment, a party must satisfy the rules provided by the state where enforcement is sought. These rules will dictate the conditions for the recognition and enforcement of foreign civil judgments. In most cases, the legal sources are found in domestic civil procedure laws, bilateral or multilateral treaties, and international treaties. China has not established a complete system of rules governing the recognition and enforcement of foreign judgments. However, Articles 281 and 282 of the Civil Procedure Law stipulate that international treaties and the principle of reciprocity are to be treated as the legal basis for the implementation of foreign judgments. However, foreign judgments sought to be enforced may not breach mandatory legal principles, sovereignty, national security, and the social interests of China. China has yet to ratify any international convention for the recognition and enforcement of foreign judgments at the date of writing, despite China having signed the 2005 Hague Choice of Court Convention in 2017[27] and the Convention of 2 July 2019 on the Recognition and Enforcement of Foreign Judgments in Civil or Commercial Matters. To date, China has entered into bilateral treaties or agreements on civil and commercial judicial assistance with 39 states. The treaties or agreements with Singapore, South Korea, Thailand, and Belgium make no mention of the relevant rules that apply to the recognition and enforcement of foreign judgments. The remaining treaties primarily establish conditions for rejecting the enforcement of foreign judgments. However, the function performed by bilateral treaties or agreements remains restricted as the amount in controversy sufficient to trigger jurisdiction is small, and some states having close trading ties with China are not included. For states which have no effective enforcement treaties with China, enforcement of foreign judgments in China follows the reciprocal principle prescribed in Article 281 of the Civil Procedure Law.

B. Assessment of Indirect Jurisdiction

In considering the enforcement of a foreign judgment, a Chinese court will first assess whether the foreign court issuing the ruling had jurisdiction. The reciprocal principle and bilateral treaties are the primary authorities consulted by Chinese courts in examining indirect jurisdiction. However, the criteria justifying indirect jurisdiction in those bilateral treaties are the main source of controversy. Different treaties use different criteria to assess whether the requesting court has

[27] The Hague Convention of 30 June 2005 on Choice of Court Agreements, as well as the newly published Convention of 2 July 2019 on the Recognition and Enforcement of Foreign Judgments in Civil or Commercial Matter, excluded their application in anti-monopoly (competition) matters, which reflects the difficulty in seeking unification in the areas of domestic public law such as competition law.

appropriate jurisdiction.[28] Under the judicial assistance agreements with Argentina, Bulgaria, Poland, France, Cuba, Mongolia, Brazil, UAE, and Romania, the foreign court has jurisdiction over the case according to the domestic law of the requested party. The judicial assistance agreements with Russia, Kyrgyzstan, Tadzhikistan and Ukraine only set out that the foreign judgment shall not violate the exclusive jurisdictional provisions of the requested party. Lastly, the agreements with states such as Laos, Cyprus, Tunisia, Spain, Italy, and Vietnam explicitly list concrete standards that the foreign judgment must meet and provide that exclusive jurisdiction rules of the requested states prevail as well.[29]

The effects doctrine is among the reasons for rejecting indirect jurisdiction as the basis for the enforcement of foreign competition judgments. In the Chinese civil procedural law, the territorial principle is the primary basis justifying a court's jurisdiction in competition infringement cases, and the effects doctrine has yet to be officially adopted when justifying the court's jurisdiction over cross-border competition disputes. Therefore, most of the foreign decisions regarding competition infringement, based on the effects doctrine, may be rejected by Chinese courts in accordance with indirect jurisdiction rules. If China is to adopt the effects doctrine in competition infringement as a basis for jurisdiction, it is a necessity, on the reciprocal basis, to admit the foreign courts' jurisdiction granted by the effects doctrine when a foreign judgment is to be enforced in China. Otherwise, Chinese judgments may face the same risk of being rejected by foreign courts. This problem should receive the attention of the Chinese legislature.

C. Enforcement of Punitive Damages

In the private enforcement of competition law, common law courts, in particular the US courts, impose punitive damages. The US uses a tripartite damages system, while the majority of common law jurisdictions employ the principle of indemnity to compensate for actual losses (full compensation). The causes of this difference are reflected in the purpose of private enforcement. In the US, private enforcement appears to have been aimed at both offering compensation to victims and serving as a deterrent to wrongdoers.[30] For instance, the Clayton Act endorses private enforcement through measures such as treble damages. The major purpose of US competition private enforcement is to defend public interests.[31] Conversely, private implementation in the EU functions as a positive supplement to public enforcement and aims at offering compensation based on private interests. Public enforcement is considered as sufficient to ensure compliance within the internal market in the EU dimension. EU competition law thus adopts full compensation in private enforcement.[32] China has not enforced a foreign judgment containing

[28] HY Shen, 'Waiguo Minshangshi Panjue Chengren He Zhixing Ruogan Yinan Wenti Yanjiu' [The research on several issues regarding the recognition and enforcement of foreign judgments on civil and commercial matters] (2018) 5 *Journal of Law Application* 10.

[29] In cases of contract dispute and tort, the standards means the court in the requesting party has jurisdiction over the case if: (1) the defendant has domicile or residence in the requesting party; (2) the defendant accepted in writing form that the court in the requesting party had jurisdiction or did not challenge the jurisdiction when arguing in the court; (3) the place where the contract was/is signed or performed is within the territory of the requesting party; or (4) the place where the tort happened or the consequence of the tort was located in is within the territory of the requesting party.

[30] Jones, Sufrin, Dunne, *EU Competition Law* (n 13) 1023.

[31] ibid., 1025.

[32] Directive 2014/104/EU of the European Parliament and of the Council of 26 November 2014 on certain rules governing actions for damages under national law for infringements of the competition law provisions of the Member States [2014] OJ L349/1.

punitive damages.[33] Nevertheless, Chinese legislation does recognise punitive damages in certain cases, especially where the issues closely affect public interests. For example, Article 148(2) of the Food Safety Law[34] stipulates that, apart from claiming damages, a consumer may require a producer of food failing to comply with food safety standards, or a trader consciously dealing in such food, to pay an indemnity of ten times the price paid or three times the loss; or if the amount of the additional compensation does not exceed 1,000, it shall be RMB 1,000, except where the non-compliance is a defect in the labels or instructions of the food which neither impairs food safety nor misleads consumers. Article 47 in the Tort Liability Law (revised in 2010) also specifies that where a manufacturer or seller, knowing of any defect in a product, continues to manufacture or sell the product and the defect causes a death or any serious damage to the health of another person, the victim has the right to claim the corresponding punitive compensation. Research reveals that the imposition of punitive damage in China depends on the following elements in addition to the provisions of the Civil Procedure Law. First, punitive damages are imposed in cases of infringement of tort law but not in breach of contract cases. Chinese courts will not impose punitive damages based on contract breach which is contradictory to the legislative spirit of the Civil Procedure Law. Second, punitive damages shall be paid to the infringed rather than to the government. Judicial practice in China and other jurisdictions usually rejects compensation paid to the government. Third, the amount of punitive damages should be within a reasonable range. Chinese courts can reject a quantum of punitive damages regarded as unfair and unreasonable by domestic standards.[35] Thus, in theory, punitive damages can be applied in the enforcement of foreign competition infringement judgments.

V. Conclusion

Global competition is complex because of the diversity of national competition regimes and the difficulties of coordinating between different jurisdictions. Private international law is among the tools employed to resolve the problems caused by global trade and competition. It mainly focuses on private enforcement but has been subject to influence from public enforcement theories and practice. The effects doctrine has been debated by commentators in public enforcement and has a long-standing record of judicial application in the US. Other jurisdictions, like Europe, have applied a qualified effects doctrine in their judicial practices. In the meantime, comity is treated as an approach to reduce conflicts and intense relations resulting from effects doctrine. As for China, the AML and AUCL have relatively short histories in comparison with competition law in the US and the EU.

China's market is significant to global markets so its competition law in relation to cross-border disputes must be modified and extended to take account of new realities. First, current jurisdiction provisions in China provide little legal basis for enforcement if a competition infringement occurs abroad but has detrimental effects in the Chinese market. The qualified effects doctrine should be applied in the jurisdiction of adjudication. Second, there remains a lack of separately

[33] YP Xiao, HM Qin, 'Lun Waiguo Chengfaxing Sunhai Peichang Panjue De Bufen Chengren Yu Zhixing' [Partial recognition and enforcement of foreign punitive damage] (2017) 3 *Jiangxi Social Sciences* 162.

[34] Regulation on the Implementation of the Food Safety Law of the People's Republic of China, Amendment edition effect from 1 December 2019.

[35] SQ Zhao, 'Lun Waiguo Fayuan Chengfaxing Peichang Panjue De Chengren Yu Zhixing' [The recognition and enforcement of punitive damage judgment of foreign courts] (2016) 1 *Commercial Arbitration* 7.

applicable rules to regulate competition infringement. The effects doctrine should be adopted in the choice of law rules, which will reduce the hostility from other states. Third, collaboration on implementing foreign judgments in civil and commercial cases remains in progress. Both the 2005 Hague Convention on Choice of Court Agreement and the 2017 Convention on the Recognition and Enforcement of Foreign Judgments in Civil or Commercial Matters excluded anti-monopoly issues. Therefore, the enforcement of foreign competition judgments in China is now primarily dependent on domestic civil procedure law, bilateral or multilateral treaties, and agreements to examine the indirect jurisdiction of the requiring foreign court. In the meantime, China has yet to apply punitive damages in competition cases. Nevertheless, punitive damages might be adopted in the future given the public function and impact of AML.

20

Recognition

ZHENGYI ZHANG, ZHEN ZHANG

In accordance with the principle of state sovereignty, a court's decision on a foreign-related case can only be legally effective within its own territory. However, globalisation is daily increasing the cross-border flows of personnel, information, and assets. In order to meet the needs of all countries for international communication and cooperation, countries often recognise and implement the judgments of foreign courts on foreign-related civil cases in certain ways. As for the theoretical basis of recognition and enforcement of foreign court judgments, there have been many theories, such as 'doctrine of international comity', 'acquired right theory', 'debt theory', 'obligation theory', 'reciprocity theory', 'theory of res judicata', etc. There is still no unified understanding in the international community. As for the legal basis for the recognition and enforcement of foreign court judgments, each country has different domestic laws for its own interests. Underpinning the theoretical and legal bases is a tension between, on the one hand, the interest of countries to safeguard their judicial sovereignty and insist on the protection of their national rights and, on the other hand, the need to integrate into the tide of economic globalisation. The reality is that the recognition and enforcement of foreign court judgments is necessarily mainly due to the survival and development needs of the country. With closer exchanges between countries, countries increasingly recognise that foreign civil and commercial judgments have legal effect in their own countries, thus giving rise to the need to properly handle foreign civil and commercial cases, to protect the legitimate rights of parties, and to promote the development of friendly relations between countries.[1] In other words, the need for survival and development has prompted the legislatures of various countries to provide for mutual recognition and enforcement of judgments of foreign courts under certain conditions.[2]

The recognition and enforcement of foreign court judgments are often amalgamated. However, though they are interrelated, they are distinct concepts. Enforcement – the execution of a judgment – is premised on the recognition of the judgment, but the recognition of a judgment does not necessarily include its enforcement. In some cases, the court of the home country only needs to affirm the validity of the judgment of the foreign court, recognising that the judgment has the same effect in the home country as the judgment of the domestic court, and does not

[1] J Lu, *Guoji Sifa zhi Lilun Yu Shijian [Theory and practice of private international law]* (Zhongguo Zhengfa daxue chubanshe, 2004).

[2] SY Li, SS Xie, *Guoji Minshi Susongfa Gailun* [*Introduction to International Civil Procedure Law*] (Wuhan daxue chubanshe, 2001).

require the public power of the country to enforce the judgment, for example, in cases of simple divorce, where there are usually no enforcement issues. The conditions for recognition of foreign court judgments are lower than those for the enforcement of foreign judgments. It is impossible to execute judgments without an authoritative act granted by a domestic court to permit the execution of the judgment, either after a new hearing of the case, or after a new judgment, or to register the foreign judgment in the book. In addition, conditions for admission are virtually the same as those for enforcement.[3]

I. Recognition in Bilateral and Multilateral Treaties and Conventions

International law does not obligate states to recognise and enforce foreign court judgments. According to the principle of equality among states, all countries are equal in sovereignty. The courts of a country can only exercise jurisdiction within its own territory. The principle would be violated if jurisdiction were extended to other countries, or if one state could give orders to other states to enforce its judgments. Yet international engagement will be difficult if there is no effective way to ensure the recognition and enforcement of foreign court decisions. To solve this impasse, it is necessary for states to be willing to recognise judgments of other states, as a basis for those other states to show reciprocal recognition. This mutual or multilateral recognition will be embodied in the form of a treaty. For all valid treaties on the basis of sovereign equality and full expression of the parties' will, all parties must interpret their treaties in good faith and faithfully fulfill their treaty obligations.[4] To this end, it is hoped that all countries, including China, will actively participate in the signing of bilateral or multilateral treaties to ensure the stability and continuity of judicial assistance in the field of recognition of foreign judgments. At present, China's conventions on mutual recognition and enforcement of court judgments mainly exist in bilateral treaties on judicial assistance, Regulations on Interregional Judicial Assistance in China, the Hague Conventions, and other conventions.

A. Bilateral Treaties on Judicial Assistance

To date, China has not acceded to any multinational international conventions on the recognition and enforcement of judgments of foreign courts. Instead, China has mainly signed bilateral mutual legal assistance treaties to achieve mutual legal recognition and enforcement of court judgments. At present, China has signed 39 bilateral treaties which contain arrangements for judgment recognition and enforcement, out of which 37 have been ratified by the Chinese legislature.[5] Details are shown in the table below at the end of this chapter. These bilateral judicial assistance treaties predominantly regulate civil and commercial matters. They constitute the principal basis for Chinese courts to recognise and enforce foreign courts' civil and commercial judgments. For example, the Ningbo Intermediate People's Court issued a final ruling on

[3] M Wolf, HP Li and ZS Tang, *Guoji Sifa [Private International Law]* (Peking University Press, 2009) 282–283.

[4] Article 26 of the Vienna Convention on the Law of Treaties (*United Nations Treaty Series vol 1155, 23 May 1969*) www.refworld.org/docid/3ae6b3a10.html accessed 13 August 2020.

[5] 'The ministry of foreign affairs of the People's Republic of China: judicial assistance treaty to schedule' (*Ministry of foreign affairs*) www.fmprc.gov.cn/web/ziliao_674904/tytj_674911/tyfg_674913/t1215630.shtml accessed 3 June 2019.

12 March 2014, recognising a civil judgment made by the Wroclaw Appeal Court of Poland on 8 April 2009.[6]

The above bilateral judicial assistance treaties mainly stipulate the scope of civil and commercial adjudications, such as judgments, rulings, decisions, mediation documents and even arbitration awards, along with application requests, conditions of recognition and enforcement or refusal of recognition and enforcement, indirect jurisdiction, procedure, and the effect of recognition and enforcement. The specifics are as follows. First, the scope of the recognition and enforcement of the judgments. There is no major dispute on the scope of recognition and enforcement of foreign judgments, including the decisions in civil cases, rulings on compensation in criminal cases, and civil mediation documents. However, regarding the definition of the 'judgment', there are three major differences:

(1) Treaties signed between China and other countries clearly define the meaning of 'judgment' inter se. For example, in Article 17 of the bilateral treaty between China and Ukraine, 'judgment of courts' refers to judgments, rulings, decisions and mediation documents issued by the court on civil matters and the ruling on damages in criminal cases in the PRC; and it refers to judgments on damages in criminal cases rendered by courts, civil judgments, rulings, decisions and mediation documents, as well as judgments and rulings made by arbitration courts in Ukraine.[7]
(2) Some countries have made general agreements with China about the meaning of 'judgment'. For example, Article 17, Paragraph 2 of the Treaty with the United Arab Emirates states that 'judgment', regardless of the name, refers to any decision made by the competent courts of both parties in the judicial process, which also includes Kuwait.[8]
(3) Most countries have agreed with China to adopt enumerated methods, which are stipulations that determine which types of specific awards can be recognised and enforced, and which cannot. Examples include Article16 in the treaty between China and Poland.[9]

Second, the standard of jurisdiction for the recognition and enforcement of judgments. In the bilateral judicial assistance treaties between China and various countries, different countries have

[6] See typical cases of the first batch of the Supreme People's Court of China providing judicial services and security for the construction of "One Belt And One Road" (Supreme People's Court, Case 8) http://cicc.court.gov.cn/html/1/218/62/163/641.html accessed 8 December 2019.

The facts of this case are as follows: Ningbo Yongchang Company filed sale contract disputes against Frigball Company in 2004 and 2006 successively in the district court of the green mountain city and the district court of Opole, asking Frigball company to pay US$65,454 and related interest. All the above Polish courts ruled against Ningbo Yongchang, but the Polish Wroclaw appeals court ruled in his favour. The Polish Supreme Court then quashed the ruling of the appeals court and remanded the case. On 8 April 2009, the Wroclaw court of appeal of Poland (Case no IACa231/9) ruled against Ningbo Yongchang's request and ordered it to return the US$54,521 and related litigation costs that had been paid to it by the Wroclaw court of appeal. The final judgment by the court of appeal in Wroclaw, Poland, took effect on 12 May 2009. On 8 April 2011, Frigball sent an application to the Ningbo intermediate court for recognition and enforcement of documents related to the execution of Polish court decisions.

[7] Treaty between the People's Republic of China and Ukraine on Civil and Criminal Justice Assistance, Art 17.

[8] Agreement between the People's Republic of China and the State of Kuwait on Judicial Assistance in Civil and Commercial Matters, Art 17.

[9] Agreement between the People's Republic of China and the People's Republic of Poland on Civil and Criminal Judicial Assistance, Art 16:

1. The Contracting Parties shall recognize or implement the following judgments made in the territory of the other Contracting Party after the entry into force of this Agreement in accordance with the conditions stipulated in this Agreement: (1) The court's decision on civil cases; (2) The court's decision on the compensation request in the criminal case; (3) The ruling made by the competent authority on the succession case; (4) The award made by the arbitral tribunal.
2. The 'judgment' referred to in this agreement also includes a mediation statement.

different ways of determining jurisdiction standards, the standards for determining jurisdiction are different, and there are the following three main methods:

(1) Enumeration method. That is, the enumeration method is adopted to stipulate how to determine that the foreign court which has made the judgment has jurisdiction. Judicial assistance treaties that stipulate jurisdiction standards of recognition and enforcement of judgment in this way include bilateral treaties signed between China and Italy, Spain, Egypt, Cyprus, Vietnam, Laos, etc.[10] In the treaties signed with these countries, 10 jurisdiction determination standards are listed in detail.
(2) The exclusion method. This method is to judge whether the court of the original trial country has jurisdiction based on whether the requested country has exclusive jurisdiction over the case. This is adopted by the judicial assistance treaties concluded between China and Russia, Ukraine, Belarus, Kazakhstan and other countries. For example, the Civil Judicial Assistance Treaty between China and Russia uses the *exclusive* jurisdiction of the applicant country over the case as one of the reasons for refusing to recognise and enforce the court's judgment.[11] This method is relatively clear, that is, the jurisdiction of the foreign court is not recognised only when the law of the requested country provides exclusive jurisdiction over the case.
(3) The third method is to directly judge whether the court of the requesting country has jurisdiction according to the laws of the requested country. This method is adopted in the judicial assistance treaties signed by China with France, Poland, Mongolia, Cuba, Romania and other countries. That is, if 'according to the law of the requested party, the court of the requesting party does not have *qualified* jurisdiction over the case', then the court of the requested country may refuse to recognise the judgment.[12] In addition, some treaties that have criteria for listing jurisdiction, also stipulate that the criteria for determining jurisdiction does not affect the exclusive jurisdiction cases under the domestic law of the applicant country.[13] In other words, some countries have adopted the method of listing and adding negative lists to check whether the jurisdiction is qualified.

Third, the conditions for recognition and enforcement of the judgments or its refusal. In the bilateral judicial assistance treaties between China and various countries, the conditions for recognition and enforcement of a judgment mainly adopt two methods: one is the affirmative form, which lists the specific conditions for recognition and enforcement, such as the bilateral treaties between China and Cyprus, and Hungary;[14] the other is the negative form, which lists the specific circumstances for refusal to recognise and enforce the judgment, such as the bilateral treaties between China and Belarus, Bulgaria etc.[15] Whether affirmative or negative, Regarding the conditions for recognition and enforcement of foreign court judgments, the following main aspects will be included in these bilateral judicial assistance treaties:

(1) Validity of the foreign judgment. According to the law of the country where the judgment was originally made, the judgment may not be recognised and enforced if the judgment has not been determined or has no adjudication force. Different countries have different

[10] Treaty between the People's Republic of China and the Italian Republic on Civil Judicial Assistance, Art 22.

[11] Treaty between the People's Republic of China and the Russian Federation on Civil and Criminal Justice Assistance, Art 20.

[12] Agreement between the People's Republic of China and the Republic of Cuba on Civil and Criminal Judicial Assistance, Art 25.

[13] Treaty between the People's Republic of China and the kingdom of Spain on Civil and Criminal Justice Assistance, Art 20(2).

[14] Treaty between the People's Republic of China and the Republic of Hungary on Judicial Assistance in Civil and Commercial Matters, Art 17.

[15] Treaty between the People's Republic of China and the Republic of Belarus on Civil and Criminal Judicial Assistance, Art 21.

opinions on the validity of the judgment. In the treaties, there are two kinds of provisions for the judgments applied for recognition and enforcement. One is that the judgment must be effective and enforceable, and the other is that the judgment is final and enforceable.

(2) The judgment is not recognised and enforced by a court without jurisdiction.

(3) A judgment made under the following circumstances is not recognised and enforced: in the absence of a judgment, the losing party has not been legally summoned by the court or has not been legally represented when he has no capacity for litigation;

(4) A judgment which impairs the sovereignty, security or public policy of the requested contracting party shall not be recognised and enforced.

Fourth, procedures for recognition and enforcement of judgments. There are two main types of procedures for recognition and enforcement of awards:

(1) Regarding the procedures for recognition and enforcement of arbitral awards, the contracting parties apply the laws of their respective countries, such as the provisions of bilateral treaties between China and Cyprus and Egypt.[16]

(2) The recognition and enforcement of court judgments shall be conducted by the court of the requested contracting party in accordance with the procedures provided for in its national laws, such as the provisions of the bilateral treaties concluded by China with Belarus, Bulgaria, Cuba, Greece etc.[17]

The judicial assistance agreements signed between China and other countries provide firm bases for reciprocal recognition and enforcement of civil and commercial judgments.

B. Regulations on Interregional Judicial Assistance in China

In addition to international civil and commercial mutual judicial assistance treaties, the existence of different special administrative regions in China and the corresponding development of economic value and trade with these special administrative regions has resulted in arrangements for the regional circulation of judgments.

On the recognition and enforcement of judgments in the mainland of China and Taiwan, the Supreme People's Court issued the Provisions of the Supreme People's Court on Recognition and Enforcement of the Civil Judgments of Courts of the Taiwan Region.[18] It provides that the parties to a civil judgment of a court of the Taiwan Region may, in accordance with the aforementioned provisions, apply to the People's Court of the mainland as an applicant for recognition and enforcement of the civil judgment of the relevant court of the Taiwan Region.[19] The conditions for recognition and enforcement of judgments mostly coincide with those in the above-mentioned bilateral treaties. However, the provision emphasises that where recognition of the civil judgment violates the principle of China or any other fundamental principle of the laws of the state, or

[16] Agreement between the People's Republic of China and the Arab Republic of Egypt on Civil, Commercial and Criminal Judicial Assistance, Art 25(1).

[17] Agreement between the People's Republic of China and the Republic of Greece on Civil and Criminal Justice Assistance, Art 24(1).

[18] Provisions of the Supreme People's Court on Recognition and Enforcement of the Civil Judgments of Courts of the Taiwan Region (Supreme People's Court, Fa Shi [2015] 13, 1 July 2015) www.chinacourt.org/law/detail/2015/06/id/148295.shtml accessed 20 May 2020.

[19] Provisions of the Supreme People's Court on Recognition and Enforcement of the Civil Judgments of Courts of the Taiwan Region, Art 1.

damages social and public interests, the People's Court shall issue a ruling not to recognise it. In order to give better play to the functional roles of the People's Courts in serving, guaranteeing, and promoting cross-straits economic and cultural exchanges, cooperation and integrated development, on 25 March 2019 the Supreme People's Court issued the Several Measures for Providing Judicial Services to Deepen the Cross-Straits Integrated Development.[20] This provides that an application for the recognition and enforcement of a civil judgment and arbitration award made in the Taiwan Region shall be examined in a legal and timely manner, and that a civil judgment of the Taiwan Region that is recognised by ruling shall have the same legal force as an effective judgment of the People's Court. This demonstrates China's determination to legally, comprehensively, and equally safeguard the lawful rights and interests of its Taiwan compatriots.

Regarding the recognition and enforcement of judgments between the Mainland and the Macao Special Administrative Region, according to Article 93 of the Basic Law of the Macao Special Administrative Region of the People's Republic of China, the Supreme People's Court reached the Arrangement between the Mainland and the Macao Special Administrative Region on the Mutual Recognition and Enforcement of Civil and Commercial Judgments with the Macao Special Administrative Region, and it came into force as of 1 April 2006.[21] First of all, the arrangement stipulates its scope of application, including the mutual recognition and enforcement of judgments in civil and commercial cases (including labour dispute cases in the Mainland and civil labour cases in the Macao Special Administrative Region) between the Mainland and the Macao Special Administrative Region, as well as verdicts of civil damages involved in criminal cases.[22] Second, the arrangement stipulates in detail the conditions and procedures for the recognition and enforcement of judgments, especially concerning the issue of parallel litigation. When the court of the requested party has disposed any similar action, the judgment shall not be recognised if the aforesaid action had been put forward prior to the judgment to be recognised, and the court of the requested party has jurisdiction.[23] When accepting a request for recognition of a judgment, if the court of the requested party has a pending litigation in the same case, two conditions must be met to refuse recognition of the other party's judgment: (1) the court of the requested party has jurisdiction over the lawsuit; (2) the court of the requested party accepted the case first, which had been put forward prior to the judgment to be recognised. This resolved the problem of jurisdiction in parallel litigation.

Finally, in terms of the recognition and enforcement of judgments in the Mainland and the Hong Kong Special Administrative Region, the legal systems of the Mainland and the Hong Kong Special Administrative Region belong to the civil law system and the common law system respectively. Pursuant to Article 95 of the Basic Law of the Hong Kong Special Administrative Region of the People's Republic of China, the Supreme People's Court and the Hong Kong Special Administrative Region ('HKSAR') reached the Arrangement between the Mainland and the Hong Kong Special Administrative Region on Reciprocal Recognition and Enforcement of the

[20] Notice of the Supreme People's Court on Issuing the Several Measures for Providing Judicial Services to Deepen the Cross-Straits Integrated Development (Supreme People's Court, Fa Fa [2019] 9 Hao, 25 March 2019) www.court.gov.cn/fabu-xiangqing-148032.html accessed 21 May 2020.

[21] Arrangement between the Mainland and the Macao Special Administrative Region on the Mutual Recognition and Enforcement of Civil and Commercial Judgments (Supreme People's Court, Fa Shi (2006) 2, 1 April 2006) www.chinacourt.org/law/detail/2006/03/id/107944.shtml accessed 25 May 2020.

[22] Arrangement between the Mainland and the Macao Special Administrative Region on the Mutual Recognition and Enforcement of Civil and Commercial Judgments, Art 1.

[23] Arrangement between the Mainland and the Macao Special Administrative Region on the Mutual Recognition and Enforcement of Civil and Commercial Judgments, Art 11(1).

Decisions of Civil and Commercial Cases under Consensual Jurisdiction, which was signed on 14 July 2006 and came into force as of 1 August 2008.[24] The arrangement provides that for a final decision of payment with executive force made by a people's court in the Mainland and a court of the HKSAR in a civil or commercial case under a written jurisdiction agreement, the party concerned may apply to the people's court in the Mainland or the HK court for the recognition and enforcement of the decision.[25] In January 2019, the Supreme People's Court and the Department of Justice of Hong Kong signed the Arrangement on Reciprocal Recognition and Enforcement of Judgments in Civil and Commercial Matters by the Courts of the Mainland and of the Hong Kong Special Administrative Region in Beijing, which made provisions on mutual recognition and enforcement of civil and commercial case judgments. Upon commencement of this arrangement, the earlier arrangement between the Mainland and the Hong Kong Special Administrative Region on Reciprocal Recognition and Enforcement of the Decisions of Civil and Commercial Cases under Consensual Jurisdiction was terminated. The arrangement of 2019 contains 31 articles, which stipulate the scope and content of mutual recognition and enforcement of judgments in civil and commercial cases, procedures and methods for applying for recognition and enforcement, examination of the jurisdiction of the original court, circumstances of non-recognition and enforcement, etc. This arrangement expands the scope of mutual recognition and enforcement of judgments in civil and commercial cases as far as possible. It includes non-monetary rulings and judgments in some intellectual property cases in the scope of mutual recognition and enforcement. Virtually all significant fields are covered.[26]

China's various regions may be separated by legal systems, but they share common national interests. All regions have the responsibility and mission of safeguarding the country's overall interests, are subject to the same constitution, are under the national legal system, and are unified by the state's sovereignty. In the process of regional economic integration, the free circulation of judgments can ensure the free circulation of goods, personnel, services, and capital, and that judgments across regions meet the country's political and economic needs. This is called the 'interregional characteristics'.[27] To enable the free circulation of judgments, it is necessary to maximise the scope of recognition and enforcement of court judgments, to give lax treatment to the conditions of recognition and enforcement of court judgments, and to simplify the procedures for recognition and enforcement of court judgments.[28] The arrangements of recognition and enforcement by inter-regional courts between the Mainland and the HKSAR, the Macao Special Administrative Region and Taiwan Region are matters of mutual judicial assistance within a state, and establish a relatively complete judicial assistance system.

[24] Arrangement of the Supreme People's Court between the Mainland and the HKSAR on Reciprocal Recognition and Enforcement of the Decisions of Civil and Commercial Cases under Consensual Jurisdiction (Supreme People's Court, Fa Shi [2008] 9 Hao, 1 August 2008) www.chinacourt.org/law/detail/2008/07/id/127153.shtml accessed 25 May 2020.

[25] Arrangement of the Supreme People's Court between the Mainland and the HKSAR on Reciprocal Recognition and Enforcement of the Decisions of Civil and Commercial Cases under Consensual Jurisdiction, Art 1.

[26] Media headquarters of the people's court: the mainland and Hong Kong today signed a mutual recognition and enforcement of civil and commercial cases judgment arrangement: Yang Wanming, Teresa Cheng represent both signed (*Supreme People's Court*, 18 January 2019) www.court.gov.cn/zixun-xiangqing-139481.html accessed 19 February 2019.

[27] ZH Yu, 'Neidi Yu Xianggang Tequ Minshangshi Panjue Chengren Yu Zhixing Wenti Fenxi' [Analysis on the Recognition and Enforcement of Civil and Commercial Judgments in the Mainland and Hong Kong Special Administrative Region] (2015) 11 *Jinan Journal Philosophy and Social Science* 5.

[28] ZH Yu, 'Shilun Zhongguo De Quyu Jingji Yitihua Yu Panjue De Ziyou Liudong' [On the Regional Economic Integration of China and the Free Circulation of Judgment], (2011) 11 *Zheng Fa Lun Cong* 55.

C. Convention of the Hague Conference on Private International Law

For a long time, the global enforceability of domestic court decisions had not been effectively addressed. In the 1970s, the Hague Conference on Private International Law adopted the Convention on the Recognition and Enforcement of Foreign Judgments in Civil and Commercial Matters.[29] However, as only Albania and Kuwait have ratified the convention,[30] it was not ratified by a sufficient number of countries. The legal requirements for its entry into force have not yet been met so the Convention has not entered into force.[31] Therefore, the Convention has had little success in promoting the recognition and enforcement of international civil judgments. In the context of cross-border civil and commercial disputes, especially the international jurisdiction of the court and the recognition and implementation of its judgments abroad, the Hague Conference on Private International Law launched the 'Judgments Project' in 1992, hoping to develop a wide range of international conventions on the two major issues of international jurisdiction, recognition and implementation.[32] Recognition has been dealt with by the 2005 Convention on Choice of Court Agreements.[33] The Convention, adopted by the 20th diplomatic conference of the Hague Conference on Private International Law on 30 June 2005, aims to ensure the validity of the choice of court agreement made by the parties (or 'court selection clause'), and has been ratified by the US and the vast majority of EU countries. China signed the Convention on 12 September 2017, although it has yet to be ratified. It is worth noting that the focus of developing countries represented by China is different from that of Europe and the US. Developing countries attach special importance to the issues of jurisdiction and the nature of national sovereignty decided by the court, and do not give way to jurisdiction easily.[34]

The Convention on Choice of Court Agreements sets three obligations for the courts of member countries of the Convention where parties have made a choice of court. First, the court chosen by the parties is obliged to hear the dispute. Second, other courts are obliged to refuse to exercise jurisdiction in such a dispute. Third, judgments rendered by courts chosen by the parties shall be recognised and enforced in the courts of other countries. Therefore, the convention establishes for the first time a global legal framework for civil and commercial judgments, and effectively dealt with the recognition and enforcement of judgments arising from the parties' choice of court jurisdiction. To this end, the Judgments Project was launched again in 2012. On 2 July 2019, the 22nd diplomatic conference of the Hague Conference on Private International Law discussed the adoption of the Convention on Recognition and Enforcement of Foreign Judgments in Civil and Commercial matters. The scope and definition of the Convention are explained at the beginning of Chapter I. Defining the scope of application of the Convention is particularly important for a comprehensive understanding of the it. The scope of the Convention includes both positive definition and negative exclusion. Article 1

[29] HCCH: Convention of 1 February 1971 on the Recognition and Enforcement of Foreign Judgments in Civil and Commercial Matters www.hcch.net/en/instruments/conventions/full-text/?cid=78accessed 12 December 2019.

[30] Cyprus, Portugal and the Netherlands have signed but not ratified the Convention.

[31] HCCH: Convention of 1 February 1971 on the Recognition and Enforcement of Foreign Judgments in Civil and Commercial Matters www.hcch.net/index_en.php?act=conventions.status&cid=78 accessed 23 April 2020.

[32] 'On the Judgments Project' www.hcch.net/en/projects/legislative-projects/judgments accessed 7 Feb 2019. On the problems encountered in drafting a double convention, see G Tu, *A Study on a Global Jurisdiction and Judgments Convention* (Sweet & Maxwell, 2009).

[33] HCCH: Overview of the Judgments Project www.hcch.net/en/projects/legislative-projects/judgments/overview-judgments accessed 7 Feb 2019.

[34] T Du, 'Zhongguo Pizhun Haiya Xunaze Fayuan Xieyi Gongyue De Falv Wenti He Duice' [Legal Issues and Solutions of China's Ratification on Choice of Court Agreement Convention] (2016) 4 *Wuhan University Journal (Social Science)* 94.

defines the scope of its application, namely the recognition and implementation of judgments related to civil and commercial affairs, and the geographical scope of its application. Article 2 excludes 17 matters that are not covered by the Convention. Chapter II on Recognition and Enforcement, contains 12 clauses. These constitute the main content of the document and provide relatively comprehensive provisions on the system of recognition and implementation.[35] In the future, China's ratification of the Convention will help establish an effective dispute resolution mechanism among states' parties to international trade and investment agreements, and help remedy the current institutional deficiencies in the system of extraterritorial recognition and enforcement of Chinese judgments, especially monetary judgments. In the context of a new round of economic globalisation and 'One Belt and One Road' international cooperation, parties should be more active in participating in international civil and commercial exchanges.[36]

In addition to the aforementioned conventions, China has joined other conventions drafted by the Hague Conference on Private International Law. For example, the Convention on the Service Abroad of Judicial and Extrajudicial Documents in Civil or Commercial Matters,[37] and the Convention on the Taking of Evidence Abroad in Civil or Commercial Matters.[38] These conventions also address the recognition and enforcement of judgments of extraterritorial courts.

D. Other International Conventions

Provisions for the recognition and enforcement of foreign judgments generally appear in the form of special chapters or articles in international conventions addressing a specialised field. In some international treaties on the unification of substantive law, the international community has provided for the recognition and enforcement of foreign court judgments. For example, Article 31 of the 1956 International Convention on Contracts for the Carriage of Goods by Road, Article 10 of the 1969 International Convention on Civil Liability for Oil Pollution Damage, and Article 58 of the 1970 Convention on Contracts for the Carriage of Goods by Rail.[39] Some specialised international conventions to which China has acceded also contain provisions on the mutual recognition of court judgments of contracting states. As provided for in Article 10 of the 1969 International Convention on Civil Liability for Oil Pollution Damage:

> A judgment rendered by a court of jurisdiction having the provisions of Article 10, which may be applied in the country of origin without the need for the usual review procedure, shall be recognized by the states parties unless: (1) the judgment was obtained by deception; (2) the defendant was not given

[35] HCCH: Convention of 2 July 2019 on the Recognition and Enforcement of Foreign Judgments in Civil or Commercial Matters www.hcch.net/en/instruments/conventions/full-text/?cid=137 accessed 5 Oct 2019.

[36] RS Liu, 'Woguo Pizhun Xuanze Fayuan Xieyi Gongyue De Wenti Yu Duice' [Issues and Solutions of China's Ratification on Choice of Court Agreement Convention] (2018) 4 *Chinese Journal of Law* 201.

[37] HCCH: Convention of 15 November 1965 on the Service Abroad of Judicial and Extrajudicial Documents in Civil or Commercial Matters www.hcch.net/en/instruments/conventions/full-text/?cid=17 accessed 2 January 2020.

[38] HCCH: Convention of 18 March 1970 on the Taking of Evidence Abroad in Civil or Commercial Matters www.hcch.net/en/instruments/conventions/full-text/?cid=82 accessed 2 January 2020.

[39] Article 10(1) of International Convention on Civil Liability for Oil Pollution Damage (United Nations Treaty Series vol 973, 29 November 1969) 3: Any judgment given by a Court with jurisdiction in accordance with Article IX which is enforceable in the State of origin where it is no longer subject to ordinary forms of review, shall be recognized in any Contracting State, except:

(a) where the judgment was obtained by fraud; or
(b) where the defendant was not given reasonable notice and a fair opportunity to present his case.

> reasonable notice or fair opportunity to state his or her position. A judgment confirmed in accordance with paragraph 1 of this article shall be executed immediately in each contracting state upon completion of the formalities prescribed by that state. The formalities do not permit any repetition of the facts of the case.

It is noteworthy that the above-mentioned international conventions to which China has acceded are very limited in number, and are not comprehensive in their areas of application. Therefore, international conventions have little practical significance for China's approach to the recognition and enforcement of foreign judgments. China's recognition and enforcement of foreign court judgments in accordance with multilateral international conventions is also very limited. In practice, recognition is normally pursuant to bilateral mutual legal assistance treaties, not multilateral treaties.

II. Indirect Jurisdiction

Jurisdiction of a country's court over a case is an important embodiment of national judicial sovereignty. In order to protect their national sovereignty, all countries attach great importance to provisions of jurisdiction. As a corollary, when determining whether to recognise and enforce a foreign judgment, most countries believe that the court of the original state must have appropriate jurisdiction. That is, to obtain the recognition and enforcement of the requested contracting party's decision, the court in which the requesting party receives the decision must have jurisdiction over the case. This is known as indirect jurisdiction.[40] Generally speaking, the international community should respect the judicial sovereignty of all countries. However, if the judgment needs to be recognised and enforced in the requested state, this will inevitably affect that state's interests. Therefore, it is necessary for the court to determine whether the foreign court which produced the judgment itself had jurisdiction.[41] Indirect jurisdiction is a prerequisite for the recognition and enforcement of foreign court decisions in several documents formulated by the Hague Conference on private international law.

The circumstances set out in Article 5 of the Convention on Recognition and Enforcement of Foreign Judgments in Civil and Commercial Matters apply only to indirect jurisdiction and do not take into account the direct jurisdiction of the country where the court of the first instance is located.[42] Where the indirect jurisdiction requirement is met, this Article is divided into three paragraphs. The first paragraph lists 13 indirect jurisdiction bases, for example, habitually resident of the defendant, the principal place of business of the natural person, jurisdiction based on consent, the defendant maintained a branch, agency, or other establishment, and jurisdiction based on request and jurisdiction of the court of the first instance etc. The second paragraph provides some protective elements for weak parties to consumer contracts and employment contracts, and excludes the application of certain jurisdictional bases in paragraph 1. The third paragraph provides for the exclusive jurisdiction of the location of the real estate for the lease and registration of real estate. In continuance of the earlier Hague texts, the convention adopted

[40] T Du, *Guoji Sifa Yuanli [Principles of Private International Law]* (Fudan University Press, 2018) 315.

[41] J Shen, 'Zailun Haiya Minshangshi Guanxiaquan He Waiguo De Panjue Chengren Yu Zhixing Gongyue Caoan Ji Zhongguo De Kaoliang' [Further Discussion on the Drafts of the Hague Convention on Jurisdiction and Recognition and Enforcement of Foreign Judgments in Civil and Commercial Matters and Considerations from Chinese Perspective] (2016) 6 *Study of International Law* 98.

[42] 'On the Jurisdiction Project' www.hcch.net/en/projects/legislative-projects/jurisdiction-project accessed 12 January 2020.

'habitual residence' as one of the connecting factors in determining whether the state of origin has jurisdiction over the case, rather than the 'domicile' or 'nationality' factors commonly used in domestic legal systems. Recently, one of the requirements of indirect jurisdiction – the 'mirror principle' – has received attention.[43] The principle requires that the reasons for indirect jurisdiction should be consistent with the reasons for applying direct jurisdiction in the same country, so as to prevent discrimination against foreign judgments.[44] However, the mirror principle does not appear in relevant legal documents at present.

Indirect jurisdiction ensures that there is a certain link between the country where the decision is made and the defendant or the matter in dispute. Indirect jurisdiction is also called international jurisdiction, because it includes the internationally accepted reasons for the court to have jurisdiction over the defendant or the lawsuit. But there is difficulty in accurately defining these reasons.[45] A number of documents prepared by the Hague Conference on Private International Law prescribe a minimum standard for mutual recognition or enforcement of judgments, the specific content is as follows:

(i) the state of the court is the habitual residence of the accused, or the defendant's principal place of business or the place where the defendant has set up branches or agents, as long as the aforesaid place is closely related to the place of the action;
(ii) the defendant has no objection to the jurisdiction or has invoked the jurisdiction of the court to bring a counterclaim to acknowledge the jurisdiction of the court by a clear agreement or asserting entity;
(iii) a judgment that ruled on a residential lease of immovable property (tenancy) or ruled on the registration of immovable property is eligible for recognition and enforcement only if it was given by a court of the State where the property is situated;
(iv) the non-contractual obligations related to the litigation and the acts causing the damage occurred in the state of the trial court.[46]

Chinese domestic law on jurisdiction is contained in the Supreme People's Court 1991 'Provisions on the Procedure of Chinese Citizens' Application for Recognition of Divorce Judgments in Foreign Courts.'[47] The provisions clarify that if the country where the case is heard does not have jurisdiction over the case, China can refuse to recognise and enforce the judgment. Bilateral judicial assistance agreements signed by China and foreign states follow the basic requirements of indirect jurisdiction. For an example, see the detailed provisions on jurisdiction in Article 18 of the Treaty between the People's Republic of China and the Socialist Republic of Vietnam on Civil and Criminal Judicial Assistance.[48] The jurisdiction standards stipulated in the bilateral

[43] 'Introduction: Towards a System for the Recognition and Enforcement of Judgments' in A Reyes (ed), *Recognition and Enforcement of Judgment in Civil and Commercial Matters* (Hart Publishing, 2019) 30.

[44] ibid, 22.

[45] ibid, 19.

[46] HCCH: Draft Convention on the recognition and enforcement of foreign judgments in civil or commercial matters prepared by the Special Commission on the Judgments Project of May 2018, Art 5 www.hcch.net/en/instruments/conventions/specialised-sections/judgments/special-commission accessed 13 August 2020.

[47] Article 12 of Provisions on Issues concerning the Procedures for Chinese Citizens to Apply for the Recognition of the Divorce Judgments Made by Foreign Courts www.law-lib.com/law/law_view.asp?id=7763 accessed 15 August 2020: *Upon review, if the divorce judgment of a foreign court has one of the following circumstances, it will not be recognized: (2) The foreign court that made the judgment has no jurisdiction over the case.*

[48] Article 18 of the Treaty between the People's Republic of China and the Socialist Republic of Vietnam on Civil and Criminal Judicial Assistance: In one of the following circumstances, the court of the Contracting Party that made the decision shall be deemed to have jurisdiction over the case in accordance with this Treaty: (1) at the time of initiating a lawsuit, the defendant is in the territory of that party or residence; (2) when proceedings are brought, the defendant

mutual legal assistance treaties concluded by China are different again. There are three main legislative methods. First, specifying the scope of jurisdiction in detail, such as in the bilateral judicial assistance agreements concluded by China with Italy, Spain, Egypt, Cyprus and other countries.[49] Second, adopting the method of 'exclusive jurisdiction exclusion', such as the treaty between China and Russia on civil and criminal justice assistance.[50] Third, directly applying the law of the requested country, such as the treaties signed between China and France, Turkey and other countries.[51]

Among the three methods, the first two are consistent with the Convention on Recognition and Enforcement of Foreign Judgments in Civil and Commercial matters established by the Hague Conference on Private International Law. Hence, China has a legal basis for accepting the convention in the future. Regarding the recognition and enforcement of international civil and commercial cases, the standards for the jurisdiction of the courts of different countries are also different. Although most countries choose to adopt their own laws to examine the jurisdiction of the court of the original state, the regulations on direct jurisdiction of each country are not uniform. Many problems have arisen in judicial practice, making jurisdictional conditions a real obstacle in the recognition and enforcement of international civil and commercial judgments.

III. Principle of Reciprocity

In the absence of treaty relations, states generally recognise and enforce foreign court judgments on the basis of reciprocity. Due to the existence of the principle of reciprocity, the review standard of a judicial recognition and enforcement of a foreign judgment not only affects whether a foreign court's judgment can be recognised and enforced by domestic courts, but also whether the domestic courts' judgments can be recognised and enforced in that foreign country. In accordance with the provisions of the Civil Procedure Law and the relevant judicial interpretation, if a legally effective judgment or written order made by a foreign court requires recognition and enforcement by a Chinese court, the domestic court shall generally examine the judgment in accordance with the international treaties concluded or acceded to by the PRC or with the principle of reciprocity. The exception is where the parties apply to the people's court for recognition of a legally effective divorce judgment made by a foreign court. In 1995, the applicant, Wuwei Huang, a Japanese citizen, applied to the Dalian Intermediate People's Court in Liaoning Province, China, requesting recognition and enforcement of a Japanese judgment. The Supreme

has a representative office in the territory of the said party; (3) the defendant has expressly accepted the jurisdiction of the court in writing; (4) the defendant entered a plea on the merits of the dispute and did not raise any objection to the question of jurisdiction; (5) in the event of a contractual dispute, the contract is concluded or has been or should have been performed within the territory of the said party, or the subject matter of the action is within the territory of the said party; (6) in the case of infringement outside the contract, the infringing act or result occurs within the territory of the party concerned; (7) in a case of status relations, the litigant has a domicile within the territory of the said party; (8) in a case of maintenance obligation, the debtor has a domicile in the territory of the said party; (9) in a case of succession, the domicile or main estate of the decedent is within the territory of the said party at the time of his death; or (10) the subject matter of the proceedings is real property located within the territory of that party.

[49] Treaty between the People's Republic of China and the Italian Republic on Civil Judicial Assistance, Art 22.

[50] Treaty between the People's Republic of China and the Russian Federation on Civil and Criminal Justice Assistance, Art 20; Agreement between the People's Republic of China and the Republic of Cuba on Civil and Criminal Judicial Assistance, Art 25.

[51] Treaty between the People's Republic of China and the Russian Federation on Civil and Criminal Justice Assistance, Art 20. Agreement between the People's Republic of China and the Republic of Cuba on Civil and Criminal Judicial Assistance, Art 25.

People's Court of China issued its opinion on 26 June 1995, holding that the Japanese court's judgment would not be recognised and enforced because there was no relevant international treaty between China and Japan, nor was there a reciprocal fact of mutual recognition and enforcement of each other's court decisions. Therefore, the Dalian Intermediate People's Court rejected Wuwei Huang's request according to the Supreme People's Court's opinion.

Since there is no precedent system in China, it is particularly important to confirm the existence of legal reciprocity between China and foreign countries when China changes from de facto reciprocity to legal reciprocity.[52] The courts at all levels followed the Supreme People's Court's opinion and established the principle of reciprocity based on the fact that the country in which the foreign judgment was made had recognised Chinese judgments.[53] In recent years, there has been reciprocal recognition by Chinese courts of judgments made by courts in Singapore and the US.[54] Recently, the Supreme People's Court of China signed a memorandum of cooperation with the Supreme Court of Singapore.[55] The memorandum states the conditions for the courts of China and Singapore to consider the recognition and enforcement of their respective judgments. Conditions include the finality of the judgment sought to be enforced and whether the requirements of indirect jurisdiction are met. The memorandum is seen as an important demonstration of mutually beneficial relations between China and other states. Although the memorandum is not legally binding, it could provide a reference for other common law countries to establish mutually beneficial relations with China and to facilitate the recognition and enforcement of judgments. In addition, Article 7 of the Nanning Statement in the second session of the China-ASEAN Judicial Forum observed that as long as the court of another state did not refuse to recognise or enforce a state's judgments based on the lack of reciprocity, the relationship of reciprocity can be presumed to exist.[56]

The adoption of the Nanning Statement shows that Chinese courts and courts of ASEAN states have reached an effective consensus on the 'presumption of reciprocity' in the mutual recognition and implementation of civil and commercial judgments.[57] Although the Nanning Declaration

[52] J Huang, 'Reciprocal Recognition and Enforcement of Foreign Judgments in China: Promising Developments, Prospective Challenges and Proposed Solutions' (2019) *Nordic Journal of International Law* 10.

[53] A Chong, 'Recognition and Enforcement of Foreign Judgments in Asia' (2017) *Asia Business Law Institute* 67.

[54] Jiangsu Nanjin Intermediate People's Court Decision *Kolmar Group AG v Jiangsu Textile Industry (Group) Import and Export Co Ltd* (2016) Su-01 Xie Wai Ren No 03. In this case, on 9 December 2016, the Nanjing intermediate people's court in accordance with the principle of mutual recognition and enforcement recognised the Singaporean court judgment on 22 October 2015, Singapore 013 civil judgments, the reason being that in 2014, Singapore's High Court admitted and executed a Suzhou intermediate people's court decision in its [2014] SGHC16 judgment. Hubei Wuhan Intermediate People's Court Decision *Liu Li v Tao Li and Tong Wu* (2015) Yue Wuhan Zhong Min Shang Wai Chu Zi No 00026 (30 June 2017). In this case, on 30 June 2017, the intermediate people's court of Wuhan, Hubei province recognised and implemented the judgment No EC62608 issued by the superior court of Los Angeles county, California, US.

[55] The memorandum of guidance between the Supreme Court of the People's Republic of China and the Supreme Court of the Republic of Singapore on the recognition and enforcement of monetary judgments in commercial cases 2018 (SG).

[56] Article 7 of Nanning Statement of the 2nd China-ASEAN Justice Forum (2017): Regional cross-border transactions and investments require a judicial safeguard based on appropriate mutual recognition and enforcement of judicial judgments among countries in the region. Subject to their domestic laws, Supreme Courts of participating countries will keep good faith in interpreting domestic laws, try to avoid unnecessary parallel proceedings, and consider facilitating the appropriate mutual recognition and enforcement of civil or commercial judgments among different jurisdictions. If two countries have not been bound by any international treaty on mutual recognition and enforcement of foreign civil or commercial judgments, both countries may, subject to their domestic laws, presume the existence of their reciprocal relationship, when it comes to the judicial procedure of recognising or enforcing such judgments made by courts of the other country, provided that the courts of the other country had not refused to recognise or enforce such judgments on the ground of lack of reciprocity.

[57] T Du, 'Tuiding Huhui Guanxi: Cujin Yidai Yilu Susong Jiufen Jiejue' [The presumption of reciprocity and promotion of 'One Belt And One Road' litigation and dispute resolution] (2017) 2 *People's Court of Justice* 1.

is also not legally binding, it still provides a useful reference for promoting the establishment of legal reciprocity, promoting the common business cooperation between China and ASEAN states, and even possibly applying the reciprocity principle to the regional or global trends in the future. In addition, the announcement of the Opinions of the Supreme People's Court Regarding Further Providing Judicial Services and Guarantees by the People's Courts for the Belt and Road Initiative on 27 December 2019 reflects the further transformation of the application of the principle of reciprocity in China.[58] The opinion directly states that 'The people's courts in China shall adopt a judicial attitude of presumption of reciprocity to continuously promote the mutual recognition and enforcement of international commercial court judgments.' The opinion expresses that the Chinese courts will change the traditional and conservative concept of reciprocity, establish the idea of legal reciprocity, and handle international judicial assistance in line with a more active and open reciprocal attitude. With the gradual deepening and implementation of the 'Belt and Road' initiative, China will expand the principle of reciprocity to enable more foreign judgments to be recognised and enforced in China. It is foreseeable that legislative and judicial practice in China will be more positive towards the principle of reciprocity in the future.[59]

IV. Grounds for Refusal

Reaching consensus on the mutual recognition and enforcement of court judgments among various countries not only helps to secure the rights and interests of the parties, but also facilitates all-round cooperation between countries in the political, economic, and judicial fields. However, because of the issue of sovereign equality, it is necessary to attach some review conditions to this cooperation. These are found in the reasons for refusing to recognise and enforce foreign judgments. The following reasons for refusal to recognise and enforce foreign judgments are listed in the Hague Conference on Private International Law Convention on Recognition and Enforcement of Foreign Judgments in Civil and Commercial Matters: lack of indirect jurisdiction, denial of due process (including procedural fraud to obtain a verdict), violation of public policy, and the existence of prior *res judicata*.[60] China's Supreme People's Court's Notice of Several Issues on Trial and Enforcement of Foreign-related Civil and Commercial Cases stresses that the courts are expected to maintain an image of national judicial dignity and to comply with the rule of law, to recognise the importance of foreign-related enforcement, to strengthen the enforcement of foreign cases, to pay attention to the method of execution, to improve the enforcement efficiency, and to pay attention to the effect of enforcement.[61] In order to facilitate the recognition and enforcement of judgments made by foreign courts in China, in both domestic legislation and bilateral judicial assistance treaties, China has made specific provisions on the recognition and

[58] Opinions of the Supreme People's Court Regarding Further Providing Judicial Services and Guarantees by the People's Courts for the Belt and Road Initiative (Supreme People's Court, Fa Fa (2019) 29 Hao, 12 September 2019) www.court.gov.cn/fabu-xiangqing-212931.html accessed 6 May 2020.

[59] YJ Zhang and L Yang, 'Sifa Jiguan Xianghu Chengren Zhixing Minshangshi Panjue De Xintansuo' [New exploration of mutual recognition and enforcement of civil and commercial judgments by judicial organs] (2019) 13 *Renmin Sifa* 22.

[60] HCCH: Draft Convention on the recognition and enforcement of foreign judgments in civil or commercial matters prepared by the Special Commission on the Judgments Project of May 2018, Art 7 www.hcch.net/en/instruments/conventions/specialised-sections/judgments/special-commission accessed 13 August 2020.

[61] Notice on several issues that should be paid attention to in the trial and execution of foreign-related civil and commercial cases, Art 3 (Supreme People's Court, Fa [2000] 51, 17 April 2000) www.pkulaw.cn/fulltext_form.aspx?Db=alftwotitle&Gid=1549574260750815bdfb accessed 21 January 2020.

enforcement of civil and commercial judgments of foreign courts in China. This reflects China's attitude to strengthen cooperation in dealing with judgments of foreign courts.

Among the above-mentioned 37 bilateral mutual judicial assistance agreements signed by China, four do not provide for the recognition and enforcement of foreign court judgments, namely Singapore, South Korea, Thailand and Belgium. The rest contain specific provisions on the conditions for refusal of recognition and enforcement. These provisions mainly include: (1) according to the law of the requested country, the court of the country where the judgment is made must have had jurisdiction; (2) the judgment of the foreign court must be effective and enforceable; (3) there were no unfair circumstances in the proceedings of the foreign court; (4) there is no parallel litigation; and (5) there is no violation of the public policy of the requested state. Turning to domestic law, the Supreme People's Court judicial interpretation in 1991 on the Provisions on the Procedure of Chinese Citizens' Application for Recognition of Divorce Judgments in Foreign Courts observed that a foreign court divorce judgment will not be recognised and enforced in any of the following circumstances:[62] the judgment has not become legally effective; the foreign court making the judgment has no jurisdiction over the case; the verdict was given in the absence of the defendant and without a lawful summons; the divorce case between the parties is being heard or has been decided by a Chinese court, or the Chinese courts have recognised a third country judgment on the divorce of the parties; or the judgment violates the basic principles of China's laws or endangers China's national sovereignty, security, and social and public interests. Since divorce cases involve special status relationships, the recognition and enforcement of divorce judgments in China is relatively special. The recognition and enforcement of non-divorce judgments are mainly stipulated in the Civil Procedure Law and its judicial interpretation.

A. Finality of the Foreign Judgment

Almost all legal systems allow the debtor to challenge the recognition and enforcement of the judgment of another state. Among the restrictions, the most important is that the judgment must be 'effective'.[63] That is, according to the laws of the original country, if the judgment has not been determined or has no adjudicative power, it may not be recognised and enforced. It is common practice in the international community to require foreign court judgments to have legal effect. The lack of legal effect will seriously affect the validity of foreign judgments. If the judgment of a court cannot be recognised and enforced in the original judgment country, it is even less likely to be recognised and enforced in the requested country. As far as Chinese regulations are concerned, under China's Civil Procedure Law and its judicial interpretation,[64] it is a condition for the recognition and enforcement of a foreign judgment that the judgment has come into force. In the

[62] Provisions on Issues Concerning the Procedures for Chinese Citizens to Apply for the Recognition of the Divorce Judgments Made by Foreign Courts Art 12 (Supreme People's Court, Fa Min [1991] 21, 13 August 1991) www.chinacourt.org/law/detail/1991/08/id/13301.shtml accessed 21 January 2020.

[63] P Hay, *Advanced Introduction to Private International Law and Procedure* (Edward Elgar Publishing, 2018) 113.

[64] Article 281 of the Civil Procedure Law of the People's Republic of China: Where an effective judgment or ruling of a foreign court requires recognition and enforcement by a people's court of the People's Republic of China, a party may apply directly to the intermediate people's court of the People's Republic of China having jurisdiction for recognition and enforcement or apply to the foreign court for the foreign court to request recognition and enforcement by the people's court in accordance with the provisions of an international treaty concluded or acceded to by the People's Republic of China or under the principle of reciprocity.

Supreme People's Court judicial interpretation in the 1990s on the Provisions on the Procedure of Chinese Citizens' Application for Recognition of Divorce Judgments in Foreign Courts, one reason for refusing to recognise and enforce a foreign divorce judgment is that the judgment has not yet taken legal effect. For example, in the case of Fang Lixin and Zeng Linxiang,[65] because the court could not confirm whether the court judgment of Tajikistan Republic submitted by the applicant Fang Lixin had been effective, the court considered that the application of the applicant Fang Lixin did not meet the condition of recognition and enforcement of foreign civil judgment in China, and rejected the applicant's request.

B. International Parallel Litigation

Parallel litigation refers to conflicts between domestic and foreign court judgments and two (or more) foreign court judgment conflicts that may arise when the domestic court (the court of the requested country) examines the application for recognition and enforcement of foreign civil judgments.[66] The laws of various countries and relevant international conventions regard the absence of international parallel litigation as an important condition for the recognition and enforcement of judgments of foreign courts. In essence, international parallel litigation is the result of conflicting claims of jurisdiction due to the diversity of jurisdictional rules in various countries' laws. The specific reasons are as follows: (1) the facts or elements that constitute 'disputes' are implicated in several countries; (2) there are various types of jurisdiction systems, and countries are trying to expand their jurisdictions under the drive of judicial sovereignty, but there are no uniform international rules of civil and commercial jurisdiction; (3) the parties have sufficient freedom and rights to choose the court, often considering the choice of court based on their own interests.

The Convention on Recognition and Enforcement of Foreign Judgments in Civil and Commercial matters lists the existence of parallel litigation as one reason for the refusal to recognise and enforce foreign court judgments.[67] It also stipulates how to deal with pending litigation in the requested country. Similar provision is found in the domestic Article 533 of

[65] Hunan Changsha Intermediate People's Court Decision *Fang Lixin v Zeng Linxiang* (2018) Xiang-01 Xie Wai Ren No 03: When the applicant Fang Lixin worked in the Republic of Tajikistan, he established a labour relationship with The Benling Co Ltd, which is registered in the Republic of Tajikistan. Because Ben Ling Co Ltd had not paid the applicant's labour fees, the applicant filed a lawsuit in the Sino District Court of the Republic of Tajikistan, and the court decided to enforce the court judgment against Zeng Linxiang, general manager of Ben Ling Co Ltd. However, it was verified that Zeng Linxiang was no longer in his place of residence in Dushanbe, rendering the debt unenforceable. Therefore, the applicant applied to the Chinese People's Court for recognition of the judgment in accordance with the provisions of Treaty between the People's Republic of China and the Republic of Tajikistan on Civil and Criminal Justice Assistance. http://wenshu.court.gov.cn/website/wenshu/181107ANFZ0BXSK4/index.html?docId=38efc6873b2f4f9680d1a9bd00673cdc accessed 15 August 2020.

[66] SD Zhang, 'Lun Waiguo Minshi Panjue Chengren Yu Zhixing Zhong De Susong Jinghe Shencha' [Parallel Proceedings Review in the Recognition and Enforcement of Foreign Civil and Commercial Judgments] (2017) 1 *Wuhan University International Law Review*, 87.

[67] Article 7(2) of the HCCH: Convention of 1 February 1971 on the Recognition and Enforcement of Foreign Judgments in Civil and Commercial Matters www.hcch.net/en/instruments/conventions/full-text/?cid=78: Recognition or enforcement may be postponed or refused if proceedings between the same parties on the same subject matter are pending before a court of the requested State, where –

(a) the court of the requested State was seized before the court of origin; and
(b) there is a close connection between the dispute and the requested State.

Interpretation of Civil Procedure Law.[68] In China's judicial practice, there are cases where foreign judgments have not been recognised and enforced due to the existence of parallel litigation. For example, in the case of the applicant Americhip Inc applying for recognition and enforcement of Civil Judgment NZHC1864 of the New Zealand High Court on 11 August 2016,[69] the respondent Dean replied that case No 1864, tried by the New Zealand court, and Case No 2125 (2016) Yue 0391 Minchu, tried by the Shenzhen Qianhai Court had 'parallel litigation', therefore case No 1864 could not be recognised and enforced by the Chinese courts. The court of this case also noted that the applicant had filed a lawsuit against the same defendants, Dean and Chen Juan, in the Qianhai Court before the case was accepted. Comparing the two lawsuits filed by Americhip Inc in the New Zealand High Court and Qianhai Court respectively, both are against Dean and Chen Juan's action of obtaining Americhip Inc funds by taking advantage of their work. It can be concluded that Americhip Inc's petition to the New Zealand High Court and Qianhai Court is the same dispute. As the dispute between the parties was still in the process of trial in a Chinese court, in order to ensure that China's courts independently exercise jurisdiction and adjudication, and to avoid conflicts between the review results of the High Court of New Zealand judgment and the judgment results of the litigation cases accepted by the Qianhai Court, the court considered it inappropriate to review the judgment of the Court of New Zealand based on the principle of reciprocity, so it rejected the applicant's application.

C. Due Process

Countries generally require that foreign judgments, to be recognised and enforced, must comply with principles of procedural justice. This is to ensure that the country's citizens are tried fairly when involved in cases abroad. If the domestic court finds that a foreign judgment is tainted by procedural unfairness, or fails to effectively protect the legitimate rights and interests of the citizens of the country, the court may have the right to refuse to recognise and enforce the foreign judgment, even if the foreign court had jurisdiction. Unfair procedures are mainly reflected in two aspects: (1) timely and adequate notice; (2) effective protection of rights. Article 7 of the Convention on the Recognition and Enforcement of Foreign Judgments in Civil and Commercial Matters adopted by the Hague Conference on Private International Law in 2019 lists the circumstances under which the court of the requested state may refuse recognition and enforcement of foreign judgments. Under the Convention, procedural justice is violated if: (1) the defendant was not notified in sufficient time and in such a way as to enable them to arrange for their defence;

[68] Article 533 of Interpretation of the Supreme People's Court on the Application of the Civil Procedure Law of the People's Republic of China (Supreme People's Court, Fa Shi [2015] 5): where a party applies to an intermediate people's court of the PRC having jurisdiction for recognition and enforcement of an effective judgment or ruling of a foreign court, if the home country of the foreign court has neither concluded or jointly acceded to an international treaty nor has a relationship of reciprocity with the PRC, the court shall rule to dismiss the application, unless the party applies to the people's court for recognizing an effective divorce judgment rendered by a foreign court.

[69] Guangdong Shenzhen Intermediate People's Court Decision *Americhip Inc v Jason Charles Dean and Juan Chen* (2018) Yue-03 Min Chu No 420. In this case, the applicant, Americhip Inc, is a company incorporated in California with limited liability. In September 2013, the applicant sued New Zealand citizen Mr Dean and Chinese citizen Ms Chen Juan in the New Zealand High Court, requesting the court to order Chen Juan and Dean to return the fraudulent US$12.9 million and pay interest. The New Zealand High Court issued judgment No 1864 on 11 August 2016 and ordered Chen Juan and Dean to compensate the applicant for US$15,796,253.02 (including interest of US$2,866,906.00) and pay the applicant a litigation fee and related costs of NZ$28,333. Chen Juan herself lives in China and has property for execution in China. Therefore, the applicant applied to the court for recognition and enforcement of judgment No 1864 in accordance with the provisions of the Civil Procedure Law of the People's Republic of China.

or (2) the defendant was notified in the requested state in a manner that is incompatible with fundamental principles of the requested state concerning service of documents. The first category protects the interests of the defendant. The second protects the interests of the requested country.

In the Provisions on Issues Concerning the Procedures for Chinese Citizens to Applying for the Recognition of Judgments on Divorce by Foreign Courts, the Provisions on Issues concerning People's Courts Accepting the Application for the Recognition of Divorce Judgments Made by Foreign Courts, and bilateral mutual judicial assistance treaties, China has provided rules requiring fairness of trial procedures in foreign judgments. The basic contents include that if the defendant fails to attend the trial of the case due to untimely delivery, or if other litigation rights are not guaranteed, the foreign judgment rendered will not be recognised and enforced by the Chinese court. In addition, bilateral judicial assistance agreements concluded by China all use due process as a condition for recognition and enforcement, generally stating that if one of the parties who has not been legally summoned under the law of the state party and does not meet the procedural justice, the judgment will not be recognised and enforced, such as in the provisions of bilateral treaties between China and Turkey and Argentina.[70]

D. Fraud

Much national legislation and many relevant international treaties stipulate that foreign court judgments obtained by fraudulent methods will not be recognised and enforced. Judicial judgments in favour of oneself obtained through fraudulent means are a kind of injustice.[71] Fraud will generally be procedural. For example, during the course of litigation there may be deception of the court, acceptance of bribes by the court, destruction of evidence, etc which violates the right to procedural fairness. Article 7 of the Convention on the Recognition and Enforcement of Foreign Judgments in Civil and Commercial Matters stipulates that if a judgment is obtained by fraud, the court of the requested state may refuse to recognise and enforce the judgment.[72] The regulations on fraud in China are also reflected in the Arrangement on Reciprocal Recognition and Enforcement of Judgments in Civil and Commercial Matters by the Courts of the Mainland and of the Hong Kong Special Administrative Region, which stipulates that when the judgment was obtained by fraud, after being examined and verified by the court of the requested state, it shall not be recognised and enforced.

E. Public Policy

The reservation of public policy is a condition generally adopted by judicial practice in various countries to exclude the recognition and enforcement of judgments of foreign courts.

> [I]t means that the courts of a state should apply foreign law in accordance with their conflicting norms, but its application will be excluded because its application will conflict with the major interests, basic policies, basic concepts of morality or basic principles of law of the state where the court is located.[73]

[70] Treaty between the People's Republic of China and the Argentine Republic on Judicial Assistance in Civil and Commercial Matters, Art 18(3).

[71] HY Guo, 'Waiguo Fayuan Panjue Chengren Yu Zhixing Yanjiu' [Research on the Recognition and Enforcement of Foreign Court Judgments] (2011) *Ocean University of China* 20.

[72] Article 7(1) of the Convention on the Recognition and Enforcement of Foreign Judgments in Civil and Commercial Matters states that recognition or enforcement may be refused if: (b) the judgment was obtained by fraud.

[73] DP Han, *Guoji Sifa Xinlun [New Theory of Private International Law]* (Wuhan University Press, 1997) 617.

In the conflict of laws, if the result of applying foreign law would violate the domestic public order, the court may refuse to apply the foreign law in accordance with the principle of reservation of public order, and instead apply mandatory provisions of domestic law.[74] Hence, the principle of reservation of public policy is actually intended to protect the terms of national sovereignty. In the field of recognition and enforcement of foreign judgments, public order reservation is applied for similar reasons. The public order reservation is stipulated in Article 282 of China's current Civil Procedure Law, which defines the 'public policy' as 'the basic principles of the laws of the People's Republic of China or national sovereignty, security, and social public interest'.[75]

In the civil and commercial bilateral judicial assistance treaties concluded by China, the conditions for mutual recognition of judgments between the relevant contracting states generally have a 'reservation of public order' clause, such as the provisions of bilateral treaties between China, France and Tajikistan.[76] As mentioned above, when a judgment made by a foreign court violates the fundamental interests of the domestic country or the basic principles of law and morality, the domestic court can refuse to recognise and enforce the foreign court's judgment. Therefore, the public order reservation clause is the final safeguard of the concept of justice in a national legal system, which has the function of 'safety valve'. In view of the diversity of foreign judgments, it may be the best way to apply the public order reservation clause as the final cover clause.

F. Procedures

Requirements for the recognition and enforcement of foreign judgments include compliance with relevant procedural provisions. Regardless of whether the foreign court's judgment has been effective and enforceable and whether the foreign court's proceedings are justified, it is necessary to submit corresponding supporting documents to the domestic court where recognition or enforcement is sought. China's Civil Procedure Law and its judicial interpretations contain provisions regarding the procedures for applying for recognition and enforcement of foreign judgments.[77] They include:

(1) the parties or the court that made the judgment should apply to the intermediate people's court with jurisdiction in China;
(2) with regard to the submitted materials, a translation in Chinese or other languages as stipulated in the international treaty is required;

[74] YZ Fu, 'Chengren Yu Zhixing Waiguo Minshangshi Fayuan Panjue Shi De Gonggong Zhixu Shencha' [Review of Public Policy in Recognition and Enforcement of Judgments of Foreign Civil and Commercial Courts] (2015) *Western Law Review*, 15.

[75] Article 282 of the Civil Procedure Law of the People's Republic of China states that after examining an application or request for recognition and enforcement of an effective judgment or ruling of a foreign court in accordance with an international treaty concluded or acceded to by the People's Republic of China or under the principle of reciprocity, a people's court shall issue a ruling to recognize the legal force of the judgment or ruling and issue an order for enforcement as needed to enforce the judgment or ruling according to the relevant provisions of this Law if the people's court deems that the judgment or ruling does not violate the basic principles of the laws of the People's Republic of China and the sovereignty, security and public interest of the People's Republic of China. If the judgment or ruling violates the basic principles of the laws of the People's Republic of China or the sovereignty, security or public interest of the People's Republic of China, the people's court shall not grant recognition and enforcement.

[76] Treaty between the People's Republic of China and the Republic of Tajikistan on Civil and Criminal Justice Assistance, Art 20(5).

[77] Article 543 of Interpretation of the Supreme People's Court on the Application of the Civil Procedure Law of the People's Republic of China states that where the applicant applies to the people's court for recognition and enforcement of an effective judgment or ruling of a foreign court, the applicant shall submit a written application, to which the original or

(3) at the time of filing the application, in addition to the application form, the applicant shall submit at the same time the original effective judgment, or a certified copy and a Chinese translation;
(4) the people's court shall form a collegial bench to examine the case of recognition and enforcement of an effective judgment, etc.

In practice, there are cases in which the applicant fails to obtain recognition and enforcement from the Chinese court due to the fact that the applicant has failed to provide authentic and valid judgment documents, as well as the certification documents on a legal summons from the foreign court, etc. For example, in a 2019 case,[78] the court held that Xu Xinlin had failed to provide the certification documents required by judgment No 395/2014 issued by the primary court of Parla, Spain,. The applicant could not prove the evidence and therefore the court refused to recognise and enforce the judgment of the primary court of Parla.

Table 1 List of treaties on judicial assistance in civil and commercial affairs signed by China with foreign states

No	State	Treaty Name	Signature Date	Effective Date
1	Iran	Treaty between the People's Republic of China and the Islamic Republic of Iran on Judicial Assistance in Civil and Commercial Matters	23 January 2016	Not yet in force
2	Ethiopia	Treaty between the People's Republic of China and the Federal Democratic Republic of Ethiopia on Judicial Assistance in Civil and Commercial Matters	4 May 2014	3 January 2018
3	Bosnia-Herzegovina	Treaty between the People's Republic of China and Bosnia and Herzegovina on Civil and Commercial Judicial Assistance	18 December 2012	12 October 2014
4	Algeria	Treaty between the People's Republic of China and the Democratic People's Republic of Algeria on Civil and Commercial Judicial Assistance	10 January 2010	16 June 2012

(continued)

the certified error-free duplicate and Chinese translation of the effective judgment or ruling of the foreign court shall be affixed. If the judgment or ruling rendered by the foreign court is a default judgment or ruling, the applicant shall, at the same time, submit the certification documents on a legal summons from the foreign court, unless the judgment or ruling has expressly stated the fact.

Article 548 of Interpretation of the Supreme People's Court on the Application of the Civil Procedure Law of the People's Republic of China states that the people's court shall form a collegial bench to examine a case of recognition and enforcement of an effective judgment or ruling of a foreign court or a foreign arbitration award.

[78] Zhejiang Wenzhou Intermediate People's Court Decision *Xu Xinlin v Xiao Shaofen* (2019) Zhe-03 Xie Wai Ren No 07. The Applicants Xu Xinlin and Xiao Shaofen were married in 2001 in the Civil Affairs Bureau of Ouhai District, Wenzhou City, Zhejiang Province. Later, based on the grounds of the feelings between the two parties, they applied for a divorce to the Primary Court of Parla, Spain, and the court issued a divorce judgment on 11 July 2014. Applicant Xu Xinlin requested the Wenzhou Intermediate People's Court to recognise the divorce judgment No 395/2014 made by the Primary Court of Parla.

Table 1 ***(Continued)***

No	State	Treaty Name	Signature Date	Effective Date
5	Brazil	Treaty between the People's Republic of China and the Federative Republic of Brazil on Judicial Assistance in Civil and Commercial Matters	19 May 2009	16 August 2014
6	Peru	Treaty between the People's Republic of China and the Republic of Peru on Judicial Assistance in Civil and Commercial Matters	19 March 2008	25 May 2012
7	Kuwait	Agreement between the People's Republic of China and the State of Kuwait on Judicial Assistance in Civil and Commercial Matters	18 June 2007	6 June 2013
8	United Arab Emirates	Agreement between the People's Republic of China and the United Arab Emirates on Judicial Assistance in Civil and Commercial Matters	21 April 2004	12 April 2005
9	North Korea	Treaty between the People's Republic of China and the Democratic People's Republic of Korea on Civil and Criminal Judicial Assistance	19 November 2003	21 January 2006
10	Korea	Treaty between the People's Republic of China and the Republic of Korea on Judicial Assistance in Civil and Commercial Matters	7 July 2003	27 April 2005
11	Argentina	Treaty between the People's Republic of China and the Argentine Republic on Judicial Assistance in Civil and Commercial Matters	9 April 2001	9 October 2011
12	Lithuania	Treaty between the People's Republic of China and the Republic of Lithuania on Civil and Criminal Judicial Assistance	20 March 2000	19 January 2002
13	Tunisia	Treaty between the People's Republic of China and the Republic of Tunisia on Judicial Assistance in Civil and Commercial Matters	4 May 1999	20 July 2000
14	Laos	Treaty between the People's Republic of China and the Lao People's Democratic Republic on Civil and Criminal Justice Assistance	25 January 1999	15 December 2001
15	Vietnam	Treaty between the People's Republic of China and the Socialist Republic of Vietnam on Civil and Criminal Judicial Assistance	19 October 1998	25 December 1999

(continued)

Table 1 ***(Continued)***

No	State	Treaty Name	Signature Date	Effective Date
16	Uzbekistan	Treaty between the People's Republic of China and the Republic of Uzbekistan on Civil and Criminal Judicial Assistance	11 December 1997	29 September 2000
17	Singapore	Treaty between the People's Republic of China and the Republic of Singapore on Judicial Assistance in Civil and Commercial Matters	28 April 1997	27 June 1999
18	Tajikistan	Treaty between the People's Republic of China and the Republic of Tajikistan on Civil and Criminal Justice Assistance	16 September 1996	2 September 1998
19	Kyrgyzstan	Treaty between the People's Republic of China and the Kyrgyz Republic on Civil and Criminal Judicial Assistance	4 July 1996	26 September 1997
20	Morocco	Agreement between the People's Republic of China and the Kingdom of Morocco on Judicial Assistance in Civil and Commercial Matters	16 April 1996	26 November 1999
21	Hungary	Treaty between the People's Republic of China and the Republic of Hungary on Judicial Assistance in Civil and Commercial Matters	9 October 1995	21 March 1997
22	Cyprus	Treaty between the People's Republic of China and the Republic of Cyprus on Civil, Commercial and Criminal Judicial Assistance	25 April 1995	11 January 1996
23	Greece	Agreement between the People's Republic of China and the Republic of Greece on Civil and Criminal Justice Assistance	17 October 1994	29 June 1996
24	Egypt	Agreement between the People's Republic of China and the Arab Republic of Egypt on Civil, Commercial and Criminal Judicial Assistance	21 April 1994	31 May 1995
25	Thailand	Agreement between the People's Republic of China and the Kingdom of Thailand on Mutual Legal Assistance and Arbitration Cooperation between Civil and Commercial Affairs	16 March 1994	6 July 1997
26	Bulgaria	Agreement between the People's Republic of China and the Republic of Bulgaria on Civil Judicial Assistance	2 June 1993	30 June 1995
27	Kazakhstan	Treaty between the People's Republic of China and the Republic of Kazakhstan on Civil and Criminal Judicial Assistance	14 January 1993	11 July 1995

(continued)

Table 1 ***(Continued)***

No	State	Treaty Name	Signature Date	Effective Date
28	Belarus	Treaty between the People's Republic of China and the Republic of Belarus on Civil and Criminal Judicial Assistance	11 January 1993	29 November 1993
29	Ukraine	Treaty between the People's Republic of China and Ukraine on Civil and Criminal Justice Assistance	31 October 1992	19 January 1994
30	Turkey	Agreement between the People's Republic of China and the Republic of Turkey on Civil, Commercial and Criminal Judicial Assistance	28 September 1992	26 October 1995
31	Russia	Treaty between the People's Republic of China and the Russian Federation on Civil and Criminal Justice Assistance	19 June 1992	14 November 1993
32	Italy	Treaty between the People's Republic of China and the Italian Republic on Civil Judicial Assistance	20 May 1991	1 January 1995
33	Romania	Treaty between the People's Republic of China and Romania on Civil and Criminal Justice Assistance	16 January 1991	22 January 1993
34	Mongolia	Treaty between the People's Republic of China and the People's Republic of Mongolia on Civil and Criminal Justice Assistance	31 August 1989	29 October 1990
35	Belgium	Agreement between the People's Republic of China and the Kingdom of Belgium on Civil Judicial Assistance	20 November 1987	Not yet in force
36	Poland	Agreement between the People's Republic of China and the People's Republic of Poland on Civil and Criminal Judicial Assistance	5 June 1987	13 February 1988
37	France	Agreement between the People's Republic of China and the French Republic on Civil and Commercial Judicial Assistance	4 May 1987	8 February 1988
38	Spain	Treaty between the People's Republic of China and the kingdom of Spain on Civil and Criminal Justice Assistance	2 May 1992	1 January 1994
39	Cuba	Agreement between the People's Republic of China and the Republic of Cuba on Civil and Criminal Judicial Assistance	24 November 1992	26 March 1994

21

Enforcement of Judgments

ZHENGYI ZHANG

The essence of international civil and judicial procedure is the recognition and enforcement of foreign judgments. Such recognition reflects national sovereignty, being more strictly territorial. Judgments rendered by foreign courts can only be recognised and enforced in China by the courts of the relevant countries through international civil judicial assistance. While the previous chapter addressed the requirements for recognition and enforcement of foreign judgments generally, this chapter addresses the mechanisms by which judgments are enforced in China, and the procedure for securing recognition and enforcement of a foreign judgment.

I. How China Enforces Judgments

China's Civil Procedure Law and relevant Judicial Interpretations begin by identifying the civil judgments and rulings made by foreign courts that may be recognised and enforced. Bilateral agreements on judicial assistance to which China is a party generally stipulate that a foreign court's ruling in civil cases and ruling by the competent foreign court on compensation in civil damages in criminal cases may also be recognised and enforced in China.[1] Some bilateral agreements on judicial assistance also adopt the concept of 'ruling' by the court, which mainly includes a variety of forms of decisions such as court judgments, rulings, and mediation awards. The rest of this section discusses the enforcement mechanisms available in respect of both domestic and foreign judgments.

A. Enforcement Measures

The parties to a legally effective civil judgment or written order must adhere to the judgment. If one party refuses to perform, the other party may apply to the people's court for enforcement, or the judge may transfer the matter to the appropriate executive officer for enforcement. The parties must perform their obligations where the conciliation statement and other legal documents require it to be judicially enforced. If one party refuses to perform, the other party may

[1] Treaty between the People's Republic of China and Hungary on Civil and Criminal Justice Assistance, Art 16. Treaty between the People's Republic of China and Italy on Civil and Criminal Justice Assistance, Art 20. Treaty between the People's Republic of China and Vietnam on Civil and Criminal Justice Assistance, Art 15.

apply to the people's court for enforcement in China.[2] If the person who is required to perform fails to fulfil their obligations specified in the legal document following notice, they are required to report the status of their property both at the time of notice and one year before the date of notice. If the person who is required to perform refuses to make a report or makes a false report, the people's court may, according to the seriousness of the circumstances, impose a fine or detain such person, their legal representative, the principal person in charge of the unit concerned, or the person directly responsible. On the whole, China's Civil Procedure Law shows that the scope of the inquiry into the characteristics of the relevant property is wider, the subject of assistance in enforcement is larger and the enforcement measures are greater, compared with last version of Civil Procedure Law in 2012. The principle of value equivalence limits the extent of enforcement.[3]

Enforcement measures detailed in Chapter 21 of the Civil Procedure Law mainly include those discussed in the following sub-sections.[4]

i. Inquiry into, Seizure, Freezing, Transfer, and Conversion of Financial Assets[5]

If the person subjected to enforcement fails to fulfill their obligations as specified in the legal document according to the notice, the court has the power to inquire into the person's deposits, bonds, stocks, fund shares, and other properties. The court has the power to seize, freeze, transfer, or change the value of such property, depending upon the circumstances. The court's inquiry, seizure, freezing, transfer, or conversion of property may not exceed the scope of the obligations of the person subjected to enforcement.

ii. Withholding of Earnings[6]

If the person subjected to enforcement fails to fulfill the obligations specified in the notice, the court has the power to withhold or withdraw part of that person's income to the extent of their obligations. However, such person may retain necessary living expenses.

iii. Sealing Up and Seizing Property[7]

When the people's court seals up or seizes property of a Chinese citizen, it must notify them or an adult member of their family to be present and the person's affiliation or the grass-roots organisation at the locality of his property shall send persons to participate. If the person subjected to enforcement is a legal entity or any other organisation, its legal representative or principal person-in-charge shall be notified to be present. Refusal to attend shall not affect the operation of enforcement. The enforcement officer must make a list of the sealed-up or distrained property, which shall be signed or sealed by the persons on the scene and submitted to the person subjected to enforcement. If a citizen is subjected to enforcement, a copy may also be submitted to an adult member of their family. The enforcement officer may designate the person subjected to enforcement to take charge of the sealed property. The person subjected to enforcement shall bear any losses caused by their fault.

[2] Civil Procedure Law of the People's Republic of China, most recently amended at the 28th session of the Standing Committee of the 12th National People's Congress on 27 June 2017, Art 236.

[3] BX Jiang, *Understanding and Application of Enforcement Provisions* (China Legal Publishing House, 2018) 358–360.

[4] Civil Procedure Law of the People's Republic of China, ch 21.

[5] ibid, Art 242.

[6] ibid, Art 243.

[7] ibid, Arts 244–246.

iv. Auction or Sale of the Property[8]

After the property is sealed or distrained, the enforcement officer must instruct the person subjected to enforcement to perform the obligations specified in the legal document within the specified period. If the person subjected to enforcement fails to perform within the time limit, the court shall auction off the sealed or distrained property. If an auction is not suitable or if both parties agree not to conduct an auction, the court may entrust the relevant unit to off items by itself. Items that may not legally be traded freely shall be purchased by the unit concerned at a price set by the state.

v. Specify Delivery[9]

The enforcement officer must summon both parties that delivery concerned to deliver the property or negotiable instruments specified in the legal document in person, or the enforcement officer must hand them over and the person to whom they are to be delivered shall sign for and receive them. If the unit concerned holds the property or negotiable instrument, it shall, according to the notice for assistance in enforcement issued by the people's court, turn it over to the recipient for signature. If a citizen concerned holds the property or negotiable instrument, the people's court shall notify the citizen to hand it over. If they refuse to surrender it, they will be subject to compulsory enforcement.

vi. Forced Eviction[10]

In the case of forced eviction from premises or forced withdrawal from land, the President of the people's court must issue a public notice ordering the person subjected to enforcement to perform within the specified period. If the person subjected to enforcement fails to perform within the time limit, the enforcement officer will enforce the execution. If at the time of compulsory enforcement, the person subjected to enforcement is a citizen, they or an adult member of their family shall be notified to be present. If the person subjected to execution is a legal entity or any other organisation, its legal representative or principal person-in-charge shall be notified to be present. Refusal to attend will not affect the enforcement. If the person subjected to enforcement is a citizen, their work unit or the grass-roots organisation in the locality of the citizen's house or land shall send persons to participate. The enforcement officer will make a written record of the compulsory enforcement, which must be signed or sealed by the persons present. The people's court shall send persons to transport the property removed from the premises and deliver it to the person subjected to enforcement. If the person subjected to enforcement is a citizen, they may also be handed over to an adult member of their family. The person subjected to enforcement shall bear losses caused by their refusal to accept the property.

vii. Continued Performance[11]

If the person subjected to enforcement is still unable to repay their debts after the enforcement measures have been taken to seal, detain, freeze, transfer, or convert financial assets, detain or

[8] ibid, Art 247.
[9] ibid, Art 249.
[10] ibid, Art 250.
[11] ibid, Art 254.

extract income, seal, detain, freeze, auction or sell off the property of the person subjected to enforcement, the person must continue to perform his obligations. If the creditor finds that the person subjected to enforcement has other property, the creditor may at any time request enforcement at the people's court.

viii. Restrictive Measures for Persons Subjected to Enforcement[12]

If the person subjected to enforcement fails to fulfill the obligations specified in the legal document, the court may take, or notify the relevant units to assist in taking, measures such as restricting exit from the boundary of China, recording the event in the credit investigation system, publishing the information of non-performance through the media, or taking other measures prescribed by law. The adoption of enforcement measures, including sealing up and seizure directly involve the person subjected to enforcement and his related interests. The people's court shall, on the one hand, guarantee the implementation of effective legal documents, and, on the other hand, ensure that the legitimate property rights and interests of the person subjected to enforcement are not infringed.[13]

B. Enforcement Organ

The Chinese courts shall, when necessary and when authorised by the provisions of relevant law, set up an enforcement organ to be specifically responsible for enforcement. The enforcement organ shall be responsible for the enforcement of the following effective legal documents: civil and administrative judgments, rulings, conciliation statements, civil sanctions decisions, payment orders, and civil judgments, rulings and conciliation statements attached to criminal cases; decisions on administrative penalties and administrative handling that should be executed by the court according to law; arbitration awards and conciliation statements issued by the Chinese arbitration organisation; the award of property preservation and evidence preservation made by the court in accordance with the relevant provisions of the arbitration law of the People's Republic of China; a document of creditor's rights on recovery of debts and articles that has been legally given the effect of compulsory enforcement by the notary office; a judgment or written order of a foreign court acknowledging its effectiveness by a people's court, or an arbitration award by a foreign arbitration institution; other legal documents provided by law for enforcement by the people's court.

II. Procedures for Recognition and Enforcement of Judgments of Foreign Courts

A person requesting the recognition and enforcement of a judgment of a foreign court in China must submit their request to a Chinese court. Either the party concerned or the foreign court may apply for the execution of the judgment.

[12] ibid, Art 255.
[13] LH Ding, *Civil Execution Procedure Treatise* (China Democratic Legal System Press, 2019) 668.

A. Submission of the Request for Recognition and Enforcement

i. Subject and Basis of the Request

The request may be made directly by the parties concerned, or by the original court through the central organ of the court with jurisdiction over the requested state in accordance with the treaty concluded or acceded to by both parties, or based on the principle of reciprocity.[14] Legally effective judgments or written orders rendered by the foreign court, submitted for recognition and enforcement of the PRC, can be submitted by the parties seeking enforcement directly to the intermediate people's court having jurisdiction over the matter. Submission can also be made by a foreign court in accordance with the provisions of the international treaties concluded or acceded to by the relevant country and the PRC or under the principle of reciprocity.[15]

ii. Documents to be Submitted

Applicants for the recognition and enforcement of foreign judgments or written judicial orders must submit a copy of the original or certified correct foreign judgment or judicial order and a version translated into Chinese. If the judgment or order to be enforced has been made by default, the applicant shall submit documentary evidence that has been compiled by the foreign court, except where the judgment or order has clearly stated default as the basis for judgment. Where effective international treaties provide rules for the submission of documents, such provisions shall apply.[16]

iii. Period of Recognition and Execution

The Civil Procedure Law's provisions on the period of application for enforcement apply to the parties' application for recognition and enforcement. If the party applies for recognition only but does not apply for enforcement at the same time, the period in which enforcement may be applied for is counted anew from the date when the ruling made by the people's court on the application for recognition becomes effective.[17] The period of application for enforcement is two years. An application for suspension of the period shall be governed by the provisions of the law on the suspension or suspension of the limitation of action on Article 239 of the Civil Procedure Law. The period of application is counted from the last day of the period of performance specified in the legal document. Where a legal document prescribes performance by stages, the period of application in respect of each stage of performance shall be counted from the last day of each prescribed period of performance. If the period for performance is not specified in the legal document, the application period shall be counted from the date when the legal document enters into force.[18]

[14] Civil Procedure Law of the People's Republic of China, most recently amended in 2017, Art 280(1), 281.

[15] ibid, Art 281.

[16] The Interpretation of the Supreme People's Court on the Application of the Civil Procedure Law of the republic of China, adopted at the 36th session of the Judicial Committee of the Supreme People's Court on 18 December 2014 (2015 Interpretation), is promulgated for implementation on 4 February 2015, Art 543.

[17] 2015 Interpretation, Art 547.

[18] Civil Procedure Law of the People's Republic of China, most recently amended in 2017, Art 239.

B. Review of Judgments of Foreign Courts

According to Article 268 of the Civil Procedure Law of China and the provisions of bilateral agreements on judicial assistance signed by China, China only conducts a formal review of foreign judgments[19] if the people's court determines that the judgment to be enforced does not violate the basic principles of the laws of the PRC, nor harms national sovereignty, security, or social public interests, it may enforce the judgment. Judgments that violate the basic principles of the laws of the PRC or endanger state sovereignty, security, or public interests may not be recognised and enforced.[20] If the foreign court's country and the PRC are not parties to a bilateral judicial assistance agreement, and do not have a relationship of reciprocal recognition, the application shall be rejected, unless the parties apply to the people's court for recognition of a legally effective divorce judgment made by a foreign court. If the application for recognition and enforcement is rejected by written order, the party concerned may bring a suit in a people's court.[21]

Article 546 of the judicial interpretation on the application of the Civil Procedure Law issued by the Supreme People's Court in 2015 stipulates that if a legally effective judgment, ruling, or foreign arbitration award made by a foreign court needs to be executed by a court of the PRC, the party concerned shall first apply to the people's court for recognition. After the people's court has examined the case and made an order of recognition, it shall enforce the case in accordance with the provisions of Part 3 of the Civil Procedure Law. If a party only applies for recognition but does not apply for enforcement at the same time, the people's court shall only examine whether the judgment should be recognised and make a ruling accordingly. People's courts shall form collegial panels to review cases that recognise and enforce legally effective judgments or orders made by foreign courts or foreign arbitration awards. The people's court shall serve the application for recognition and enforcement on the respondent. The respondent may state his opinion. A ruling made by a people's court becomes legally effective upon service.[22]

There are restrictions on the Chinese review of foreign judgments in addition to the procedures provided in international treaties or the system of reciprocity and public order. The basic principles and structure of the Civil Procedure Law basic system, and current international common practice, hold that the recognition and enforcement of a foreign judgment in China requires that the civil or commercial judgment to be enforced must have been the result of a trial in a country that has jurisdiction over the case; the trial procedures must have been in strict compliance with that country's procedural rules; and the respondent must have been provided with a full opportunity to appear in court to answer the lawsuit. The litigation and judgment may also not be in conflict with ongoing or terminated litigation in China. The bilateral treaties on judicial assistance concluded between China and foreign countries have made clear provisions with respect to these matters. Examples are Article 22 of the 1987 agreement between the PRC and France on judicial assistance in civil and commercial affairs, and Article 22 of the 1991 agreement between the PRC and Romania on judicial assistance in civil and criminal affairs.

[19] The agreement on judicial assistance requires the application to be accompanied by the judicial documents and related documents, and does not mention the review of the contents of the judicial documents.

[20] Civil Procedure Law of the People's Republic of China, most recently amended in 2017, Art 282.

[21] 2015 Interpretation, Art 544.

[22] 2015 Interpretation, Art 548.

22

Interregional Judicial Assistance

JUN CHEN

I. Introduction

A. Interregional Conflict of Laws in China

China has been a unitary socialist legal system with only one jurisdiction since the founding of the People's Republic of China (PRC) in 1949. However, the political concept of 'one country, two systems' was introduced when:

(1) China and Britain signed the 'Joint Statement of the People's Republic of China and the Government of the United Kingdom of Great Britain and Northern Ireland on Hong Kong' on 19 December 1984; and
(2) China and Portugal signed the 'Joint Statement of the Government of the People's Republic of China and the Government of the Republic of Portugal on the Macao Issue' on 26 March 1987.

In order to implement this concept, the Third Session of the National People's Congress passed the 'Basic Law of the Hong Kong Special Administrative Region of the People's Republic of China' on 4 April 1990, and on 31 March 1993, the First Session of the Eighth National People's Congress passed the 'Basic Law of the Macao Special Administrative Region of the People's Republic of China.' These laws and statements left the original laws of Hong Kong and Macao unchanged under 'one country, two systems' after the Chinese Government resumed sovereignty over Hong Kong and Macao in 1997 and 1999 respectively. The peaceful return of the Taiwan area would create a new situation in China: one country, two systems, three legal systems, and four legal jurisdictions.[1] In this way, inter-regional conflicts of law will inevitably arise between the laws of Hong Kong, Macao and Taiwan and the laws of mainland China.

China's interregional legal conflicts of law rules have several unique characteristics:[2]

(1) The rules address legal conflicts under two different economic systems. The Mainland system is socialist. Hong Kong, Macao and Taiwan are capitalist.
(2) The rules cover conflicts among three different legal systems. The Mainland uses the socialist system, Hong Kong uses the common law system, and Macao and Taiwan use the civil law system.

[1] J Huang, *Discussion on Interregional Legal Issues in China* (China University of Political Science and Law Press, 2012) 4.
[2] ibid, 125.

(3) The rules apply in different international contexts. This includes conflicts between the legal systems of various jurisdictions and conflicts between the laws of one jurisdiction and the international treaties that apply to other jurisdictions. According to the annexes of the Sino-British, Sino-Portuguese Joint Declaration and the two Basic Laws, Hong Kong and Macao may separately sign and implement international agreements with other countries, regions and relevant international organisations around the world in the names, respectively, of 'Hong Kong, China' and 'Macau, China' in all fields except national defence and diplomacy. The central government in Beijing may also decide to conclude treaties for the two regions under certain circumstances.
(4) The rules deal with conflicts that arise with the independent exercise of judicial power and final adjudication power in various jurisdictions. Each jurisdiction has its own Court of Final Appeal, and there is no unified Court of Final Appeal with authority in all jurisdictions. Hence, coordination of the highest judicial organs in resolving international conflicts requires mutual assistance agreements signed by each jurisdiction.

B. Interregional Judicial Assistance in China

Judicial assistance between different jurisdictions, especially between different legal systems within a country, is different from international judicial assistance and judicial assistance between different regions within a unified jurisdiction. China does not have a specialised law to resolve inter-regional conflicts of law. In principle, the resolution of legal conflicts between different jurisdictions refer to the Law on the Law Applicable to Foreign-Related Civil Relationships.[3] This principle is easier to apply to determine the applicable law and jurisdiction since the issue of mutual cooperation between Hong Kong, Macao and China does not usually arise in this context. Ordinarily, courts in a given jurisdiction only need to determine the jurisdiction and applicable law in accordance with their own laws. However, it is difficult to implement procedures in international civil litigation that deal with cross-border delivery, service of process, taking of evidence, and the recognition and enforcement of judgments. These functions are usually carried out through mutual legal assistance between countries, and such judicial assistance is mostly based on the provisions of bilateral or multilateral treaties between countries or through diplomatic channels.

This principle does not work in China because the Mainland, Hong Kong, Macao, and Taiwan are governed under the same national framework and international treaties and diplomatic channels do not exist. Hong Kong and Macao joined the international treaties dealing with private international law under the governance of the UK and Portugal before they were returned to China. According to the Sino-British Joint Declaration and the Hong Kong Basic Law,[4] these treaties continue to apply to Hong Kong after 1997, even if the Beijing Government has not acceded to them.[5] But Hong Kong and Macao have never been independent parties to these treaties. Hong Kong and Macao are now governed by the Mainland, so the relationship between them cannot be determined by the provisions of international treaties. The Taiwan region is not a subject of

[3] (Supreme People's Court, Fa Shi (2015) 5, adopted on the 1636th meeting on 18 December 2014).

[4] 'Sino-British Joint Declaration on the Question of Hong Kong' (1984) 7 *Loyola of Los Angeles International and Comparative Law Review* 139 http://digitalcommons.lmu.edu/ilr/vol7/iss1/6 accessed 31 August 2020, Art 3(3); *The Basic Law of the Hong Kong Special Administrative Region of the People's Republic of China* (Joint Pub (HK) Co, 1991) Arts 8, 96.

[5] T Du, *Principles of Private International Law* (Fudan University Press, 2018) 339.

international law so it cannot independently participate in any international treaty. Therefore, the issue of interregional mutual legal assistance among China, Taiwan, Hong Kong, and Macao can only be resolved by applying the respective laws and regulations of each region and the cooperation arrangements between each region.

II. Service of Process

A. Between the Mainland and Hong Kong

Article 95 of the Basic Law of the Hong Kong Special Administrative Region of the People's Republic of China states: 'The Hong Kong Special Administrative Region may, in consultation with the judicial organs of other parts of the country, conduct judicial contacts and provide assistance in accordance with the law.' Pursuant to this provision, the Supreme People's Court, after consultation with representatives of the Hong Kong region, reached 'The Arrangement of the Supreme People's Court on the Mutual Commissioning of the Service of Civil and Commercial Documents by the Courts in the Mainland and HKSAR', which was issued in the form of a judicial interpretation by the Supreme People's Court in the Mainland.[6] The arrangement stipulates that the courts of the Mainland and the Hong Kong courts entrust the service of judicial documents through the High People's Courts and the High Court of the Hong Kong Special Administrative Region. Mainland judicial documents include: (i) a copy of the bill of complaint; (ii) a copy of the appeal; (iii) a power of attorney; (iv) a summons; (v) a judgment; (vi) a mediation; (vii) a ruling; (viii) a decision; (ix) a notice; (x) a certificate; (xi) a service receipt, etc. The judicial documents of Hong Kong include: (i) copies of complaints; (ii) copies of appeals; (iii) subpoenas; (iv) adverbials; (v) affidavits; (vi) judgments; (vii) awards; (viii) notices; (ix) court orders; (x) communication notes, etc.[7]

The judicial documents of the Supreme People's Court can also be directly entrusted for service to the High Court of the Hong Kong Special Administrative Region. When the entrusting party wishes to serve the judicial documents, it must issue a power of attorney in Chinese. Regardless of whether the date or the time limit for the appearance in the judicial document has passed, the entrusted party shall serve the judicial document.[8] Upon receipt of the power of attorney, the entrusted party shall complete the delivery in a timely manner, no later than two months from the date of receipt of the power of attorney. After the completion of the delivery, a certificate of delivery or a certificate of service shall be issued. If the entrusting party is unable to deliver the judicial instrument, it shall indicate the reasons for the rejection and the date and return the power of attorney and all the attached documents in a timely manner.

B. Between the Mainland and Macao

In 2001, pursuant to the provisions of Article 93 of the Basic Law of the Macao Special Administrative Region of the People's Republic of China, the Supreme People's Court, in consultation with representatives of the Macao region, reached a 'Plan of the Supreme People's Court for

[6] (Supreme People's Court, Fa Shi (1999) 9, adopted on 30 December 1998).
[7] ibid, Art 9.
[8] ibid, Art 4.

Mutual Entrustment in Civil and Commercial Matters for the Service of Judicial Documents and Investigation and Evidence Obtainment Between the Mainland and Macau Special Administrative Region.' Pursuant to this provision, the Arrangement for Investigating Evidence was issued in the form of a judicial interpretation by the Supreme People's Court. It is effective as of 15 September 2001.[9] The provisions on the delivery of the arrangement are similar to the arrangements with the Hong Kong Special Administrative Region that are described above.[10] In addition, the much-awaited Arrangement for Mutual Service of Judicial Documents in Civil and Commercial Cases between the Hong Kong Special Administrative Region and the Macao Special Administrative Region, which was signed three years ago on 5 December 2017, will come into force from 1 August 2020.[11]

C. Several Provisions of the Supreme People's Court on the Delivery of Judicial Documents Concerning Commercial Cases in Hong Kong, Macao, and China

The 1,643rd meeting of the Judicial Committee of the Supreme People's Court passed the 'Several Provisions of the Supreme People's Court on the Delivery of Judicial Documents Concerning Hong Kong, Macao, Taiwan, and Taiwan Business Cases' on 16 February 2009 in order to further standardise the delivery of judicial documents related to Hong Kong and Macao.[12] Article 8 stipulates that the people's court may serve the addressee by fax, e-mail, or in any other appropriate way by which receipt can be confirmed. Article 10 stipulates that the people's court may simultaneously serve the person to be served in a variety of other legal ways in addition to delivering notice. The date of delivery shall be determined in accordance with the method of first delivery if these other methods are also employed.

D. Between the Mainland and Taiwan

There is no bilateral mutual legal assistance arrangement between the Mainland and Taiwan. However, when the cross-strait courts tried to deal with cases involving each other, they encountered the bottleneck problem of service of process. To this end, the Supreme People's Court unilaterally promulgated the 'Several Provisions on the Delivery of Civil Litigation Documents Concerning Taiwan' on 22 April 2008 and implemented it on 23 April 2008.[13] This Regulation contains 12 articles. The main contents are: (i) the scope of application; (ii) the types of civil litigation documents delivered by law or on behalf of the people; (iii) the ways and means for the people's courts to send legal civil litigation documents to the local Taiwanese parties; (iv) provisions

[9] (Supreme People's Court, Fa Shi (2001) 26, took effect on 15 September 2001). This was revised by the Plan of the Supreme People's Court for Mutual Entrustment in Civil and Commercial Matters for the Service of Judicial Documents and Investigation and Evidence Obtainment Between the Mainland and Macau Special Administrative Region (2020 Amendment) (Supreme People's Court, Fa Shi (2020) 1, took effect on 1 March 2020).

[10] (Supreme People's Court, Fa Shi (1999) 9, adopted on 30 December 1998), Art 5.

[11] Arrangement for Mutual Service of Judicial Documents in Civil and Commercial Cases between the Hong Kong Special Administrative Region and the Macao Special Administrative Region (*Hong Kong Department of Justice*, 5 December 2017) www.doj.gov.hk/eng/mainland/intracountry.html.

[12] (Supreme People's Court, Fa Shi (2009) 2, took effect on 16 March 2009).

[13] (Supreme People's Court (2008), 4, took effect on 23 April 2008).

for the delivery of lien-delivery, fax, and e-mail; (v) in the case of cross-strait courts mutual entrustment, specific requirements for the subject of delivery and the letter of entrustment; and (vi) specific provisions for the publication of the civil litigation documents in Taiwan.

On 26 April 2009, the Association for Relations across the Taiwan Straits and the Taiwan Strait Exchange Fund signed the Agreement on Combating Crimes across the Straits and Mutual Legal Assistance.[14] The agreement requires the two parties to do their best to assist each other in serving judicial documents and to cooperate with each other in investigating and obtaining evidence. In order to implement this agreement and further promote the development of mutual legal assistance across the Taiwan Straits, the 1,506th meeting of the Judicial Committee of the Supreme People's Court passed the 'Provisions of the Supreme People's Court on the handling of cross-strait service documents and investigations and evidence-seeking mutual legal assistance cases by the people's courts.'[15] According to this regulation, the people's courts can handle the service documents and the investigation and collection of evidence, and provide mutual legal assistance in civil, criminal, and administrative cases litigated across the Taiwan Straits. The Supreme People's Court is the first-level window for liaison with Taiwanese authorities in cross-straits judicial mutual assistance. The director of the Taiwan Judicial Affairs Office of the Supreme People's Court is the liaison person appointed by the Supreme People's Court. The Supreme People's Court authorised the Higher People's Court to establish a secondary window for handling cross-strait documents and to establish liaison with the competent Taiwanese authorities. The intermediate people's courts and the grassroots people's courts shall appoint special persons to be responsible for cross-strait judicial mutual assistance. Article 7 provides that the people's court may serve civil and administrative litigation documents to the parties residing in the Taiwan area. The following methods may be used:

(1) It shall be served directly if the person to be served resides in the Mainland. If the person to be served is a natural person who was not at the scene at the time, the document can be signed by adult family members living with him or her. If the person to be served is a legal person or other organisation, the legal representative of the legal person, the principal person in charge of the other organisation, or the legal person or other person responsible for the reception may sign. The document also can be delivered directly if the person to be served does not live in the Mainland but is in the Mainland when the document was to be delivered.
(2) If the person to be served has an agent in the Mainland, service shall be made on the agent unless the person to be served clearly indicates in a power of attorney that his agent has no right to receive it on his or her behalf.
(3) If the person to be served has a designated collector, it shall be served on the collector.
(4) If the person to be served has a representative office, branch or business agent in the Mainland, it shall be served on the representative office or the branch that has been expressly authorised to accept the service by the person to be served.
(5) The people's court can ask the relevant organisation in Taiwan to serve the documents through the cross-strait judicial mutual assistance method determined by the agreement.
(6) If the address of the person to be served in Taiwan is definite, it can be delivered by post.
(7) If there is a definite fax number or e-mail address, it can be delivered to the recipient by fax or email.

[14] (Association for Cross-Strait Relations, Group Regulations, effective as of 25 June 2009).
[15] (Supreme People's Court, Fa Shi (2011) 15).

If the above methods cannot be used or the whereabouts of the party in Taiwan are unknown, the documents may be served on the public notice. If the people's courts need to serve criminal justice documents on parties in the Taiwan area, they may ask the Taiwan region to serve these documents using the cross-strait judicial mutual assistance method determined by the agreement. Article 8 provides that when the people's court assists the Taiwan District Court in serving judicial documents, it shall adopt the law of the Civil Procedure Law, the Criminal Procedure Law, the Administrative Litigation Law, and other relevant judicial interpretations, and shall adopt the direct delivery method as much as possible, but shall not use the announcement delivery method.

III. Taking Evidence

A. Between the Mainland and Hong Kong

On 29 December 2016, the Supreme People's Court and the Department of Justice of the Hong Kong Special Administrative Region signed the 'Arrangement on the Entrustment of Evidence between the Mainland and Hong Kong Special Administrative Regions on Civil and Commercial Cases' in Shenzhen.[16] The Arrangement stipulates the scope of application, liaison organs, procedures, and other matters. The purpose of the Arrangement is to provide clear guidelines and institutional arrangements for the mutual entrustment and evidence collection work between the two places. After the Arrangement comes into effect, the parties to civil and commercial cases may separately request the assistance of witnesses, documents, detained property, sampling, and identification through the liaison offices of the two places. This will greatly reduce the obstacles faced by the court cases involving each other in the civil and commercial fields. The liaison offices designated by the Mainland are the High People's Courts and the liaison office designated by Hong Kong is the Administration Department under the Office of the Chief Secretary for Administration.

B. Between the Mainland and Macao

The Supreme People's Court's Arrangement of the Courts of the Mainland and the Macao Special Administrative Region on the Mutual Entrustment of Judicial Documents and Investigations in Civil and Commercial Cases stipulates that the entrusted court can only request evidence related to the lawsuit.[17] The scope of evidence obtained by the entrusted party includes: interrogating the parties, witnesses and appraisers, conducting identification and judicial investigations on behalf of the parties, and obtaining other evidence related to the litigation. In addition, according to Article 11 of the Supreme People's Court's 'Several Provisions on Evidence in Civil Proceedings',[18] where the evidence provided by the parties to the people's court is formed in Hong Kong, Macao, or Taiwan, relevant certification procedures must be performed. This requires the relevant parties to follow the rules for evidence formed in Hong Kong, Macao and Taiwan.

The specific methods are as follows. Litigation materials submitted or entrusted by the Hong Kong parties who do not have a residence in the Mainland must be notarised by Hong Kong lawyers entrusted by the Ministry of Justice of the People's Republic of China. A notarial

[16] (Supreme People's Court, Fa Shi (2017) 4).
[17] (Supreme People's Court, Fa Shi (2001) 26, adopted on the 1,186th meeting on 7 August 2001).
[18] ibid.

certificate transferring Hong Kong notary documents should be stamped with the special seal of China Legal Services (Hong Kong) Co Ltd. Litigation materials submitted or entrusted handed to the Mainland by Macao parties who do not have a place of residence in the Mainland must be stamped with a special seal for the certification of China Legal Services (Macau) Co Ltd. Litigation materials submitted or entrusted by the parties in Taiwan who do not have a domicile in Mainland China must be issued by the local notary public in Taiwan or other departments, civil organisations, or lawyers, and the individual may issue a certificate from his or her work unit. Authentication of the notarised documents shall be performed in accordance with the provisions of the Cross-Strait Co-Certification Agreement for the Use of Cross-Strait Certificates signed on 29 April 1993 and the use of the cross-strait notary certificate issued by the Ministry of Justice on 11 May 1993. In addition, Taiwanese parties can also apply for notarisation using the methods adopted by the parties in Hong Kong and Macao.

C. Between the Mainland and Taiwan

According to the 'Regulations of the Supreme People's Court on the handling of cross-strait service documents and investigations and evidence-seeking mutual legal assistance cases by the people's courts',[19] the people's court, in obtaining evidence related to litigation, is limited to the following assistance from the Taiwan District Court in handling cross-strait investigation and evidence collection and mutual legal assistance business: (i) obtaining testimony and statements; (ii) providing documentary evidence; (iii) physical evidence and audio-visual materials; (iv) determining the location of the person concerned or confirming the person's identity, and obtaining previous records of illegal crimes if such records exist; and (v) conducting inquests, inspections, seizures, identification procedures, and inquiries. The people's court may also assist the Taiwan District Court in investigating and collecting evidence, and shall adopt the methods of the Civil Procedure Law, the Criminal Procedure Law, the Administrative Litigation Law, and other relevant judicial interpretations. The people's court shall endeavour to assist in the investigation and collection of evidence, assisting as much as possible in accordance with the content and form of the Taiwan regional request without prejudice to the law and relevant regulations, without prejudice to the public interest, and without prejudice to the ongoing litigation procedures.[20]

IV. Recognition and Enforcement of Court Judgments and Arbitral Awards

A. Between the Mainland and Hong Kong

i. Arrangements for Mutual Recognition and Enforcement of Arbitral Awards between the Mainland and the Hong Kong Special Administrative Region

The Mainland and the Hong Kong Special Administrative Region have gone through two stages in the recognition and enforcement of arbitral awards. The demarcation point is 1 July 1997.

[19] (Supreme People's Court, Fa Shi (2011) 15).

[20] Typical Case of Mutual Legal Assistance of the People's Court in Taiwan in 2014 (Supreme People's Court, 1 July 2015) 3–4.

Prior to the reunification of Hong Kong on 1 July 1997, arbitral awards of the Chinese Mainland could be recognised and enforced in Hong Kong in accordance with the provisions of the New York Convention. After 1 July 1997, China resumed its sovereignty over the Hong Kong Special Administrative Region so that the New York Convention no longer applied between the Mainland and Hong Kong. On 21 June 1999, the Supreme People's Court and the Hong Kong Special Administrative Region Government reached an 'Arrangement of the Supreme People's Court on Mutual Enforcement of Arbitral Awards between the Mainland and the Hong Kong Special Administrative Region.'[21] The Arrangement was issued and implemented on the Mainland through judicial interpretations issued by the Supreme People's Court. The Hong Kong Special Administrative Region implemented the amendments by amending the Arbitration Ordinance, which is roughly the same as the New York Convention.

ii. Recognition and Enforcement of Judgments on the Mainland and in Hong Kong

The issue of recognition and enforcement of Mainland and Hong Kong judgments has a long history. There are significant historical differences in the social and legal systems of Hong Kong and the Mainland.[22] This presents a direct obstacle to the recognition and enforcement of judgments. In addition, the lack of understanding of each other's legal system and the lack of mutual trust between the two territories also provide obstacles to the recognition and enforcement of judgments. Mainland courts have heard several representative Hong Kong cases after resuming sovereignty over the island, including cases involving the application of recognition and enforcement of the Civil Judgment of the High Court of the Hong Kong Special Administrative Region.[23] In the case of the Japan Pipe Material Center Column Association and Beijing Zhuangsheng Real Estate Development Co Ltd in 2008,[24] the Japan Pipe Material Center Column Association filed an appeal as the court of first instance denied the judgment of the Hong Kong court. The Beijing High Court as the Court of Final Appeal court rejected the party's request on the ground that the Mainland court and Hong Kong court had not made arrangements for mutual recognition and enforcement of civil judgments, and instead informed the parties of their right to re-litigate in the people's court with jurisdiction on the Mainland. Hong Kong believed that the Mainland judgment did not meet the conditions of a final judgment due to the Mainland retrial system, so it determined that the Mainland judgment could not be enforced in Hong Kong. In the cases of *Lin Zhemin v Lin Zhitao*,[25] and *Chi You Bank v Chen Tianjun*,[26] decided by the High Court of Hong Kong, the Hong Kong courts refused to enforce the judgments of the two Mainland courts based on the applicant's failure to provide evidence to prove the judgment was final and irrevocable.

[21] (2000) 2 *Gazette of the Supreme People's Court* 59–60. Adopted at the 1,069th meeting of the Judicial Committee of the Supreme People's Court on 18 June 1999.

[22] See ZH Yu, 'Analysis of the Recognition and Enforcement of Civil and Commercial Judgments in the Mainland and Hong Kong Special Administrative Region' (2015) 37(11) *Journal of Jinan Philosophy and Social Sciences Edition* 8.

[23] See, eg, Supreme People's Court, China Institute of Applied Law, [*Selected Cases of the People's Court*] (People's Court Press, 2001).

[24] Beijing Higher People's Court Decision *Japan Pipe Center Co Ltd v Beijing Zhuangsheng Real Estate Development Co Ltd*. Sales contract dispute case (2009) No 919.

[25] *Lin Zhemin v Lin Zhitao* (CACV 354/2001, 2001).

[26] *Chiyu Banking corporation Limited v Chan Tin Kwun* [1996] 2 HKLR 395.

There has been no agreement on the recognition and enforcement of judgments between the two places after Hong Kong's return. The situation did not improve after reunification, and Hong Kong litigants cannot rely upon Mainland courts to recognise and enforce their judgments. The Mainland and Hong Kong have held long-term consultations to address these issues. The Hong Kong Secretary for Home Affairs drafted an advisory opinion on 'Mutual Implementation of Commercial Judgments in the Mainland of Hong Kong Special Administrative Region' in March 2002.[27] After several consultations, the Supreme People's Court and the Department of Justice of the Hong Kong Special Administrative Region signed the 'Arrangement on Mutual Recognition of Mainland and Hong Kong Special Administrative Region Courts and Enforcement of Judgments in Civil and Commercial Cases under the Agreement of the Parties' in Hong Kong on 14 January 2006.[28] The Arrangement has 19 articles, the main contents of which are: (i) the scope of application; (ii) the final judgment with enforcement power; (iii) the identity of the accepting court and the conditions for acceptance; (iv) the reasons for refusal of recognition and enforcement; (v) the time limit for application; and (vi) the property preservation during the acceptance period aspect. Mainland courts have recognised and enforced a number of Hong Kong court judgments following this arrangement. Hong Kong courts rarely have the opportunity to reciprocate due to limitations in the Arrangement itself. The Hong Kong High Court formally recognised a civil mediation letter from the Shenzhen Intermediate People's Court in *Wu Zuocheng v Liang Li* on 16 February 2016 and has since done so in several other cases.[29]

Since the return of Hong Kong, personnel exchanges between the two places have been closer and cross-border marriages have also increased year by year. However, the Arrangement does not apply to matters of marriage and family, so the Mainland courts have refused to recognise and enforce applications for divorce. In 2010, in an historically significant case, the Hong Kong Court of Final Appeal for the first time acknowledged a divorce judgment issued by a Mainland court.[30] The man filed for divorce with the Shenzhen court in October 2006 and filed a request to split the common property of the husband and wife. In November 2007, the Shenzhen court issued a ruling dissolving the marriage and dividing the common property of the husband and wife. In 2008, the man applied to the Hong Kong court for recognition and enforcement of the judgment made by the Shenzhen court. In 2010, the Hong Kong Court of Final Appeal acknowledged the termination of the marriage in accordance with Hong Kong's Marriage Proceedings Ordinance. On 15, December 2010, the Hong Kong Legislative Council amended the Marriage Proceedings and Property Ordinance, confirming the legal effect of a divorce judgment approved by a Mainland court. The Department of Justice of Hong Kong stated that discussions on the establishment of arrangements for mutual recognition and enforcement of marriage judgments would be held in the Mainland in order to achieve parity of treatment of marriage judgments between the two places.[31] On 20 June 2017, the Supreme People's Court and the Hong Kong Special Administrative Region signed the 'Arrangement on Mutual Recognition and Enforcement of Judgments in Civil Cases in Marriage and Family between the Mainland and Hong Kong Special Administrative Region Courts'.

[27] See Hong Kong Legislative Council Paper CB (2) 2020/01-02 (01).

[28] On the Mainland, see (Supreme People's Court, Fa Shi (2008) 9, 3 July 2008). The Arrangement was adopted at the 1,390th meeting of the Judicial Committee of the Supreme People's Court on 12 June 2006. In Hong Kong, the Hong Kong Legislative Council formally passed the Mainland Judgment (Reciprocal Enforcement) Ordinance (Cap 597) on 23 April 2008, which came into effect on 1 August 2008.

[29] See, eg, [*Wu Zuo Cheng v Leung Lai Ching Margaret*] (HCMP 2080/2015, 2016). The case approved the Shenzhen Intermediate People's Court Foreign-related Civil Mediation (2014) Shen Zhong Fa She Wai Chu Zi No 91.

[30] *ML v YJ* (FACV, 20/2009, 2009).

[31] Legislative and Legal Affairs Committee of the Hong Kong Legislative Council, *Information on Mutual Recognition and Enforcement of Marriage Judgments between the Mainland and Hong Kong*, CB (2) 1781/10-11 (04).

The Mainland and Hong Kong have signed three mutual legal assistance arrangements regarding the recognition of civil and commercial cases. They are respectively:

(1) The 'Arrangement on the Judgment of Civil and Commercial Jurisdictions under the Mutual Recognition and Enforcement of the Agreement of the Parties between the Mainland and the Hong Kong Special Administrative Region Courts' signed in 2006 ('Arrangement on Jurisdiction of Agreements');[32]
(2) the 'Arrangement on Mutual Recognition and Enforcement of Marriage and Family Civil Cases between the Mainland and Hong Kong Special Administrative Region Courts' signed in 2017 ('Marriage and Family Arrangements') (which will not take effect until the Supreme Court issues a judicial interpretation and Hong Kong completes the relevant procedures);[33] and
(3) the 'Arrangement on Mutual Recognition and Enforcement of Judgments in Civil and Commercial Cases between the Mainland and Hong Kong Special Administrative Region Courts' signed in 2019 ('Mutual Recognition Arrangement of Civil and Commercial Judgments') (which also will not be effective until the Supreme Court issues a judicial interpretation and Hong Kong completes the relevant procedures).[34]

The Arrangement on Jurisdiction of Agreements provides for the mutual recognition and enforcement of civil and commercial judgments in the case of a written jurisdiction agreement. The Marriage and Family Arrangement provides for mutual recognition and enforcement of partial marriage and family judgments. However, the Mutual Recognition Arrangement of Civil and Commercial Judgments contains the situations the parties agree to govern, and the scope of mutual recognition and enforcement is broader. Therefore, the Arrangement on Jurisdiction of Agreements shall be repealed at the same time as the implementation of the Mutual Recognition Arrangement of Civil and Commercial Judgments. However, a transitional period sustaining the arrangement has also been established if the parties have signed a written jurisdiction agreement referred to in the Arrangement on Jurisdiction of Agreements.[35] The Marriage and Family Arrangement remains applicable to enforcement of judgments in the cases stipulated in the Marriage and Family Arrangement.

B. Between the Mainland and Macao

i. Arrangements for the Mutual Recognition and Enforcement of Civil and Commercial Judgments between the Mainland and the Macao Special Administrative Region

On 28 February 2006, the 'Inter-Regional and Macao Special Administrative Region Arrangement for Mutual Recognition and Enforcement of Civil and Commercial Judgments' was signed in

[32] (Supreme People's Court, Fa Shi (2008) 9, 3 July 2008).

[33] The Executive Vice President of the Supreme People's Court Shen Deyong and the Secretary of Justice of the Hong Kong Special Administrative Region Government Yuan Guoqiang respectively signed the 'Arrangements on the Mutual Recognition and Enforcement of Judgments in Marriage and Family Civil Cases by the Courts of the Mainland and the Hong Kong Special Administrative Region' in the Hong Kong Special Administrative Region.

[34] Adopted at the 1,759th meeting of the Judicial Committee of the Supreme People's Court.

[35] Arrangement on Mutual Recognition and Enforcement of Judgments in Civil and Commercial Cases between the Mainland and Hong Kong Special Administrative Region Courts, Art 33.

Macao and became effective in the Mainland on 1 April 2006.[36] The Arrangement includes a total of 24 articles, mainly concerning: (i) the jurisdiction of courts that accept applications for recognition and enforcement; (ii) the simultaneous application for enforcement and coordination in the two places; (iii) the procedure for accreditation; (iv) the refusal of recognition; (v) the remedies of the parties; (vi) the acceptance; and (vii) the execution of the request, property preservation, separate litigation, and other issues. Regarding the scope of recognition and enforcement, according to Article 1 of the Arrangement, the Mainland and the Macao Special Administrative Region may mutually recognise and enforce their respective judgments in civil and commercial cases (including labour dispute cases in the Mainland and labour civil cases in the Macao Special Administrative Region). The 'judgments' referred to in the Arrangement include judgments, rulings, decisions, mediations, and payment orders in the Mainland; rulings of rulings, judgments, confirmations of settlements, and decisions of judges or instructions in the Macao Special Administrative Region. Regarding the accepting court, the intermediate people's courts where the applicant's domicile, permanent residence, or property is located have the power to accept applications for the execution of judgments in the Mainland. The intermediate courts of the Macao Special Administrative Region have the power to accept applications for recognition of judgments, and the junior courts have the power to enforce them.

Regarding the review of judgment of application for recognition and enforcement, the Arrangement stipulates that the court that is asked to review the case shall review the request for recognition and enforcement as soon as possible and make a ruling. The ruling will not be recognised if one of the following circumstances exists:

(1) according to the law of the requesting party, the matters confirmed by the judgment belong to the exclusive jurisdiction of the requested court;
(2) the same lawsuit already exists in the requested court, the lawsuit was filed before the action for recognition of the judgment, and the requested court has jurisdiction over the lawsuit;
(3) the requested court has recognised or enforced a judgment or arbitral award made by a different court or arbitration institution for the same lawsuit;
(4) the losing party is not legally summoned, or a person without litigation capacity is not legally represented;
(5) the judgment that the court is being asked to recognise and enforce has not yet taken effect, or execution has been suspended due to retrial;
(6) recognition and the enforcement of the judgment in the Mainland would violate the basic principles of Mainland law or the public interest or recognition and enforcement of the judgment in the Macao Special Administrative Region would violate the basic principles or public order of the laws of the Macao Special Administrative Region.

The applicants may not refile or file a new application for recognition and enforcement if the judgment applied for falls within provisions (1), (4), or (6). However, according to the law of the requested party, if the court is asked to have jurisdiction, the parties may file a separate lawsuit with the local court for the same case if permitted. In cases of non-acceptance due to the presence of item (5), the applicant may file an application for recognition and enforcement after the judgment has become effective. Since the entry into force of the Arrangement, the Mainland courts have recognised and implemented many judgments of the Macao courts. Judgments of the Macao court can also be used as evidence in a relevant case by the Mainland court.

[36] (Supreme People's Court, Fa Shi (2006) 2).

ii. Arrangements for Mutual Recognition and Enforcement of Arbitral Awards between the Mainland and the Macao Special Administrative Region

According to Article 93 of the Basic Law of the Macao Special Administrative Region of the People's Republic of China, the Supreme People's Court and the Macao Special Administrative Region have reached an 'Arrangement on Mutual Recognition and Enforcement of Arbitral Awards between the Mainland and the Macao Special Administrative Region', signed on 30 October 2007 and implemented in the Mainland since 1 January 2008.[37] The Arrangement contains sixteen articles, addressing: (i) the scope of application; (ii) the level of the court that accepts the application; (iii) the content of the application for approval and execution and the specific documents submitted; (iv) the conditions for the approval and enforcement of the arbitral award; (v) the time limit for the application for execution; and (vi) the precautionary measures and the like. The Arrangement permits the recognition and implementation of civil and commercial arbitral awards in the Mainland and the Macao Special Administrative Region made, respectively, by the arbitral tribunals and arbitrators of the Macao Special Administrative Region according to the Macao Special Administrative Region Arbitration Regulations and the civil and commercial arbitration awards made by the Mainland arbitration institutions in accordance with the Arbitration Law of the People's Republic of China, unless otherwise specifically provided.

If an executor has property in the Mainland and the Macao Special Administrative Region, the parties may submit applications for recognition and enforcement to the courts of the Mainland and the Macao Special Administrative Region respectively. The selected court shall conduct examinations in accordance with the law. If the application is approved, the court may take enforcement measures to seize, detain, or freeze the property of the person subject to enforcement. The local court where the arbitration was made shall first perform the execution. The total amount of property executed by the courts of the Mainland and Macao Special Administrative Region shall not exceed the amount of the judgment. If one party applies to a local court for the enforcement of an arbitral award and the other party applies to another court for revocation of the arbitral award, the enforcement court shall suspend the execution on the condition that the person against whom the judgment is to be executed applies for the suspension of execution and provides a sufficient guarantee of the judgment. In addition, arbitral awards made after the return of Macao but before the implementation of the Arrangement can be enforced in the Mainland. The time limit during which a party may apply for such recognition and enforcement begins on the date the Arrangements were implemented. The signing of the Arrangement demonstrates that the relationship between the Mainland and Macao has become increasingly close and the scope of mutual assistance has also expanded, laying the foundation for further judicial cooperation.

C. Between the Mainland and Taiwan

i. Provisions of the Supreme People's Court on the Approval and Enforcement of Civil Judgments of Taiwan District Courts

On 2 June 2015, the 1,653th meeting of the Judicial Committee of the Supreme People's Court passed the 'Provisions of the Supreme People's Court on the Recognition and Enforcement of Civil Judgments in Taiwan District Courts', which took effect on 1 July 2015.[38] Following this, the

[37] (Supreme People's Court, Fa Shi (2007) 17).
[38] (Supreme People's Court, Fa Shi (2015) 13).

Supreme People's Court's Provisions on the People's Courts' Approval and Enforcement of Civil Judgments of Relevant Courts in Taiwan,[39] the Supreme People's Court's Reply on the Acceptance of the People's Court by the People's Court in the Handheld of the Court's Payment Order to the People's Court,[40] and the Supreme People's Court Supplementary Provisions of the People's Court Approving the Civil Judgments of the Courts in Taiwan were abolished.[41] The Provision contains the following:

(1) The Provision applies to all civil judgments of the Taiwan District Court, including effective civil judgments, rulings, reconciliation transcripts, mediation transcripts, and payment orders, and all effective criminal judgments, rulings, and reconciliation transcripts of civil damage compensation made in criminal cases, as well as to the transfer documents issued by the mediation committees of townships and cities in Taiwan and approved by the Taiwan District Court.
(2) The court of the applicant's domicile – the place of usual residence or the place where the respondent resides or the place of usual residence – or the intermediate people's court where the property is located, or the special people's court, shall accept cases asking for recognition of the Taiwan District Court's civil judgments.
(3) Article 9 provides that if an applicant asks for the recognition of a Taiwan District Courts' civil judgment, the applicant shall provide the relevant supporting documents and prove that the judgment is true and has entered into force.
(4) Before or after the People's Court accepts an application for the recognition of a Taiwan civil judgment, it may, in accordance with the provisions of the Civil Procedure Law and relevant judicial interpretations, order preservation measures.

The civil ruling of the Taiwan District Court will not be recognised under the following circumstances:

(1) The civil judgment for which recognition is applied is made in the absence of the respondent without legal summons, or when the respondent has no capacity for litigation and is not properly represented.
(2) The case falls within the exclusive jurisdiction of the people's court.
(3) The parties signed a valid arbitration agreement and have not waived the jurisdiction of the arbitration.
(4) The people's court has already made a judgment, or the arbitral tribunal on the Mainland has already made an arbitral award in the case.
(5) The court of The Hong Kong Special Administrative Region, the court of the Macao Special Administrative Region, or a foreign court has already rendered a judgment in the same dispute that has been recognised by the people's court.
(6) The arbitral tribunal of the Taiwan region, the arbitral tribunal of the Hong Kong Special Administrative Region, the arbitral tribunal of the Macao Special Administrative Region, or a foreign arbitral tribunal has already made an arbitral award for the same dispute which has been recognised by the people's court.

The people's court will not recognise a civil judgment if such recognition violates the basic principles of the national law such as the 'One-China' principle or otherwise damages the public interest.

[39] (Supreme People's Court, Fa (1999) No 10).
[40] (Supreme People's Court, Fa (2001) No 13).
[41] (Supreme People's Court, Fa (2009) No 4).

Civil judgments of the Taiwan District Court recognised and enforced by the people's court have the same effect as a judgment of the people's court.

ii. Judicial Practice in the Mainland and Taiwan

In the Mainland, there are no legal obstacles to the recognition and enforcement of Taiwan's court decisions in the Mainland since the promulgation of the Supreme People's Court's Provisions of the People's Court on the Recognition of Civil Judgments of Relevant Courts in Taiwan in 1998 (Law [1998] No 11). Arbitral awards made by Taiwan's arbitration institutions are also be recognised in the Mainland in accordance with the above provisions. In the Taiwan region, courts began to recognise the divorce judgment of the Mainland court earlier. On 20 September 1995, the Banqiao local court in Taiwan approved a divorce judgment made by the Nanjing Intermediate People's Court in Jiangsu, becoming the first divorce judgment recognised by the Taiwan court.[42] Although there are increasingly more judgments from Mainland courts being recognised by Taiwan, the Supreme Court of Taiwan stated its opinion in a 2007 judgment that after a civil judgment made by the Mainland is recognised, it has only enforcement power and no power to make judgments on non-enforcement issues.[43]

[42] See GX Wang and C Zhou, 'Liang an min shi pan jue de ren ke yu zhi hang wen ti yan jiu' [Research on the Recognition and Enforcement of Civil Judgments on Both Sides of the Strait] (2010) 3 *Law Research*.

[43] Supreme Court of the Republic of China Decision *Zhejian Textiles Import & Export Group Co Ltd v Evergreen International Storage & Transport Corp* ((2007) No 2531).

23

International Commercial Arbitration

SHUO FENG

I. Jurisdictional Requirements in International Commercial Arbitration

A. Requirements for Valid Arbitration Agreements

The arbitration agreement is the cornerstone of international commercial arbitral jurisdiction.[1] Both international commercial arbitral theories and legislation hold that an arbitration agreement is a prerequisite for conducting arbitration proceedings. This principle is generally agreed upon by both international commercial arbitral legislation and practice. For example, Article II (3) of the New York Convention clearly specifies that:

> The court of a Contracting State, when seized of an action in a matter in respect of which the parties have made an agreement within the meaning of this article, shall, at the request of one of the parties, refer the parties to arbitration, unless it finds that the said agreement is null and void, inoperative or incapable of being performed.

Article VII of the UNCITRAL Model Law contains similar provisions. The contents of arbitration agreements directly impact on the agreements' validity.[2] In general, a complete arbitration agreement should cover at least the following substantive requirements, set out at I.A.i to I.A.v.

i. An Expression of Intention to Apply for Arbitration

The expression of intention to apply for arbitration is generally regarded as the fundamental element of arbitration agreements.[3] In the modern arbitral system, the expression of an intention to apply for arbitration must be clear and unmistakable.[4] If an arbitration agreement confers jurisdiction to the arbitral tribunal and the court at the same time, the agreement will be invalid. Generally, the parties must conclude an arbitration agreement at their true will. For instance, Article 17 of the PRC Arbitration Law stipulates that if one party coerced the other party into concluding the arbitration agreement, the arbitration agreement shall be null and void.

[1] E Gaillard, *Legal Theory of International Arbitration* (Martinus Nijhoff Publishers, 2010) 21.
[2] M Rubino-Sammartano, *International Arbitration Law and Practice* 2nd edn (Kluwer Law International 2001) 214.
[3] UNCTAD, *Dispute Settlement: International Commercial Arbitration, 5.2 The Arbitration Agreement*, (United Nations 2005) 40.
[4] D Horton, 'Arbitration About Arbitration' (2018) 70 *Stanford Law Review* 363, 419.

ii. Subject Matters for Arbitration

The subject matter of an arbitration agreement also plays an important role in arbitration. If the parties have not agreed on the arbitral matter in their arbitration agreement, it is impossible for any tribunal to hear the arbitration and make an award. Moreover, the matter submitted by parties must be arbitrable. In general, the domestic arbitration law provides for the scope of arbitrability. If the matter falls beyond the scope of arbitrable matters, the court must refuse to give an arbitral award.

iii. Seat or Place of Arbitration

A vital element for any international arbitration agreement is the designation of the 'seat' (or 'place') of the arbitration. This specifies the state where the arbitration has its formal legal or juridical seat, and where the arbitral award will formally be made.[5]

First, the seat of the arbitration directly relates to the law governing the validity of the arbitration agreement. In international commercial arbitration, requirements for the validity of arbitration agreements vary across different countries, resulting in a large number of legal conflicts on validity. Generally, the law of the country where the seat of arbitration is located is the applicable law for arbitration agreements unless the parties have made other provisions.[6] Thus, the determination of the validity of arbitration agreements depends largely on the provisions in the seat of arbitration.[7] Second, according to the territorial principle, the seat of arbitration affects the procedural rules governing arbitral proceedings. If the parties do not make a choice of law, the law of the arbitral seat is usually applied.[8] Finally, the seat of arbitration affects the substantive law which will govern the arbitration. If the parties do not make a clear choice of the applicable substantive law, the tribunal will determine the applicable law by reference to the conflicts rules dictated by the law of the seat of arbitration.[9] In some cases, where the parties have not made a choice of law, this will result in the tribunal applying the substantive law of the arbitral seat.

iv. Arbitration Rules

Arbitration rules, also known as arbitration procedure rules, are the procedural rules that should be followed by the parties and the tribunal throughout the arbitral process. They govern jurisdiction, the application for arbitration, the arguments, the appointment of arbitrators, the composition of the arbitral tribunal, the arbitration awards, etc. Procedural rules relate directly to the protection of the arbitration process and influence the substantive rights of the parties. In practice, the choice of arbitration rules varies due to differences among arbitral modes. For institutional arbitration, the parties usually agree to arbitrate according to the rules of the arbitral institution, since leading institutions all formulate their own rules for the parties. As for ad hoc arbitration, the parties must choose or design rules in their arbitration agreement.

[5] GB Born, *International Arbitration: Law and Practice* (Kluwer Law International, 2012) 37.
[6] ibid, 56.
[7] J Han, *Theory and Practice of Modern International Commercial Arbitration* 2nd edn (Law Press·China, 2000) 91.
[8] G Petrochilos, *Procedural Law in International Arbitration* (Oxford University Press, 2004) 23.
[9] N Blackaby, C Partasides, et al, *Redfern and Hunter on International Arbitration* 5th edn (Oxford University Press, 2009) 233.

v. *Choice-of-Law Clauses*

International arbitration can give rise to tortuous choice-of-law questions. As a consequence, many arbitration agreements contain a choice-of-law clause which specifies the substantive law applicable to the parties' dispute.[10] Similarly, the agreement may dictate certain procedural requirements, such as the language of the arbitration; the number of arbitrators; the method of selection and qualifications of arbitrators. These elements are fundamental to obtaining jurisdiction for arbitral tribunals. The parties may also adopt model arbitration clauses provided by arbitral institutions to prevent the arbitration agreement from being invalid for not satisfying substantive requirements.

B. Application of Parties

A valid arbitration agreement does not by itself allow the tribunal to obtain jurisdiction. Generally, the parties must make an application, after which the arbitration institution will conduct a formal inspection of jurisdiction over the dispute. At this stage, arbitration institutions only inspect the formal validity of arbitration agreements. As long as it can be proved prima facie that the parties have a formally valid arbitration agreement, the tribunal may accept the case.[11] After acceptance by an arbitration institution, the parties can select arbitrators according to arbitration agreements or rules. Arbitral tribunals are thus finally composed and arbitral jurisdiction is formally established.

C. The Scope of Arbitral Jurisdiction

The scope of arbitral jurisdiction differs from the scope of the jurisdiction of courts, and most countries restrict the arbitral jurisdiction. For example, Article 2 of PRC Arbitration Law stipulates that:

> Contractual disputes and other disputes over rights and interests in property between citizens, legal persons and other organisations that are equal subjects may be arbitrated.

And Article 3 stipulates that:

> The following disputes may not be arbitrated, (a) marital, adoption, guardianship, support and succession disputes; (b) administrative disputes that shall be handled by administrative organs as prescribed by law.

II. Objection to Arbitral Jurisdiction

A. Who can Object to Arbitral Jurisdiction

The parties have the right to object to arbitral jurisdiction. In arbitral proceedings, it is usually the respondents who appeal against the jurisdiction of the arbitral institution or tribunal.

[10] GB Born, *International Arbitration and Forum Selection Agreements: Drafting and Enforcing* 3rd edn (Kluwer Law & Business 2010) 79–80.

[11] XH Liu, *Theoretical and Practical Legal Aspects of International Commercial Arbitration Agreements* (The Commercial Press, 2005) 92–95.

Moreover, some scholars deem that arbitration institutions or arbitral tribunals also have the power to refuse to exercise their jurisdiction in accordance with their functions, but this is still inconclusive.[12]

B. Time Limit of Objection

After the commencement of arbitral proceedings, according to major international arbitration laws and arbitral institutional rules, if one party objects to the entire or partial jurisdiction of an arbitration institution or arbitral tribunal, they must propose an objection in time.[13] Permitting objections to jurisdiction maintains party autonomy and the rule of law. Requiring objections to be timely ensures that jurisdiction is established in a timely manner, avoiding waste of the parties' time and money.[14]

C. Reasons for Objection

i. *The Arbitration Agreement is Invalid*

The most significant reason for objection is invalidity of arbitration agreements. For example, Article 4.3(e) of the ICC Arbitration Rules 2021 and Article 20.3 of the UNCITRAL Arbitration Rules both clearly stipulate that a party must submit the arbitration agreements or arbitral clauses between the parties when it applies for an arbitration. If the parties do not have an agreement or the agreement is invalid, arbitration institutions cannot accept the case.[15]

ii. *The Scope of Agreement on Disputed Matters*

The jurisdiction of the arbitral tribunal is also limited by the scope of the parties' arbitration agreement. If the parties only agree to address matter A by arbitration, tribunals will not have jurisdiction over disputes on matter B.

D. Who can Determine Arbitral Jurisdiction

i. *Arbitration Institutions*

Arbitration institutions do not have the power, or the practical ability, to conduct substantive examination. The arbitral jurisdiction includes the power to solve substantive disputes and the power to decide on procedural matters. Thus, the integrity of jurisdiction of arbitral tribunals will be violated if the challenges are handled by arbitration institutions.[16]

[12] GB Born, *International Arbitration: Law and Practice* (Kluwer Law International, 2012) 48.

[13] UNCITRAL Model Law, Art 16, UNCITRAL Arbitration Rules, Art 23.2, SIAC Arbitration Rules 2016, Art 28.3.

[14] XH Liu and FQ Yuan, *Cases of International Commercial Arbitration* (Beijing University Press, 2017) 90.

[15] ML Moses, *The Principles and Practice of International Commercial Arbitration* (Cambridge University Press, 2008) 17.

[16] M Rubino-Sammartano, *International Arbitration Law and Practice* 2nd edn (Kluwer Law International, 2001) 371.

ii. Arbitral Tribunals

The competence-competence rule provides a theoretical basis for arbitral tribunals in determining jurisdiction. The rule means that an arbitral tribunal can determine its own jurisdiction and the existence and validity of arbitration agreements without going through the court.[17] The effects of this rule are obvious. To a large extent, it prevents parties from dealing with jurisdictional issues through the lengthy process of the courts in an attempt to delay or destroy the arbitral proceedings. Hence, it increases arbitral effectiveness and contributes to the realisation of arbitral values. Shuangyuan Li, a leading Chinese scholar of international private law, has stated that the competence-competence rule can ensure the existence of the validity of arbitration agreements between parties, and save time in resolving disputes.[18]

iii. Courts

The decision of the arbitral tribunal on jurisdiction is not the end; arbitration agreements shall accept examination by the court. In theory, the courts have final authority to determine the validity of arbitration agreements. Appropriate supervision of arbitration by courts is accepted by consensus among most arbitrators despite the contractual nature of arbitration, and the fact that the realisation of arbitral values is not a proper function of the courts.[19] Practice proves that an objection to the tribunal's jurisdiction can be submitted during or after the determination of the award, subject to time limits.[20] Normally, a party will apply to the court following a failed objection to jurisdiction before the tribunal. Although most national legislation and the majority of relevant international conventions state that arbitral tribunals have the power to decide questions of jurisdiction, their decisions will be supervised judicially by the courts. Article II(3) of the New York Convention stipulates that:

> The court of a Contracting State, when seized of an action in a matter in respect of which the parties have made an agreement within the meaning of this article, shall, at the request of one of the parties, refer the parties to arbitration, unless it finds that the said agreement is null and void, inoperative or incapable of being performed.

This rule demonstrates that decisions of arbitral tribunals on their own jurisdiction are subordinate to the courts' decisions.

III. Chinese Legislation with Respect to Arbitration Jurisdiction

Article 5 of the PRC Arbitration Law states that, where the parties have concluded an arbitration agreement and a party institutes proceedings in a people's court, the people's court shall not accept the case unless the arbitration agreement is null and void. This article establishes the basic principle that arbitration agreements may grant jurisdiction to arbitral tribunals. Article 20 of the PRC Arbitration Law states that, a party who challenges the validity of an arbitration agreement

[17] P Binder, *International Commercial Arbitration and Mediation in UNCITRAL Model Law Jurisdictions* 4th edn (Kluwer Law International 2019) 253–254.

[18] SY Li, *A New Theory of Law and Practice on International Economy and Trade* (Hunan University Press, 1996) 396.

[19] J Zhao, *Research on Judicial Supervision over International Commercial Arbitration* (Law Press·China, 2000) 15–18.

[20] P Binder, *International Commercial Arbitration and Mediation in UNCITRAL Model Law Jurisdictions* 4th edn (Kluwer Law International, 2019) 257–258.

may either request the Arbitration Commission to make a decision or apply to the people's court for a ruling. This article gives arbitration institutions the power to decide the validity of arbitration agreements and gives the Arbitration Commission competence-competence jurisdiction.[21] The second half of Article 20 of the PRC Arbitration Law then stipulates that if one party requests the Arbitration Commission to make a decision on jurisdiction and the other party applies to the people's court for a ruling, the people's court shall give a ruling. Hence, the court has final jurisdiction over arbitration and may have significantly influenced Chinese arbitration rules.[22]

IV. Choice of Law

A. Procedural Rules

Most countries adopt Article 19 of the UNCITRAL Model Law to govern procedures. This establishes party autonomy as the primary principle and, where there is no agreement between the parties, gives the arbitral tribunal the power to identify the relevant procedural laws. The principle of party autonomy in the choice of procedural law is supported by a number of international documents (including international conventions, model laws, and institutional arbitration rules). The main international commercial arbitration institutions recognise this principle. For example, Article 21 of the ICC Arbitration Rules 2021 and Article 27 of the Arbitration Institute of the Stockholm Chamber of Commerce Arbitration Rules 2017 both affirm the priority of party autonomy in the application of relevant laws, including arbitration procedural law. Party autonomy gives parties the right to agree upon arbitral procedures, but this right is generally subjugated to mandatory national law. In theory, autonomy in the civil and commercial fields cannot disturb the basic legal order maintained by mandatory law.[23]

Although international commercial arbitration does not belong to any state, both the composition of arbitral tribunals and the advancement of the arbitral proceedings are, in practice, linked to some specific legal systems. If the parties do not choose the applicable procedural law in their arbitration agreement and cannot reach a unanimous agreement after the dispute occurs, the arbitration tribunal is required to determine which procedural laws to apply.[24] When arbitrators choose the applicable procedural laws, the first factor to be considered is the law of the arbitral seat. In addition, the arbitral tribunal will consider the recognition and enforcement of an award made by the state concerned.[25] Therefore, an award made through domestic procedural law is more easily enforced than an award made through the law of a foreign country. Moreover, when an arbitrator has the authority to choose the procedural law, it is more convenient to choose a mature municipal legal system.[26]

[21] SS Xie, *Commercial Arbitration* (Higher Education Press, 2003) 69.

[22] CIETAC Arbitration Rules (2000), Art 4; Chin Maritime Arbitration Commission (CMAC) Arbitration Rules (2001), Art 4.

[23] XH Liu and S Feng, 'Conflict and Coordination between Institutional Management Power and Parties Autonomy in International Commercial Arbitration' (2018) 33(5) *Journal of Shanghai University of Political Science & Law* 1, 6.

[24] G Vial, 'Influence of the Arbitral Seat in the Outcome of an International Commercial Arbitration' (2017) 50(2) *The International Lawyer* 334–335.

[25] AJ Belohlávek, 'Importance of the Seat of Arbitration in International Arbitration: Delocalization and Denationalization of Arbitration as an Outdated Myth', (2013) 31 *ASA Bulletin* 262–265.

[26] MS Kurkela, S Turunen, and Conflict Management Institute (COMI), *Due Process in International Commercial Arbitration* (Oxford University Press, 2010) 156.

The procedural law of a state must be applied when litigation is proposed to be conducted in that state, under the *locus regit actum* doctrine in private international law. The application of this principle in international commercial arbitration means that any activities in arbitration must be governed by the law of the arbitral seat.[27] The *locus regit actum* doctrine has widespread support. Article V(1)(a) and (d) of the New York Convention are representative in the context of international law. In terms of domestic law, the UK Arbitration Act 1996 clearly prescribes that the parties cannot breach its mandatory requirements by contrary agreement with respect to any English arbitral award. Swedish and German legislations have similar provisions.[28] The international consensus has accepted the arbitral seat as the *lex causae* of arbitration procedures.

i. Other Applicable Procedural Laws and Rules

In general, an arbitral tribunal is not bound to apply the law of the arbitral seat unless it is contrary to the mandatory conditions of the law of arbitral seat. Switzerland's Federal Code on Private International Law 1989 allows the parties to choose the arbitration procedures and, in the absence of party agreements, the tribunal shall identify the arbitral procedures, either directly or in accordance with domestic procedural law and arbitration rules. An example of the rules of main arbitral institutions is Article 14.5 of the LCIA Arbitration Rules 2014 which stipulates,

> The Arbitral Tribunal shall have the widest discretion to discharge these general duties, subject to such mandatory law(s) or rules of law as the Arbitral Tribunal may decide to be applicable.

B. Chinese Legislation on the Choice of Law in Arbitration Procedures

i. Rules of Procedure

Chinese arbitration law does not directly stipulate how to determine procedural rules in international commercial arbitration. Article 4 of the CIETAC Arbitration Rules 2012 provides that:

> Where the parties agree to refer their dispute to CIETAC for arbitration but have agreed on a modification of these Rules or have agreed on the application of other arbitration rules, the parties' agreement shall prevail unless such agreement is inoperative or in conflict with a mandatory provision of the law applicable to the arbitral proceedings. Where the parties have agreed on the application of other arbitration rules, CIETAC shall perform the relevant administrative duties.

Therefore, the parties enjoy full autonomy in international commercial arbitrations conducted in China. They can make an agreement on the procedural rules binding the arbitral tribunal by invoking or tailoring relevant arbitration rules, but such agreements cannot violate the mandatory provisions of the law of the arbitral seat.[29]

ii. Supervision of Arbitration by the Court

The Arbitration Law adopts the geographical principle with respect to external rules of arbitration. According to Article 65 of the PRC Arbitration Law, arbitration concerning disputes arising from

[27] ZD Chen, *International Commercial Arbitration* (Law Press·China, 1998) 206.

[28] Mr Liangyi Yang cited cases from 10 different countries in his book to illustrate that the arbitral seat law applicable to arbitral procedure has been widely respected in the courts. See LY Yang and others, *Arbitration Law: From the UK Arbitration Act (1996) to International Commercial Arbitration* (Law Press·China, 2006) 95.

[29] L Yang, *A Study of Procedure of International Commercial Arbitration* (Law Press·China, 2011) 104–105.

foreign economic, trade, transportation, and maritime affairs shall be governed by provisions of Chapter 7 of the PRC Arbitration Law (special provisions for foreign-related arbitration). If there is no corresponding provision in Chapter 7 of the PRC Arbitration Law, other relevant provisions of the Arbitration Law shall apply. Article 70 of the PRC Arbitration Law stipulates that the courts exercise jurisdiction over procedural review of arbitral awards made by Chinese foreign-related arbitration institutions. Therefore, in general, international commercial arbitration conducted in China must abide by the mandatory provisions of the PRC Arbitration Law and must accept the jurisdiction of the courts in China on procedural review of revoking the arbitral award.[30]

C. Rules Applicable to Substantive Disputes

i. Party Autonomy

In general, the laws of different countries all allow parties to agree on the law applicable to international commercial transactions. This reflects the principle of party autonomy and has generally been applied in international private law arbitration.[31] For example, Article VII.1 of European Convention on International Commercial Arbitration declares that:

> The parties shall be free to determine, by agreement, the law to be applied by the arbitrators to the substance of the dispute. Failing any indication by the parties as to the proper law, the arbitrators shall apply the proper law under the conflict of laws rules that the arbitrators deem applicable.

Article 28 of the UNCITRAL Model Law provides that the arbitral tribunal shall decide the dispute in accordance with such rules of law as are chosen by the parties as applicable to the substance of the dispute. In practice, the power of arbitral institutions to hear commercial disputes derives from authorisation by the parties.[32] The arbitral tribunal should generally respect the choice of the parties unless the action fails to meet mandatory conditions of the relevant domestic law. For example, Article 22.3 of the LCIA Arbitration Rules 2014 stipulates that:

> The Arbitral Tribunal shall decide the parties' dispute in accordance with the law(s) or rules of law chosen by the parties as applicable to the merits of their dispute. If and to the extent that the Arbitral Tribunal decides that the parties have made no such choice, the Arbitral Tribunal shall apply the law(s) or rules of law which it considers appropriate.

Thus, in international commercial arbitration, the 'law or rules of law agreed by the parties' usually refers to substantive law, not including the conflict of law rules of the jurisdiction.[33]

ii. Limits to Party Autonomy

The parties have the right to choose substantive law to settle their disputes in international commercial arbitration,[34] but their autonomy is limited. First, the choice made by the parties

[30] XF Yu, *Judicial Supervision and Assistance in International Commercial Arbitration: on Legislation and Judicial Practice of China* (Intellectual Property Publishing House Co Ltd, 2006) 393–395.

[31] A Mills, *The Confluence of Public and Private International Law: Justice, Pluralism and Subsidiarity in the International Constitutional Ordering of Private Law* (Cambridge University Press, 2009) 291.

[32] ZX Wang and X Zheng, *Autonomy and Intervene Research on the International Commercial Arbitration Consensus* (Law Press·China, 2016) 80–81.

[33] KP Berger, *International Economic Arbitration* (Kluwer Law and Taxation Publishers, 1993) 816–817.

[34] N Blackaby, C Partasides, et al, *Redfern and Hunter on International Arbitration* 5th edn (Oxford University Press, 2009) 203.

must be 'in good faith and lawful'.[35] The parties may not choose substantive law for the purpose of evading another law. Second, the parties cannot violate the mandatory laws or public policies of the state of arbitral seat. Last, the substantive law chosen by the parties must have some connection with the contract. Most countries enumerate this requirement in legislation, though some, such as the UK and France, do not demand that the substantive law chosen by the parties have a reasonable connection with the contract. As a matter of practice, arbitral tribunals rarely overrule the parties' choice of substantive law due to a lack of connection with the contract.[36] When the parties adopt arbitration as a means of resolving disputes, they are free to decide which laws should be applied between themselves at the time they enter into their contract or agreement. But there are different opinions on whether the parties have this right to make a choice of law subsequent to a dispute arising. Some scholars hold that the spirit of party autonomy allows the parties to delay making such choices or to modify existing decisions.[37] In practice, even if the parties modify such pre-determined decisions, the arbitral tribunal and arbitrators generally respect the parties' choice.

There are two methods of choosing substantive law – express and implied. Express choices have been widely accepted by many countries, but the attitudes of different countries are inconsistent with respect to implied choices. In practice, the universal approach is to presume that the parties intend to apply the law of the arbitral seat. However, with the development of practice, elements of irrationality in this approach have been gradually exposed. Despite this, some countries such as the US still acknowledge when the parties choose the law impliedly.

D. Decisions by the Arbitral Tribunal

i. *Applicable Conflict of Laws Rules*

The traditional view is that when the parties do not make a choice about the applicable law, the arbitral tribunal should choose the substantive law based on the conflict rules of the state where the arbitration is seated.[38] However, in practice, it may be difficult to determine the arbitral seat. The arbitration may be heard in several countries, conducted online, or the arbitral seat may change temporarily, etc, all of which complicate the determination of the arbitral substantive law. In China, Article 28(2) of the UNCITRAL Model Law makes clear that the arbitral tribunal may determine the law according to the conflict of laws rules it considers most appropriate in the absence of an agreement by the parties. This mode has been adopted by the European Convention on International Commercial Arbitration. Article 46(3) of the UK Arbitration Act 1996 also stipulates that if, or to the extent that, there is no such choice or agreement, the tribunal shall apply the law determined by the conflict of laws rules that it considers most appropriate. The UNCITRAL Arbitration Rules and the ICC Arbitration Rules both illustrate this mode, providing that the arbitral tribunal may choose 'applicable' or 'appropriate' conflict of laws rules to determine the substantive law when the parties have not made a choice.

[35] L Kou, *Research on the Application of Contemporary International Commercial Arbitral Law* (Intellectual Property Publishing House Co Ltd, 2013) 121.

[36] XH Liu and FQ Yuan, *Cases of International Commercial Arbitration* (Beijing University Press, 2017) 195.

[37] N Blackaby, C Partasides, et al, *Redfern and Hunter on International Arbitration* 5th edn (Oxford University Press, 2009) 197.

[38] AFM Maniruzzaman, 'International Commercial Arbitration: The Conflict of Laws Issues in Determining the Applicable Substantive Law in the Context of Investment Agreements' (1993) 40 *Netherlands International Law Review* 201, 206.

ii. *Applicable Substantive Rules: Accordance with the Most Significant Relationship*

Germany and Switzerland are among the countries adopting this mode. The Code of Germany Civil Procedure stipulates that when the parties have failed to determine the law applicable to substantive disputes, the arbitral tribunal shall apply the law of the state that has the most significant relationship with the subject matter of the arbitration.[39] Article 187 of Switzerland's Federal Code on Private International Law is similar, providing that the arbitral tribunal shall apply the legal rules chosen by the parties or, in the absence of a choice made by the parties, the legal rules which have the most significant relationship with the dispute. In international commercial arbitration, when the parties have not made a choice regarding the law, the tribunal may identify the substantive law by reference to the conflict of laws rules of the country which has the most significant relationship with the dispute. For example, in a case of ICC Arbitration the arbitrator applied the Italian conflicts of laws rules on the grounds that the Italian legal system has the most significant relationship with the dispute.[40]

iii. *Applicable Substantive Rules: Substantive Laws of the Arbitral Seat*

In the US, if the parties have not chosen the law to be applied, it is presumed that they agree to apply the substantive law of the arbitral seat. However, this method has gradually lost favour because the arbitral seat serves as the place to resolve the dispute, instead of a location that designates the regulation of the parties' rights and obligations. Especially in international commercial arbitration, the direct application of the law of the seat may result in the impairment of the autonomy of the arbitration and render it no different from litigation in the arbitral seat.[41] However, if this method is adhered to, the parties need to think more deeply about choosing the arbitral seat. On the other hand, the parties' autonomy will be undermined to a certain degree when the arbitration institution or the arbitral tribunal determines the arbitral seat.

iv. *Applicable Substantive Rules: Uniform Commercial Laws*

Uniform commercial laws refer to unified substantive normative systems composed of international treaties concluded or jointly participated in by all the countries around the world to adjust their international economic and trade activities. The purpose of these uniform rules is to avoid legal conflicts arising from the differences amongst diverse national laws and the uncertainties of the legal rules caused by changes in domestic laws. Typical uniform commercial laws include the United Nations Convention on Contracts for the International Sale of Goods (CISG). The CISG allows parties to choose to resolve their disputes by applying the convention. They may limit their choice to particular provisions of the convention and even modify some of the provisions. This shows significant flexibility and respect for party autonomy.[42]

[39] K Herbert, 'Most Significant Relationship, Governmental Interests, Cultural Identity, Integration: "Rules" at Will and the Case for Principles of Conflict of Laws' (2004) 9 *Uniform Law Review* 467, 475.

[40] [1966] ICC Arbitration Tribunal 1422, [1974] 101 Journal de Droit International 162.

[41] P Sanders, *International Arbitration: Liber amicorum for Martin Domke* (Martinus Nijhoff, 1967) 161.

[42] P Schlechtriem and P Butler, *UN Law on International Sales: The UN Convention on the International Sale of Goods* (Springer, 2009) 18–19.

v. Applicable Substantive Rules: General Principles of Law

Article 38 of the Statute of The International Court of Justice stipulates that general principles of law can be used as bases for the Court's judgments. General principles of law used in international commercial arbitration are no different from those used in public international law.[43] For example, *pact sunt servanda*, fairness and good faith, and estoppel are all general principles of law. However, the use of general principles of law makes it difficult to guarantee the certainty and accuracy of awards in the field of commercial arbitration.

vi. Applicable Substantive Rules: Amiable Composition

Amiable composition, also known as arbitration *ex aequo et bono*, means that the arbitrator, with the authorisation of both parties, may make an award based on criteria the arbitrator considers to be fair and reasonable.[44] The parties give authorisation to the arbitral tribunal to make an award in accordance with *ex aequo et bono*, and so must bear the consequences of the arbitral tribunal making an award without referring to any legal rules. Amiable arbitration has been recognised by a number of international treaties and arbitration rules, such as the European Convention on International Commercial Arbitration, ICC Arbitration Rules, and the China (Shanghai) Pilot Free Trade Zone Arbitration Rules. The International Centre for Settlement of Investment Disputes Convention also allows for the handling of relevant investment disputes on the basis of *ex aequo et bono* even in international investment arbitration. The use of *ex aequo et bono* gives the arbitral tribunal wide discretion, and thus many countries impose restrictions on the exercise of this power, to prevent abuse of power or arbitrary judgments.[45]

vii. Applicable Substantive Rules: Commercial Customary Law

Commercial customary law is derived from the Latin *lex marcatoria*, which also translates into merchant customary law, commercial customary law, etc. It mainly appears in the following forms. The first is international trade practice, including trade customs and practices that are repeatedly applied internationally, as well as written uniform practices formed by long-term trade activities, such as the International Rule for the Interpretation of Trade Terms (INCOTERMS) and the Uniform Customs and Practice for Documentary Credits (UCP), which were developed by the ICC in 1936 and revised several times. The second is the standard form contract, which is prepared for the parties by an international organisation or professional company. The parties have the right to modify and supplement standard form contracts, and they can use the contents of the standard form contract as the basis for their rights and obligations.[46] Chinese law also reflects the reference to and absorption of merchant customary law. For example, the General Provisions of the Civil Law of the PRC, promulgated in 2017, incorporates 'customs' into the official origins of the civil law in China, which shows the influence of the merchant customary law on Chinese legislation.

[43] KP Zhu, *Application of Law in International Commercial Arbitration* (Law Press·China, 1999) 177.
[44] DP Han, *Monograph on Private International Law Issues* (Wuhan University Press, 2004) 410.
[45] S Feng, 'Reflection and Choice of the Application of Amiable Arbitration in International Investment Arbitration' (2018) 2(3) *The South China Sea Law Journal* 94, 103.
[46] SM Yang, *International Commercial Arbitration* (Chongqing University Press, 2002) 164.

E. Chinese Legislation on the Choice of Substantive Arbitration Law

Article 7 of the PRC Arbitration Law stipulates that disputes shall be fairly and reasonably settled by arbitration on the basis of facts and in accordance with the relevant provisions of law. Article 47.1 of the CIETAC Arbitration Rules (2012) states that:

> The arbitral tribunal shall independently and impartially render a fair and reasonable arbitral award based on the facts of the case and the terms of the contract, in accordance with the law, and with reference to international practices.

According to these provisions, Chinese arbitration institutions decide on substantive disputes in accordance with laws, contractual provisions, and international practices. In foreign-related disputes, the applicable substantive law is determined according to rules on conflicts in Chinese legislation such as the Contract Law and the Regulations on the Application of Foreign-Related Legal Relations. For general foreign-related contract disputes, the arbitration institutions of China will first apply the law chosen by the parties. Where the parties have not chosen the law, the law of the country that has the most significant relationship with the contract will be applied.[47] But Chinese law must apply directly when it comes to the implementation of Sino-foreign joint venture contracts, Sino-foreign cooperative venture contracts, and Sino-foreign exploration and development natural resource contracts, as well as contracts for other types of foreign direct investment in China.[48] At present, Chinese arbitration law and rules of arbitration institutions do not provide for the possibility of amiable arbitration, which has not been adopted in China.

V. Recognition and Enforcement of International Commercial Arbitral Awards in China

A. International Treaties

Since China's accession to the New York Convention in 1987, the Convention has become the most important legal basis for the recognition and enforcement of foreign commercial arbitration in China. However, when China acceded to the New York Convention, it made two declarations of reservations. One is the Declaration of Reciprocity Reservation, and the other is the Declaration of Commercial Reservations.[49] In addition to the Convention, some bilateral trade

[47] Law of the People's Republic of China on Choice of Law for Foreign-related Civil Relationships, Art 41 'The parties concerned may choose the laws applicable to contracts by agreement. If the parties do not choose, the laws at the habitual residence of the party whose fulfillment of obligations can best reflect the characteristics of this contract or other laws which have the closest relation with this contract shall apply.'

[48] See PRC Contract Law, Art 126 'For a Chinese-foreign equity joint venture contract, a Chinese-foreign contractual joint venture contract, or a contract for Chinese-foreign joint exploration and development of natural resources which is performed within the territory of the PRC, the law of the PRC shall be applied.'

[49] SPC's Notice on the Implementation of China's Accession to the Convention on the Recognition and Enforcement of Foreign Arbitral Awards, Fa (Jing) Fa [1987] No 5, Art 1: '(1) In accordance with the reciprocity reservation declaration made by China upon its accession to this Convention, China will only apply this Convention to the recognition and enforcement of arbitral awards made in the territory of another contracting state. In case of any discrepancy between the provisions of this Convention and the provisions of China's Civil Procedure Law (Trial Implementation), this Convention prevails; (2) Where an arbitral award made within the territory of a non-contracting state needs to be recognized and enforced by a Chinese court, Article 204 of the PRC Civil Procedure Law (Trial Implementation) shall apply.'; Art 2: 'In accordance with the commercial reservation declaration made by China upon its accession to this Convention, China will apply the Convention only to differences arising out of legal relationships, whether contractual or not, which are

treaties, investment protection treaties, and judicial assistance treaties concluded between China and other countries also involve the recognition and enforcement of foreign arbitral awards. These bilateral treaties can be applied when China and the applicant's country or the country where the foreign arbitral award was made have not jointly acceded to multilateral international conventions governing the recognition and enforcement of foreign arbitral awards.[50]

B. Domestic Law

China's provisions on the recognition and enforcement of foreign arbitral awards are scattered in the PRC Arbitration Law, the PRC Civil Procedure Law, and Judicial Interpretations, notifications and approvals promulgated by the SPC. The contents of various judicial interpretations, notifications, and approvals promulgated by the SPC mainly involve the refusal to recognise and enforce foreign arbitral awards, the determination of organs of arbitration agreements and jurisdiction, fees for recognising and enforcing foreign arbitral awards, the time limit for examination, and the validity of arbitration agreements for ad hoc arbitration. These legal documents make up for the unclear legal provisions exposed in judicial practice, and function as a supplementary basis for China to recognise and enforce foreign arbitral awards.

C. The Principle of Reciprocity

In practice, except in the case of divorce judgments, Chinese courts must examine whether there is a reciprocal relationship between the state of the judgment and China, with regard to other civil and commercial judgments made by foreign courts. Chinese courts once rejected the 'legal reciprocity' approach which requires recognising and enforcing Chinese judgments under the law of the other countries, and adopted the 'factual reciprocity' standard which considers whether the other country in fact reciprocally recognises and enforces Chinese judgments and arbitral awards.[51] However, the SPC has now issued the 2015 Opinions of the SPC on Providing Judicial Services and Guarantees for the Belt and Road Construction. This document was the first to put forward a 'presumption of reciprocity', that is, it is presumed that there is reciprocity in recognition as long as China can confirm that a foreign country has not refused to accept the precedent of its court decisions. In October 2017, the SPC put forward the Provisions on the Recognition and Enforcement of Civil and Commercial Judgments of Foreign Courts (Draft for Opinions), which further provided for the determination of reciprocity, and showed a tendency to introduce 'presumptive reciprocity' or 'legal reciprocity' as separate from 'factual reciprocity'.[52]

considered commercial under the national law of the People's Republic of China. "Legal relationships, whether contractual or not, which are considered commercial" means the economic rights and obligations arising from contracts, torts or relevant legal provisions, such as purchase and sale of goods, lease of property, project contracting, processing, technology transfer, equity or contractual joint adventure, exploration and development of natural resources, insurance, credit, labor service, agency, consultation service, marine, civil aviation, railway or road passenger and cargo transportation, product liability, environment pollution, marine accident, and ownership disputes, except disputes between foreign investors and the host government.'

[50] XQ Qi, *Study on Recognition and Enforcement of Foreign Arbitral Awards* (Law Press·China, 2010) 35.

[51] T Du, 'Reciprocity Principle and Recognition and Enforcement of Foreign Judgments' (2007) 29(1) *Global Law Review* 117,118.

[52] WG Xu, 'Paths of Recognition and Enforcement of Foreign Court Judgment System in China – Also on the Change of Attitudes towards the Determination of Reciprocal Relationship' (2018) 35(2) *Studies in Law and Business* 171, 179.

Reciprocity in the recognition and enforcement of foreign commercial arbitral awards is still necessary. This change of attitude by China towards the recognition of reciprocal relationships may be an effective way to highlight China's support for arbitration.[53]

D. Procedures for Recognising and Enforcing Foreign Arbitral Awards

i. Jurisdiction

According to Article 283 of the PRC Civil Procedure Law, a party seeking recognition and enforcement of a foreign arbitral award must apply directly to the intermediate people's court at the place of domicile of the party against whom enforcement is sought, or at the place where the relevant property is located. The SPC has ruled that the application of the parties should be accepted by the intermediate people's courts in the following places: (i) the domicile or residence of the person against whom the application is sought, if that person is a natural person; (ii) the place of principal office if the person is a legal entity; or (iii) the place where the person's property is located, if the person has no domicile, residence or main office in China, but has property in China.[54]

ii. Time Limits

The recognition and enforcement of foreign arbitral awards in China is governed by Article 239 of the PRC Civil Procedure Law concerning time limits on applications for enforcement. As with the recognition and enforcement of foreign-related arbitral awards, the application period for enforcement by the parties is two years, and the application for suspension or interruption of the limitation of execution shall be governed by the provisions of the law relating to the suspension or interruption of the limitation of action. The period of application for enforcement begins from: (i) the last day of the performance period specified in a legal instrument; (ii) the last day of each specified performance period if a legal instrument requires performance in instalments; or (iii) the effective date of a legal instrument if the legal instrument does not specify a period of performance.

iii. Documents

Where a party applies to have a foreign arbitral award recognised and enforced, it must generally submit to the court an application, an original arbitral award, and an arbitration agreement or a duly certified or certified copy thereof. In addition, the applicant must provide, amongst other materials, the applicant's identity certificate, a document on the power of attorney for foreign applicants to employ Chinese lawyers. Otherwise, Chinese courts may refuse to accept the application, order supplementary materials to be accepted after meeting the application requirements, or reject the action. The documents submitted by the applicant must be made in Chinese and certified as required.[55]

[53] S Feng, 'The Difficulties and Solutions of Applying for Property Preservation during the Examination of Recognition and Enforcement of Foreign Arbitral Awards' (2018) 106(4) *Beijing Arbitration Quarterly* 18, 32–33.

[54] The Notice of the Supreme People's Court on Implementing the Convention on the Recognition and Enforcement of Foreign Arbitral Awards Acceded to by China (1987).

[55] Art 21.2 of Provisions of the SPC on Several Questions Concerning Enforcement Work of People's Courts (Trial Implementation) provides that, when applying for enforcement of arbitral awards of foreign arbitration institutions, the text of arbitral awards certified by Chinese embassies and consulates abroad or notarised by Chinese notary organs shall be submitted.

E. Legal Reasons for Non-Recognition and Non-Enforcement of Foreign Arbitral Awards

i. Validity of the Arbitration Agreement

Article V(1)(a) of the New York Convention on arbitration agreements has always been the focus of China's examination in the recognition and enforcement of foreign commercial arbitral awards. In the case of *Xuplin International Engineering Co Ltd v Wuxi Wooke General Engineering Rubber Co Ltd of China* (2003),[56] the arbitration clause agreed by the parties in the contract provided for 'arbitration in Shanghai under ICC arbitration rules'. After disputes occurred between the two sides, the German party, while filing arbitration with the ICC, submitted a request to the People's Court of Wuxi New District to confirm the validity of the arbitration agreement. The case eventually reached the SPC, which ruled that the arbitration clause was invalid on the grounds that it did not specify an arbitration institution that had received the SPC's approval. At the same time, the ICC recognised its jurisdiction on the basis of the principle of competence-competence and made an award in favour of the German company, which was later applied to the Wuxi Intermediate People's Court for recognition and enforcement. After nearly two years of trial, the Wuxi Intermediate Court refused to recognise or enforce the arbitral award. The court held that though the arbitration award belonged to the 'non-domestic award' category stipulated in the New York Convention, the arbitration clause did not clearly stipulate the proper law, meaning that the validity of the clause should be determined by the place of arbitration, that is, under Chinese law. However, the arbitration clause did not stipulate a clear arbitration institution, so the court refused to recognise and enforce the award.

ii. Due Process

A determination that an arbitration violates due process generally refers to the failure of the respondent to receive proper notice of the appointment of an arbitrator or of the arbitration procedure, or other non-respondent actions which cause the respondent to fail to make a reasonable statement for the case.[57] For example, in the case of *Refusing to Recognise and Enforce the Tokyo 05-03 Arbitration Award of the Japan Commercial Arbitration Association*, the respondent was Tianjin Xinmao Technology Co Ltd. Xinyue Company claimed that after its 'Application for Amendment of Claim' was submitted to the arbitral tribunal on 31 August 2005, the Arbitration Association had sent the Request for Opinion to Xinmao Company by international express on 21 October 2005. However, Xinmao denied receiving the relevant 'Request for Opinions' sent by the arbitral tribunal, and Xinyue failed to submit evidence that the arbitral tribunal did perform the above notification. At the same time, there was no evidence that the arbitral tribunal had mailed the documents concerning the application for amendment of Xinyue Company to Xinmao Company on 21 October 2005. Xinmao Company also failed to provide evidence on the change of Xinyue Company's application. Article 20 of the Arbitration Rules provides that:

> (a) The claimant may apply to the Association for amendment of the same arbitration agreement and change the content of his application. If the amendment is made after the composition of the arbitral tribunal, the application for amendment shall be submitted to the arbitral tribunal and the approval of the arbitral tribunal shall be obtained.

[56] (2003) Xilimin Zhongzi Civil Ruling No 074.

[57] A Reyes, *The Practice of International Commercial Arbitration: A Handbook for Hong Kong Arbitrators* (Informa Law from Routledge, 2018) 11–12.

Xinmao had the right to comment on the subject matters of the claim after the Xinyue amendment, and the notice of the alteration should have been an important part of the arbitration procedure. The failure of the arbitral tribunal to notify Xinmao of the amendment of claim deprived Xinmao of its right and opportunity to make an argument, which fell within Article V(1)(b) of the New York Convention. The court refused to recognise and enforce the arbitral award.[58]

iii. Arbitral Awards beyond the Scope of Arbitration Agreements

If the respondent proves that the arbitration tribunal has made an award based on disputes other than those stipulated in the arbitration agreement, the people's court may refuse to recognise and enforce the arbitration award. If the invalid part can be separated from the parts entitled to arbitration, the court may only refuse to recognise and enforce the invalid part of the award. In the case of *American GMI's Application for Recognition of the London Metal Exchange Arbitration Award*,[59] the arbitration clause in the sales contract between GMI and Wuhu Smelter allowed the arbitration tribunal only to rule on disputes arising from the sales contract between GMI and Wuhu Smelter. But the application of GMI listed Wuhu Hengxin Copper Group Co Ltd. which had no arbitration agreement with GMI as a respondent. The arbitration tribunal's ruling on the disputes over the sales contract between GMI and Wuhu Hengxin was clearly beyond the scope of the arbitration agreement. The arbitral tribunal had jurisdiction to decide only the part of the award for which Wuhu Smelter was solely responsible, which it held was divisible from the overruling part. The court could not distinguish the separate responsibilities of Wuhu Smelter in other parts of the application that used the term 'respondent' to include both Wuhu Smelter and Wuhu Hengxin. Therefore, the people's court refused to recognise the indistinguishable part of the award.[60]

iv. Improper Composition of the Arbitral Tribunal or Improper Arbitration Procedure

An improper composition of the arbitral tribunal or improper arbitration procedure means that the composition of arbitral tribunal or the conduct of the arbitration procedure violates the agreement of the parties or, in cases where the parties have no agreement, the law of the seat.[61] In the case of *Application of Laibao Resources International Private Limited for Recognition and Enforcement of the Arbitral Award* decided by the SIAC in Singapore,[62] the arbitration clause signed between Laibao Resources International Private Limited and Shanghai Xintai International Trade Co Ltd stipulated that 'disputes and claims shall be submitted to arbitration in Singapore in accordance with the arbitration rules of the SIAC in force at that time; the arbitral tribunal shall consist of three arbitrators'. The arbitration rules applicable to the submission of disputes to arbitration are the fifth edition of the Arbitration Rules of the SIAC in 2013, in which

[58] SPC's Reply on the Ruling of Non-Recognition and Enforcement of the Arbitration Decision No 05-03 Tokyo Made by Japan Commercial Arbitration Association.

[59] SPC's Reply on American GMI's Application for Recognition of the London Metal Exchange Arbitration Award.

[60] See EX Wan and XH Xia, 'Reasons for the Refusals of the Recognition and Enforcement of Foreign Arbitral Awards in Chinese Courts – New York Convention Case Studies' (2010) 13(2) *Wuhan University International Law Review* 1, 16–17.

[61] XL Gao, 'Positive Practice of Chinese Courts on Recognition and Enforcement of Foreign Arbitral Awards' (2018) 5 *Journal of Law Application* 2, 3.

[62] (2016) Hu 01 Xiewairen No 01.

Article 5 stipulates 'expedited procedure'. In its reply No 50 to the Shanghai Higher People's Court (2017), the Supreme People's Court pointed out that the SIAC applied 'expedited procedure' for arbitration on the basis of the written application of Laibao Resources, which conformed to the provisions of the Arbitration Rules. The parties in this case clearly agreed in the arbitration clause that the arbitration tribunal should be composed of three arbitrators and did not exclude the application of 'expedited procedure' in the arbitration. Therefore, the application of 'expedited procedure' did not affect the basic procedural rights of the parties to obtain three arbitrators for arbitration in accordance with the arbitration clause. The SIAC decided to adopt the form of a sole arbitrator despite the arbitration clause, and the Shanghai Xintai expressly opposed the sole arbitration, thus creating a situation in which 'the composition of the arbitration tribunal was inconsistent with the agreement between parties'. Consequently, the SPC refused to recognise and enforce the arbitral award under Article V(1)(d) of the New York Convention.

v. Other Reasons

Article V(2) of the New York Convention on the non-arbitrability of disputes and violation of public policy gives the court of the place where the arbitral award is recognised and enforced the power to examine the award on its own initiative. In its Reply No 33 (2009), the SPC pointed out that the dispute in that case arose because the claimant Wu Chunying, as the legal heir of her deceased husband, claimed his right to a Mongolian arbitration award. Mongolian arbitration was provided for in the arbitration clause of the contract involved. Arbitral awards that do not involve matters of inheritance may be recognised and enforced. Article 3 of the PRC Arbitration Law stipulates that inheritance disputes cannot be arbitrated. The arbitral award in question confirmed Wu Chunying's status as the legal heir and her investment property rights arising from that status. Therefore, the arbitration award was not recognised or enforced in accordance with Article V(2) of the New York Convention.[63]

Chinese courts insist on a cautious approach to the examination of public policy. There has only been one case where a court refused to recognise and enforce a foreign arbitral award on this basis. In the case of *Applying for Recognition and Enforcement of Arbitral Awards made by ICC by Haimufam Corporation, Mag International Trading Company and Sulamo Media Company Limited, In its reply to the Shandong High People's Court No 11* (2008), the SPC held that the arbitration clauses agreed upon in the joint venture contract between Haimufam, Mag International, Sulamo Media, and Yongning only covered disputes between the parties to the joint venture, and not the lease dispute between Yongning and the joint venture company. In arbitrating disputes over joint venture contracts, the ICC heard and adjudicated disputes over lease contracts between Yongning and the joint venture company which went beyond the scope of the arbitration agreement. The ICC adjudicated the disputes over the lease contract despite the fact that a Chinese court had decided to preserve the property of the joint venture company and made a decision on the lease contract dispute between Yongning and the joint venture company. This action infringed on China's judicial sovereignty and the jurisdiction of the Chinese courts. Accordingly, the court refused to recognise and enforce the arbitral award in accordance with Article V(1)(c) and 2(b) of the New York Convention.[64]

[63] No 4 Civil Tribunal of Supreme People's Court, *Guide on Judgment of Foreign-Related Commercial and Maritime Cases* (People's Court Press, 2009) 97.

[64] (2008) MinSi TaZi No 11.

F. Internal Reporting System of Non-Recognition and Non-Enforcement of Foreign Arbitral Awards

According to the SPC Notice on Dealing with Issues Relating to Foreign-Related Arbitration and Matters Related to Foreign-Related Arbitration promulgated on 28 August 1995:

> Where a party applies to the people's court for the enforcement of an award by China's foreign-related arbitration institutions, or for the recognition and enforcement of an award by foreign arbitration institutions, if the people's court considers that China's foreign-related award meets the circumstances set out in Article 258 of the PRC Civil Procedure Law, or if the foreign arbitral award does not comply with the provisions of the international conventions to which China is a party or the principle of reciprocity, the application must be submitted to the Higher People's Court under its jurisdiction for examination before the people's court decides not to enforce or refuse to recognize and enforce it; if the Higher People's Court agrees to not enforce or to not recognise or enforce, it shall be reported to the SPC. Only after the SPC has replied can the decision of non-enforcement or refusal to recognise or enforce be made.

Accordingly, the people's court must implement this internal reporting system before refusing to enforce foreign-related arbitral awards, and before refusing to recognise or enforce foreign arbitral awards.[65]

G. Recognition and Enforcement of Arbitral Awards Made by Mainland China and Hong Kong

The New York Convention was extended to Hong Kong by the British Government. After China's accession to the New York Convention, and the provisions of the New York Convention naturally applied to the recognition and enforcement of arbitral awards between the Mainland and Hong Kong.[66] The New York Convention still applies to Hong Kong after the city's return to China, but cannot be applied to the recognition and enforcement of arbitral awards between the Mainland and Hong Kong. Therefore, the Hong Kong Arrangements was published.[67] Its main contents are as follows.

i. Basis of Enforcement

The courts of the Hong Kong Special Administrative Region (SAR) have agreed to enforce awards made by Mainland arbitration institutions (a list is provided by the Legal Office of the State Council through the Hong Kong and Macao Affairs Office of the State Council) in accordance with the Arbitration Law of China, and the people's courts of the Mainland have agreed to enforce the awards made in the Hong Kong Special Administrative Region in accordance with the Arbitration Ordinance of the Hong Kong Special Administrative Region.

[65] XH Liu and FQ Yuan, *Cases of International Commercial Arbitration* (Beijing University Press, 2017) 273.

[66] H Song, *Recognition and Enforcement of Arbitral Awards in International Commercial Arbitration* (Law Press·China, 2000) 248–249.

[67] XH Liu, 'Study on Mutual Recognition and Enforcement of Mainland and Hong Kong Arbitral Awards' (2001) 3 *Journal of Law Application* 19.

ii. Jurisdictional Courts

'Jurisdictional courts' are those courts which are competent to recognise and enforce arbitral awards. In the Mainland this refers to the intermediate people's courts in the place where the respondent resides or the property is located, while in the Hong Kong Special Administrative Region this refers to the High Court of the Hong Kong Special Administrative Region. Where the respondent's places of residence or property is both in the Mainland and the Hong Kong Special Administrative Region, the applicant may not apply to the competent courts in both places at the same time. Only when the enforcement of one court is insufficient to repay its debts can the insufficient part be applied to the other court for enforcement. The total amount of arbitral awards enforced successively by the courts of the two places may not exceed the original amount of the awards.

iii. Application of Enforcement

According to the Articles 3–5 of the Hong Kong Arrangements, an applicant who applies to the competent court for enforcement of an arbitral award made in the Mainland or the Hong Kong Special Administrative Region must submit an application for enforcement, the relevant document for the arbitral award, and the arbitration agreement. After receiving the application from the applicant, the court shall handle and execute the application in accordance with the legal procedures at the place of enforcement.

iv. Refusal of Enforcement

According to the Article 7 of the Hong Kong Arrangements, where the respondent submits evidence to prove that any of the following circumstances exist, the competent court may, upon verification, rule to refuse enforcement of the arbitral award.

(a) The parties to the arbitration agreement were, under the law applicable to them, under some incapacity; or the arbitration agreement is not valid under the law to which the parties have subjected it or, failing any indication thereon, under the law of the place where the award was made.
(b) The respondent was not given proper notice of the appointment of the arbitrator or was otherwise unable to present its case.
(c) The award deals with a difference not contemplated by or not falling within the terms of the submission to arbitration, or it contains decisions on matters beyond the scope of the submission to arbitration, provided that, if the decisions on matters submitted to arbitration can be separated from those not so submitted, that part of the award which contains decisions on matters submitted to arbitration shall be enforced.
(d) The composition of the arbitral tribunal or the arbitral procedure was not in accordance with the agreement of the parties, or, failing such agreement, was not in accordance with the law of the place where the arbitration took place.
(e) The award has not yet become binding on the parties or has been set aside or suspended by a court of or under the law of the place in which that award was made.
(f) If the court in the Mainland finds that the enforcement of the arbitral award would be contrary to the public interest of the Mainland, or the court of the Hong Kong SAR decides that the enforcement of the arbitral award in the Hong Kong SAR would be contrary to the public policy of the Hong Kong SAR, the enforcement of the award may be refused. If the competent court finds that the subject matter of the dispute is not capable of settlement by arbitration under the law of the place of enforcement, the enforcement of the arbitral award may be refused. Where the court in the Mainland finds that enforcement of the arbitral award would be contrary to the public interest of

the Mainland, or the court of the Hong Kong SAR decides that enforcement of the arbitral award in the Hong Kong SAR would be contrary to the public policy of the Hong Kong SAR, enforcement may be refused.

H. Recognition and Enforcement of Arbitral Awards Made by Mainland China and Macao

On 30 October 2007, the SPC and the Macao Special Administrative Region, through consultation, reached and signed the Macao Arrangement in accordance with Article 93 of the Basic Law of the Macao Special Administrative Region. According to the provisions of the Macao Arrangement, both civil and commercial arbitral awards are mutually recognised and enforced by the Mainland and Macao. Meanwhile, the awards of the Macao SAR include not only the awards made by the Macao arbitration institutions in accordance with the Macao arbitration regulations, but also the awards made by the Macao arbitrators in accordance with the Macao arbitration regulations.[68] The main contents of the agreement are as follows.

i. Jurisdictional Court

The competent courts in the place of residence, habitual residence, or property of the respondent have jurisdiction to recognise and enforce arbitral awards. Among them, in the Macao SAR, the intermediate courts have the right to accept applications for admitting arbitration awards, and the lower courts have the right to enforce arbitration awards. If any of the place of domicile, the place of residence or the locality of the property of the parties against whom an application is filed is located on Mainland or the Macao SAR, the applicant may file the application for recognition and enforcement with the competent court in one place or the competent courts in both places. If the application is filed with the competent courts in both places, both courts shall make examinations according to law. Should the application be approved, the courts will take such means of execution as sealing up, detaining, or freezing the property of the parties against whom the order is to be executed. The court at the place of arbitration must first enforce the payment of the debt; the court at the other place shall, after receiving the certificate issued by the court at the place of arbitration proving that the creditor's right is not paid off, enforce the payment to the applicant for the unpaid portion. The total amount of the payment enforced by both courts may not exceed the amount prescribed in the award and any related legal provisions.[69]

ii. Application for Enforcement

The applicant must submit to the competent court: an application form for the admission and enforcement an arbitration award; their identity certificate; the arbitration agreement; and the arbitration award. Where any of the above-mentioned documents is not prepared in Chinese, an officially notarised translated Chinese version must be submitted.

[68] FD Simoes, 'Recognition and Enforcement of Foreign Arbitral Awards in Macao' (2014) 44 *Hong Kong Law Journal* 563, 579–581.

[69] J Pien, 'Creditor Rights and Enforcement of International Commercial Arbitral Awards in China' (2007) 45 *Columbia Journal of Transnational Law* 586, 589.

iii. Refusal of Enforcement

Specific reasons for reviewing the court's refusal to recognise and enforce the relevant arbitration award are generally similar to those for the review of the Hong Kong arbitration award.

iv. Protective Measures

A court may, before or after accepting an application for admitting and enforcing an arbitration award, take protective measures against the property of the parties against whom the application is filed in accordance with the legal provisions where the court is situated if the application requests the court to do so.

I. Recognition and Enforcement of Arbitral Awards Made by Mainland China and Taiwan

With the relaxation of cross-strait relations after the 'reform and opening up', the recognition and enforcement of arbitral awards is becoming possible.[70] Therefore, the SPC promulgated the Taiwan Provisions in 2015. Its main contents are as follows.

i. The Scope of Application

A party to an arbitral award of the Taiwan Region may, in accordance with these Provisions, apply to the people's court for recognition and enforcement of the arbitral award of the Taiwan Region. The term 'arbitral awards of the Taiwan Region' means the arbitral awards on civil or commercial disputes issued by the relevant permanent arbitration institutions or temporary arbitral tribunals in the Taiwan Region in accordance with provisions of the Taiwan Region on arbitration, including arbitration judgments, arbitration settlements, and arbitration mediations.

ii. Jurisdictional Courts

A case involving an application for recognition of an arbitral award of the Taiwan Region shall be accepted by the intermediate people's court or a special people's court at the place where the applicant is domiciled or habitually resides, where the respondent is domiciled or habitually resides, or where the relevant property is located. Where the applicant applies for recognition to two or more people's courts having jurisdiction, the case shall be heard under the jurisdiction of the people's court which dockets the case first. Where the applicant applies for recognition to the people's court at the place where the respondent's property is located, the relevant evidence on existence of such property shall be provided.

iii. Protective Measures

Before or after the people's court accepts an application for recognition of an arbitral award of the Taiwan Region, it may issue a rule to adopt preservation measures in accordance with the Civil

[70] H-Soo Ha, 'A Study on Enforcement of Arbitral Awards between China and Taiwan', (2009) 19 *Journal of Arbitration Studies* 45, 47.

Procedure Law and relevant judicial interpretations and on the basis of the applicant's application. Where, after the people's court accepts an application for recognition of an arbitral award of the Taiwan Region, a party institutes an action regarding the same dispute, the people's court shall reject it. Where a party does not apply for recognition but institutes an action in the people's court regarding the same dispute instead, the people's court shall not accept it unless the arbitration agreement is invalid. After the people's court accepts an application for recognition of an arbitral award of the Taiwan Region, if the applicant requests to withdraw the application before a ruling is issued, the people's court may issue a ruling to allow withdrawal.[71]

iv. Refusal of Recognition and Enforcement

The reasons for refusing to recognise and enforce Taiwan's arbitration award are similar to those for examining Hong Kong's arbitration award.

v. Decision to Enforce

According to the Articles 17 and 18 of the Taiwan Provisions, where the court of the Taiwan Region revokes the arbitral award, the people's court shall issue a ruling to reject the arbitral award or issue a ruling to terminate enforcement. Where the court of the Taiwan Region dismisses the claim of arbitral award revocation, the people's court shall resume the recognition or enforcement procedure. Where the people's court issues a ruling to reject an arbitral award of the Taiwan Region and the applicant files another application, the people's court shall reject it. However, a party may apply for arbitration on the basis of a new arbitration agreement that the parties have entered into, or institute an action in the people's court with respect to the same dispute.

[71] XH Liu, 'Examination and Amendment of The System of Mutual Recognition and Enforcement of Arbitration Awards on Both Sides of the Taiwan Strait' (2011) 12 *Law Science* 86, 88–89.

24

Investment Treaty Arbitration

JUNRONG SONG, MIN HAN

Traditionally, investment disputes between a host state and foreign investors are mainly resolved through diplomatic protection of the investor's home state, local remedies in the host state and litigation at foreign courts. All of these dispute resolution methods have disadvantages or limitations. Therefore, a new method of dispute resolution has arisen, by which investors directly initiate arbitration procedures against the host state – international investment arbitration. Like international commercial arbitration, the consent of the host state and investors to settle their dispute by arbitration is a necessary condition for the arbitral tribunal to have jurisdiction.[1] In practice, consent to arbitration is mainly realised in three ways.[2] The first way is to include an arbitration clause in the investment contract entered into by the investor and the host government. In *SCB HK v TANESCO*, a dispute was submitted to the International Centre for the Settlement of Investment Disputes (ICSID) on the basis of the Implementation Agreement between the Government of Tanzania and Independent Power Tanzania Limited dated 8 June 1995 and the ICSID Convention.[3] The second way is for legislation of the host state to stipulate that foreign investors have the right to initiate arbitration procedures. For example, Article 8.2 of the Albanian Law No 7764 of 2 November 1993 provides:

> If the dispute arises out of or relates to expropriation, compensation for expropriation, or discrimination and also for the transfers in accordance with Article 7, then the foreign investor may submit the dispute for resolution and the Republic of Albania hereby consents to the submission thereof, to the International Centre for Settlement of Investment Disputes established by the Convention on the Settlement of Investment Disputes between States and National of Other States, done at Washington, March 18, 1965.[4]

As long as the legislation is still valid, the investor may express their consent by initiating an arbitration proceeding. The third way is to include an arbitration clause in the bilateral or multilateral investment treaties concluded between the host state and the investor's home state, which stipulates that nationals of one party can apply for arbitration against the other party's government. For example, Article 8.2 of the China-South Korea BIT provides: 'If a dispute cannot thus be settled within six months, it shall, upon the request of either Contracting Party, be submitted

[1] JS Yu, *Guoji Jingji Fa Gailun* [*International Economic Law*] (Higher Education Press, 2019) 411.
[2] ibid, 412.
[3] *Standard Chartered Bank (Hong Kong) Limited v Tanzania Electric Supply Company Limited (TANESCO)*, ICSID Case No ARB/15/41, Decision on Jurisdiction (12 February 2014), [1].
[4] Law for Foreign Investment (Albanian Law No 7764), Art 8.2.

to an ad hoc arbitral tribunal.'[5] Similar to the second way, the arbitration clause in the international investment treaty only indicates that the host state agrees to the 'offer' of arbitration, and the 'signing' and validity of the arbitration agreement is still needed to obtain the 'commitment' of the investor. Such commitment is generally manifested in the investor's submission of arbitration claims. Investment treaty arbitration is based on this third method. Since the mid-1990s, the number of investment treaty arbitration cases has increased dramatically as arbitration has become the main way to resolve disputes between host states and foreign investors.

Investment treaty arbitrations are usually divided into two types: ad hoc arbitrations and administered arbitrations.[6] In ad hoc arbitrations, the arbitral tribunals are appointed by the parties or by an appointing authority chosen by the parties. In administered arbitration, the arbitration will be administered by a professional arbitration institution providing arbitration services, such as the International Centre for the Settlement of Investment Disputes (ICSID), the ICC International Court of Arbitration, the Arbitration Institute of the Stockholm Chamber of Commerce, the Singapore International Arbitration Centre, or the London Court of International Arbitration. The China International Economic and Trade Arbitration Commission also provides an arbitration service for investor-state disputes. ICSID has administered the majority of all international investment cases. As a member of the World Bank Group, ICSID was established in 1966 by the Convention on the Settlement of Investment Disputes between States and Nationals of Other States. It has 155 member states as of 9 June 2020.[7] Many states have agreed to designate ICSID as a forum for investor-state dispute settlement in international investment treaties and in numerous investment laws and contracts. A number of international organisations and arbitration institutions, including the UNCITRAL, have developed arbitration rules that can be incorporated into investment agreements.

I. Jurisdiction of the Arbitration Tribunal

The jurisdiction of the arbitral tribunal for international investment is established on the basis of the arbitration agreement between the parties to the dispute, which authorises the arbitral tribunal to exercise the judgment function and establishes the scope of the hearing, covering: (1) jurisdiction *ratione materiae*; (2) *ratione personae*; and (3) *ratione temporis*.

A. Jurisdiction Ratione Materiae

Jurisdiction *ratione materiae* refers to the scope of disputes over which the arbitral tribunal has the right to hear and adjudicate. Disputes submitted to ICSID for arbitration in accordance with an international investment treaty must meet the requirements of both the Convention and international investment treaty.

[5] Agreement between the Government of the People's Republic of China and the Government of the Republic of Korea on the Promotion and Protection of Investments (signed 7 September 2007, entered into force 1 December 2007) ('China-South Korea BIT') Art 8.2.

[6] JS Yu, *International Economic Law* (n 1) 416.

[7] 'The List of Contracting States and Other Signatories of the Convention' (ICSID/3) (*ICSID*, 2020) https://icsid.worldbank.org/en/Pages/icsiddocs/List-of-Member-States.aspx accessed 26 June 2020.

i. Provisions of the ICSID Convention – Investment

According to Article 25.1 of the ICSID Convention, the jurisdiction of the Centre shall extend to any legal dispute arising directly out of an investment, between a Contracting State and a national of another Contracting State, which the parties to the dispute consent in writing to submit to the Centre.[8] Article 25.1 of the ICSID Convention does not clearly define the term 'investment'. In international investment agreements, 'investment' is described in various ways. For example, Article 1 of the Canada-China BIT provides:[9]

> '[I]nvestment' means:
>
> (a) an enterprise;
> (b) shares, stocks and other forms of equity participation in an enterprise;
> (c) bonds, debentures, and other debt instruments of an enterprise;
> (d) a loan to an enterprise
>   (i) where the enterprise is an affiliate of the investor, or
>   (ii) where the original maturity of the loan is at least three years;
> (e) notwithstanding sub-paragraphs (c) and (d) above, a loan to or debt security issued by a financial institution is an investment only where the loan or debt security is treated as regulatory capital by the Contracting Party in whose territory the financial institution is located;
> (f) an interest in an enterprise that entitles the owner to share in the income or profits of the enterprise;
> (g) an interest in an enterprise that entitles the owner to share in the assets of that enterprise on dissolution;
> (h) interests arising from the commitment of capital or other resources in the territory of a Contracting Party to economic activity in such territory, such as under
>   (i) contracts involving the presence of an investor's property in the territory of the Contracting Party, including turnkey or construction contracts, or concessions to search for and extract oil and other natural resources, or
>   (ii) contracts where remuneration depends substantially on the production, revenue or profits of an enterprise;
> (i) intellectual property rights; and
> (j) any other tangible or intangible, moveable or immovable, property and related property rights acquired or used for business purposes; but 'investment' does not mean:
> (k) claims to money that arise solely from
>   (i) commercial contracts for the sale of goods or services, or
>   (ii) the extension of credit in connection with a commercial transaction, such as trade financing, other than a loan covered by sub-paragraph (d); or
> (l) any other claims to money, that do not involve the kinds of interests set out in sub-paragraphs (a) to (j).

The earliest award to consider the meaning of 'investment' in depth was *Fedax NV v Venezuela*.[10] The tribunal adopted an approach suggested by Schreuer to define 'investment', ie the use of five criteria: duration, regularity of profit and return, assumption of risk, substantial commitment, and

[8] Convention on the Settlement of Investment Disputes between States and Nationals of Other States (opened for signature 18 March 1965, entered into force 14 October 1966) ('ICSID Convention') Art 25.1.

[9] Agreement Between the Government of Canada and the Government of the People's Republic of China for the Promotion and Reciprocal Protection of Investments (signed 8 September 2012, entered into force 1 October 2014) ('Canada-China BIT') Art 1.

[10] *Fedax NV v The Republic of Venezuela*, ICSID Case No ARB/96/3, Decision on Jurisdiction (9 March 1998).

significance for the host state's development.[11] *Fedax* was then applied by a subsequent tribunal whose reference to the five criteria has caused them to become known ever since as the *Salini* criteria. The dispute in *Salini* arose out of an agreement which was concluded between two Italian construction companies and the Government of Morocco.[12] The two Italian companies agreed to build a highway in Morocco's capital, Rabat. However, the delivery of the project had been delayed for various reasons and the Moroccan Government had therefore refused to fulfil its payment obligations. After several fruitless negotiations, the two Italian companies, as joint applicants, submitted the dispute to ICSID for arbitration. They claimed for actual fulfilment of the contract and compensation. The tribunal ruled that the investment under Article 25.1 of the ICSID Convention must simultaneously meet four elements: contribution, duration of certain contract performance, commitment to transaction risk and contribution to the economic development of the host state. The construction project in this case meets the above requirements and thus constitutes a qualified investment. The *Salini* criteria have been used in a series of subsequent investment arbitration cases, but some other tribunals have rejected them. In *BUCG v Yemen*, the tribunal endorsed a 'double keyhole' test under which the definition of 'investment' must meet the requirement of both the ICSID Convention and the China-Yemen BIT. Then the tribunal adopted the *Salini* criteria and held that the definition of 'investment' in BIT does not exceed what is permissible under the ICSID Convention. In the view of the tribunal, BUCG's contribution to the Sana's International Terminal project resulted in it now asserting 'claims to any performance having an economic value' within the meaning of Article 1 of the BIT. Thus, it is sufficient to bring the claimant's claim within the jurisdiction of the Tribunal under both the BIT and the ICSID Convention.[13]

ii. Provisions of the ICSID Convention – Legal Disputes

In *Mavrommatis Palestine Concessions* (*Greece v UK*), the Permanent Court of International Justice defined a dispute as 'a disagreement on a point of law or fact, a conflict of legal views or of interests between two persons'.[14] The general situation is that two parties communicate with each other but fail to reach an agreement on the settlement of dispute, or one party fails to respond to the request of the other party. The ICSID Convention does not provide for what constitutes a legal dispute. However, the Report of the Executive Directors on the ICSID Convention deals with this issue. It states that a legal dispute must concern the existence or scope of a legal right or obligation, or the nature or extent of the reparation to be made for breach of a legal obligation.[15] A mere conflict of interests or political dispute cannot constitute a legal dispute. If the investor initiates arbitration on the ground that the host state has violated its rights under a BIT or investment contract, it shall generally be considered a legal dispute.

iii. Provisions of the ICSID Convention – The Dispute's Direct Relation with an Investment

The legal dispute that the applicant submits to ICSID for arbitration must arise directly from the investment. That the relevant legal disputes do not arise directly from investment and thus

[11] C Schreuer, 'Commentary on the ICSID Convention' (1996) 11 ICSID *Review Foreign Investment Law Journal* 318.
[12] *Salini Costruttori S.P.A. and Italstrade S.P.A. v Kingdom of Morocco*, ICSID Case No ARB/00/4, Decision on Jurisdiction (31 July 2001).
[13] *Beijing Urban Construction Group v Yemen*, ICSID Case No ARB/14/30, Decision on Jurisdiction (31 May 2017), [136].
[14] *Mavrommatis Palestine Concessions (Greece v UK)* [1924] PCIJ Rep Series B No 3, [19].
[15] *Report of the Executive Directors on the ICSID Convention* 1 ICSID Reports 28, [26].

jurisdiction is found wanting is one of the common jurisdictional objections raised. In *CSOB v Slovakia*, the applicant provided a loan to a collection company under the guarantee of the Slovak Ministry of Finance. Afterwards, the collection company failed to repay, so CSOB initiated arbitration proceedings under the ICSID Convention against Slovakia. Slovakia argued that the applicant's request was not directly related to the loan and therefore did not fall under the jurisdiction of the ICSID. The tribunal noted that an investment was often a very complex activity consisting of a variety of interrelated matters, which may not all fit the definition of an investment. However, if a transaction is part of an investment activity, the Centre considered that disputes based on the transaction are directly related to investment, even if the transaction itself is not an investment.[16] Argentina has argued in a number of ICSID cases that its actions are general measures aimed at improving the welfare of the whole country rather than specific investment activities, and that the disputes are not directly related to investment. Nevertheless, these arguments have been rejected. The tribunals considered that, as long as macroeconomic instruments had a direct impact on investments, it's entitled to examine whether they violated commitments made by the host state to investors in treaties, laws or contracts.[17] It can be extrapolated that if the measures taken by the host state have a direct impact on investment and violate specific commitments or obligations, the host state cannot claim for exemption on the basis of the macroeconomic characteristic of the measures.

iv. Provisions of International Investment Treaties

Arbitration clauses in international investment treaties generally provide for the coverage of disputes which could be submitted for arbitration. Some treaties have relatively broad provisions covering disputes arising not only from the violation of an investment treaty but also from the violation of an investment agreement signed by the host state and the investor. For example, Article 24.1 of the 2012 US model BIT makes clear that the investor's claim to arbitration may be based on the host state's breach of either: (a) Articles 3 to 10 of the agreement; (b) an investment authorisation; or (c) an investment agreement.[18] Other treaties have relatively limited coverage of the disputes which could be submitted for arbitration. For example, Article 14.1 of the ASEAN-China Investment Agreement provides that:

> This Article shall apply to investment disputes between a Party and an investor of another Party concerning an alleged breach of an obligation of the former Party under Article 4 (National Treatment), Article 5 (Most-Favoured-Nation Treatment), Article 7 (Treatment of Investment), Article 8 (Expropriation), Article 9 (Compensation for Losses) and Article 10 (Transfers and Repatriation of Profits), which causes loss or damage to the investor in relation to its investment with respect to the management, conduct, operation, or sale or other disposition of an investment.[19]

[16] *CSOB v The Slovak Republic*, ICSID Case No ARB/97/4, Decision on Jurisdiction (1997), [72].

[17] *CMS Gas Transmission Company v The Republic of Argentina*, ICSID Case No ARB/01/8, Decision on Jurisdiction (17 July 2003), [33]; *LG&E Energy Corp v The Argentine Republic*, ICSID Case No ARB/02/1, Decision on Jurisdiction (30 April 2004), [67]; *Sempra Energy International v The Argentine Republic*, ICSID Case No ARB/02/16, Decision on Jurisdiction (11 May 2005), [71].

[18] 2012 US Model Bilateral Investment Treaty ('US Model BIT') www.state.gov/documents/organization/188371.pdf accessed 22 August 2020.

[19] Agreement on Investment of the Framework Agreement on Comprehensive Economic Cooperation Between the People's Republic of China and the Association of Southeast Asian Nations (signed 1 Jan 2010) ('ASEAN-China Investment Agreement') Art 14.

A claimant who submits a dispute to the ICSID on the basis of an investment treaty must ensure that the dispute qualifies for coverage not only under the ICSID Convention but also under the investment treaty.

B. Jurisdiction Ratione Personae

If a dispute is submitted to the ICSID on the basis of an international investment treaty, each party must qualify for coverage under the relevant provisions of the ICSID Convention as well as the international investment treaty.

i. Provisions of the ICSID Convention – The State Party

Article 25.1 of the ICSID Convention restricts the jurisdiction of the ICSID to investment disputes between a Contracting State and a national of another Contracting State.[20] The state party must be a Contracting State of the ICSID Convention. In the case of any constituent subdivision or agency of a Contracting State, two requirements must be satisfied. First, the subdivision or agency must have been designated to the Center by that state. Second, the consent of the subdivision or agency to the Centre for arbitration must have been approved by that state unless it notifies the Centre that such approval is not required.[21]

ii. Provisions of the ICSID Convention – The National of Another Contracting State

As the claimant, the investor will have the nationality of a Contracting State other than the state party to a dispute. According to the Article 25.2 of the ICSID Convention, 'national of another contracting state' means:[22]

(a) any natural person who had the nationality of a Contracting State other than the State party to the dispute on the date on which the parties consented to submit such dispute to conciliation or arbitration as well as on the date on which the request was registered pursuant to paragraph (3) of Article 28 or paragraph (3) of Article 36, but does not include any person who on either date also had the nationality of the Contracting State party to the dispute; and
(b) any juridical person which had the nationality of a Contracting State other than the State party to the dispute on the date on which the parties consented to submit such dispute to conciliation or arbitration and any juridical person which had the nationality of the Contracting State party to the dispute on that date and which, because of foreign control, the parties have agreed should be treated as a national of another Contracting State for the purposes of this Convention.

In accordance with these provisions, a natural person must hold the nationality of a Contracting State other than the state party to the dispute. Nationality has to be acquired in conformity with the law of the home state. As for timing, an eligible natural person must hold this nationality on: (a) the date the parties consented to submit their dispute to arbitration; and (b) the date the dispute was registered. Generally, the two dates are the same.

[20] ICSID Convention, Art 25.1.
[21] ibid.
[22] ibid, Art 25.2.

As regards the eligible juridical person, there are two categories.[23] The first category is a juridical person holding the nationality of a Contracting State other than the state party to the dispute on the date the parties consented to submit their dispute to arbitration. The second category is a juridical person holding the nationality of the Contracting State which is party to the dispute on that date. Because of foreign control, the parties to the Convention have agreed that this person should be treated as a national of another Contracting State for the purposes of the arbitration. As Aron Broches noted, the ICSID Convention gave the greatest possible latitude to the parties to decide under what circumstances a company could be treated as a 'national' of another Contracting State.[24] This is called the 'subjective test'. It turns on whether the BIT (or other investment instrument) provides the host state company with the opportunity, for the purposes of the ICSID Convention, to be considered a home state national because of the Contracting Parties' agreement to include a 'foreign control' test, and that the host state company has, by the terms of that agreement, fulfilled its requirements.[25] If the BIT requirement is met, the subjective test is satisfied. Nevertheless, this does not necessarily mean that the arbitral tribunal's jurisdiction *ratione personae* has been established. The decisions in some recent ICSID cases have held that a corporation claimant holding host state nationality must satisfy not only a 'subjective test', but also an 'objective test'.

The *National Gas* award explained the 'objective test' in the following terms:

(1) The objective test is raised by the phrase 'because of foreign control' in Art 25(2) (b).
(2) Once it is determined that the juridical person of the host state has met the terms of the parties' agreement, it must next be determined if, objectively, the host state juridical person is controlled by a national of the home state.
(3) That is, the mere agreement of the Contracting Parties is insufficient to satisfy the objective test. It must be investigated whether the host state company is actually controlled directly or indirectly by nationals of a third, non-Contracting State or nationals of the host state.[26]

No matter if a corporation claimant falls within the first or the second category under Article 25(2)(b) of the ICSID Convention, its nationality has to be determined. However, the ICSID Convention is silent on the method to be employed for the determination of a juridical person's nationality. Traditionally, arbitral tribunals have adopted the tests of incorporation or the seat of a corporation. Recent arbitral decisions have shown a tendency to use the test of control. Nevertheless, the test of control is subject to controversy.[27] One question is what signifies control. Control is generally understood to mean the actual ownership of more than 50 per cent of a company's shares or the power to appoint a majority of the directors or otherwise exercise actual control over their activities. Nevertheless, in some cases the qualification of minority shareholders as claimants were confirmed by the arbitral tribunals. In *Azurix v Argentina*, the tribunal found that 'given the wide meaning of investment in the definition in Article I.1(a), the provisions of the BIT [US-Argentina] protect indirect claims'.[28]

[23] ibid.
[24] See 'History of the ICSID Convention' II (2) 360 https://icsid.worldbank.org/en/Pages/resources/The-History-of-the-ICSID-Convention.aspx.,last accessed 26 June 2020.
[25] C Mclachlan, L Shore and M Weiniger, *International Investment Arbitration: Substantive Principles* 2nd edn (Oxford University Press, 2017) 197.
[26] *National Gas SAE v Arab Republic of Egypt*, ICSID Case No ARB/11/7, Decision on Jurisdiction (3 April 2014), [133].
[27] M Casas, 'Nationalities Of Convenience, Personal Jurisdiction, and Access To Investor-State Dispute Settlement' (2004) 49 *New York University Journal of International Law and Politics* 63, 106.
[28] *Azurix v Argentine Republic*, ICSID Case No ARB/01/12, Decision on Jurisdiction (8 December 2003), [73].

The other question is the qualification of indirect shareholders as claimants. Tribunals have not been consistent on this issue. In *Amco v Indonesia*, the claimant is a company incorporated in the US, but is directly controlled by a Hong Kong company which is further controlled by a private Dutch investor. Therefore, Indonesia contended that the claimant, Amco, should not be treated as an American company and is not entitled to claim the protection of US law. However, the tribunal ultimately rejected Indonesia's argument and pointed out that in determining jurisdiction and the nationality of the investor, the nationality of the foreign shareholder controlling the local company should not be considered.[29] In other words, the tribunal refused to pierce the corporate veil. In *SOABI v Senegal*, the tribunal took the opposite position. In this case, the claimant SOABI was a company incorporated in Senegal. Senegal raised jurisdictional objections based on the nationality of SOABI. The tribunal found that SOABI was directly controlled by a Panamanian company FLEXA, which was under direct control of a Belgian investor. Although Panama is not a contracting party to the ICSID Convention, Belgium is a contracting party to the ICSID Convention. In the end, the tribunal rejected Senegal's objection on jurisdiction, finding that SOABI was entitled to initiate arbitration because it was under indirect control of an investor of a contracting party to the ICSID Convention, thereby substantially meeting the nationality requirement of the ICSID Convention.[30] The tribunals' holdings in these two cases are seemingly different. However, they can be distinguished in that the Panamanian company in *SOABI* was just a holding company whereas the US company in *Amco* was far more substantial. This suggests that tribunals will look through holding companies to determine control but will not look through companies pursuing activities in the jurisdiction in which they are incorporated.[31]

iii. Provisions of International Investment Treaties

International investment treaties generally limit the arbitral tribunals' jurisdiction to investment disputes between one Party and an investor of another Party. Generally, an investor of a Party means a natural person or a juridical person of a Party that is making or has made an investment in the territories of the other Parties. A natural person of a Party normally refers to any natural person possessing the nationality or citizenship of the Party, or a right of permanent residence in the Party in accordance with its laws and regulations. As a claimant, a natural person investor should not have the nationality of the state Party to a dispute. When the nationality of natural person investors is in dispute, the issue is subject to substantial review by the arbitral tribunal. In other words, certificates or other legal documents issued by relevant countries constitute no more than *prima facie* evidence.[32]

International Investment Treaties adopt a variety of tests to determine whether a corporation is qualified as an investor of a Party. Some treaties set a low threshold, such as the requirement of incorporation in the home Contracting State. For example, Article 1.4 of the China-Singapore BIT prescribes: 'The term "company" means: (a) in respect of the People's Republic of China,

[29] *Amco Asia Corp v Republic of Indonesia*, ICSID Case No ARB/81/1, Decision on Jurisdiction (25 Dec 1983), [14].

[30] *Société Ouest Africaine des Bétons Industriels v Republic of Senegal*, ICSID Case No ARB/82/1, 2 ICSID Reports 181, 182, 184.

[31] R Wisner, N Gallus, 'Nationality Requirements in Investor-State Arbitration' (2003) 5 *Journal of World Investment & Trade* 927, 936.

[32] *Waguih Elie George Siag and Clorinda Vecchi v The Arab Republic of Egypt*, ICSID Case No ARB/05/15, Decision on Jurisdiction, and Partial Dissenting Opinion of Professor Francisco Orrego Vicuña (11 April 2007), [153].

a company or other juridical person incorporated or constituted in its territory in accordance with its laws.'[33] Some treaties set a higher standard, requiring that the putative corporation investor should not only be incorporated in the home Contracting State, but have its 'seat', 'domicile' or 'headquarters' in the home state. For example, Article 1.2 of the China-Germany BIT provides that the term 'investor' means:

> (b) in respect of the People's Republic of China: [...] economic entities, including companies, corporations, associations, partnerships and other organizations, incorporated and constituted under the laws and regulations of and with their seats in the People's Republic of China, irrespective of whether or not for profit and whether their liabilities are limited or not.[34]

Some treaties contain a further requirement that the corporation has substantial business activities in the home Contracting State. For example, Article 1.1 of the ASEAN-China Investment Agreement provides that 'juridical person of a Party' means:

> any legal entity duly constituted or otherwise organized under the applicable law of a Party, whether for profit or otherwise, and whether privately-owned or governmentally-owned, and engaged in substantive business operations in the territory of that Party, including any corporation, trust, partnership, joint venture, sole proprietorship or association.[35]

Finally, some treaties apply the test of control.

As a claimant, the investor may only refer to international investment treaties to which the state of its nationality is a contracting party. Yet the more than 3,000 existing international investment treaties differ from each other in their treatment of investors. As a result, investors are motivated to seek the application of the treaties that are more favourable to them by means of artificial change of nationality, transfer of shares, establishment of shell companies, etc. In response, international investment treaties of the new generation usually contain 'denial of benefits' clauses.[36] For example, Article 15.1 of the ASEAN-China Investment Agreement prescribes: 'Subject to prior notification and consultation, a Party may deny the benefits of this Agreement to:

> (a) investors of another Party where the investment is being made by a juridical person that is owned or controlled by persons of a non-Party and the juridical person has no substantive business operations in the territory of another Party; or
> (b) investors of another Party where the investment is being made by a juridical person that is owned or controlled by persons of the denying Party.'[37]

Such a clause excludes treaty protections from companies that have no connection to the home state other than the simple fact of their incorporation, or are owned or controlled by investors from a country with which a Contracting State has no diplomatic relations or otherwise prohibits transactions.

In *Tza Yap Shum v Peru*, a special issue regarding the application of Peru-China BIT to Hong Kong residents was raised. The claimant was a national of China and had been a Hong Kong resident since 1972. He cited the Peru-China BIT as the legal basis for his claim. However, Peru

[33] Agreement Between the Government of the People's Republic of China and the Government of the Republic of Singapore on the Promotion and Protection of Investments (signed 21 November 1985, entered into force 7 February 1986) ('China-Singapore BIT') Art 1.4.

[34] Agreement between the Federal Republic of Germany and the People's Republic of China on the Encouragement and Reciprocal Protection of Investments (signed 1 December 2003, entered into force 11 November 2005) ('China-Germany BIT') Art 1.2.

[35] ASEAN-China Investment Agreement, Art 1.1.

[36] SX Huang, 'Treaty Shopping in International Investment Arbitration' (2014) 1 *Law Science* 62.

[37] ASEAN-China Investment Agreement, Art 15.1.

objected and alleged that he was excluded from the Peru-China BIT scope of application.[38] The tribunal held that the text of the Peru-China BIT did not contain any provision explicitly excluding Chinese nationalities with residence in Hong Kong from the scope of application thereof. In the view of the tribunal, the respondent had not proven convincingly that the parties to the Peru-China BIT had such an intention.[39] The claimant finally prevailed on this issue. The tribunal's decision has been broadly criticised by Chinese scholars. Article 153 of the Basic Law of the Hong Kong Special Administrative Region of the People's Republic of China provides:

> The application to the Hong Kong Special Administrative Region of international agreements to which the People's Republic of China is or becomes a party shall be decided by the Central People's Government, in accordance with the circumstances and needs of the Region, and after seeking the views of the government of the Region.[40]

Accordingly, international agreements to which the PRC is or becomes a party shall not be applied to the Hong Kong SAR automatically. Only after the Central Government seeks the views of the government of the Hong Kong SAR and decides that such an agreement shall be applied to the region can the agreement be applied to the Hong Kong SAR. The Sino-British Joint Statement also confirms such an arrangement.[41] However, the Central Government never adopted any such measures to extend the application of the Peru-China BIT to the Hong Kong SAR. Therefore, as a resident of Hong Kong SAR, Tza Yap Shum is not entitled to enjoy the protection of the Peru-China BIT.

C. Temporal Jurisdiction

In principle, an investment treaty can only apply to the measures or events that take place after it enters into force. Article 28 of the Vienna Convention on the Law of Treaties makes it clear that:

> Unless a different intention appears from the treaty or is otherwise established, its provisions do not bind a party in relation to any act or fact which took place or any situation which ceased to exist before the date of the entry into force of the treaty with respect to that party.[42]

Therefore, the consent made by contracting parties to an investment treaty to arbitration should in principle only apply to the disputes arising after the entry into force of the treaty. For example, Article 14.2 of the ASEAN-China Investment Agreement provides that: 'this article shall not apply to investment disputes arising out of events which occurred, or to investment disputes which had been settled, or which were already under judicial or arbitral process, prior to the entry into force of this Agreement'.[43] In addition, the dispute settlement provisions of international investment

[38] *Tza Yap Shum v Republic of Peru*, ICSID Case No ARB/07/6, Decision on Jurisdiction and Competence (19 June 2009), [31], [40].

[39] ibid [71], [74], [77].

[40] The Basic Law of the Hong Kong Special Administrative Region of the People's Republic of China (1997).

[41] A Chen, 'Queries to the Recent ICSID Decision on Jurisdiction upon the Case of Tza Yap Shum v Republic of Peru: Should China-Peru BIT 1994 Be Applied to Hong Kong SAR under "One Country Two Systems"' (2009) 17(1) *The Journal of International Economic Law* 10.

[42] Vienna Convention on the Law of Treaties (*United Nations Treaty Series vol 1155, 23 May 1969*) www.refworld.org/docid/3ae6b3a10.html accessed 13 August 2020.

[43] ASEAN-China Investment Agreement, Art 14.2.

treaties also provide for the limitation of arbitration. For example, Article 9.7 of the China-South Korea BIT of 2007 states:

> Notwithstanding the provisions of paragraph 3 of this Article, an investor may not make a claim pursuant to paragraph 3 of this Article if more than three years have elapsed from the date on which the investor first acquired, or should have first acquired, knowledge that the investor had incurred loss or damage.[44]

To sum up, the arbitral tribunal's temporal jurisdiction depends on two conditions. First, the dispute must have occurred after the entry into force of the international investment treaty relied on by the claimant. Second, the application for arbitration must not have exceeded the limitation of arbitration stipulated by the international investment treaty relied on by the claimant.

In practice, disputes over the temporal jurisdiction of the arbitral tribunal mainly focus on two aspects. One is timing of the dispute. The other involves the replacement of international investment treaties. In *Maffezini v Spain*, the respondent challenged the tribunal's temporal jurisdiction, arguing that the dispute predated the entry into force of the Argentine-Spain BIT. The tribunal found that disagreement between the two parties occurred many years before the Argentine-Spain BIT came into force, but that did not necessarily mean that the whole dispute predated the treaty. The tribunal stated:

> There tends to be a natural sequence of events that leads to a dispute. It begins with the expression of a disagreement and the statement of a difference of views. In time these events acquire a precise legal meaning through the formulation of legal claims, their discussion and eventual rejection or lack of response by the other party. The conflict of legal views and interests will only be present in the latter stage, even though the underlying facts predate them.[45]

In the end, the arbitral tribunal held that the dispute in this case began to take shape technically and legally after the BIT came into force, rejecting the respondent's objection to jurisdiction.[46]

There are two other special situations that need special attention. First, although the host state's violation of an international investment treaty may have occurred before the treaty's entry into force, the violation and its legal consequences may continue until the treaty's entry into force.[47] The investor can request for arbitration against such a violation based on the treaty. Second, the situation where the host state's violation of an international investment treaty is a combination of a series of specific violations, some of which took place after the entry into force of the treaty, and some of which took place before the entry into force of the treaty. The investor can still request for arbitration against such a violation based on the treaty. In *Tecmed v Mexico*, the arbitral tribunal followed this principle, holding that the host state's series of acts initiated before the entry into force of the BIT should be subject to the jurisdiction of the arbitral tribunal, and that the host state should bear the corresponding international responsibility for violating the treaty. In this case, Tecmed claimed that the successive acts or omissions by INE (an agency of the Federal Government of the United Mexican States within the Ministry of the Environment, Natural Resources and Fisheries) in connection with permits or authorisations relating to the operation of the Las Víboras landfill which belonged to one and the same course of conduct.

[44] China-South Korea BIT, Art 9.7.

[45] *Emilio Agustín Maffezini v The Kingdom of Spain*, ICSID Case No ARB/97/7, Decision on Jurisdiction (25 January 2000) [96].

[46] ibid. [98], [99].

[47] *SGS Société Genérale de Surveillance SA v Republic of the Philippines*, ICSID Case No ARB/02/6, Decision of the Tribunal on Objections to Jurisdiction (29 January 2004) [167].

Although INE's initial behaviour took place before the effecting date of the Spain-Mexico BIT, INE's failure to update the licence occurred after the BIT entered into force. The arbitral tribunal decided that the respondent's successive acts constituted combined acts which violated the BIT and that the respondent should be liable for such a violation.[48]

In the case of the replacement of a BIT, it is common for the new BIT to contain different arbitration provisions. When this happens, a problem may arise as to which treaty the investor should base its claim on for arbitration regarding a dispute arising in the transition period. Some treaties are explicit and specific on this issue. For example, the China-South Korea BIT of 2007 stipulates that the old BIT terminates as of the effecting date of the new BIT and the new BIT will not apply to disputes that occurred prior to its entry into force.[49] However, some treaties are vaguer on this issue. For example, the China-Switzerland BIT of 2010 only stipulates that the new BIT replaces the old BIT. Some other treaties have a gap. For example, the China-Belgium-Luxembourg Economic Union BIT of 2009 stipulates that the new BIT replaces the old BIT, and the new BIT shall not apply to any investment-related dispute or claim which was already under judicial or arbitral process before its entry into force.[50] Such disputes and claims shall continue to be settled according to the old BIT. This provision leaves one situation unsolved, namely where a dispute arises, but has not yet entered judicial or arbitral proceedings, before the entry into force of the new BIT. The ambiguity and omission of the BIT transition clauses is one of the important reasons leading to the dispute of the temporal jurisdiction in the arbitration practice.

Ping An v Belgium is such a case. Between October 2007 and July 2008, China Ping An acquired shares in the Fortis Group in the open market for an aggregate sum of more than €2 billion, and became Fortis' single largest shareholder. Later, due to the impact of the global financial crisis, Fortis group's banking business has suffered serious liquidity problems. Since September 2008, the Belgian Government has injected more than €4.7 billion into FBB, acquiring a 49.93 per cent stake. Unfortunately, such a measure did not resolve FBB's liquidity crisis. Finally, Belgium took the remaining shares in FBB for €4.7 billion and transferred 75 per cent of the shares in FBB to BNP Paribas, in exchange for new shares to be issued in the latter, valued at €8.25 billion. China Ping An considered that its investment in FBB was completely expropriated as a result of these transactions.[51]

On 14 October 2008, China Ping An submitted its first letter to Belgium through the Chinese Embassy in Brussels, expressing its dissatisfaction with Belgium's 'market rescue measures'. On 14 October 2009, China Ping An sent a letter to the Belgian Embassy in China, stating clearly that its letter dated 14 October 2008 constituted a notice concerning the investment dispute under the Article 10.1 of the China-Belgium-Luxembourg BIT of 1986, and for the first time alleged the Belgian Government's intervention measures constituted expropriation without reasonable compensation and due process.[52] On 3 July 2012, China Ping An wrote to the Belgian Embassy in China again, claiming that the letter it sent on 14 October 2009 constituted a notice under

[48] *Técnicas Medioambientales Tecmed, SA v The United Mexican States*, ICSID Case No ARB (AF)/00/2, Award of the Tribunal (29 May 2003), [38]–[47], [172].

[49] China-South Korea BIT, Art 12.

[50] Agreement between the Belgium-Luxembourg Economic Union and the Government of the People's Republic of China on the reciprocal promotion and protection of investments (signed 6 June 2005, entered into force 1 December 2009) ('China-Belgium-Luxembourg Economic Union BIT of 2009') Art 10.2.

[51] *Ping An Life Insurance Company of China, Limited; Ping An Insurance (Group) Company of China, Limited (China Ping An) v Kingdom of Belgium*, ICSID Case No ARB/12/29, Award of Tribunal (30 April 2015), [51]–[65].

[52] Agreement between the Government of the People's Republic of China and the Belgium-Luxembourg Economic Union on the Encouragement and Reciprocal Protection of Investments (signed 4 June 1984, entered into force 5 October 1986) ('China-Belgium-Luxembourg BIT of 1986').

Article 8.1 of the China-Belgium-Luxembourg Economic Union BIT of 2009.[53] On 7 September 2012, China Ping An filed a request for arbitration against Belgium, relying on the 1986 BIT for the substance of its claim and on the 2009 BIT for the jurisdiction of the Tribunal.[54] Belgium raised objections to jurisdiction, one of which was an objection *ratione temporis*. Belgium argued that the dispute between the parties arose before the entry into force of the 2009 BIT on 1 December 2009 so was excluded from the Tribunal's jurisdiction *ratione temporis*. The tribunal noted that the general principle in international law, in the absence of provision to the contrary, is non-retroactivity.[55] Article 10.2 of the 2009 BIT provided:

> The present Agreement shall apply to all investments made by investors of either Contracting Party in the territory of the other Contracting Party, whether made before or after the entry into force of this Agreement, but shall not apply to any dispute or any claim concerning an investment which was already under judicial or arbitral process before its entry into force. Such disputes and claims shall continue to be settled according to the provisions of the Agreement of 1984 mentioned in paragraph 1 of this Article.

In the view of the Tribunal, there was nothing in the wording of the 2009 BIT to justify on the basis of its express language, or an implication or inferences, the conclusion that the remedies under the 2009 BIT would be available to pre-existing disputes that had been notified under the 1986 BIT but not yet begun the arbitral or judicial process.[56] China Ping An finally failed in this case. However, the analysis of the tribunal is not without flaw.[57] The wording of the 2009 BIT only expressly excludes the disputes which were already under judicial or arbitral process. It is submitted that short of such exclusion, all other cases should fall within the scope of the dispute resolution mechanism of the 2009 BIT, including the dispute in this case.

II. Application of Law

A. Rules Governing the Application of Law

The application of law in investment treaty arbitration mainly involves the choice of substantive law. Generally speaking, the parties' agreement is the first choice. For example, Article 42.1 of the ICSID Convention states that the tribunal shall decide the dispute in accordance with the rules of law which may be agreed by the parties. Article 35 of the UNCITRAL and Article 21 of the ICC Arbitration Rules have provisions to the same effect.[58] In investment treaty arbitration, the parties generally agree on the application of law through two steps. First, the host state incorporates provisions on the application of arbitration law in the international investment treaty reached

Article 10.1 of the 1986 BIT provides: 'All disputes relating to investments shall be notified in writing, accompanied by a sufficiently detailed memorandum, by the investor of one Contracting Party to the other Contracting Party.' Furthermore, Art 10.3 of the 1986 BIT limits the disputes which the investor may submit to international arbitration to those relating to the amount of compensation payable in case of expropriation, nationalisation or any other measure similarly affecting investment.

[53] Article 8 of the China-Belgium-Luxembourg Economic Union BIT of 2009 extends the disputes which the investor may submit to international arbitration to any legal disputes arising between an investor of one contracting party and the other contracting party.

[54] *Ping An v Belgium* (n 51) [38].

[55] ibid, [167].

[56] ibid, [231].

[57] Y Liu, 'China Ping An v Belgium From the Perspective of Inter-temporal Law of the Application of Treaties' (2016) 4 *Global Law Review*, 166.

[58] 2017 International Chamber of Commerce Rules of Arbitration ('ICC Arbitration Rules').

with the investor's home state. Second, the investor expresses their consent to the above provisions by submitting an arbitration request. There are two types of provisions on the application of law in international investment treaties. One provides for the application of international law, including only the substantive rules of the treaty itself, and the other includes both the domestic laws of the host state and international law. The 2012 US Model BIT is more elaborate, with different provisions on the application of law for different matters.[59] If the arbitration matter is a violation of the BIT by the host state, only the BIT and certain rules of international law apply. If the subject matter of the arbitration is a breach of the investment licence or investment contract by the host state, the laws set forth by the investment licence or investment contract or otherwise agreed by the parties shall apply.

If the applicable laws are not specified and the parties have not otherwise agreed, the laws of the respondent (including the rules on conflict of laws) and applicable rules of international law apply. The applicable rules of international law may include normative resolutions of the United Nations General Assembly, international practices and other supplementary sources of international law. The China-Canada BIT has different rules. It only authorises investors to submit violations of BIT by Contracting States for arbitration.[60] In dealing with such disputes, the tribunal shall apply not only the BIT and applicable rules of international law, but also, where appropriate, the laws of the host state.[61]

If the parties do not agree on the application of laws, it shall be determined in accordance with the rules of arbitration procedure chosen by the parties. For example, Article 42 of the ICSID Convention makes it clear that if the parties fail to agree on the application of the law, the tribunal shall apply the laws of the Contracting State party (including their rules on conflict of laws) along with the applicable rules of international law. The arbitral tribunal may not make a finding of *non liquet* – that is, that there is no applicable law – on the ground of silence or obscurity of the law. A tribunal may decide a dispute *ex aequo et bono* if the parties so agree – that is, to consider the case in accordance with the notion of 'fundamental fairness'. Such a principle makes it possible for the arbitral tribunal to set aside the current conflicting legal rules and reach a mutually acceptable decision, so as to maintain the normal relationship between the disputing parties. From this perspective, *ex aequo et bono* is consistent with the purpose of ICSID arbitration mechanism. However, the principle is highly elastic and therefore can easily be abused. In practice, when applying this principle, the arbitral tribunal always takes into account the laws which are originally applicable to the dispute. The exclusive application of the principle is often limited to the calculation of the amount of compensation.[62]

B. Problems Arising in Arbitration Practice

The application of the above provisions in arbitration practice is likely to cause four problems. First, if the applicable law is the domestic law of the host state and the host state modifies the relevant law after the investor has made an investment, should the arbitral tribunal apply the old law or the new law? With the aim to balance the legislative power of the host state and protection

[59] The 2012 US Model BIT, Art 30.
[60] China-Canada BIT, Art 21.
[61] ibid, Art 30.
[62] Y Zhou, 'A Study on Substantive Applicable Law in ICSID Arbitration' [2015] Dissertation of PhD degree Wuhan University, 66–67.

of the interests of investors, some Chinese scholars advocate that the new law should be applied, with three exceptions:[63] (i) if the new law conflicts with the obligations of the host state under an investment treaty, only the treaty can be applied; (ii) when the limitation clause in the new law provides that the old law applies, the old law applies; (iii) where the parties have agreed in advance to apply the laws at the time of conclusion of the contract, the new law shall not apply.

Second, if the applicable law includes both the law of the host state and international law, to what matters should the former be applied, and to what matters should the latter be applied? In *Maffezini v Spain*, the arbitral tribunal did not discuss this issue in detail, but directly applied international law to some matters and the law of the host state to others. As to whether SODIGA was a state entity, the arbitral tribunal mainly applied Spanish law. For the environmental impact assessment, the tribunal applied Spanish law, relevant EC directives and Argentine-Spain BIT. As to whether there was an effective disinvestment contract between the investor and SODIGA, the arbitral tribunal applied the Spanish Civil Code and the Spanish Commercial Code.[64] In *Antoine Goetz v Burundi*, the arbitration tribunal applied both the domestic law and international law on the same matter, because the Belgium-Burundi BIT clearly listed Burundi's domestic law as the applicable law, and in turn Burundi's domestic law had incorporated an international treaty of which Burundi was a Contracting State. The arbitral tribunal first analysed the dispute in accordance with Burundian law and concluded that the conduct of the host state was consistent with Burundian law. Then, the arbitral tribunal analysed the dispute from the perspective of international law and concluded that the legitimacy of the act of the host state depended on whether the host state had made sufficient and effective compensation, finding that in fact the host state had not made compensation to the investors.[65]

Third, if the applicable law includes both the domestic law of the host state and the international law, and the result of applying the former is different from applying the latter, what law should be applied finally? This involves the hierarchy of the host state's domestic law and international law. Unfortunately, the existing international investment treaties rarely contain explicit provisions on this issue, and nor does the ICSID Convention. At present, the widely accepted theory is that international law is the supplement and correction of domestic law. In *Amco v Indonesia*, the ad hoc committee stated: 'Article 42(1) of the Convention authorises an ICSID tribunal to apply rules of international law only to fill up lacunae in the applicable domestic law and to ensure precedence to international law norms where the rules of the applicable domestic law are in collision with such norms.'[66] In other words, international law plays a supplemental and corrective role in relation to the law of the host state as substantive applicable law. In *LG&E v Argentina*, the tribunal emphasised that a state cannot justify its violation of international obligations by invoking its own laws, and international law takes precedence over domestic law when they conflict with each other.[67] However, some arbitral tribunals hold different opinions, endowing international law with a higher status than mere complementary or corrective applicable law. In *Wena v Egypt*, the ad hoc committee stated that the use of the word 'may' in the second sentence of Article 42.1 of the ICSID Convention indicated that the Convention did not draw a

[63] XL Shi and H Qi, 'International Investment Law' [2009] *China University of Political Science and Law Publishing House*, 280.

[64] *Emilio Agustín Maffezini v The Kingdom of Spain*, ICSID Case No ARB/97/7, Award of the Tribunal (13 Nov 2000) [50], [52], [57], [77], [83], [89], [90].

[65] *Antoine Goetz v Burundi*, ICSID Case No ARB/95/3, Award Embodying the Parties' Settlement Agreement (10 February 1999) [94]–[99], [120]–[133].

[66] *Amco Asia Corp v Republic of Indonesia*, ICSID Case No ARB/81/1, Decision on Annulment (16 May 1986) [2]0.

[67] *LG&E Energy Corp v The Argentine Republic*, ICSID Case No ARB/02/1, Decision on Liability (3 October 2006) [94].

sharp line for the distinction of the respective scope of international and of domestic law and, correspondingly, that this had the effect of conferring on to the Tribunal a certain margin and power for interpretation. The committee further concluded that both the international law and the domestic law played a role. In particular, the rules of international law that directly or indirectly relate to the state's consent prevail over domestic rules that might be incompatible with them. In applying the rules of the Agreement for the Promotion and Protection of Investments entered into by the UK and Egypt on 11 June 1975 in the instant case, the tribunal did not exceed its powers.[68]

Fourth, if the rules of international law apply, what rules of international law should apply? Most arbitral tribunals interpret the 'rules of international law' in Article 42.1 of the ICSID Convention in accordance with Article 38.1 of the Statute of the International Court of Justice and conclude that they should cover international conventions, international customs, general principles of law, judicial decisions and the teachings of the most highly qualified publicists.[69] Among them, international conventions are the sources of international law most frequently applied by arbitral tribunals, especially the international investment treaties concluded or approved jointly by the host state and the investor's home state. The application of international customs mainly involves such issues as the treatment of investors, expropriation and compensation, prohibition on denial of justice, and the state responsibility for the infringement of foreigners. General principles of law are mainly used to fill gaps in treaties and international customs.

III. Recognition and Enforcement of Arbitral Awards

A. Recognition and Enforcement of ICSID Arbitral Awards

Articles 53 to 55 of the ICSID Convention are focused on the recognition and enforcement of ICSID arbitral awards, establishing a self-governing and self-sufficient recognition and enforcement mechanism.[70] Article 53 establishes the basic principle that ICSID arbitral awards are binding on the parties and expressly prohibits the parties from appealing or taking any other remedies other than those provided for in the convention. Such obligations apply only to the parties, whereas the obligations under Article 54 apply to all Contracting States and are activated only if the losing party refuses to fulfil the ICSID arbitral award. Article 54 was considered by Aron Broches, the chief draftsman of the convention, to be one of the most important provisions of the convention and one of its most exciting innovations.[71] It requires Contracting States to recognise an ICSID arbitral award as binding, to enforce the pecuniary obligations imposed by that award within its territories as if it were a final judgment of a court, and to notify the Secretary-General of the designation of the competent court or other authority for this purpose. Accordingly, Contracting States shall not refuse to recognise ICSID arbitration awards for any reason, even public policy. It makes ICSID arbitral awards more final than those made by other

[68] *Wena Hotels Limited v Arab Republic of Egypt*, ICSID Case No ABR /98 /4, Decision on Annulment (5 February 2002) [39]–[4].

[69] ibid, [37].

[70] AJ van den Berg, 'Some Recent Problems in the Practice of Enforcement under the New York and ICSID Conventions' (1987) 2 *ICSID Review Foreign Investment Law Journal* 439, 441.

[71] A Broches, 'Awards Rendered Pursuant to the ICSID Convention: Binding Force, Finality, Recognition, Enforcement, Execution' (1987) 2 *ICSID Review Foreign Investment Law Journal* 287, 299.

arbitral tribunals. However, the enforcement obligations of Contracting States do not apply to all ICSID arbitral awards but are limited to awards that impose pecuniary obligations. As for other decisions made by ICSID arbitral tribunals, such as those requiring the host state to amend or revoke its domestic laws and return the seized property, the Contracting States do not assume compulsory enforcement obligations. In addition, the enforcement of arbitral awards by Contracting States is governed by their existing law concerning the enforcement of court decisions. In other words, how a Contracting State enforces an arbitral award depends entirely on the provisions of its domestic law. Furthermore, at the request of the US, Article 54 allows a Contracting State with a federal constitution to enforce an award in or through its federal courts and to provide that such courts shall treat the award as if it were a final judgment of the courts of a constituent state.[72] Finally, Article 54 stipulates the procedural obligation of the winning party to apply for recognition of an ICSID arbitral award, namely, providing a copy of the arbitral award verified by the Secretary-General. Since the obligations under Article 54 are binding upon all Contracting States to the convention, the winning party may choose any one of them to apply for recognition of an arbitral award. In making such a choice, the overriding concern is usually the enforceability of the assets of the losing party in the Contracting State concerned.

Article 55, which deals with sovereign execution immunity, confirms that the rules of the domestic law of Contracting States relating to sovereign execution immunity prevail over Article 54. This means that ICSID arbitral awards can only be enforced if the domestic law of the country where the winning party seeks for execution allows it. So far, China still adheres to the principle of absolute immunity. In *FG Hemisphere Associates LLC v The Democratic Republic of the Congo*, the Hong Kong Court of Final Appeal requested the Standing Committee of the National People's Congress to interpret the relevant law on the issue of sovereign immunity. According to the Committee's interpretation, the Hong Kong Special Administrative Region should adhere to a doctrine of absolute sovereign immunity in line with the Central Government. Finally, the court held that the courts of Hong Kong had no jurisdiction over the Democratic Republic of the Congo.[73]

B. Recognition and Enforcement of Other Arbitral Awards

The recognition and enforcement of awards rendered by arbitral tribunals administered by other international arbitral institutes, including awards based on the ICSID Additional Facilitation Rules, and awards rendered by ad hoc arbitral tribunals must comply with the domestic laws of the country where the enforcement is requested and the provisions of the New York Convention. Article 3 of the New York Convention provides that each Contracting State shall recognise arbitral awards as binding and enforce them in accordance with the rules of procedure of the territory where the awards are relied upon, under the conditions laid down in this convention. Article 5 of the New York Convention provides that recognition and enforcement of a foreign arbitral award

[72] ICSID, 'History of the ICSID Convention, Documents Concerning the Origin and the Formulation of the Convention on the Settlement of Investment Disputes Between States and Nationals of Other States' 900 https://icsid.worldbank.org/apps/ICSIDWEB/resources/Documents/History%20of%C20ICSID%C20Convention%20-%20VOLUME%20II-1.pdf accessed 30 June 2020.

[73] *FG Hemisphere Associates LLC v The Democratic Republic of the Congo* [2010] FACV 5-7/2010 (On appeal from CACV 373/2008 & 43/2009).

may be refused in two situations. First, where the party against whom recognition and enforcement of an arbitral award is invoked proves that:

(a) the parties were under some incapacity, or the arbitration agreement is not valid; or
(b) the party against whom the award is invoked was not given proper notice of the appointment of the arbitrator or of the arbitration proceedings or was otherwise unable to present his case; or
(c) the award deals with a difference not contemplated by or not falling within the terms of the submission to arbitration, or it contains decisions on matters beyond the scope of the submission to arbitration, provided that, if the decisions on matters submitted to arbitration can be separated from those not so submitted, that part of the award which contains decisions on matters submitted to arbitration may be recognised and enforced; or
(d) the composition of the arbitral authority or the arbitral procedure was not in accordance with the agreement of the parties, or, failing such agreement, was not in accordance with the law of the country where the arbitration took place; or
(e) the award has not yet become binding on the parties, or has been set aside or suspended by a competent authority of the country in which, or under the law of which, that award was made.

Second, where the competent authority in the country where recognition and enforcement is sought finds that: (a) the subject matter of the difference is not capable of settlement by arbitration under the law of that country; or (b) recognition or enforcement of the award would be contrary to the public policy of that country.

The Chinese Government has made a declaration of 'commercial reservations' to the New York Convention, stating that 'China applies this Convention only to disputes arising from contractual and non-contractual commercial legal relations in accordance with our laws [...] but excluding disputes between foreign investors and host governments.'[74] In other words, it excludes the application of the New York Convention in the recognition and enforcement of international investment arbitration awards involving Chinese investors and the Chinese Government.

[74] Notice of the Supreme People's Court on the Implementation of the 'Convention on the Recognition and Enforcement of Foreign Arbitral Awards' Acceded to by China (Supreme People's Court, Fafa (1987) 5, 10 April 1987).

25

China's Role in the Work of International Organisations

ZHENGYI ZHANG, YANNAN LIU

I. China and HCCH

A. HCCH Overview

The charter of the Hague Conference on Private International Law (effective on 15 July 1955) adopted by the 7th Hague Conference on Private International Law (the 'Hague Conference', HCCH) in 1951 established the Hague Conference as a permanent international organisation, with the aim of 'gradual unification of the rules of private international law'. The Hague Conference is the most important intergovernmental international organisation engaged in the international unification of private international law rules. In the years since its establishment, the Hague Conference has been committed to promoting the international unification of private international law rules through the negotiation and formulation of international conventions on private international law. At present, the HCCH has 85 members, including 84 states and one regional economic integration organisation.[1] In addition, there are 70 non-member states which have nonetheless signed, ratified, or acceded to one or more Hague conventions or are in the process of becoming members.[2] The Hague Conference and its conventions regarding private international law have greatly enriched the theories of private international law, promoted the international unification of private international law rules, and promoted the development of private international law practice in various countries, including China. Furthermore, recent developments in the Hague Conference for the unification of the private international law rules of private international law of business (including the promotion of the party autonomy principle of the Hague Convention on Court Choice Agreements in 2005, the Principles of Choice of Law of International Commercial Contracts in 2015, and the Convention on the Recognition and Enforcement of Foreign Civil and Commercial Judgments in 2019) will help to overcome the traditional barriers to international economic and financial activities.

[1] The Hague Conference on Private International Law (HCCH), 'HCCH Members and Parties: HCCH Members' www.hcch.net/en/states/hcch-members accessed 4 March 2020.

[2] HCCH, 'HCCH Members and Parties: Other Connected Parties' www.hcch.net/en/states/other-connected-parties accessed 4 March 2020.

In recent years, the Hague Conference has formulated the Convention on Choice of Court Agreements and the Principles for Choice of Law in International Commercial Contracts, as well as a series of Hague conventions on child abduction, child adoption, and child maintenance which are in constant response to the challenges brought by globalisation in the fields of commerce, trade, natural persons, and families. There are also the complex issues of cross-border surrogacy agreements and the role of private international law in temporary migration matters, the environment, and climate change. Upon China's resumption of the exercise of sovereignty over Hong Kong and Macao in 1997 and 1999, respectively, experts from the Hong Kong and Macao special administrative regions participated in the Hague Conference on Private International Law as members of the Chinese delegation. Some treaties that had already applied to Hong Kong or Macao continued to apply after the resumption of sovereignty. In addition, the establishment of the Asia-Pacific regional office of the Hague Conference on Private International Law has made an extraordinary contribution to the work in the conference. Regional offices in Buenos Aires (2005) in Latin America and in Hong Kong (December 2012) in the Asia-Pacific region have both given strong support to the Hague Conference on Private International Law and its work within their respective regions.

B. China's Participation

On 3 July 1987, China officially joined the Hague Conference on Private International Law. Since then, China has actively participated in the negotiation of treaties formulated by the Hague Conference.[3] The few Hague treaties on private international law currently in force in China are limited to the Convention on the Service Abroad of Judicial and Extra-Judicial Documents in Civil or Commercial Matters, the Convention on the Taking of Evidence Abroad in Civil or Commercial Evidence, and the Convention on the Protection of Children and Cooperation in Respect of Intercountry Adoption. The Hague Service Convention and The Hague Evidence Convention, which aim at improving the efficiency of the administration of justice and formulating rules for mutual assistance between states' parties in the service of documents and obtaining evidence in the civil or commercial matters, have greatly expanded the scope of the target countries for judicial assistance in the civil and commercial affairs and have played an important role in China's judicial trials. The Hague Convention on Child Adoption, which came into force in China on 1 January 2006, has facilitated the development of alternative child care policies in China, and the number of domestic adoptions has since increased. In addition to the aforementioned three conventions, there are several Hague conventions that are only applicable in the Hong Kong Special Administrative Region and the Macao Special Administrative Region. Among them are: (i) the Convention Abolishing the Requirement of Legalization for Foreign Public Documents and the Convention on the Civil Aspects of International Child Abduction in force both in Hong Kong and Macao; (ii) the Convention on the Conflicts of Laws Relating to the Form of Testamentary Dispositions, the Convention on the Recognition of Divorces and Legal Separations, and the Convention on the Law Applicable to Trusts and on their Recognition which are applicable in Hong Kong only; and (iii) the Convention on Civil Procedure, the Convention on the Law Applicable to Maintenance Obligations Towards Children, and the Convention Concerning the Powers of Authorities and the Law Applicable in Respect of the Protection of

[3] See also App 1 below.

Infants only effective in Macao.[4] Besides these conventions, China has signed the Convention on the Choice of Court and the Convention on Civil and Commercial Judgment Recognition and Enforcement, which will take effect in China and will, to a certain extent, make up for the deficiencies of the current Chinese civil and commercial judicial assistance mechanism. They will provide a new legal basis for China in the field of civil and commercial judgment recognition and enforcement of foreign cooperation.

China's private international law has made great progress in legislation, judicial practice, and in theoretical research, and the country has rapidly shifted from a bystander to an important participant in the Hague Conference on private international law; the improvement in its status has been closely linked with the development of domestic private international law, altogether forming distinct characteristics.

II. China and UNIDROIT

A. UNIDROIT Overview

The International Institute for the Unification of Private Law ('UNIDROIT') is an independent intergovernmental organisation with its seat in Rome. Set up in 1926 as an auxiliary organ of the League of Nations, the Institute was, following the demise of the League, re-established in 1940 on the basis of a multilateral agreement, the UNIDROIT Statute. Membership in UNIDROIT is restricted to states which have acceded to the UNIDROIT Statute. UNIDROIT's 63 member states are drawn from the five continents and represent a variety of different legal, economic, and political systems as well as different cultural backgrounds.[5] On the basis of such a complex and diverse composition of states, UNIDROIT has made great achievements by seeking common ground and reserving space for differences to formulate and promote the unification of private law. The purpose of UNIDROIT is to study needs and methods for modernising, harmonising and coordinating private and, in particular, commercial law between states and groups of states and to formulate uniform law instruments, principles, and rules to achieve those objectives.

The first and primary task of UNIDROIT is to unify contract law. The most widespread contracts are those with international trade domain applications; hence, this is the most vital and basic type of law in international trade development. UNIDROIT has been working on the unification of contract law for 30 years. In addition, two Hague conventions came into being in 1964. One is the convention on the establishment of a uniform law of contracts for the international sale of goods, and the other is the convention on the uniform law on the international sale of goods. The former is about the formation of a contract and the latter is about the sale of goods. Since the 1970s, UNIDROIT has been studying the Principles of International Commercial Contracts ('PICC'). In 1971, three experts from France, Britain, and Romania, representing the civil law system, the Anglo-American law system and the socialist law system, formed a guiding group to study the feasibility of formulating a uniform law on international commercial contracts and to provide guidance on this law's purposes and scope. In 1980, UNIDROIT formally established

[4] Ministry of Foreign Affairs of the People's Republic of China, 'List of China's participation in HCCH Conventions' (Ministry of Foreign Affairs, 16 July 2014) www.mfa.gov.cn/web/ziliao_674904/tytj_674911/tyfg_674913/t1201153.shtml accessed 5 September 2019.

[5] International Institute for the Unification of Private Law (UNIDROIT), 'History and Overview' www.unidroit.org/about-unidroit/overview accessed 4 March 2020.

a working group to draft various chapters of the PICC. The PICC is the representative work of the UNIDROIT and is its most important creation. In 1994, the drafting of the UNIDROIT Principles 1994 was largely completed, with a revision in 2004 to cover a wider range of topics.[6] In 2016, the steering committee adopted the revised draft of the 2010 Principles of International Commercial Contracts as revised by the working group on long-term contracts, and authorised the secretariat to publish a new version of the 2016 Principles of International Commercial Contracts of the UNIDROIT. The latest version of the PICC was published in 2016.

The PICC, formulated by the UNIDROIT as a 'non-domestic law rule' that does not represent the interests of any specific country, has provided a set of neutral and applicable rules for parties to international commercial contracts. Judgments applying the Principles are not uncommon and are widely distributed; according to data from the UNILEX database, as of 13 July 2019 there are 460 judgments which apply or consider the general rules, including courts in more than 30 countries and a number of arbitral bodies including the ICC. Among them, there are: (i) four cases concerning the general rules' material scope of application; (ii) 410 cases concerning the applicability of the Principles, including those relating to the legal principles governing contracts, provisions as part of contracts, those which provide a means of supplementing and interpreting domestic laws, and those relating to CISG; (iii) 42 cases involving the Principles and related instruments; and (iv) four cases involving the relevant editions of the Principles.[7] The UNILEX database is not comprehensive, so the real number of cases applying or considering the Principles will be higher. Regardless, the number and variety of cases demonstrate that the general principles have been widely accepted and recognised.

B. China's Participation

In 1983, on the invitation of UNIDROIT, the Chinese Government sent representatives to a diplomatic conference held in Geneva to discuss a convention on the agency for the International Sale of Goods and to establish contacts with UNIDROIT. China formally accepted the constitution of UNIDROIT on 23 July 1985 and officially became a member on 1 January 1986, sending experts to participate in the drafting and deliberation of the convention organised by the association. As the latest achievement of the movement for the international unification of private law, the PICC has aroused with its persuasiveness the attention of legislators, jurists, and scholars in China,[8] and has exerted a significant positive influence on the development of Chinese contract law. In addition, the Chinese delegation has participated in discussions on the formulation of a number of documents, including the convention on substantive rules for intermediated securities, the convention on international financial leasing, the convention on international interests in mobile equipment, the protocol to the convention on international interests in mobile equipment on matters specific to aircraft equipment, and the protocol on space assets.

[6] YQ Zhang, 'Yi Bu Xian Dai Tong Yi Zhi He Tong Fa Ping Jia "Guo Ji Shang Shi He Tong Tong Ze" 2004' [A Modern Unified Contract Law – Commentary on the 2004 Principles of International Commercial Contracts] (2005) 4 *Beijing Arbitration Quarterly*.

[7] UNIDROIT, 'Article Preamble, UNIDROIT Principles: Selected Cases by Article and Issues' www.unilex.info/principles/cases/article/102#article_102 accessed 13 July 2019.

[8] Seminar titled 'The BRI and Dispute Resolution: Focusing on UNIDROIT Principles International Arbitration and Judicial Adjudication' co-organised by UNIDROIT, UIBE and CIETAC was held in Beijing on 31 March 2017. www.ccpit.org/contents/channel_3528/2017/0410/786140/content_786140.htm accessed 19 October 2020.

III. China and UNCITRAL

A. UNCITRAL Overview

Established in 1966, the United Nations Commission on International Trade Law ('UNCITRAL') is a subsidiary body of the General Assembly of the United Nations with the general mandate to further the progressive harmonisation and unification of the law of international trade. Since its establishment, UNCITRAL has prepared a wide variety of conventions, model laws, and other instruments dealing with substantive law regulating trade transactions or other aspects of commercial law that affect international trade. UNCITRAL convenes annually, alternating between New York and Vienna. The 60 member countries include 14 African countries, 14 Asian countries, eight Eastern European countries, 10 Latin American and Caribbean countries, and 14 Western European and other countries, with this structure intended to ensure that the various regions and major economic and legal systems of the world are represented.[9] UNCITRAL is one of the most important bodies of the United Nations in its role discussing the formulation of Trade Law norms. It is not only committed to harmonising and unifying laws between different jurisdictions in the world, but also to studying the latest developments in international trade law. The achievements and roles of UNCITRAL have been recognised all over the world. A series of conventions and model laws formulated under its auspices have been adopted in many countries, which has greatly promoted the development of international trade. UNCITRAL's representative publications on the development of private international law theory and practice include the Model Law on Secured Transactions, the Model Law on Electronic Transferable Records, the Model Law on Public Procurement, and the Model Law on International Commercial Arbitration.[10] UNCITRAL's ideas for the development of international commercial arbitration and mediation mainly are embodied in the following normative documents:[11] the United Nations Treaty on the Conciliation of the International Convention on the Settlement Agreement (draft), the UN Treaty Arbitration Based on Transparency Between Investors and the National Convention (2014, New York) ('the Convention on Mauritius Transparency'), and the Convention on the Recognition and Enforcement of Foreign Arbitral Awards (1958, New York) ('the New York Convention').

B. China's Participation

The Chinese Government has taken an active part in the work of the six working groups of UNCITRAL and has arranged for domestic judges, government officials, and experts to participate in various special activities of UNCITRAL. In addition, the Chinese Government sends timely information on each session and activity of UNCITRAL to relevant agencies to disseminate the progress and achievements of UNCITRAL. China has also called on the general assembly to give more support to the work of UNCITRAL so that it can be carried out in a sustained and efficient manner.[12] Chinese representative Shi Xiaobin spoke at the Sixth Committee of

[9] ibid.

[10] UNCITRAL, 'UNCITRAL Publications' https://uncitral.un.org/en/library/publications accessed 3 January 2019.

[11] UNCITRAL, 'International Commercial Arbitration' https://uncitral.un.org/en/texts/arbitration accessed 4 January 2019.

[12] J Guan, 'Statement by Mr. J Guan (representative of China) on the Report of the United Nations Commission on International Trade Law on the Work of its Thirty-sixth session' (Sixth Committee of the 58th session of the General Assembly, 6 October 2003).

the 70th Session of the UN General Assembly on the 'Report on the Work of the 48th Session of the United Nations Commission on International Trade Law', stating that:

> The Chinese government has fully participated in the drafting of legal documents of the UNCITRAL working groups, in domestic legislation, drawing on the contents of the UNCITRAL model law or legislative guide, and actively promoting the work of UNCITRAL in China.[13]

Speaking at the Sixth Committee of the 65th Session of the UN General Assembly on the 'Report on the Work of the 43rd Session of the United Nations Commission on International Trade Law', Chinese representative Yang Yuya pronounced that:

> The Chinese Government has always attached importance to the work of the United Nations Commission on International Trade Law and fully participated in drafting the laws of the UNCITRAL Working Groups. China has drawn on the UNCITRAL model law or legislative guide in drafting domestic legislation, and has actively promoted UNCITRAL.[14]

The United Nations International Trade Law considered and adopted the following documents at that annual session: the revised version of the Committee's Arbitration Rules, the UNCITRAL Legislative Guide on Secured Transactions, the draft supplement to intellectual property rights, and the UNCITRAL Legislative Guide on Insolvency Law on the treatment of bankruptcy of enterprise groups.[15]

In the final draft of the technical guidelines on dispute resolution in cross-border e-commerce transactions, the UNCITRAL Working Group III adopted a Chinese proposal that reflects China's needs and takes into account the legal differences between the EU and the US.[16]

IV. China and ICSID

A. Overview

The International Centre for Settlement of Investment Disputes ('ICSID') was established in 1966 by the Convention on the Settlement of Investment Disputes between States and Nationals of Other States (the 'ICSID Convention') and is the world's first institution devoted to international investment dispute settlement. ICSID has a simple structure consisting of a Secretariat and Administrative Council, with each member state having one representative on the Administrative Council. ICSID is one of the five organisations of the World Bank Group and has independent legal personality. According to Article 1(2) of the ICSID Convention, 'the purpose of the Centre shall be to provide facilities for conciliation and arbitration of investment disputes between Contracting States and nationals of other Contracting States in accordance with the provisions of this Convention'. ICSID contributes to the aforementioned goal through its particular work, examples of which include encouraging developed countries to make investments in developing countries and providing for the settlement of disputes between investors and states.

[13] XB Shi, 'Statement by Mr. XB Shi (representative of China) on the Report of the United Nations Commission on International Trade Law on the Work of its Forty-eighth session' (Sixth Committee of the 70th session of the General Assembly, 19 October 2015).

[14] YY Yang, 'Statement by Ms. YY Yang (representative of China) on the Report of the United Nations Commission on International Trade Law on the Work of its Forty-third session' (Sixth Committee of the 65th session of the General Assembly, 11 October 2010).

[15] ibid.

[16] L Han, '"China's Voice" in the United Nations Commission on International Trade Law' *China News Network* (Chongqing, 29 March 2016) www.chinanews.com/gn/2016/03-29/7816096.shtml accessed 8 January 2019.

ICSID is firmly established as the preeminent global institution for the resolution of investment disputes. The vast majority of all known international investment cases have been administered by ICSID, with strong demand for the Centre's services.[17] The ICSID Convention and the ICSID Additional Facility represent the most advanced international practice in many aspects, such as procedure design, public trial, list of arbitrators, seat of arbitration, and transparency of arbitration procedures. As of March 2020, ICSID had registered 76 cases under the ICSID Convention and Additional Facility Rule. As such disputes grow increasingly common, the number of cases registered by the Centre has increased as well, which makes ICSID an even more prominent player in investor-state dispute settlement ('ISDS'). By March 2020, ICSID had 155 member states, with an additional eight signatory states.[18] ICSID's growing membership and reach is as much a sign of its growing global reach as is its growing caseload. ICSID seeks to resolve international investment disputes by providing arbitration, mediation, and fact-finding. Considering the special nature of international investment disputes and the particularity of the parties to the disputes, ICSID pays special attention to the balance of interests between investors and host countries in the design of procedures. More than 700 such cases have been administered by ICSID to date.[19]

As mentioned, ICSID is involved in contract investment disputes among contracting state institutions. The dispute settlement mechanism of the national or international investment arbitration is distinct from international arbitration between countries and between private subjects of international commercial arbitration. The arbitration body is for the sovereign state and the other nation, but in disputes over commercial activities, investors are allowed to bring the host state to arbitration directly. International investment arbitration, which has inherited and innovated from the traditional arbitration form, has raised new questions and brought new challenges to the international commercial dispute legal system. ICSID, as the institution which most often accepts international investment arbitration cases, has set forth rules and regulations which promote international capital flow. In the latest of the ICSID convention overhauls, the rule amendment project will modernise and streamline ICSID's procedural rules, while also reducing the time, cost and environmental footprint of cases. ICSID is also addressing a number of topics that were raised by member states and other stakeholders during the consultation process. These include third-party funding, transparency, and security for costs.[20] Such efforts will not only improve the efficiency of ICSID itself, but also distinguish ICSID as a model in the field of international arbitration.

B. China's Participation

On 9 February 1990, China signed the ICSID Convention, which became effective on 6 February 1993. The instrument of ratification declared that, in accordance with Article 25(4) of the ICSID Convention, in disputes over compensation issues resulting from expropriation and nationalisation, the Chinese Government would only consider submitting to the jurisdiction of the ICSID. So far, Chinese investors have initiated six arbitration cases against ICSID, among which five have been settled and one is still being handled.[21] The first ICSID case involving China (ARB/07/6)

[17] ICSID, '2019 ICSID Annual Report: Excellence in Investment Dispute Resolution' https://icsid.worldbank.org/sites/default/files/publications/annual-report/en/ICSID_AR19_CRA_Web_Low_DD.pdf accessed 25 August 2020.

[18] ICSID, 'Database of ICSID Member States' https://icsid.worldbank.org/about/member-states/database-of-member-states accessed 17 June 2020.

[19] ICSID, 'About ICSID' https://icsid.worldbank.org/about/ICSID accessed 25 August 2020.

[20] ICSID Secretariat, '2020 Annual Report: Excellence in Investment Dispute Resolution', https://icsid.worldbank.org/sites/default/files/publications/ICSID_AR20_CRA_Web.pdf, accessed 19 October 2020.

[21] See also App 2 below.

was initiated on 12 February 2007 by Tza Yap Shum, a Chinese citizen. The Tribunal rendered the award in favour of the investors on 7 July 2011. Subsequently, the Republic of Peru requested initiation of the annulment process; the request was rejected by the ICSID ad hoc committee on 12 February 2015.[22] In the cases of *Standard Chartered Bank (Hong Kong) Limited v Tanzania Electric Supply Company Limited* (ARB/10/20)[23] and *Standard Chartered Bank (Hong Kong) Limited v United Republic of Tanzania* (ARB/15/41),[24] which were initiated by the same claimant, the Tribunal's awards were consistent in requiring the respondent to pay the claimant. Conversely, in the case of *Ping An Life Insurance Company of China, Limited and Ping An Insurance (Group) Company of China, Limited v Kingdom of Belgium* (ARB/12/29), the Tribunal rendered its award in support of the respondent, finding that it lacked jurisdiction over the applicant's request. Accordingly, the Tribunal in that case did not express any view on the substantive issues.[25] As for the case *Beijing Urban Construction Group Co Ltd v Republic of Yemen* (ARB/14/30), as both parties agreed to suspend the proceedings the Tribunal issued a procedural order taking note of the discontinuance of the proceeding pursuant to ICSID Arbitration Rule 43(1) on 7 June 2018.[26] The aforementioned pending case (ADHOC/17/1) was initiated by Sanum Investments Limited, with the latest development being on 29 April 2020, and the Tribunal having decided on the Claimants' request as denying expropriation on 20 April 2020.[27]

In recent years, with the deepening of China's 'One Belt and One Road' initiative and the acceleration of enterprises' exporting from China, China has gradually transformed from a traditional capital importing country to possessing the dual status of capital importing country and capital exporting country. This also means that in ICSID, in addition to the number of disputes initiated by Chinese investors against the host state, the probability of China passively accepting arbitration as the home country of investors will be greatly increased.[28] Malaysia-based Ekran Berhad was the first company to break China's 45-year record of not accepting a lawsuit from a foreign investor against the Chinese Government. Its application for arbitration against China was registered on 24 May 2011. Four months after the registration of the case, the arbitration procedure was suspended by agreement between the two parties. Two years later, the Secretary-General issued a procedural order taking note of the discontinuance of the proceeding pursuant to ICSID Arbitration Rule 43(1).[29] On 4 November 2014, Ansung Housing Co Ltd initiated the second arbitration of an investment dispute against China. China accepted the award rendered by the constituted Tribunal. On 9 March 2017, an ICSID arbitration tribunal rendered an award and rejected all of the claims. The Tribunal supported China's position on important legal issues such as the time limitation of arbitration and the scope of application of MFN treatment clauses.[30] Another case in which China is a respondent has not been settled. The latest progress is that the Claimant filed a rejoinder on jurisdiction on 18 May 2020.[31]

[22] *Señor Tza Yap Shum v The Republic of Peru*, ICSID Case No ARB/07/6, Decision (12 February 2015).

[23] *Standard Chartered Bank (Hong Kong) Ltd v Tanzania Electric Supply Company Ltd*, ICSID Case No ARB/10/20, Decision (22 August 2018).

[24] *Standard Chartered Bank (Hong Kong) Ltd v United Republic of Tanzania*, ICSID Case No ARB/15/41, Award (11 October 2019).

[25] *Ping An Life Insurance Company Ltd and Ping An Insurance (Group) Company Ltd v The Government of Belgium*, ICSID Case No ARB/12/29, Award (30 April 2015).

[26] *Beijing Urban Construction Group Co Ltd v Republic of Yemen*, ICSID Case No ARB/14/30, Decision (31 May 2017).

[27] *Sanum Investments Ltd v Lao People's Democratic Republic*, ICSID Case No ADHOC/17/1 https://icsid.worldbank.org/en/Pages/cases/casedetail.aspx?CaseNo=ADHOC/17/1 accessed 27 June 2020.

[28] See also App 3 below.

[29] *Ekran Berhad v People's Republic of China*, ICSID Case No ARB/11/15, Procedural Order No 1 (16 May 2013).

[30] *Ansung Housing Co Ltd v People's Republic of China*, ICSID Case No ARB/14/25, Award (9 March 2017).

[31] *Hela Schwarz GmbH v People's Republic of China*, ICSID Case No ARB/17/19 https://icsid.worldbank.org/cases/case-database/case-detail?CaseNo=ARB/17/19 accessed 24 August 2020.

In addition, in 2017 China successfully recommended and appointed four Chinese arbitrators and four Chinese mediators to the ICSID, which marked the deepening of China's participation in the international investment dispute settlement mechanism and the enhancement of China's influence and voice in the international investment dispute settlement mechanism.[32] In June 2018, the Shenzhen International Arbitration Court ('SCIA') and ICSID signed a cooperation agreement. According to the agreement, ICSID and SCIA will provide each other with supporting facilities, translation, and secretarial services. At the same time, the two sides will jointly promote arbitration, mediation, and other alternative dispute resolution mechanisms in the business and legal communities, and exchange information and organise activities in this field.

Appendices

Appendix 1 A chronicle of events of China's proposal in HCCH

Date	The Meeting
September–October 1987	To participate in the third special committee meeting on drafting a convention on the application of law on foreign-related inheritance.
June 1990	First meeting of the AD hoc committee on the drafting of an international convention on intercountry adoption of children.
May 1993	To participate in the diplomatic conference on the elaboration of the convention on intercountry adoption and protection of children.
June 1996	To participate in the drafting of civil and commercial jurisdiction and enforcement of judgments.
September 1996	To participate in amending the Hague convention on jurisdiction and application of law for the protection of minors.
April 1999	New York convention for the consideration of recourse for maintenance.
October 1999	To participate in the seventh AD hoc committee meeting on the drafting of a convention on international civil and commercial jurisdiction and the effectiveness of foreign judgments.
30 November 2000	Signing of the convention on the protection of children and cooperation in intercountry adoption.
December 2003	To participate in the drafting of the convention on court choice agreements.
March 2004	To participate in the informal consultation on the drafting of the convention on the choice of courts.
April 2005	To attend the drafting committee meeting of the exclusive court choice agreement.
May 2007	To participate in the special committee meeting on the drafting of the convention on the obligation of maintenance.
12 September 2018	To sign the Hague Convention on Choice of Courts.
2 July 2019	To sign the Convention on the Recognition and Enforcement of Foreign Judgments in Civil or Commercial Matters.

[32] The Ministry of Commerce of the People's Republic of China, 'The Construction of Commercial Rule of Law is Improving Day by Day' (Ministry of Commerce, 20 October 2017) www.mofcom.gov.cn/article/zt_dlfj19/fbdt/201710/20171002657439.shtml accessed 2 February 2019.

Appendix 2 Arbitration Cases Delivered to ICSID by Chinese Investors

Arbitration Cases Delivered to ICSID by Chinese Investors			
No	**Case No**	**Parties**	**Arbitration Procedure and Status Quo**
1	ARB/07/6	*Tza Yap Shum v Republic of Peru*	Concluded. The case was initiated on 12 February 2007 by Tza Yap Shum, a Chinese citizen. The Tribunal rendered the award in favour of the investors on 7 July 2011. Subsequently, the Republic of Peru requested the initiation of the annulment process. The ICSID ad hoc committee rejected the request on 12 February 2015. This was the first ICSID case involving China or a Chinese investor.
2	ARB/10/20	*Standard Chartered Bank (Hong Kong) Limited v Tanzania Electric Supply Company Limited*	Concluded. In this case, the Tribunal rendered its award on 12 September 2016, confirming its jurisdiction over the case and requiring the respondent to pay the claimant US$1,484,000,000 plus interest. On 6 January 2017, the respondent requested the initiation of the annulment proceeding, and the tribunal unanimously rejected the application on 22 August 2018.
3	ARB/12/29	*Ping An Life Insurance Company of China, Limited and Ping An Insurance (Group) Company of China, Limited v Kingdom of Belgium*	Concluded. On 30 April 2015, the Tribunal rendered its award in support of the Belgian Government's objection to jurisdiction in this case, finding that it lacked jurisdiction over the applicant's request. It did not express its views on the substantive issues.
4	ARB/14/30	*Beijing Urban Construction Group Co Ltd v Republic of Yemen*	Concluded. The Respondent in this case contended that the Tribunal lacked jurisdiction both *ratione personae* and *ratione materiae*. The Tribunal made a decision to confirm its jurisdiction on 31 May 2017. In January 2018, both parties agreed to suspend the proceedings. On 7 June 2018, the Tribunal issued a procedural order taking note of the discontinuance of the proceeding pursuant to ICSID Arbitration Rule 43(1).
5	ARB/15/41	*Standard Chartered Bank (Hong Kong) Limited v United Republic of Tanzania*	Concluded. The Tribunal in this case rendered its award on 11 October 2019, confirming its jurisdiction over the case and requiring the respondent to pay the claimant US$185,449,440.04 plus interest.
6	ADHOC/17/1	*Sanum Investments Limited v Lao People's Democratic Republic*	Pending.
7	ARB/20/26	*Fengzhen Min v Republic of Korea*	Pending.

Appendix 3 The ICSID arbitration cases against China

No	Case No	Parties	Arbitration Procedure and Status Quo
1	ARB/11/15	*Ekran Berhad v PRC*	Concluded. Malaysia-based Ekran Berhad was the first company to break China's 45-year record of not accepting a lawsuit from a foreign investor against the Chinese Government. Its application arbitration against China was registered on 24 May 2011. Four months after the registration of the case, the arbitration procedure was suspended due to the agreement made between the two parties. Two years later, the Secretary-General issued a procedural order taking note of the discontinuance of the proceeding pursuant to ICSID Arbitration Rule 43(1).
2	ARB/14/25	*Ansung Housing Co Ltd v PRC*	Concluded. Ansung Housing Co Ltd initiated arbitration of an investment dispute against China on 4 November 2014. It is the second international investment arbitration case brought against China and the first case in which the constituted Tribunal rendered an award. On 9 March 2017, an ICSID arbitration tribunal rendered an award and rejected all of the claims. The Tribunal supported China's position on important legal issues such as the time limitation of arbitration and the scope of application of MFN treatment clauses.
3	ARB/17/19	*Hela Schwarz GmbH v PRC*	Pending. On 21 June 2017, German company Hela Schwarz GmbH initiated an arbitration against the Chinese Government in the ICSID. The case is still pending. The latest progress was in December 2018, when the Tribunal issued the No 3 procedural order concerning the Respondent's request to address the objections to jurisdiction as a preliminary question. As a result, the objections to jurisdiction were joined to the merits of the dispute.
4	ARB/20/22	*Macro Trading Co., Ltd v People's Republic of China*	Pending.

26

The Belt and Road Initiative and Chinese Private International Law

ZHENGYI ZHANG

I. The Belt and Road Initiative

An increasing number of countries have responded enthusiastically to China's Belt and Road Initiative ('BRI'). Jointly building the BRI is becoming a way for China to participate in globalisation, improve the global economic governance system, promote global common development and prosperity, and build a community based on a shared future for mankind.[1] The origin, core meaning, and contents of cooperation of the Belt and Road Initiative have attracted much attention.[2]

A. The Origin of the Belt and Road Initiative

On 7 September 2013, Chinese President Xi Jinping delivered a speech titled 'Carry Forward the Friendship of the People and Create a Better Future' at Nazarbayev University in Kazakhstan, proposing to build the Silk Road Economic Belt with the rest of the world and on 3 October 2013, President Xi Jinping delivered a speech titled 'Working Together to Build a Community of Shared Future between China and the Association of Southeast Asian Nations (ASEAN)' in the Indonesian Parliament, proposing to jointly build the '21st Century Maritime Silk Road'. Together these form the Silk Road Economic Belt and the twenty-first Century Maritime Silk Road (One Belt and One Road) Initiative. The ancient Silk Road, spanning thousands of miles and extending over millennia, symbolised peace and cooperation, openness and inclusiveness, mutual learning and mutual benefit, reciprocity and 'win-win' results. This is the precious heritage of human civilisation. The BRI has become one of the world's most popular global public goods, but also one of the best prospective platforms for international cooperation.[3]

[1] C Zhao and B An, 'Xi Jinping attended the symposium on the 5th anniversary of the promotion of the "Belt and Road" programme and delivered an important speech' (Xinhua News Agency, 27 August 2018) www.yidaiyilu.gov.cn/xwzx/xgcdt/63963.htm accessed 31 January 2019.

[2] By the end of July 2019, the Chinese Government had signed 195 intergovernmental cooperation agreements with 136 countries and 30 international organisations. Illustration: One Belt and One Road Initiative Six-year Report Card (Belt and Road Portal, 9 September 2019) www.yidaiyilu.gov.cn/xwzx/gnxw/102792.htm accessed 15 October 2020.

[3] National Information Centre, 'What is the "Belt and Road"?' (Belt and Road Portal) www.yidaiyilu.gov.cn accessed 31 January 2019.

B. The Core Meaning of the Belt and Road Initiative

China is willing to work with international partners to jointly to build the BRI. Through this new platform for international cooperation, China intends to add fresh impetus to common global development and build the BRI into a road of peace, prosperity, openness, environmental health, innovation, and civilisation.[4] Within the framework of international cooperation under the Belt and Road Initiative, all parties, upholding the principles of consultation, joint contribution, and sharing, will join hands to meet the challenges that the world economy is facing and create new opportunities for development. This is the original intention of this initiative and the ultimate goal to be achieved.[5] Guided by these objectives, the top-level framework of the BRI covers five directions: the three directions of the Silk Road Economic Belt and the two directions of the twenty-first Century Maritime Silk Road. The main framework is 'Six Corridors, Six Roads, Many Countries and Many Ports'. This means the construction of six international economic cooperation corridors – by road, railway, shipping, aviation, pipeline, and a space-integrated information network. The goal is to demonstrate early success in the countries who have already joined the project by jointly building important ports and node cities, and to make maritime cooperation prosperous for all.

C. Contents of Cooperation in the Belt and Road Initiative

Cooperation in the Belt and Road Initiative includes policy communication, facility connectivity, unimpeded trade, financing, and people-to-people exchanges. China has signed cooperation documents for jointly building the BRI with the United Nations Development Programme ('UNDP'), the Economic and Social Commission for Asia and the Pacific ('ESCAP'), and the World Health Organization ('WHO'). In addition, China has signed cooperation agreements for the BRI with more than 100 countries and international organisations. Facility connectivity includes cooperation in the construction of railways, highways, ports, aviation facilities, postal services, energy facilities, and information infrastructure, and the connection of quality systems and technical systems. To achieve unimpeded trade, China has carried out activities such as investment and trade facilitation, created free trade area networks, and engaged in global cooperation in increasing production capacity, constructing overseas parks, and establishing and improving China-European Union train links. In terms of financing, China will accelerate the construction of new cooperation platforms, cooperate with multilateral banks, utilise existing financial cooperation mechanisms, and support developmental, policy-based financial institutions. For example, the Asian Infrastructure Investment Bank ('AIIB') is a multilateral development bank with a mission to improve social and economic outcomes in Asia. Headquartered in Beijing, operations began in January 2016 and have now grown to 103 approved members worldwide.[6] People-to-people exchanges are mainly reflected in cultural exchanges, tourism exchanges, education, science and technology, ecological and environmental protection, hygiene and health, poverty reduction support, and other areas.

[4] JP Xi, 'Keynote speech by Jinping Xi at the opening ceremony of the 2018 China-Africa cooperation forum summit in Beijing (full text)' (Xinhua News Agency, 3 September 2018) www.yidaiyilu.gov.cn/xwzx/xgcdt/64809.htm accessed 31 January 2019.

[5] JP Xi, Open up a new starting point for cooperation and seek new impetus for development' (Xinhua News Agency, 15 May 2017) www.yidaiyilu.gov.cn/xwzx/xgcdt/13629.htm accessed 31 January 31, 2019.

[6] Asian Infrastructure Investment Bank ('AIIB'), 'Introduction' (AIIB Portal) www.aiib.org/en/about-aiib/index.html accessed 15 October 2020.

The BRI takes enterprises as the main body of market-oriented operations. Enterprises must participate fairly and abide by international rules and the laws and regulations of the country where the enterprise is located, and the country where the project is located. It is foreseeable that the process of advancing the BRI will also promote the corresponding development of China's private international law in the aspects of jurisdiction, law application, recognition, and implementation.

II. The Belt and Road Initiative and International Civil and Commercial Dispute Settlement

As more and more countries support and join the BRI, the geographical area involved is expanding and the cultural traditions of the countries and regions involved are becoming more and more diverse. Disputes are inevitable in the process of implementation because the BRI covers a wide range of complex areas in economy and trade, and confronts significant cultural differences among the participating countries. Since most of the countries along the BRI are developing countries, the establishment of independent dispute settlement mechanisms also helps to better integrate developing countries into the mainstream of the world economy.[7] China has made significant advances in improving both judicial and non-litigation dispute settlement mechanisms.

A. International Commercial Courts under the Belt and Road Initiative

In order to hear international commercial cases in a timely and fair way in accordance with the law, fairly protect the legitimate rights and interests of Chinese and foreign parties, and create a stable, fair, transparent, and convenient business environment governed by law, the Supreme People's Court of China has established international commercial courts. The first international commercial court was established in Shenzhen, Guangdong province, and the second in Xi'an, Shaanxi province. The fourth Civil Trial Court of the Supreme People's Court is responsible for coordinating and guiding the work of the two international commercial courts. Cases are heard by a collegial bench composed of three or more judges. The international commercial courts conclude a case with one trial, and the judgment or ruling given has legal effect.

The main features of the international commercial courts are as follows.[8] First, judgments and rulings of the international commercial courts are legally effective. Second, the international commercial courts have developed an organic connection between litigation, mediation, and arbitration, forming a convenient, fast, and low-cost 'one-stop' dispute settlement platform. China should establish a mediation system composed of international commercial mediation institutions, international commercial arbitration institutions and international commercial tribunals. A one-stop international commercial dispute resolution mechanism has been formed through an integrated platform of settlement, arbitration and litigation.[9] Third, the international commercial courts actively encourage international civil and commercial judicial assistance, and

[7] GG Wang, 'Study on the Dispute Settlement Mechanism of "Belt and Road" [2017] 6 China Legal Science 68.

[8] The International Commercial Court, 'Introduction to the International Commercial Court', (The International Commercial Court, 28 June 2018) www.cicc.court.gov.cn/html/1/218/19/141/index.html accessed 31 January 2019.

[9] Y Xue, YQ Chen, 'China's "one-stop" international commercial dispute settlement mechanism with the international commercial tribunal as the core' (2020) 1 *Journal of Political Science and Law* 149.

work to develop an efficient and smooth international judicial assistance mechanism. Fourth, the international commercial courts make full use of information in the settlement of international commercial disputes. Fifth, the international commercial courts aim at fairness, efficiency, convenience, and low cost. Sixth, the international commercial courts deal with international commercial disputes between equal subjects. Seventh, the judges of the international commercial courts are selected by the Supreme People's Court from senior judges who have rich trial experience and are familiar with international treaties, international practices, and international trade and investment practices, and can skilfully use both Chinese and English as working languages. Eighth, the international commercial court forms the international commercial expert committee using Chinese and foreign legal experts who are proficient in international law and domestic law and who have rich practical experience and strong international reputation. So far, 31 Chinese and foreign experts have been invited.

The range of cases accepted by the international commercial courts includes the following. First, international commercial cases of the first instance in which the parties choose the jurisdiction of the Supreme People's Court by agreement in accordance with the provisions of civil procedure law, and the amount of money in dispute is more than RMB300 million. Second, applications for arbitration preservation, cancellation, or enforcement of international commercial arbitration rulings in accordance with the provisions of the Supreme People's Court on Several Issues Concerning The Establishment of the International Commercial Courts. Third, international commercial cases of the first instance under the jurisdiction of the Supreme People's Court which the Court decides should be adjudicated in an international commercial court. Fourth, international commercial cases of the first instance which are of national significance. Fifth, other international cases which the Supreme People's Court considers should be tried by the international commercial court. In addition, 'international commercial cases' accepted by the international commercial court must meet one of the following conditions:[10] (i) one or both parties are foreigners, stateless persons, foreign enterprises, or organisations; (ii) the habitual residence of one party or both parties is outside the territory of the People's Republic of China (PRC); (iii) the legal facts that create, alter, or terminate commercial relations take place outside the territory of the PRC; (iv) the subject matter is outside the territory of the PRC.

In response to the BRI, China's Supreme People's Court published a total of 18 cases in two batches as typical cases of people's courts providing judicial services and guarantees for the Belt and Road construction. In addition, the international commercial court of the Supreme People's Court has formally accepted a number of international commercial disputes in accordance with the Civil Procedure Law of the People's Republic of China and the provisions of the Supreme People's Court on several issues concerning the establishment of international commercial courts.[11]

B. Diversified Dispute Settlement Mechanisms under the Belt and Road Initiative

Besides litigation, diversified dispute settlement mechanisms including arbitration and mediation will safeguard economic and trade cooperation under the BRI, provide efficient and fair

[10] International Commercial Court, 'Introduction' (China International Commercial Court, 28 June 2018) http://cicc.court.gov.cn/html/1/218/19/141/index.html accessed 15 October 2020.

[11] International Commercial Court, 'The Supreme Court of International Commercial Court has accepted a number of international commercial disputes' (China International Commercial Court, 29 December 2018) www.cicc.court.gov.cn/html/1/218/149/192/1150.html accessed 31 January 2019.

legal services, and enhance China's influence in fashioning dispute settlement mechanisms. The construction of the BRI multi-channel dispute settlement mechanism should be sensitive to the diversity of legal cultures and legal traditions of countries alongside the BRI and provide targeted institutional guarantees for such diversity. This requires that the construction of the BRI multi-channel dispute settlement mechanism should consider absorbing the arbitration institutions of countries alongside the BRI.[12] In 2016, the Belt and One Road (China) arbitration Court initiated by the Wuhan arbitration commission was established in Beijing. This is the first professional arbitration court in China to serve the Belt and Road Initiative. With the increase of Chinese enterprises' investment scale and infrastructure projects in countries alongside the Belt and Road, various types of contract and cooperation disputes are on the rise. In its early days, the arbitration Court focused on settling cases where both parties were Chinese enterprises.[13] Given that the major investment projects of Chinese enterprises in countries alongside the Belt and Road are infrastructure construction, the arbitrators and members of the expert consultation committee of the arbitration Court are mostly experts in the field of construction engineering.

On 20 December 2018, the United Nations General Assembly passed the United Nations Convention on International Settlement Agreements Resulting from Mediation (also known as the 'Singapore Convention on Mediation'). The Convention, drafted by the second working group of the United Nations Commission on International Trade Law, aims at establishing a framework for the reconciliation of international agreements resulting from mediation that is acceptable to states with different legal, social, and economic systems and will be conducive to the development of harmonious international economic relations and cross-border civil and commercial dispute mediation. Mediation is also known as the 'treasure of the East' because it can improve the efficiency of dispute settlement and avoid the waste of resources.[14] The flexible use of mediation in litigation or arbitration has become popular in China's judicial and arbitral practice. It is foreseeable that the promotion of the Singapore Convention on Mediation and its model law will contribute to the understanding of mediation as a non-litigation dispute resolution mechanism with Chinese characteristics.

For example, a special agency, the One Belt and One Road Service Mechanism Mediation Committee, and the 'Belt and Road' International Commercial Mediation Centre have been established in China to resolve BRI commercial disputes.[15] The responsibility of the Mediation Centre is to assist parties to resolve BRI-related international commercial disputes. The functions of the Mediation Centre are: (i) selecting qualified mediators; (ii) organising training to qualify mediators; (iii) providing mediation services for members of the BRI as well as governments, enterprises, and other commercial organisations and individuals in Belt and Road countries; (iv) promoting a culture of harmony, mutual benefit, and equality through online and offline mediation in the Belt and Road international business subjects, and promoting the good economic order of Belt and Road; (v) cooperating with governments, judicial organs, and mediation and

[12] BP Chu, 'The present and future of the construction of "Belt and One Road" multi-dispute settlement centre' (2017) 6 *China Legal Science* 74.

[13] SHIPA, 'Arbitration Court of "Belt and Road" (China) has been founded' (China Council for the Promotion of International Trade, 8 November 2016) www.ccpit.org/Contents/Channel_3586/2016/1108/715570/content_715570.htm accessed 31 January 2019.

[14] L Liao, 'Research on the innovation of "Belt and One Road" dispute settlement mechanism – a perspective of international law and comparative law' (2018) 2 *Law Review* 172.

[15] Belt and Road Service Mechanism Mediation Committee, Belt and Road International Commercial Conciliation Centre: Mediation Centre Introduction (Belt and Road Service Mechanism Mediation Committee, Belt and Road International Commercial Conciliation Centre) www.bnrmediation.com/Home/Center/index/aid/150.html accessed 30 January 2019.

arbitration organisations of Belt and Road countries to promote the development of international commercial mediation and its connections with judicial procedures, including the connection of litigation with mediation, judicial confirmation, and the execution of mediation agreements. With the increasing acceptance of the Singapore Convention and its model law by the international community,[16] mediation services in China will be further opened up so as to be more widely used in the settlement of international commercial disputes.

In the process of constructing the Belt and Road diversified dispute settlement mechanism, attention should also be paid to creating a connecting platform to meet the parties' diversified judicial needs. Specific measures include: making full use of the parties' characteristics to achieve a variety of combinations of negotiation, mediation and adjudication; strengthening the effective connections among mediation, arbitration, and litigation; and establishing an information-based office platform for relevant institutions to realise rapid exchange and transfer of documents between institutions.[17]

[16] 53 states have signed United Nations Convention on International Settlement Agreements Resulting from Mediation, among which Belarus, Ecuador, Fiji, Qatar, Saudi Arabia, Singapore have ratified. Status: United Nations Convention on International Settlement Agreements Resulting from Mediation (Texts and Status International Commercial Mediation) https://uncitral.un.org/en/texts/mediation/conventions/international_settlement_agreements/status accessed 15 October 2020.

[17] GM Xu, 'Diversified settlement of commercial disputes under the backdrop of "Belt and Road" People's Court Daily (Beijing, 15 September 2017).

27

The Future of Private International Law

GUOJIAN XU, ZHENGYI ZHANG

I. The Future of Law Application

The Law of the People's Republic of China on Choice of Law for Foreign-related Civil Relationships[1] and its judicial interpretation provide rules on choice of laws in the fields of civil subjects, marriage and family, inheritance, real rights, creditors' rights and intellectual property. Clearly, this is not a complete code. Judicial interpretation influences how the rules are understood, and other legislation contains relevant choice of law rules. Three kinds of legislative norm can be identified. First, generally-applicable provisions. For example, Chapter 8 of the General Principles of the Civil Law (the application of law for foreign-related civil relations) provides substantive conflict rules of general application, while the fourth part of the Civil Procedure Law provides rules of civil procedure concerning foreign affairs. Second, special chapters of laws regulating a particular area of activity. For example, Chapter 14 of the Maritime Law, Chapter 14 of the Civil Aviation Law, Chapter 5 of the Negotiable Instruments Law, and Chapter 7 of the Arbitration Law. Third, provisions relevant to particular areas of law. For example, 'Contract Law', 'Inheritance Law', and other separate laws include provisions regarding the application of law.[2] Conflicts rules are therefore spread across legislation. However, there has been significant work towards the codification of civil law in China, of which private international law forms a part. At the bequest of the National People's Congress ('NPC'), a comprehensive Civil Law Code of China has been approved in May 2020 and will take effect from 2021. The Code, the biggest legislative project in China's history, will make the systematic integration of civil legislation a defining characteristic of China's legal system. Consequently, norms governing the application of law in foreign-related civil relations, which have long been attached to substantive civil laws, will also be developed systematically and integrally.

In addition to these formal developments, it is foreseeable that future legal provisions will become more flexible through the blending of connection points. Three points should be made. First, the triumph of flexible and open connection points over rigid and closed connection points is regarded as a major feature of the international development of contemporary private

[1] Law of the People's Republic of China on Choice of Law for Foreign-related Civil Relationships, which was adopted at the 17th session of the Standing Committee of the 11th National People's Congress on 28 October 2010, is hereby promulgated and shall come into force on 1 April 2011.

[2] W Ding, 'Analysis of the relationship between the law of the application of law for foreign-related civil relations and "other laws"' (2011) 29 *Tribune of Political Science and Law* 14.

international law. China's private international law has also begun to move away from rigidity by using flexible and open connection points. For example, use of *the lex voluntatis* and proximate connections permits conflict norms to play an active and fair role in complex multilateral international civil and commercial relations dispute resolution. Second, the use of multiple alternative connection points is noteworthy. When there are multiple connecting points, courts and tribunals have greater flexibility to enable international civil and commercial relations to validly come into force. Third, where a connection point has multiple possible meanings, courts may prefer that which gives legal effect to the parties' civil relations. For example, Chinese private international law norms explain the *lex loci delicti* as including both the law of the place where the infringement takes place and the law of the place where the infringement results. If the two are inconsistent, the people's court may choose one to apply.[3] This demonstrates that the same connection point could be used in different situations to perform different functions.

II. The Future of Judicial Assistance

Judicial assistance in its broadest sense includes the recognition and enforcement of judgments. The Hague Conference on Private International Law launched the 'Judgments Project' in 1992, hoping to develop a wide range of international conventions on international jurisdiction, recognition and implementation in the context of international commercial disputes. Among the Project's successes is the Convention on Choice of Court Agreements 2005.[4] Meetings chaired by The Hague Conference on Private International Law over the years have emphasised the importance of the Judgments Project in providing greater predictability and legal certainty for international litigation and reducing the time, cost, and complexity of the process.[5] If successful, the Project will greatly contribute to existing mechanisms for the settlement of international civil and commercial disputes.[6]

A. Prospect of the Convention on Choice of Court Agreements

The Convention on Choice of Court Agreements was the first product of the Judgments Project.[7] Adopted by the twentieth diplomatic conference of the Hague Conference on Private International Law on 30 June 2005, the Convention aims to ensure the validity of choice of court agreements (or 'choice of court clauses') and has been ratified by the vast majority of EU countries. China signed

[3] Article 187 of Opinions of the Supreme People's Court on Several Issues concerning the Implementation of the General Principles of the Civil Law of the People's Republic of China (Trial Implementation) (Supreme People's Court, Fa Ban Fa (1988) 6, adopted on 26 January 1988 and promulgated on 2 April 1988).

[4] HCCH, 'Overview of the Judgments Project' (*HCCH*) www.hcch.net/en/projects/legislative-projects/judgments/overview-judgments accessed 7 Feb 2019.

[5] HCCH, 'Conclusions and Recommendations Conference on International Litigation in the Asia Pacific Region, Wuhan, People's Republic of China' (*HCCH*, 24 Sept 2013) 11 www.hcch.net/en/projects/legislative-projects/judgments/judgments-news-wuhan accessed 7 Feb 2019.

[6] HCCH, 'Conclusions and Recommendations Conference on Cross-Border Recognition and Enforcement of Judgments, St. Petersburg, Russian Federation' (*HCCH*, 17 June 2014) 10 www.hcch.net/en/news-events/details/?varevent=367 accessed 7 Feb 2019.

[7] M Pertegas, 'HCCH in the Internet Era, Conference on Jurisdiction & Dispute Resolution in the Internet Era: Governance and Good Practice, Geneva, Switzerland' (*HCCH*, 18 June 2015) https://assets.hcch.net/docs/3ff12dff-b7a6-4a43-9189-dbccd93bd6a6.pdf accessed 8 Oct 2020.

the Convention on 12 September 2017, but has not yet ratified it. This Convention establishes the first global legal framework for the recognition and enforcement of civil and commercial judgments. China participated in the negotiation of the convention from the beginning to the end. From the perspective of China's long-term interests, ratification of the Convention will promote the transnational execution of Chinese court judgments, the perfection of the agreement jurisdiction system, and of the system of recognition and implementation of judgments. This development of China's international commercial arbitration system will enhance China's competitiveness in the international civil and commercial dispute settlement market, providing more effective legal support for the realisation of the 'One Belt and One Road' initiative and the community of shared future for mankind.[8] Disadvantages arising from ratification, for example, failure to pay due attention to the equality of parties and failure to provide the corresponding protection for parties in a weak position will be mitigated by the relative economic strength, bargaining power, and skill of Chinese parties in international commerce and trade.[9] In addition, the Hague Convention itself stipulates a set of rules and regulations to overcome its inherent disadvantages for example, the request that the chosen court exercise jurisdiction actually goes beyond the general legal principle of agreement jurisdiction, because the chosen court only has jurisdiction because of the party's choice, of which China could take advantage.

B. Prospect of the Project of Recognition and Implementation

In 2012, an expert group was invited by the Judgments Project to design the text of the Convention on the Recognition and Implementation of Judgments for the future. In June 2016, the Special Committee on the Judgment Projects began preparing the convention draft, and in the following three years four convention drafts were circulated.[10] During this period, the importance of the Judgments Project was stressed in meetings hosted by the Hague Conference on Private International Law. For example, it is stated that the Project would provide greater predictability and legal certainty in international litigation and reduce the time, cost, and complexity of international litigation.[11] If successful, the Project would greatly contribute to existing mechanisms for the settlement of international disputes in the field of civil and commercial affairs. Thus it should be continued with clear support.[12] From 1 to 9 June 2016, the Hague Conference held a special committee meeting to commence intergovernmental negotiations on the draft Convention on the Recognition and Implementation of Foreign Judgments. The 15 core articles of the draft convention were discussed and negotiated individually by 125 government representatives from 48 countries. Once adopted and implemented, the Convention will become the most important

[8] YP Xiao, 'The pros and cons of ratifying the Convention on Choice of Court Agreements and China's countermeasures' (2017) 5 *International Law Review of Wuhan University* 16.

[9] Among the many factors that affect the parties' choice of jurisdiction court, the decisive role is still the parties' bargaining power and the application of experience and skills in specific transactions.

[10] Draft of 2016, the February draft of 2017, the November draft of 2017 and the draft of 2018 respectively. Also see: HCCH, 'HCCH Special appointed' (*HCCH*) www.hcch.net/en/projects/legislative-projects/judgments/special-commission1 accessed 7 Feb 2019.

[11] HCCH, 'Conclusions and Recommendations Conference on International Litigation in the Asia Pacific Region, Wuhan, People's Republic of China' (*HCCH*, 24 Sept 2013) 11 www.hcch.net/en/projects/legislative-projects/judgments/judgments-news-wuhan accessed 7 Feb 2019.

[12] HCCH, 'Conclusions and Recommendations Conference on Cross-Border Recognition and Enforcement of Judgments, St. Petersburg, Russian Federation' (HCCH, 17 June 2014) 10 www.hcch.net/en/news-events/details/?varevent=367 accessed 7 Feb 2019.

international legal document to establish the global circulation of domestic court judgments. China sent a government delegation to participate in the negotiations, including judges from the Supreme People's Court, experts from the Department of Treaty and Law within the Ministry of Foreign Affairs, and law professors.[13] There currently is no international unified legal system regulating the global circulation of domestic court judgments in the world, which impedes global circulation of these judgments. This limits the effectiveness of domestic court judgments and hinders justice for parties in international litigation. It also restricts the positive role played by domestic justice in promoting international civil and commercial activities.

On 2 July 2019, the twenty second Diplomatic Conference of the Hague Conference on Private International Law adopted the Convention on the Recognition and Enforcement of Foreign Judgments in the Field of Civil and Commercial Affairs. The cross-border flow of judgments will ensure that judgments of courts in one country can be recognised and enforced in other countries, eliminating the divergence of the domestic rules governing the recognition and enforcement of foreign judgments between states. Through the platform provided by the Hague Conference, states have shown strong willingness to create a new international judicial system to facilitate the global circulation foreign civil and commercial judgments, and their recognition and enforcement. The experience of international legislation in this field has been rich enough that, through further negotiations approached flexibly, states may solve remaining problems and reach comprehensive consensus. Hence, the future for the international recognition and enforcement of foreign civil and commercial judgments is bright.[14]

[13] GJ Xu, 'Establishing an international legal system for the global circulation of court judgments – information, views and comments on the Draft Hague Convention on the Recognition and Enforcement of Foreign Judgments' (2017) 5 *International Law Review* 100.

[14] GJ Xu, 'Comment on Key Issues Concerning Hague Judgment Convention in 2019' (2020) 2 *Journal of Shanghai University of Political Science and Law* (The Rule of Law Forum) 39.

GLOSSARY

被请求保护地法 (Beiqingqiubaohudifa)	Lex loci protectionis
跛脚婚姻 (Bojiaohunyin)	Limping marriage
不方便法院 (Bufangbianfayuan)	Forum non conveniens
长臂管辖权 (Changbiguanxiaquan)	Long-arm jurisdiction
冲突法 (Chongtufa)	Conflict law
冲突规范 (Chongtuguifan)	Conflict rules
当事人合意选择的法律 (Dangshirenheyixuanzedefalü)	Lex voluntatis
当事人意思自治原则 (Dangshirenyisizizhiyuanze)	The principle of party autonomy
单一经济实体原则 (Danyijingjishitiyuanze)	Single economic entity doctrine
法律规避 (Falüguibi)	Evasion of law
法律确信 (Falüquexin)	Opinio juris
法律行为地说 (Falüxingweidishuo)	Locus regit actum doctrine
反致 (Fanzhi)	Renvoi
法院地法 (Fayuandifa)	Lex fori
分割法 (Fengefa)	Dépeçage
公共秩序保留 (Gonggongzhixubaoliu)	The preservation of public order
共同体领域 (Gongtongtilingyu)	Community's territory
管辖豁免 (Guanxiahuomian)	Jurisdictional immunity
管辖权选择规则 (Guanxiaquanxuanzeguize)	Jurisdiction-selection rule
国际惯例 (Guojiguanli)	International practice
国际礼让 (Guojilirang)	International comity
国际商事法庭 (Guojishangshifating)	International commercial court
国际商事仲裁 (Guojishangshizhongcai)	International commercial arbitration
国际私法 (Guojisifa)	Private international law

国际条约 (Guojitiaoyue)	International treaty
国际习惯 (Guojixiguan)	International custom
互惠原则 (Huhuiyuanze)	The reciprocal principle
级别管辖 (Jibieguanxia)	Hierarchical jurisdiction
间接管辖规则 (Jianjieguanxiaguize)	Indirect jurisdiction rule
经常居住地 (Jingchangjuzhudi)	Habitual residence
绝对主权豁免原则 (Jueduizhuquanhuomianyuanze)	Doctrine of absolute sovereign immunity
卡特尔协议 (Kateerxieyi)	Cartel agreement
跨境破产 (Kuajingpochan)	Cross-border insolvency
连结点 (Lianjiedian)	Point of contact
领事婚姻 (Lingshihunyin)	Consular marriage
临时措施 (Linshicuoshi)	Interim measures
履行地原则 (Lüxingdiyuanze)	Implementation doctrine
平等者之间无管辖权 (Pingdengzhezhijianwuguanxiaquan)	Par in parem imperium non habet
强制性规则 (Qiangzhixingguize)	Mandatory provision
侵权行为地法 (Qinquanxingweidifa)	Lex loci delicti
区际司法协助 (Qujisifaxiezhu)	Interregional judicial assistance
涉外保险法律关系 (Shewaibaoxianfalüguanxi)	Foreign-related insurance legal relationship
涉外财产关系 (Shewaicaichanguanxi)	Foreign-related property relationship
涉外公司法律关系 (Shewaigongsifalüguanxi)	Foreign-related company legal relationship
涉外海事法律关系 (Shewaihaishifalüguanxi)	Foreign-related maritime legal relationship
涉外婚姻家庭关系 (Shewaihunyinjiatingguanxi)	Foreign-related marriage and family relationship
涉外继承关系 (Shewaijichengguanxi)	Foreign-related inheritance relationship
涉外民事纠纷 (Shewaiminshijiufen)	Foreign-related civil dispute
涉外破产法律关系 (Shewaipochanfalüguanxi)	Foreign-related bankruptcy legal relationship
涉外债权债务关系 (Shewaizhaiquanzhaiwuguanxi)	Foreign-related debt relationship
涉外知识产权关系 (Shewaizhishichanquanguanxi)	Foreign-related intellectual property relationship

识别 (Shibie)	Classification
实体法 (Shitifa)	Substantive law
双重可诉规则 (Shuangchongkesuguize)	The rule of double actionability
属地管辖 (Shudiguanxia)	Territorial jurisdiction
属人法 (Shurenfa)	Lex persona
属人管辖 (Shurenguanxia)	Personal jurisdiction
司法判例 (Sifapanli)	Judicial precedent
司法外文书 (Sifawaiwenshu)	Extrajudicial documents
诉讼标的管辖权 (Susongbiaodiguanxiaquan)	Subject-matter jurisdiction
特殊地域管辖 (Teshudiyuguanxia)	Special territorial jurisdiction
特征性履行原则 (Tezhengxinglüxingyuanze)	The principle of characteristic performance
外国法的查明 (Waiguofadechaming)	Ascertainment of foreign law
外国判决的承认与执行 (Waiguopanjuedechengrenyuzhixing)	Recognition and enforcement of foreign judgments
无国籍人 (Wuguojiren)	Stateless person
物之所在地法 (Wuzhisuozaidifa)	Lex situs
先决问题 (Xianjuewenti)	Preliminary question
效果原则 (Xiaoguoyuanze)	The effects doctrine
协议管辖 (Xieyiguanxia)	Agreed jurisdiction
行为地法 (Xingweidifa)	Lex actus
选择法院 (Xuanzefayuan) forum shopping	Forum shopping
异地未决的诉讼 (Yidiweijuedesusong)	Lis alibi pendens
有限豁免原则 (Youxianhuomianyuanze)	The principle of restrictive immunity
域外送达 (Yuwaisongda)	Service abroad
征收 (Zhengshou)	Expropriation
指定管辖 (Zhidingguanxia)	Prescribed jurisdiction
直接反致 (Zhijiefanzhi)	Remission
仲裁协议 (Zhongcaixieyi)	Arbitration agreement
专属管辖 (Zhuanshuguanxia)	Exclusive jurisdiction
转致 (Zhuanzhi)	Transmission
准据法 (Zhunjufa)	Lex causae
主权豁免 (Zhuquanhuomian)	Sovereign immunity

住所地法 (Zhusuodifa)	Lex domicilii
住所地法 (Zhusuodifa)	Lex patriae
主要问题 (Zhuyaowenti)	The main issue
自裁规则 (Zicaiguize)	The competence-competence rule
最密切联系原则 (Zuimiqielianxiyuanze)	The principle of closest relationship

BIBLIOGRAPHY

Web-Based Resources

'History of the ICSID Convention' II (2) 360.
'On the Judgments Project'.
'The List of Contracting States and Other Signatories of the Convention' (ICSID/3) (ICSID, 2020).
'The ministry of foreign affairs of the People's Republic of China: judicial assistance treaty to schedule' (Ministry of foreign affairs).
'The Model Law of Private International Law of China' (China Society of Private International Law, 29th April 2014) arts 76–8, 90.
'The Protection of Intellectual Property Rights in Insolvency Proceedings INSOL International – Special Report (November 2017)', presented by Richard Chesley, Oksana Rosaluk, and Joe Riches.
'The Supreme People's Court Invited Foreign Diplomats to Attend Its Court Trial for the First Time: A Case of Appeal Concerning Capital Contribution by Foreign Shareholder was instantly adjudged in the Court (12 June 2014).
'What is Copyright?' (World Intellectual Property Organization).
Asian Infrastructure Investment Bank (AIIB), 'Introduction' (AIIB Portal).
Bonomi A, 'Preliminary Draft Protocol on the Law Applicable to Maintenance Obligations Explanatory Report' (Hague Conference on Private International Law, 33 August 2007).
Chief Judge GX Liu, 'Keynote Address' (2015 Annual Meeting of Chinese Society of Private International Law, 14 November 2015).
China Society of Private International Law, Model Law of Private International Law of the People's Republic of China (Beijing, Law Press, 2000).
China Society of Private Law, 'Model Law on International Private Law (sixth draft)' (China Society of Private Law, 2000).
Chinese Society of Private International Law (CSPIL), art 26.
Eastday, 'The Civil Affairs Bureau's Refusal to Register a Gay Marriage' (Eastday, 13 April 2016).
Guan J, 'Statement by Mr Guan Jian (representative of China) on the Report of the United Nations Commission on International Trade Law on the Work of its Thirty-sixth session' (Sixth Committee of the 58th session of the General Assembly, 6 October 2003).
Han L, '"China's Voice" in the United Nations Commission on International Trade Law' China News Network (Chong qing, 29 March 2016).
HCCH, 'Conclusions and Recommendations Conference on Cross-Border Recognition and Enforcement of Judgments, St. Petersburg, Russian Federation' (HCCH, 17 June 2014) para 10.
HCCH, 'Conclusions and Recommendations Conference on Cross-Border Recognition and Enforcement of Judgments, St. Petersburg, Russian Federation' (HCCH, 17 June 2014) para 10.
HCCH, 'Conclusions and Recommendations Conference on International Litigation in the Asia Pacific Region, Wuhan, People's Republic of China' (HCCH, 24 Sept 2013) para 11 www.hcch.net/en/projects/legislative-projects/judgments/judgments-news-wuhan.
HCCH, 'Conclusions and Recommendations Conference on International Litigation in the Asia Pacific Region, Wuhan, People's Republic of China' (HCCH, 24 Sept 2013) para 11.
HCCH, 'HCCH Members and Parties: Other Connected Parties'.
HCCH, 'Overview of the Judgments Project' (HCCH).
HCCH, 'Protocol of 23 November 2007 on the Law Applicable to Maintenance Obligations Status Table' (HCCH, 9 Dec. 2019).
HCCH: Convention of 1 February 1971 on the Recognition and Enforcement of Foreign Judgments in Civil and Commercial Matters.
HCCH: Convention of 1 February 1971 on the Recognition and Enforcement of Foreign Judgments in Civil and Commercial Matters.

HCCH: Convention of 15 November 1965 on the Service Abroad of Judicial and Extrajudicial Documents in Civil or Commercial Matters.
HCCH: Convention of 18 March 1970 on the Taking of Evidence Abroad in Civil or Commercial Matters.
HCCH: Convention of 2 July 2019 on the Recognition and Enforcement of Foreign Judgments in Civil or Commercial Matters.
HCCH: Draft Convention on the recognition and enforcement of foreign judgments in civil or commercial matters prepared by the Special Commission on the Judgments Project of May 2018, Art 5.
HCCH: Draft Convention on the recognition and enforcement of foreign judgments in civil or commercial matters prepared by the Special Commission on the Judgments Project of May 2018, Art 7.
HCCH: Overview of the Judgments Project.
ICSID Secretariat, '2020 Annual Report: Excellence in Investment Dispute Resolution'.
ICSID, '2019 ICSID Annual Report: Excellence in Investment Dispute Resolution'.
ICSID, 'About ICSID'.
ICSID, 'Database of ICSID Member States'.
ICSID, 'History of the ICSID Convention, Documents Concerning the Origin and the Formulation of the Convention on the Settlement of Investment Disputes Between States and Nationals of Other States' 900 https://icsid.worldbank.org/apps/ICSIDWEB/resources/Documents/History%20of%C20ICSID%C20Convention%20-%20VOLUME%20II-1.pdf.
Illustration: One Belt and One Road Initiative Six-year Report Card (Belt and Road Portal, 9 September 2019).
International Commercial Court, 'Introduction' (China International Commercial Court, 28 June 2018).
International Commercial Court, 'The Supreme Court of International Commercial Court has accepted a number of international commercial disputes' (China International Commercial Court, 29 December 2018) cicc.court.gov.cn/html/1/218/149/192/1150.html.
International Institute for the Unification of Private Law (UNIDROIT), 'History and Overview'.
Media headquarters of the people's court: the mainland and Hong Kong today signed a mutual recognition and enforcement of civil and commercial cases judgment arrangement: Yang Wanming, Teresa Cheng represent both signed (Supreme People's Court, 18 January 2019) www.court.gov.cn/zixun-xiangqing-139481.html.
National Information Centre, 'What is the "Belt and Road"?' (Belt and Road Portal).
Official Website of the Ministry of Foreign Affairs of the People's Republic of China.
Pertegas M, 'HCCH in the Internet Era, Conference on Jurisdiction & Dispute Resolution in the Internet Era: Governance and Good Practice, Geneva, Switzerland' (HCCH, 18 June 2015).
SHIPA, 'Arbitration Court of "Belt and Road" (China) has been founded" (China Council for the Promotion of International Trade, 8 November 2016).
Status: United Nations Convention on International Settlement Agreements Resulting from Mediation (Texts and Status International Commercial Mediation).
The Hague Conference on Private International Law (HCCH), 'HCCH Members and Parties: HCCH Members'.
The International Commercial Court, 'Introduction to the International Commercial Court', (The International Commercial Court, 28 June 2018).
The memorandum of guidance between the Supreme Court of the People's Republic of China and the Supreme Court of the Republic of Singapore on the recognition and enforcement of monetary judgments in commercial cases 2018 (SG).
The Ministry of Commerce of the People's Republic of China, 'The Construction of Commercial Rule of Law is Improving Day by Day' (Ministry of Commerce, 20 October 2017).
Typical cases of the first batch of the Supreme People's Court of China providing judicial services and security for the construction of "One Belt And One Road" (Supreme People's Court, Case 8).
UNCITRAL, 'International Commercial Arbitration'.
UNCITRAL, 'UNCITRAL Publications'.
Video recording of the hearing of TETG from 1:16:01–1:16:39.
Xi JP, 'Keynote speech by Jinping Xi at the opening ceremony of the 2018 China-Africa cooperation forum summit in Beijing (full text)' (Xinhua News Agency, 3 September 2018).
Xi JP, 'Open up a new starting point for cooperation and seek new impetus for development' (Xinhua News Agency, 15 May 2017).
Xinhua News, 'The British Consul General in Shanghai has married her Chinese Boyfriend'.
Xue L and Li Y, 'Lun zhong guo she wai zhi shi chan quan an jian guan xia quan de xian zhuang ji wan shan' [On the jurisdiction of China's Foreign-related Intellectual Property cases: Current State and Improvements] (Zhengzhou Intermediate People's Court Blog, 10th July 2012) http://zzfy.hncourt.gov.cn/public/detail.php?id=19458.
Yang YY, 'Statement by Ms Yang Yuya (representative of China) on the Report of the United Nations Commission on International Trade Law on the Work of its Forty-third session' (Sixth Committee of the 65th session of the General Assembly, 11 October 2010).

Zhao CH and An B, 'Xi Jinping attended the symposium on the 5th anniversary of the promotion of the "Belt and Road" programme and delivered an important speech'(Xinhua News Agency, 27 August 2018).

Zhong L, 'She wai zhi chan qin quan su song zhong de guan xia quan he fa lu shi yong' [Foreign-related Intellectual Property Litigation: Jurisdiction and Legal Applicability] (Ren Min Fa Yuan Bao, 31 December 2009).

Books

Bao D, 'The Misunderstanding of Extraterritoriality' in Jian W, *Western Law and Eastern Law and the Modern Reform of Chinese Law* (China University of Political Science and Law Press, 2001) 281–284.

Berger KP, *International Economic Arbitration* (Kluwer Law and Taxation Publishers 1993) 816–817.

Binder P, *International Commercial Arbitration and Mediation in UNCITRAL Model Law Jurisdictions* 4th edn (Kluwer Law International, 2019) 253–254, 257–258.

Blackaby N, Partasides C, et al., *Redfern and Hunter on International Arbitration* 5th edn (OUP, 2009) 203, 233.

Born GB, *International Arbitration and Forum Selection Agreements: Drafting and Enforcing* 3rd edn (Kluwer Law & Business, 2010) 79–80.

Chen WZ, *Bijiao Guoji Sifa* [*Comparative Private International Law*] (Law Press 2012) 6, 69.

Chen ZD, *International Commercial Arbitration* (Law Press 1998) 206.

Cheshire and North, *Private International Law* 11th edn (Butterworth 1987), 700–705.

China Institute of Applied Jurisprudence, *Ren Min Fa Yuan An Li Xuan* [*Selected Cases of the People's Court*] (People's Court Press, 2001).

Chinese Society of Private International Law, 'Model Law of Private International Law of the People's Republic of China', in Sarczvic P and Volken P (eds), *Yearbook of Private International Law* (vol 3, Sellier de Gruyter, 2001) 349.

Collins L, *Dicey & Morris on the Conflict of Laws* 15th edn (Sweet & Maxwell, 2012), Rule 156 (2).

Cuniberti G, *Conflict of Laws: A Comparative Approach* (Edward Elgar, 2017) 443–444.

Dicey AV, Morris JHC, Collins LA, and Briggs A, *Dicey, Morris and Collins on the Conflict of Laws* 15th edn (Sweet & Maxwell, 2012) 2025.

Ding LH, *Civil Execution Procedure Treatise* (China Democratic Legal System Press, 2019) 668.

Ding W, *Zhong Guo Guo Ji Si Fa He Xie Fa Zhan Yan Jiu* [*A study on the harmonious Development of Private International Law in China*] (Shanghai Academy of Social Sciences Press, 2009).

Du T, *Comments on the Act of the People's Republic of China of Application of Law to Foreign Relations* (China Legal Publishing House, 2011) 273–4, 373.

——, *Guo Ji Si Fa Yuan Li* [*Principles of Private International Law*] (Fudan University Press 2018) 3–4, 12, 21, 27–29, 157, 165, 171, 175, 315 339.

European Max Planck Group on Conflict of Laws and intellectual Property, Conflict of laws in intellectual property: the CLIP principles and commentary 1st edn (OUP, 2013).

Finch V, *Corporate Insolvency Law: Perspectives and Principles* (Cambridge University Press 2012) 21.

Fletcher I, *Insolvency in Private International Law* 2nd edn (OUP 2005) 88, 201.

——, *Insolvency in Private International Law* 3rd edn (OUP, 2007) 87, 89, 100.

Gaillard E, *Legal Theory of International Arbitration* (Martinus Nijhoff Publishers, 2010) 21.

Gao LZ, *Fu Yang Zhi Du Yan Jiu* [*Research on the Maintenance System*] (Law Press, 2006) 1.

General Principle of the Civil Law of the People's Republic of China, promulgated on 16 April 1986 (1986 GPCL); trans in Hay P, Weintraub RJ and Borchers PJ, *Comparative Conflict of Laws: Conventions, Regulations and Codes* 1st edn (Foundation Press, 2009) 316–7.

Gerber D, *Global Competition: Law, Markets, and Globalization* 1st edn (OUP 2010) 225–226, 233.

Han DP and Xiao YP, *Private International Law* 3rd edn (Higher Education Press, 2014) 20, 34, 53, 120.

——, *Private International Law* 1st edn (People's Court Press & China Social Science Press, 2004) 34.

——, *Private International Law* 2nd edn (Higher Education Press, 2007).

Han DP, *Guoji Sifa* [*Private International Law*] (Higher Education Press & Peking University Press, 2014) 53.

——, *Guoji Sifa Xinlun*, [*New Theory of Private International Law*] (Wuhan University Press, 1997) 617.

Han J, *Theory and Practice of Modern International Commercial Arbitration* 2nd edn (China Law Press, 2000) 91.

Hay P, *Advanced Introduction to Private International Law and Procedure* (Edward Elgar Publishing, 2018) 113.

Hay P, Borchers PJ and Symeonides SC, *Conflict of Laws* 6th edn (West Academic Publishing, 2018) 785–8.

Hay P, Weintraub RJ and Borchers PJ, *Comparative Conflict of Laws: Conventions, Regulations and Codes* 1st edn (Foundation Press, 2009) 316–7, 355.

He QS, *Guo Ji Si Fa Ru Men Bi Ji* [*Private International Law in a Nutshell*] (Law Press, 2019) 204, 221.

——, *International Civil Litigation in Comparative Perspective* (Higher Education Press, 2015) 128–30.

——, *Research on the Service Abroad* (Peking University Press, 2006) 199.

Huang J and Jiang RJ, *Act of the People's Republic of China of Application of Law to Foreign Civil Relations: Interpretations and Analysis* (Law Press, 2011) 21, 123–32, 230, 235.

Huang J, *Discussion on Interregional Legal Issues in China* (China University of Political Science and Law Press, 2012) 4, 125.

——, *Private International Law* (Legal Publishing House, 1999) 918.

——, *Zhonghua Renmin Gongheguo Shewai Minshi Guanxi Falv Shiyong Fa Jianyigao Ji Shuoming* [*Draft and Explanation of the law of the People's Republic of China on the Application of Law in Foreign-related Civil relations*] (Renmin University of China Press, 2011) 15, 21, 81, 136.

Huang J, *Private International Law* (Beijing, Law Press, 1999) 163.

Jiang BX, *Understanding and Application of Enforcement Provisions* (China Legal Publishing House, 2018) 358–360.

Jones A, Sufrin B, Dunne N, *EU Competition Law: Text, Cases and Materials* 7th edn (OPU, 2019) 1023, 1025, 1191, 1197.

Juenger FK, *Choice of Law and Multistate Justice* (New York, Special edn, Transnational Publishers 2005) 58.

Kurkela MS, Turunen S, and Conflict Management Institute (COMI), *Due Process in International Commercial Arbitration* (OUP, 2010) 156.

Li HP, *Collected Law Works of Li Haopei* (Law Press, 2006) 463.

——, *Selected Works of Li Haopei* (Beijing, Law Press, 2000), 45–46.

Li K, *Research on the Application of Contemporary International Commercial Arbitral Law* (Intellectual Property Publishing House Co Ltd, 2013) 121.

Li ShY, *China's General Theory of Private International Law* (Law Press, 2006) 82–83.

Li SY and Ou FY, *Guo Ji Si Fa* [*Private International Law*] (Peking University Press, 2018) 169, 174–175.

Li SY, *A New Theory of Law and Practice on International Economy and Trade* (Hunan University Press, 1996) 396.

——, *Private International* Law 3rd edn (Beijing University Publishing House, 2011) 315.

Li SY, Xie SS, *Introduction to International Civil Procedure Law* (Wuhan daxue chubanshe, 2001).

Liang HX and Chen HB, Wuquan Fa [*Property Law*] (Law Press China, 2005) 20, 38.

Liu XH and Yuan FQ, *Cases of International Commercial Arbitration* (Beijing University Press, 2017).

Liu XH, *Theoretical and Practical Legal Aspects of International Commercial Arbitration Agreements* (The Commercial Press, 2005).

LoPucki LM, *Courting Failure* (University of Michigan Press, 2005) 221–226, 232.

Lu J, *Guoji Sifa zhi Lilun Yu Shijian* [*Theory and practice of private international law*] (Zhongguo Zhengfa daxue chubanshe, 2004).

Luo GZ, *Romance of the Three Kingdoms*, ch 1.

Lv YF, *Guoji Touzi Fa* [*International Investment Law*] (Higher Education Press, 2005).

Ma HB, *Private International Law: General Part and Special Parts* 3rd edn (Ma Hanbao, 2014) 377.

Ma Y, *Explanation of the Opinions on the Application of the Civil Procedure Law* (China Procuratorate Publishing House, 1994) 217.

Mclachlan C, Shore L and Weiniger M, *International Investment Arbitration: Substantive Principles* 2nd edn (OUP, 2017) 197.

Mills A, The Confluence of Public and Private International Law: Justice, Pluralism and Subsidiarity in the International Constitutional Ordering of Private Law (Cambridge University Press 2009) 291.

Moses ML, *The Principles and Practice of International Commercial Arbitration* (Cambridge University Press, 2008) 17.

Peukert A, 'Territoriality, and Extraterritoriality in Intellectual Property Law' (2010) in Handl G, Zekoll J & Zumbansen P (eds), *Beyond Territoriality: Transnational Legal Authority in an Age of Globalization* (Queen Mary Studies in International Law, Brill Academic Publishing, 2012) 189–228.

Petrochilos G, *Procedural Law in International Arbitration* (OUP, 2004) 23.

Qi XQ, *Study on Recognition and Enforcement of Foreign Arbitral Awards* (China Law Press, 2010).

Redfern A and Hunter M, *Redfern and Hunter on International Arbitration* 5th edn (Oxford University Press, 2009) 197.

Reese WLM, 'Dépeçage: A Common Phenomenon in Choice of Law' (1973) 73 *Columbia Law Review* 58.

Reyes A, 'Introduction: Towards a System for the Recognition and Enforcement of Judgments' in Reyes A (ed), *Recognition and Enforcement of Judgment in Civil and Commercial Matters* (Hart Publishing, 2019) 19, 22.

——, *The Practice of International Commercial Arbitration: A Handbook for Hong Kong Arbitrators* (Informa Law from Routledge, 2018) 11–12.

Rubino-Sammartano M, *International Arbitration Law and Practice* 2nd edn (Kluwer Law International, 2001) 214, 371.

Sanders P, *International Arbitration: Liber amicorum for Martin Domke* (Martinus Nijhoff, 1967) 161.

Schlechtriem P and Butler P, *UN Law on International Sales: The UN Convention on the International Sale of Goods* (Springer, 2009) 18–19.

Sirafi, Abu Zayd Hasan ibn Yazid and Sulayman al-Tajir, *Ancient Accounts of India and China* (Printed for S Harding, 1733) 7–8.

Song H, *Recognition and Enforcement of Arbitral Awards in International Commercial Arbitration* (China Law Press, 2000) 248–249.

Stone P, *Stone on Private International Law in the European Union* 4th edn (Edward Elgar, 2018) 590–3.

Sun GH and Zhu JW, *Jurisprudence* 4th edn (China Renmin University Press, 2015) 63, 112.

Symeonides SC, *Codifying Choice of Law around the World: An International Comparative Analysis* (Oxford University Press 2014) 256–9, 101.

——, *'Private International Law at the End of the 20th Century: Progress or Regress?'* (Kluwer Law International, 2000) 60.

Tu G, *A Study on a Global Jurisdiction and Judgments Convention* (Sweet & Maxwell, 2009).

UNCITRAL *Model Law on Cross-Border Insolvency* (United Nations, New York 1997).

UNCITRAL *on Cross-Border Insolvency with Guide to Enactment and Interpretation* (United Nations 2013).

UNCTAD, *Dispute Settlement: International Commercial Arbitration*, 5.2 The Arbitration Agreement, (United Nations 2005) 40.

United Nations Commission on International Trade Law, *Legislative Guide on Insolvency Law* (United Nations 2005).

von Wilmowsky P, *'Choice of Law in International Insolvencies – A Proposal For Reform'*, in Jürgen Basedow J and Kono T (eds), *Legal Aspects of Globalisation: Conflict of Laws, Internet, Capital Markets and Insolvency in A Global Economy* (Kluwer Law International, 2000) 203.

Wang BS, *Guoji Sifa zhong di xianjuewenti yanjiu [Research on Preliminary Questions in Private International Law]* (Law Press, 2007).

Wan EX, *Interpretation and Application of the Provisions in the Act of Application of Law to Foreign Civil Relations* (China Legal Publishing House, 2011).

——, *Understanding and Application of Law of the People's Republic of China on Choice of Law for Foreign-related Civil Relationships* (China Legal Publishing House, 2011) 12.

Wang LM, *Wuquanfa Yanjiu [A Study of Property Law]* 3rd edn (Renmin University of China Press, 2013) 67.

Wang QX, *Employment Law* 3rd edn (Law Press, 2008) 208.

Wang ZX and Zheng X, *Autonomy and Intervene Research on the International Commercial Arbitration Consensus* (China Law Press, 2016).

Westbrook J, Booth C, Paulus C, and Rajak H, *A Global View of Business Insolvency Systems* (Martinus Nijhoff Publishers, 2010) 74–78.

Wolf M, HP and Tang ZS, *Guoji Sifa [Private International Law]* (Peking University Press, 2009) 282–283.

Wood PR, *Principles of International Insolvency* 2nd edn (Sweet & Maxwell, 2007).

Xiao YP, *Principle of Private International Law* (Beijing, Law Press China, 2003) 3, 184–5.

Xie SS, *Commercial Arbitration* (Higher Education Press, 2003) 69.

Xu DG, *Guo Ji Si Fa* (Mu Ke Ban) *[Private International Law (MOOC)]* (Peking University Press, 2016) 140.

Xu DG, *Guoji Sifa Qushi Lun [Trend of International Private Law]* (Peking University Press, 2005) 80, 161.

Xu JK, *Guoji Sifa Shang De Yisi Zizhi [Autonomy of Will in Private International Law]* (Law Press, China 2006) 216.

Xu P, *Chongtu Guifan Renyixing Shiyong Yanjiu [A Study on Facultative Application of Conflict Rules]* (Xiamen University Press, 2010).

Xu QK, *She Wai Min Shi Guan Xi Fa Lv Shi Yong Fa De Si Fa Jie Shi Wen Ti Yan Jiu [A study on the Implementation of Law of the People's Republic of China on Choice of Law for Foreign-related Civil Relationships]* (Fa Lv Chu Ban She, 2019).

Xu W, *Shewai Minshi Guanxi Falv Shiyong Fa Shishi Yanjiu [A study on the Implementation of 2010 Choice of Law Act]* (Law Press, 2019) 382.

Xu WG, *She Wai Min Shi Guan Xi Fa Lv Shi Yong Fa [A study on Law of the People's Republic of China on Choice of Law for Foreign-related Civil Relationships]* (Law Press, 2019).

Xu WG, *Shewai Minshi Guanxi Falv Shiyong Fa Shishi Yanjiu [A study on the Implementation of Law of the People's Republic of China on Choice of Law for Foreign-related Civil Relationships]* (Law Press, 2019).

Yang L, *A Study of Procedure of International Commercial Arbitration* (China Law Press, 2011) 104–105.

Yang LY and others, *Arbitration Law: From the UK Arbitration Act (1996) to International Commercial Arbitration* (Law Press, 2006) 95.

Yang SM, *International Commercial Arbitration* (Publishing House of Chongqing University, 2002) 164.

Yao MZ, *Textbook of Foreign Investment Enterprise Law* 2nd edn (Law Press, 1994) 32, 232–3.

Yu JS, *Guji Touzi Fa [International Investment Law]* 2nd edn (Law Press, 2003) 278.

——, *Guoji Jingji Fa Gailun [International Economic Law]* (Higher Education Press, 2019) 411, 412, 416.

Yu XF, *Judicial Supervision and Assistance in International Commercial Arbitration: on Legislation and Judicial Practice of China* (Intellectual Property Publishing House Co Ltd, 2006).

Yuan FQ, *Ren Quan Bao Hu Yu Xian Dai Jia Ting Guan Xi Zhong De Guo Ji Si Fa [Human Rights Protection and Private International Law in Modern Family Relations]* (Peking University Press, 2010) 81, 111, 158.

Yunguan G, 'Summary of the Evolution of Private International Law in China' (2015) 2 *Tsinghua Law Review* 3–4.

Zeng XY and Wang LM, *Guoji Sifa [International Law]* (China Renmin University Press, 2007).
Zhao J, *Research on Judicial Supervision over International Commercial Arbitration* (China Law Press, 2000) 15–18.
Zhao NN, *She Wai Hun Yin Jia Ting An Jian Lv Shi Shi Wu* [*Lawyers' Practice in Foreign-related Marriage and Family Cases*] (Law Press, 2015) 13–14, 183.
Zhao XL, *Private International Law* (China University of Political Science and Law Press, 2000) 366.
Zhao XW and Du HF, *Guo Ji Si Fa Xue Yuan Li Yu An Li Jiao Cheng* [*Principles and Case Studies of Private International Law*] (China Renmin University Press, 2016).
Zhu KP, *Application of Law in International Commercial Arbitration* (Law Press 1999) 177.

Journal Articles

Bai JF, 'Zhongguo Xiewai Falü Fazhan Kaolun' [On the Development of Foreign-Related Laws in China] [2006] *Master Thesis of China University of Political Science and Law* 8–10.
Bailey HR, 'An Assignment in Insolvency, and Its Effect upon Property and Persons out of the State' (1893) 7 *Harvard Law Review* 281, 282.
Baird J, 'A World Without Bankruptcy' (1987) 50 *Law & Contemporary Problems* 173.
Belohlávek AJ, 'Importance of the Seat of Arbitration in International Arbitration: Delocalization and Denationalization of Arbitration as an Outdated Myth', (2013) 31 *ASA Bulletin* 262–265.
Berends AJ, 'The UNCITRAL Model Law on Cross-Border Insolvency: A Comprehensive Overview' (1998) 6 *Tulane Journal of International and Comparative Law* 309.
Bogdan M, 'International Bankruptcy Law in Scandinavia' (1985) 34 *International and Comparative Law Quarterly* 49.
Broches A, 'Awards Rendered Pursuant to the ICSID Convention: Binding Force, Finality, Recognition, Enforcement, Execution' (1987) 2 *ICSID Review Foreign Investment Law Journal* 287, 299.
C Adeline, 'Recognition and Enforcement of Foreign Judgments in Asia' (2017) *Asia Business Law Institute* 67.
Casas M, 'Nationalities Of Convenience, Personal Jurisdiction, and Access To Investor-State Dispute Settlement' (2004) 49 *New York University Journal of International Law and Politics* 63, 106.
Chen A, 'Queries to the Recent ICSID Decision on Jurisdiction upon the Case of Tza Yap Shum v Republic of Peru: Should China-Peru BIT 1994 Be Applied to Hong Kong SAR under "One Country Two Systems"' (2009) 17(1) *The Journal of International Economic Law* 10.
Chen GJ 'Lun Yisi Zizhi Zai Dongchan Shiyong Zhong De Xianzhi' [On the limitation of the principle of Autonomy of Will in the application of the law of real right of chattel] (2017) 5 *Political Science and Law* 122, 122–131.
——, 'Lun Dui Waizi Guoyouhua De Buchang Biaozhun' [On the standard of compensation for nationalization of foreign capital] (2003) 4 *Journal of Graduate School of Chinese Academy of Social Sciences* 108.
Chen W and Shi T, 'Woguo Sheli Yichan Guanli Zhidu De Shehui Jichu Jiqi Zhudu Goujian' [The Social Foundation and Institutional Construction of China's Establishment of Heritage Management System] (2013) 7 *Hebei Law Science* 19.
Chen WZ, 'Shewai Minshi Guanxi Falü Shiyong Fazhan Shi Da Liang Dian' [Ten Highlights of the Application law for Foreign-related Civil Relations] [Nov 2, 2010] *Legal Daily*.
——, 'Shewai Minshi Guanxi Falv Shiyong Fa De Zhongguo Tese' [The Chinese Characteristics of Law on the Application of Law in Foreign-related Civil Relations] (2011) 11 *Legal Forum* 48, 48–52.
Chu BP, 'The present and future of the construction of "Belt and One Road" multi-dispute settlement centre' (2017) 6 *China Legal Science* 74.
Chun HS, 'Zhongguo Wuquan Chongtu Fa Tixi Zhi Chonggou' [Reconstruction of Real Right Conflict Law System in China] (2013) 4 *Journal of Henan University of Economics and Law* 53.
Dai L, 'Woguo Fanlongduan Fayu Wai Guanxia Zhidu Chutan' [Study on the extraterritorial enforcement of China's Anti-Monopoly Law] (2010) 5 *Jurist* 133.
Danov M, 'Global competition law framework: A private international law solution needed' (2016) 12 *Journal of Private International Law* 77.
Ding W, 'Analysis of the relationship between the law of the application of law for foreign-related civil relations and "other laws"' (2011) 29 *Tribune of Political Science and Law* 14.
Ding Y, 'Absolute, Restrictive, or Something More: Did Beijing Choose the Right Type of Sovereign Immunity for Hong Kong' (2012) 29 *Emory International Law Review* 997.
Dogauchi M and Hartley TC, Explanatory Report on the 2005 Hague Choice of Court Agreements Convention 61.
Dong T and Wang TX, 'Zheng Que Ren Shi Zhuan Li Quan Xiao li Ren Ding Zhong de Xin Zheng Si Fa Zhi Quan Er Fen Fa' (2019) 3 *Intellectual Property*.

Du HF, 'Chinese Style Selection, Approval and Application of Law of Natural Person's Personal And Habitual Residence' (2015) 3 *Jurist* 163.

——, 'Chinese-style Choice, Judgment, and Application of Natural Persons' Law and Current Residence – Comment on the Article 15 of Law of the People's Republic of China on Choice of Law for Foreign-related Civil Relationships' (2015) 3 *The Jurist* 152–163.

——, 'Lun Woguo Shewai Wuquan Falv Shiyong De Wanshan' [On the Improvement of The Application of The Law on Real Right in Foreign Affairs in China] (2013) 2 *Contemporary Law* 141, 143.

Du T, 'Legal Issues and Solutions of China's Ratification on Choice of Court Agreement Convention' (2016) 4 *Wuhan University Journal* (Social Science) 94.

——, 'Lun Wuquan Guoji Sifa Zhong Dangshiren Yisi Zizhi De XianDu – Jianping Shewai Minshi Guanxi Falv Shiyong Fa Di 37 Tiao' [On the Limits of Party Autonomy in International Real Right Law: Analysis of Article 37of the Law of the Application of Law for Foreign-related Civil Relations of the People's Republic of China] (2012) 5 *Journal of Shanghai University of Finance and Economics* 31–8.

——, 'Reciprocity Principle and Recognition and Enforcement of Foreign Judgments' (2007) 1 *Global Law Review* 117, 118.

——, 'The distinction between extraterritorial jurisdiction and extraterritorial application in international antitrust litigations: A comparative analysis of recent Chinese and American cases' (2019) 1 *Journal of International Economic Law* 74.

——, 'The presumption of reciprocity and promotion of "One Belt And One Road" litigation and dispute resolution' (2017) 2 *People's Court of Justice* 1.

Ehrenzweig IA, 'The Second Conflicts Restatement: A Last Appeal for Its Withdrawal' (1964–1965) 113 *University of Pennsylvania Law Review* 1230, 1241.

Feng S, 'Conflict and Coordination between Institutional Management Power and Parties Autonomy in International Commercial Arbitration' (2018) 33(5) 1.

——, 'Reflection and Choice of the Application of Amiable Arbitration in International Investment Arbitration' (2018) 6 *The South China Sea Law Journal* 94, 103.

——, 'The Difficulties and Solutions of Applying for Property Preservation during the Examination of Recognition and Enforcement of Foreign Arbitral Awards' (2018) 106 *Beijing Arbitration Quarterly* 18, 32–33.

Fletcher IF and Wessels B, 'Shaping Rules for Cooperation in International Corporate Insolvency Cases through Dialogue' (2010) 7 *European Company Law* 149.

Fletcher IF, 'Maintaining the Momentum: The Continuing Quest for Global Standards and Principles to Govern Cross-Border Insolvencies' (2007) 32 *Brooklyn Journal of International Law* 767.

Fu CY, 'Yichan Guanli Zhidu De Sheli Jichu He Tixi Kuangjia' [Foundation and Architecture of Estate Management System] (2012) 8 *Journal of Law* 31.

Fu Q, 'Wuquan Fading Santing' [Three Questions on real right law] (1999) 1 *Law and Social Development* 30–4.

Fu YZ, 'Chengren Yu Zhixing Waiguo Minshangshi Fayuan Panjue Shi De Gonggong Zhixu Shencha' [Review of Public Policy in Recognition and Enforcement of Judgments of Foreign Civil and Commercial Courts] (2015) *Western Law Review*,15.

Gao XL, 'Positive Practice of Chinese Courts on Recognition and Enforcement of Foreign Arbitral Awards' (2018) 5 *Journal of Law Application.*

Gong MM, 'Wuquan He Zhaiquan Xianghu Ronghe Zhi Qushi Fenxi' [The Analysis on the trend of the integration of real right and creditor's right] (2008) 6 *Knowledge Economy* 16–7.

Greene J, 'Bankruptcy Beyond Borders: Recognizing Foreign Proceedings in Cross-Border Insolvencies' (2005) 30 *Brooklyn Journal of International Law* 685, 704–05.

Gropper AL, 'The Curious Disappearance of Choice of Law as an Issue in Chapter 15 Cases' (2014) 9 *Brooklyn Journal of Corporate, Financial & Commercial Law* 152, 154.

Guo HY, 'Waiguo Fayuan Panjue Chengren Yu Zhixing Yanjiu' [Research on the Recognition and Enforcement of Foreign Court Judgments] (2011) *Ocean University of China* 20.

Guo YJ and Liu YY, 'On the case of FG Hemisphere Associates LLC v the Democratic Republic of the Congo and others' (2012) 2 *Law of the Times.*

Guo YJ and Xu JT, 'A Statistical Analysis of Judicial Practice on Foreign-Related Cases in Civil and Commercial Matters in China' (2008) 11 *Chinese Yearbook of Private International Law & Comparative Law* 122.

Guzman A, 'International Insolvency: In Defense of Universalism' (2000) 98 *Michigan Law Review* 2177.

Ha H-S, A Study on Enforcement of Arbitral Awards between China and Taiwan, (2009) 19 *J Arb Stud* 45, 47.

Han XL, 'Lun Shewai Budongchan Hetong De Falv Shiyong' [On the law application of foreign real estate contract] (2012) 3 *Cross-strait Legal Science* 103.

Harding SK, 'Re Sefel Geophysical LTD: A Canadian Approach to Some Specific Problems in the Adjudication of International Insolvencies' (1990) 12 *Dalhousie Law Journal* 412, 419.

He Q, 'A Study on the Application of Foreign Same-sex Marriage Law' (2012) 10 *Hebei Legal Science* 137.

He QJ, 'Lun Guoji Touzi De Guoyouhua Buchang Biaozhun Zhi Chonggou' [On the reconstruction of international investment nationalization compensation standard] (2010) 9 *Reformation & Strategy* 165–7.

He, DP, 'Difficulties and Solutions in the Application of Laws concerning Foreign-related Same-sex Unions in China' (2013) 12 *Fujian Forum* (Humanities and Social Sciences Edition) 198.

Herbert K, 'Most Significant Relationship, Governmental Interests, Cultural Identity, Integration: "Rules" at Will and the Case for Principles of Conflict of Laws' (2004) 9 *Uniform Law Review* 467, 475.

Hitsevich N, 'Intellectual property rights infringement on the internet: an analysis of private international law implications' (Unpublished Doctoral thesis, University of London 2015).

Horton D, 'Arbitration About Arbitration' (2018) 70 *Stanford* Law Review 363, 419.

Hua Q, 'Application of Marriage Real Estate Law from the Perspective of Gender, Learning and Practice' (2015) 10 *Learning and Practice* 83.

Huang J, 'Lun Guoji Sifa Shang De Wuquan Wenti' [On the real right in private international Law] (1995) 3 *Studies in Law and Business* 51.

——, 'Reciprocal Recognition and Enforcement of Foreign Judgments in China: Promising Developments, Prospective Challenges and Proposed Solutions' (2019) *Nordic Journal of International Law* 10.

——, 'Zhongguo Shewai Minshi Guanxi Falv Shiyongfa De Zhiding Yu Wanshan' [Enactment and improvement of the Law on the Law Applicable to Foreign-Related Civil Relationships] (2011) 5 *Tribune of Political Science and Law* 7.

Huang SX, 'Treaty Shopping in International Investment Arbitration' (2014) 1 *Law Science* 62.

Janger EJ, 'Silos: Establishing the Distributional Baseline in Cross-Border Bankruptcies' (2014) 9 *Brooklyn Journal of Corporate, Financial & Commercial Law* 180, 185.

——, 'Universal Proceduralism' (2007) 32 *Brooklyn Journal of International Law* 819, 834.

——, 'Virtual Territoriality' (2010) 48 *Columbia Journal of Transnational Law* 45, 401, 408–09, 429.

Ji JX, 'Homosexuality and same-sex marriage from the perspective of freedom' (2015) 3 *Journal of Law* 90.

Jiang XM, 'Application of foreign-related adoption law in China' (2005) 6 *Global Law Review* 738.

Jiang Y, 'Legislative Choice of Personal Relationship between Husband and Wife in Contemporary Civil Code' (2019) 16 *Law and Business Studies* 37.

Jin H, 'The Choice-of Law Principles for Torts' (1989) 3 *Anhui University Journal* 70, 74.

Li H and Wang WN, 'Defects in the Effectiveness of The Act of Marriage Establishment – and the Relevant Provisions on the Draft Marriage and Family Compilation in the Civil Code' (2019) 4 *Law Studies* 103–104.

Li J, 'China's New Labor Contract Law and Protection of Workers' (2008–2009) 32 *Fordham International Law Journal* 1083, 1121–2.

Li JZ, 'Lun Shewai Yizhu Falv Shiyong Zhidu De Fazhan Qushi – Jianlun Shewai Minshi Guanxi Shiyong Fa Di 32,33 Tiao De Jieshi Yu Wanshan' [The Development Trend of the Legal Application System of Foreign-related Wills – also on the Interpretation and Improvement of Article 32 and 33 of the Law of the People's Republic of China on Choice of Law for Foreign-related Civil Relationships] (2014) 1 *Legal Science* 184.

Li QH, 'Lun Wuquan De Zhaiquanhua Qushi' [Discussion on the Trend of Obligatory Rights of Real Right] (2006) 6 *Higher Education Forum* 55–7.

——, 'Lun Zhaiquan Wuquanhua Qushi' [The Analysis on The Trend of Creditor' s Rights Turning into Property Right] (2005) 7 *Contemporary Law Review* 69, 69–71.

Li SY, Zhou HB, Huang JH, 'Qutong Zhizhong Jian Chayi – Lun Jinyibu Fengfu Woguo Guoji Sifa Wuquan Falv Shiyong Wenti De Yanjiu Neirong'[Differences are seen in convergence – On Further Enriching the Research Content of the Application of the Real Right of Chinese Private International law] (2002)1 *China Legal Science* 137–149.

Li W, 'The Analysis on Jurisdiction of Transnational Civil Litigation: Evaluating the Provisions on Jurisdiction of Transnational Civil Litigation in Civil Procedure Law of P. R. China (Amended in 2012)' (2014) 1 *Chinese Review of International Law.*

Liao L, 'Research on the innovation of "Belt and One Road" dispute settlement mechanism – a perspective of international law and comparative law' (2018) 2 *Law Review* 172.

Lin Y, 'Research on Legitimation of Illegitimate Children Concerning Foreign Elements and Relative Law Applications' (2006) 11 *Law Science Magazine* 48.

Lin YP, 'Chongtu Guifan Zai Jingzhenfa Yuwai Shiyong Zhong De Zuoyong Ji Tedian' [Effects and features of applying conflicts of rules to the extraterritoriality of competition law] (2010) *10 Legal Science* 65.

Lipstein K, 'Characteristic Performance – A New Concept in the Conflict of Laws in Matters of Contract for the EEC' (1982) 3 *Northwestern Journal of International Law & Business* 402, 405.

Liu MM, 'Reconstruction of China's Cross-border Bankruptcy Jurisdiction Distribution System' (2016) *Daqing Social Science* 1.

Liu P, 'Study on Jurisdiction of Temporary Protection Measures in International Civil Litigation' (2009) 9 *Journal of Litigation Law* 489.

Liu RS, 'Woguo Pizhun Xuanze Fayuan Xieyi Gongyue De Wenti Yu Duice' [Issues and Solutions of China's Ratification on Choice of Court Agreement Convention] (2018) 4 *Chinese Journal of Law* 201.

Liu XH and Zhou Q, 'The Principle of Actual Connection in the System of Agreement Jurisdiction and the Principle of Inconvenient Court' (2012) 12 *Law Science*.

Liu XH, 'Examination and amendment of the system of mutual recognition and enforcement of arbitration awards on both sides of the Taiwan Strait' (2011) 361 *Legal Science* 86.

Liu Y, 'China Ping An v Belgium From the Perspective of Inter-temporal Law of the Application of Treaties' (2016) 4 *Global Law Review* 166.

Liu YN, Chen S and Yuan JG, [The Preliminary Question in Private International Law] (2007) 3 *Journal of Yanshan University* (Philosophy and Social Sciences Edition).

Long XY, 'Legal Application of Foreign Same Sex Marriage in China' (2012) 6 *Journal of Central South University* (Social Science edition) 102A.

LoPucki L, 'Cooperation in International Bankruptcy: 'A Post-Universalist Approach' (1999) 84 *Cornell Law Review* 696.

Lu SP and Sun XZ, 'Lun Wuquan Chongtu Fa De Xinfazhan: ZhenShiping Lu and Xiaozhen Sun, 'On New Development of Conflict of Law of Property Law: the Law of the Place of the Relevant Intermediary Applicable to Interest in Securities' (2012) 1 *Journal of Northwest University* (Philosophy and Social Sciences Edition) 94–8.

Luo F, 'Protection of the Interests of the Weak in the Law of the People's Republic of China on Choice of Law for Foreign-related Civil Relationships' (2019) 4 *Chinese Academy of Social Sciences Graduate Journal* 51–52.

Maniruzzaman AFM, 'International Commercial Arbitration: The Conflict of Laws Issues in Determining the Applicable Substantive Law in the Context of Investment Agreements' (1993) 40(2) *Netherlands International Law Review* 201–237.

Matulionyte R, 'Enforcing Copyright Infringements Online: In Search of Balanced Private International Law Rules' (2015) 6 *Journal of Intellectual Property, Information Technology and Electronic Commerce Law* 132.

McCormack G and Hargovan A, 'Australia and the International Insolvency Paradigm' (2015) 37 *Sydney Law Review* 389, 402.

Mooney, Jr. CW, 'A Normative Theory of Bankruptcy Law: Bankruptcy As (Is) Civil Procedure' (2004) 61 *Washington & Lee Law Review* 931.

Omar P, 'The Universe of Insolvency Cooperation and the Primeo Directive' (2015) 12 *International Corporate Rescue* 32, 32.

Pan D, 'The Status of Foreign-related Gay marriage in Chinese Law' (2012) 1 *Yunnan University Law Journal* (2012) 192.

Pien J, 'Creditor Rights and Enforcement of International Commercial Arbitral Awards in China' (2007) 45 *Columbia Journal of Transnational Law* 586, 589.

Pottow J, 'Beyond Carve-outs and Toward Reliance: A Normative Framework for Cross-Border Insolvency Choice of Law' (2014) 9 *Brooklyn Journal of Corporate, Financial, and Commercial Law* 197.

——, 'Greed and Pride in International Bankruptcy: The Problems of and Proposed Solutions to 'Local Interests'' (2006) 8 *Michigan Law Review* 1899, 1902.

——, 'The Myth (and Realities) of Forum Shopping in Transnational Insolvency' (2007) 32 *Brooklyn Journal of International Law* 785.

Qiao XB, 'Applicable Laws of Foreign-related Divorce: Tradition, Reform and Development – a Concurrent Review of relevant provisions of Law of the People's Republic of China on Choice of Law for Foreign-related Civil Relationships' (2013) 6 *Jianghan Academics* 46.

Qin HM, 'Development, Problems and Suggestions for the Improvement of China's guardianship System' (2020) 3 *Journal of Zhejiang University of Science and Technology* (Social Science edition) 314.

——, 'Lun Waiguo Chengfaxing Sunhai Peichang Panjue De Bufen Chengren Yu Zhixing' [Partial recognition and enforcement of foreign punitive damage] (2017) 3 *Jiangxi Social Sciences* 162.

Ramesh K, 'The Gibbs Principle: A Tether on the Feet of Good Forum Shopping' (2017) 29 *Singapore Academy of Law Journal* 42.

Reese WLM, 'Choice of Law: Rules or Approach' (1972) 57 *Cornell Law Review* 319.

Report of the Executive Directors on the ICSID Convention 1 ICSID Reports 28, para 26.

Riesenfeld SA, 'The Status of Foreign Administrators of Insolvent Estates: A Comparative Survey' (1976) 24 *American Journal of Comparative Law* 288.

Schreuer C, 'Commentary on the ICSID Convention' (1996) 11 *ICSID Review Foreign Investment Law Journal* 318.

Shen HY, 'Waiguo Minshangshi Panjue Chengren He Zhixing Ruogan Yinan Wenti Yanjiu' [The research on several issues regarding the recognition and enforcement of foreign judgments on civil and commercial matters] (2018) 5 *Journal of Law Application* 10.

Shen J, 'Zailun Haiya Minshangshi Guanxiaquan He Waiguo De Panjue Chengren Yu Zhixing Gongyue Caoan Ji Zhongguo De Kaoliang' [Further Discussion on the Drafts of the Hague Convention on Jurisdiction and Recognition and Enforcement of Foreign Judgments in Civil and Commercial Matters and Considerations from Chinese Perspective] (2016) 6 *Study of International Law* 98.

Shi XB, 'Statement by Mr Shi Xiaobing (representative of China) on the Report of the United Nations Commission on International Trade Law on the Work of its Forty-eighth session' (Sixth Committee of the 70th session of the General Assembly, 19 October 2015).

Shi XL and Qi H, 'International Investment Law' [2009] *China University of Political Science and Law Publishing House* 280.

Simoes FD, 'Recognition and Enforcement of Foreign Arbitral Awards in Macao' (2014) 44 *Hong Kong Law Journal* 563, 579–581.

Song X, 'Tongyizhi Yu Qubiezhi De Duili Ji Jieshi' [Opposition and Interpretation between the Unitary system and the Scission System] (2011) 6 *China Law* 155.

Spiro E, 'Forum Regit Processum (Procedure Is Governed by the Lex Fori)' (1969) 18 *The International and Comparative Law Quarterly* 949.

Tan QP and Feng LK, 'Yichan Chuli Zhidu De Fansi Yu Chonggou' [Reflections and Reconstruction of The Estate Handling System] (2013) 4 *The Jurist* 124.

Tao LF and Gao YF, 'Reconstruction of the Exclusive Jurisdiction Clause over the Three Types of Contract Disputes Involving Foreign Element in China' (2013) 4 *International Business Research*.

Tian HY, 'Dashuju Shiye Xia Shewai Minshi Falv Guanxi Shiyong Fa Shishi Zhong Cunzai De Wenti Ji Jiejue Cuoshi' [Problems and Solutions in the Implementation of the Law Applicable to Foreign-related Civil Relations Law – From the Perspective of Big Data] (2018) 3 *Social Science Journal* 92–101.

Tu GJ and Li XL, 'The Chinese Approach Toward Cross-Border Bankruptcy Proceedings: One Progressive Step Ahead' (2015) 24 *INSOL International Insolvency Review* 57, 63–64.

——, 'The Second Amendment to PRC Civil Procedure Law: An International Civil Litigation Perspective' (2013) 43 *Hong Kong Law Journal* 633, 639–42.

Tung F, 'Fear of Commitment in International Bankruptcy' (2001) 33 *The George Washington International Law Review* 555, 559.

van den Berg AJ, 'Some Recent Problems in the Practice of Enforcement under the New York and ICSID Conventions' (1987) 2 *ICSID Review Foreign Investment Law Journal* 439, 441.

Vial G, 'Influence of the Arbitral Seat in the Outcome of an International Commercial Arbitration' (2017) 50(2) *The International Lawyer* 334–335.

Wan EX and Xia XH, Reasons for the Refusals of the Recognition and Enforcement of Foreign Arbitral Awards in Chinese Courts – New York Convention Case Studies (2010) 2 *International Law Review of Wuhan University*.

Wang GG, 'Study on the Dispute Settlement Mechanism of "Belt and Road"' (2017) 6 *China Legal Science* 68.

Wang GX and Zhou C, 'Liang an min shi pan jue de ren ke yu zhi hang wen ti yan jiu' [Research on the Recognition and Enforcement of Civil Judgments on Both Sides of the Strait] (2010) 3 *Law Research*.

Wang JL, 'Discussion on the Application of Law in Foreign-related Marriage and Family Relations' (2010) 4 *Modern Law* 165.

Wang L, On the Reference and Application of Identity Relationship Agreement to Civil Code Contract, (2020) 1 *Jurist* 36.

Wang LM, [The Article of the Law of the Tang Dynasty on the Incrimination of Foreigners Belongs to the Question of Private International Law and Discusses the Nature of the Criminal Code of the Tang Dynasty] (2017) 8 *Legal Science* 98.

Weizuo C, 'Shewai Minshi Guanxi Falü Shiyong di Zhongguo Te Se'[Chinese Characteristics of the Law Applicable to Foreign-related Civil Relations] [2011] *Applicable Law* 48–52.

Wessels B, 'Contracting Out of Secondary Insolvency Proceedings: The Main Liquidator's Undertaking in the Meaning of art 18 in the Proposal to Amend the EU Insolvency Regulation' (2014) 9 *Brooklyn Journal of Corporate, Financial and Commercial Law* 63, 82–83.

Westbrook JL, 'A Comment to Universal Proceduralism' (2009–2010) 48 *Columbia Journal of Transnational Law* 503, 508.

——, 'A Global Solution to Multinational Default' (2000) 98 *Michigan Law Review* 2276.

——, 'Avoidance of Pre-Bankruptcy Transactions in Multinational Bankruptcy Cases' (2007) 42 *Texas International Law Journal* 899 at 900.

——, 'Chapter 15 and discharge' (2005) 13 *American Bankruptcy Institute Law Review* 503

——, 'Choice of Avoidance Law in Global Insolvencies' (1991) 17 *Brooklyn Journal of International Law* 499, 513–14.

——, 'Locating the Eye of the Financial Storm' (2007) 32 *Brooklyn Journal of International Law* 1019.

——, 'The Control of Wealth in Bankruptcy' (2004) 82 *Texas Law Review* 796, 821

——, 'The Lessons of Maxwell Communication' (1996) 64 *Fordham Law Review* 2531, 2533–35.

——, 'Theory and Pragmatism in Global Insolvencies: Choice of Law and Choice of Forum' (1991) 65 *American Bankruptcy Law Journal* 457, 467, 468.

——, 'Universalism and Choice of Law' (2005) 23 *Penn State International Law Review* 625 at 626.

Williston S, 'The Validity of Attachments Made Abroad by Creditors of an Insolvent Debtor' (1891) 5 *Harvard Law Review* 211, 211–213.

Wisner R, Gallus N, 'Nationality Requirements in Investor-State Arbitration' (2003) 5 *Journal of World Investment & Trade* 927, 936.

Wu YH, 'On the stipulation of Article 34 of the New Civil Procedure Law to the Law Application of Foreign-related Contractual Jurisdiction' (2016) 5 *Journal of Northwest University of Political Science and Law*.

——, 'Guoji Sifa Zhong di Xianjue Wenti: Luojixue Shang de Chongxin Shenshi' [A Preliminary Question in Private International Law: A Re-examination of Logic] (2013) 1 *Western Law Review*.

Xiang D and Zhao NP, 'The Reconstruction of Family System by the Relational Contract Theory' (2017) 2 *Hebei Law Science* 103.

Xiao YP, 'The pros and cons of ratifying the Convention on Choice of Court Agreements and China's countermeasures' (2017) 5 *International Law Review of Wuhan University* 16.

Xu AG, 'The Ancient Tradition of Polygamy and the Response to Modern Law' People's Court Daily (Beijing, 11 May 2012) 005.

Xu CL, 'Guoji Touzi Fa Zhong De Zhongda Zhengyi Wenti Yu Woguo De Duice' [The major controversial issues in international investment law and China's countermeasures] (1994) 1 *Social Sciences in China* 23–38.

Xu DG, 'Humane Care and the Protection of the Interests of the Weak in Private International Law' (2004) 5 *Journal of Contemporary Law* 20.

——, 'A historical view of Actual Marriage between non-marriage and marriage' (2016) 3 *Law Review* 185.

Xu GJ, 'Comment on Key Issues Concerning Hague Judgment Convention in 2019' (2020) 2 *Journal of Shanghai University of Political Science and Law* (The Rule of Law Forum) 39.

——, 'Establishing an international legal system for the global circulation of court judgments – information, views and comments on the Draft Hague Convention on the Recognition and Enforcement of Foreign Judgments' (2017) 5 *International Law Review* 100.

Xu GM, 'Diversified settlement of commercial disputes under the backdrop of "Belt and Road" *People's Court Daily* (Beijing, 15 September 2017).

Xu Q, 'On the Trend of Justice in Conflicts Law for Torts in General and the Formulation of China's Judicial Interpretation' (2013) 3 *The Jurist* 12, 137.

——, 'The Conflicts Method to Protect Consumers' (2006) 6 *Political Science & Law* 74–8.

Xu W, 'Paths of Recognition and Enforcement of Foreign Court Judgment System in China – Also on the Change of Attitudes towards the Determination of Reciprocal Relationship' (2018) 2 *Study on Law and Business* 179.

Xue Y, Chen YQ, 'China's "one-stop" international commercial dispute settlement mechanism with the international commercial tribunal as the core' [2020] 1 *Journal of Political Science and Law* 149.

Yang DX, 'Wuquan Fading Yuanze Pipan – Jianping Zhonghua Renming Gongheguo Wuquan Fa Di Wu Tiao' [Critique of the Numerus Clausus Principle: In Addition Commenting Article 5 of Real Right Law of PRC] (2007) 4 *Law and Social Development* 20–31.

Yu F, 'Application of The Principle of Autonomy in Foreign-related Divorce' (2011) 1 *Journal of Xiamen University* (Philosophy and Social Science edition) 47.

——, 'Definition of "Principle of In Favour of" in Private International Law – Comments on the Law of the People's Republic of China on Choice of Law for Foreign-related Civil Relationships' (2012) 15 *China Annual Journal of Private International Law and Comparative Law* 67.

Yu J, 'Research on property Rights Protection of Unmarried Cohabitation of young people' (2019) 12 *China Youth Study* 36.

Yu ZH, 'Neidi Yu Xianggang Tequ Minshangshi Panjue Chengren Yu Zhixing Wenti Fenxi' [Analysis on the Recognition and Enforcement of Civil and Commercial Judgments in the Mainland and Hong Kong Special Administrative Region] (2015) 11 *Jinan Journal of Philosophy and Social Science* 5.

——, 'Analysis of the Recognition and Enforcement of Civil and Commercial Judgments in the Mainland and Hong Kong Special Administrative Region' (2015) 37(11) *Journal of Jinan Philosophy and Social Sciences Edition* 8.

Yuan FQ and Sun CG, 'Legal Symposium on the Family Affairs Concerning Foreign Elements' (2017) 1 *Law Press* 38.

Yuan FQ, 'Reflections and Reconstruction of the Protection System of the Weak in China's Private International Law' (2014) 6 *Law and Commercial Studies* 105.

Yuan XY, 'Wo Guo She Wai Zhi Shi Chan Quan Jiu Fen Fa Lu Shi Yong di Wen Ti Ji Wan Shan' [The Problems and Solutions to Applicable Laws in Foreign-Related IP Cases] (2018) 4 *Journal of East China University of Political Science and Law*.

Zhang LZ, 'A Revisit to the Relationship between the Doctrine of Characteristic Performance and the Principle of the Closest Connection – with a Comment on Article 41 of the Act of the People's Republic of China of Application of Law to Foreign Civil Relations' (2013) 15 *Chinese Yearbook of Private International Law & Comparative Law* 98, 120–3.

Zhang SD, 'Parallel Proceedings Review in the Recognition and Enforcement of Foreign Civil and Commercial Judgments' (2017) 1 *Wuhan University International Law Review* 87.

Zhang YJ and Yang L, 'Sifa Jiguan Xianghu Chengren Zhixing Minshangshi Panjue De Xintansuo' [New exploration of mutual recognition and enforcement of civil and commercial judgments by judicial organs] (2019) 13 *Renmin Sifa* 22.

Zhang YQ, 'Yi Bu Xian Dai Tong Yi Zhi He Tong Fa Ping Jia "Guo Ji Shang Shi He Tong Tong Ze" 2004' [A Modern Unified Contract Law – Commentary on the 2004 Principles of International Commercial Contracts] (2005) 4 *Beijing Arbitration Quarterly*.

Zhao SQ, 'The recognition and enforcement of punitive damage judgment of foreign courts' (2016) 1 *Commercial Arbitration* 7.

Zhao Y, 'Value Shift of Marital Property System from the Perspective of Justice' (2016) 1 *China Law* 227.

Zheng Q, 'Ziyou Jiazhi Zai Woguo Yizhu Jicheng Zhong De Dingwei Yu Luoshi' [Positioning and Implementation of The Free Value in China's Testamentary Succession System] (2016) 2 *Research on Law and Commerce* 147–8.

Zhou HC, 'Wuquan Chongtufa Zhong De Yisi Zizhi Yu Disanren Liyi Baohu' [Autonomy in Real Right Conflict Law and Protection of the Third Party's Interest] (2014)6 *Journal of Henan University of Economics and Law* 108–115.

Zhou Y, 'A Study on Substantive Applicable Law in ICSID Arbitration' [2015] Dissertation of PhD degree Wuhan University.

Zhu JG and Fan SJ, 'Lun Wuquan Fading Yu Yisi Zizhi Zhi Huanhe – Ping Woguo Shewai Wuquan Falv Shiyong Zhong Yinru Yisi Zizhi De Helixing' [On the Moderation of Numerus Clausus and Party Autonomy: On the Rationality of the Introduction of Party Autonomy into the Application of Law over China's Foreign-related Property Right] (2020) 3 *Journal of Northwest University* (Philosophy and Social Sciences Edition) 62–68.

Zhu L and Wu WL, 'She Wai Zhi Shi Chan Quan Guan Xi di Fa Lu Shi Yong' [The Applicable Law of Foreign-Related IP Cases] (2012) 9 *Journal of People's Judiciary*.

Zhu L, 'She Wai Zhi Shi Chan Quan Guan Xi di Fa Lu Shi Yong' [The Applicable Law of Foreign-Related IP Cases] (2012) 9 *Journal of People's Judiciary*.

Zhu LN, 'Legal Analysis of Conflicts of International Adoption Laws' (2011) 18 *Frontiers* 18.

Zhu WD, 'China's Codification of the Conflict of Laws: Publication of a Draft Text'(2007) 3 *Journal of Private International Law* 283, 294–6

Zhu WD, 'China's Codification of the Conflict of Laws: Publication of a Draft Text' (2007) 3 *Journal of Private International Law* 283.

Zhu ZS, 'Comments on the Protection of Children and Cooperation in International Adoption, Politics and Law' 4 (2000) 76.

Zou GY, 'The Evolution and the Latest Developments of Chinese Conflicts Law for Torts' (2014) 9 *Frontiers of Law in China* 582, 588.

Zuo ZJ, 'The Application of the Law of Same-sex Marriage in China with Foreign Elements' (2019) 12 *Modern Communication* 62.

INDEX

C